"In addition to demonstrating conclusively that Jonathan Edwards was a federal theologian, this study also provides a helpful overview of his Reformed predecessors—Johannes Cocceius, Hermann Witsius, Petrus van Mastricht, and Francis Turretin—and the development of federal theology. That historical look at the idea of a 'history of redemption,' combined with detailed examination of Edwards's exegetical basis for all the aspects of his covenant theology, makes this a landmark study in the scholarship of federal theology in general and Edwards scholarship in particular. Not only is his scholarship impeccable (and its clear style very accessible), Ryu honors the intentions of Edwards himself when he accents the important ecclesiastical, pastoral, and practical implications of covenant theology. While redemptive history is the underlying interpretive frame for understanding Edwards's theology, even more so for him, it is the structure by which to read the whole Bible for the sake of walking the Christian way. This is a valuable book for preachers and students of Scripture as well as scholars."

John Bolt,
emeritus professor of systematic theology,
Calvin Theological Seminary

T0366392

The **FEDERAL THEOLOGY** *of* **JONATHAN EDWARDS**

An Exegetical Perspective

STUDIES IN HISTORICAL
& SYSTEMATIC THEOLOGY

S H S T

The **FEDERAL THEOLOGY** *of* **JONATHAN EDWARDS**

An Exegetical Perspective

GILSUN RYU

STUDIES IN HISTORICAL AND SYSTEMATIC THEOLOGY

LEXHAM
ACADEMIC

The Federal Theology of Jonathan Edwards: An Exegetical Perspective
Studies in Historical and Systematic Theology

Copyright 2021 Gilsun Ryu

Lexham Academic, an imprint of Lexham Press
1313 Commercial St., Bellingham, WA 98225
LexhamPress.com

Scripture quotations marked (KJV) are from the King James Version. Public domain.

Print ISBN 9781683594574
Digital ISBN 9781683594581
Library of Congress Control Number 2020952119

Lexham Editorial: Todd Hains, Andrew Sheffield, John Barach
Cover Design: Owen Craft
Typesetting: Abigail Stocker, Justin Marr

To Eunseul, Hoyun, and Eunsu,
who made this work possible
through their love, patience,
and support.

CONTENTS

Part 4: Federal Theology and Ecclesiology

ACKNOWLEDGMENTS

—

No chapters of this book leave its author without the need to offer substantial thanks to several scholars. I begin by singling out the professor at Trinity Evangelical Divinity School who served as my doctoral supervisor, Dr. Douglas Sweeney, who provided helpful advice and comments at every stage of my writing. Sweeney did not spare his time as he guided me into a proper understanding of Edwards and offered insight and incisive feedback. In this respect, the primary place of honor must go to Sweeney. My second major reader and commentator was Dr. Scott Manetsch, who read the first draft and offered sage advice. I am also grateful to Dr. Richard Muller, from whom I learned the theology of Reformed orthodoxy. I regard it a great privilege to have taken Muller's class on Puritanism and Orthodoxy at Calvin Theological Seminary. A particular word of gratitude goes to Dr. Byungho Moon, from whom I inherited a love for Calvinism and Reformed theology.

Finally, I wish to express my gratitude to my family, especially my parents, Jaekoo Ryu and Sanok Lee, and parents-in-law, Sungyeon Park and Sungok Kim. My deepest gratitude goes to my wife, Eunseul, and our two children, Hoyun and Eunsu, not only for their constant support but also for their patience, sacrifice, love, and encouragement. I dedicate this book to my family.

ABBREVIATIONS

—

CH	*Church History*
CTQ	*Concordia Theological Quarterly*
EQ	*Evangelical Quarterly*
JETS	*Journal of Evangelical Theological Society*
RD	Reformed Dogmatics
TJ	*Trinity Journal*
TPT	*Theoretico-practica Theologia*
WJE	*The Works of Jonathan Edwards*
WJEO	*The Works of Jonathan Edwards Online*
WMQ	*William & Mary Quarterly*
WTJ	*Westminster Theological Journal*

FOREWORD

—

A generation ago, most Edwards scholars assumed that Harvard's Perry Miller was right to deny that Edwards stood among the federal theologians. Miller founded the Yale Edition of Edwards's *Works*, after all, and his proto-modern Edwards—a literary artist masquerading as an old-fashioned Calvinist divine—had proven useful to many late modern Western literati. The Edwards known best in the halls of academe was a philosopher, psychologist, and theological genius, not a dogmatic biblicist. He harbored little interest in the forensics of original sin and justification by faith. He was a forward-looking thinker, far ahead of his compatriots in eighteenth-century New England.

Beginning in 1975, though, with *Jonathan Edwards and the Covenant of Grace* by Carl Bogue, and continuing through the 2010s with groundbreaking work by younger scholars such as Reita Yazawa and Gilsun Ryu, a different Edwards came to light, one much more committed to his Westminsterian heritage, not least on the matter of its federal theology. This more traditional Edwards proved to be first and foremost an interpreter of Scripture. And like many of his doctrinal and commentarial sources, he divided biblical teaching with respect to sin and redemption into one eternal covenant made among the divine persons and then two historical covenants given by God to human beings as the basis of salvation. He taught that Father, Son, and Spirit had agreed from all eternity to provide a way of salvation for humanity after the fall, which God foreknew but did not will (the *covenant of redemption*). He said that Adam was on probation in the Garden of Eden: if he kept God's law, he and his progeny would have lived forever, walking with the Lord (the *covenant of works*). But he affirmed that ever since the fall, sinners had but one way of justification with God: by faith in the work of Christ, the "second Adam" of St. Paul who overcame the power of sin and death for those the Father gave Him (the *covenant of grace*). This schema was a hallmark of the Calvinist tradition. First formulated in Heidelberg and codified for Puritans in the

Westminster Confession, it was taught by William Ames and almost all of Edwards's authorities. It has come to be referred to as their federal theology.

Gilsun Ryu's book, *The Federal Theology of Jonathan Edwards*, is the most learned, accurate, and comprehensive account of this subject on offer. Well grounded in Edwards's published works and manuscript materials, it interprets his thought in relation to the federal theologies of his sources, doing more than anything else in the history of Edwards scholarship to shine a light on the nature and historical significance of his work on the covenants of redemption, works, and grace. One of my favorite things about it is its detailed attention to Edwards's biblical exegesis—another subject sorely neglected in the age of Perry Miller. Edwards spent more time on the Bible than anything else, preparing to preach, teach, and minister its truths to his people. In the hands of Gilsun Ryu, this is made crystal clear, as is Edwards's habit of maintaining doctrinal continuity with those who went before him while repackaging their teachings—even if only slightly— in relation to the intellectual culture of his day. Miller was right: Edwards was indeed a literary artist. But as Ryu has demonstrated, his medium was Scripture.

This book is essential reading for all serious Edwards scholars, historical theologians, and Reformed Bible scholars. Dr. Ryu deserves our thanks for his painstaking scholarship and lucid explanation of a key theme in Edwards's exegetical theology.

Douglas A. Sweeney
Beeson Divinity School
Samford University

1
—

INTRODUCTION

JONATHAN EDWARDS'S FEDERAL THEOLOGY

Jonathan Edwards (1703–1758), one of the most intriguing federal theologians, inherited classical federalism from Reformed orthodoxy. Federal theology is a form of Reformed covenant theology, which emphasizes the representative principle of the headship of the first and second Adams. This theology not only stemmed from earlier writers, such as Irenaeus, Augustine, and the Reformers (Ulrich Zwingli, John Calvin, Heinrich Bullinger, and others), but also was maintained and developed by Reformed orthodoxy in the sixteenth and seventeenth centuries. Since the *Westminster Confession of Faith* represented the full development of federal theology into a confessional status by clearly distinguishing between the doctrines of the covenants of works and grace, it became a theological commonplace in Reformed orthodoxy.[1]

---

1. See Mark W. Karlberg, *Federalism and the Westminster Tradition* (Eugene, OR: Wipf & Stock, 2006), 1; Karlberg, "Reformed Interpretation of the Mosaic Covenant," *WTJ* 43 (Fall 1980): 1; J. Mark Beach, *Christ and the Covenant: Francis Turretin's Federal Theology as a Defense of the Doctrine of Grace, Reformed Historical Theology* (Göttingen: Vandenhoeck & Ruprecht, 2007), 143; Peter A. Lillback, *The Binding of God: Calvin's Role in the Development of Covenant Theology* (Grand Rapids: Baker, 2001), 287, 41; Richard A. Muller, "The Covenant of Works and the Stability of Divine Law in Seventeenth-Century Reformed Orthodoxy: A Study in the Theology of Herman Witsius and Wilhelmus à Brakel," *Calvin Theological Journal* 29, no. 1 (1994): 91; *The Confession of Faith and Catechisms, Agreed upon by the Assembly of Divines at Westminster Together with Their Humble Advice Concerning Church Government and Ordination of Ministers* (London: The Sign of the Kings Head, 1649), 13. Note that the *Westminster Confession* distinguishes between the covenant of works and the covenant of grace. Through this distinction, the doctrine of the covenant of works not only played a foundational role in covenant theology but also provided a distinctive principle of Reformed hermeneutics of Holy Scripture. See I. John Hesselink, *On Being Reformed: Distinctive Characteristics and Common Misunderstandings* (Ann Arbor, MI: Servant Books, 1983), 102; Lyle D. Bierma, *German Calvinism in the Confessional Age: The Covenant Theology of Caspar Olevianus* (Grand Rapids: Baker, 1996), 11; Joel R. Beeke and Mark Jones, *A Puritan Theology: Doctrine for Life* (Grand Rapids: Reformation Heritage, 2012), 217.

Edwards neither wrote about his view of federal theology in a systematic way nor published a treatise on his exegetical method.[2] Nevertheless, his federal theology occupies a place of considerable significance in his biblical exegesis. This is clear from the fact that his use of the federal schema—the covenant of redemption, the covenant of works, and the covenant of grace—is interwoven with his biblical writings. Edwards employed the federal schema in his biblical works, including his "Blank Bible," "Notes on Scripture," "Miscellanies," typological writings, and hundreds of sermons from his extant corpus. This implies that one cannot fully understand Edwards's federal theology without his biblical exegesis.

A significant element in Edwards's federal theology is its focus on the history of redemption and the harmony of the Old and New Testaments. In formulating his doctrine of the covenant, Edwards took great pains to understand salvation history through biblical exegesis, so that he attempted to harmonize the whole Bible. This can be seen in his comments about his unfinished works *A History of the Work of Redemption* and *The Harmony of the Old and New Testaments*. First, the theme of redemptive history was of utmost importance in Edwards's theological thought. In a letter to the trustees of the College of New Jersey, Edwards writes:

> I have had on my mind and heart, (which I long ago began, not with any view to publication,) a great work, which I call a *History of the Work of Redemption*, a body of divinity in an entire new method, being thrown into the form of a history; considering the affair of Christian Theology, as the whole of it, in each part, stands in reference to the great work of redemption by Jesus Christ.[3]

Edwards's attention to the *history* project is also found in three notebooks, which Edwards wrote during the Stockbridge period (1751–1757).[4] Moreover, Edwards's interest in redemptive history is evident in his 1739 sermon

---

2. Douglas A. Sweeney, *Edwards the Exegete: Biblical Interpretation and Anglo-Protestant Culture on the Edge of the Enlightenment* (New York: Oxford University Press, 2016), ix.

3. Jonathan Edwards to the Trustees of the College of New Jersey, October 19, 1757, in *Edwards, Letters and Personal Writings*, WJE 16:727

4. During the Stockbridge period (1751–1757), Edwards wrote theological works while also ministering to Indians. For information on these notebooks, see John F. Wilson, "Jonathan Edwards's Notebooks for 'A History of the Work of Redemption,'" in *Reformation, Conformity and Dissent: Essays in Honour of Geoffrey Nuttall*, ed. R. Buick Knox (London: Epworth, 1977), 239–54.

series and the "Miscellanies."[5] From these four categories of evidence pertaining to Edwards's view of the history of redemption, the redemptive-historical theme appears to be one of the most important theological lenses through which Edwards viewed the Bible.

Edwards's view of the history of redemption can be clearly seen in his sermon series of 1739, titled *A History of the Work of Redemption*. In this work, Edwards's concept of the work of redemption is focused on the final purpose in God's design, which was made in the covenant of redemption among the persons of the Trinity. Edwards presents the purpose as follows: (1) "to put God's enemies under his feet," (2) "to restore all the ruins of the fall," (3) "to bring all elect creatures to a union in one body," (4) "to complete the glory of all the elect by Christ," and (5) "to accomplish the glory of the Trinity to an exceeding degree." This purpose is accomplished by the work of redemption as "the principal means."[6] This indicates that God's design before the creation of the world can be seen through the process of history.

One notes that Edwards's view of the redemptive-historical aspect of federal theology was not his own invention. A similar perspective on the history of redemption is found in Johannes Cocceius (1603–1669), who was one of the early federal theologians. According to Van Asselt, Cocceius's federal theology was "an attempt to move theological theorizing from the realm of eternity into the plane of history and human experience."[7] A similar view is found in Edwards's main theological authorities, such as Herman Witsius (1636–1708), Petrus van Mastricht (1630–1706), and Francis Turretin (1623–1687), who emphasized the history of God's work of redemption in their view of federal theology. As Mark W. Karlberg notes well, one of the most distinctive aspects of federalism in the Calvinistic

5. In his thirty sermons in 1739, entitled *A History of the Work of Redemption*, Edwards took great pains to portray the nature of the history of redemption, focusing on the analysis of God's work of redemption in the salvation of sinful humanity from the beginning to the end of the world. Beyond this, Edwards dealt with various topics relating to redemption throughout the "Miscellanies." For the redemption motif in the "Miscellanies," see John F. Wilson, "Editor's Introduction," in Edwards, *A History of the Work of Redemption*, WJE 9:13–17.

6. Edwards, *A History of the Work of Redemption*, 123–26.

7. Willem J. Van Asselt, *The Federal Theology of Johannes Cocceius, 1603–1669*, trans. Raymond A. Blacketer (Leiden: Brill, 2001), 2.

tradition is "its biblical-theological methods," which means "organic-historical method."[8]

Nevertheless, the idea of the history of redemption in Edwards differed significantly from those of his Reformed forebears. While he shared with his Reformed predecessors a historical approach to divine revelation regarding salvation, Edwards's concept of the history of redemption as a necessary aspect of biblical exegesis reflects the distinctiveness of his thought. As John Wilson points out, while Edwards employs the covenant scheme, he eschews "the minutiae" of covenant theology.[9] George Marsden claims that Edwards's "entire new method" referred to in the projected work would imply that his "grand comprehensive theology would imitate Scripture itself" rather than "the forms" which were used by "Thomas Aquinas or even the Reformed systematizers such as Francis Turretin or Peter van Mastricht."[10] Marsden sets the biblical Edwards over against Reformed scholastics as if Edwards is far from the method of Turretin or Mastricht. Although Marsden's description of the *history* project tends to be highly exaggerated, it is no exaggeration to suggest that the redemptive-historical perspective of the covenant is the driving force behind his reading of the Bible. In this light, David P. Barshinger mentions that the history of redemption is "the encompassing interpretive framework" by which Edwards approached the Psalms.[11]

Moreover, the redemptive-historical character of Edwards's federal theology is related to his own comprehensive understanding of the Bible through his biblical exegesis. Specifically, Edwards's emphasis upon the history of redemption comes as a necessary aspect of his view of the harmony of the Bible. In the *history* project, Edwards intended for "every divine doctrine" to "appear ... in the brightest light ... showing the admirable contexture and harmony of the whole."[12] The harmony Edwards refers to indicates something successive in all secular historical events and those

8. Karlberg, *Federalism and the Westminster Tradition*, 1; Karlberg, "Reformed Interpretation of the Mosaic Covenant," *WTJ* 43: 2.

9. Wilson, "Editor's Introduction," 54.

10. George M. Marsden, *Jonathan Edwards: A Life* (New Haven: Yale University Press, 2003), 488.

11. David P. Barshinger, *Jonathan Edwards and the Psalms: A Redemptive-Historical Vision of Scripture* (New York: Oxford University Press, 2014), 26.

12. Edwards, *Letters and Personal Writings*, 728.

recorded in the Bible. After describing the *history* project, Edwards begins to explain "another great work" which he planned to write. In the same letter, Edwards writes, "I have also for my own profit and entertainment, done much towards another great work, which I call *The Harmony of the Old and New Testament*." The harmony between the Old and New Testaments has to do with the "exact fulfillment" of the Word of God in all the historical events of the world.[13] Examining Edwards's *harmony* project, Nichols suggests that Edwards's concept of "redemption history and a covenantal system" is a framework for harmonizing the Old and New Testaments.[14] Thus, it appears that not only is the redemptive-historical lens crucial to Edwards's approach to the Bible, but the theme of the history of redemption and the covenant system is also a framework for harmonizing the whole Bible.

Edwards understood the relationship between the history of redemption and the covenant system to be focused on the biblical teaching on salvation from sin. Edwards developed his federal theology from his comprehensive understanding of the Bible in attempting the harmony between the Old and New Testaments. In doing so, Edwards examined a large body of biblical texts, not only considering etymological, cultural, theological, and practical aspects but also employing various methods, like literal, linguistic, contextual, typological, and allegorical interpretations. In examining Edwards's exegetical methods in the major prophets, especially Isaiah, Jeremiah, and Ezekiel, Yoo argues that Edwards employed more methods than merely "literal, typological, or allegorical."[15]

While Edwards finds his covenant scheme in various texts from which he extrapolates the relationship of the first Adam and the second Adam (Christ), original righteousness and original sin, total depravity, imputation of sin, and so forth,[16] one of the standard examples of the covenant schema

---

13. Edwards, *Letters and Personal Writings*, 728.

14. Stephen R. C. Nichols, *Jonathan Edwards's Bible: The Relationship of the Old and New Testaments in the Theology of Jonathan Edwards* (Eugene, OR: Pickwick, 2013), 14, 108.

15. Jeongmo Yoo, "Edwards's Interpretation of the Major Prophets," *Puritan Reformed Journal* 3, no. 2 (2011): 160–92.

16. Edwards, sermon on 2 Samuel 23:5 (Summer-Fall 1729), Box 1, F. 77, L. 4r., 3r., Beinecke; Edwards, sermon on Hebrews 9:15-16, L. 1v., 3r; Edwards, sermon on Genesis 3:11 (February 1739), Box 1, F. 2, Beinecke; Edwards, sermon on Genesis 3:24 (n.d.), Box 1, F. 3, Beinecke; Edwards, sermon on Zechariah 4:7 (n.d.), Box 13, F. 1015, L. 2r., Beinecke; Edwards, sermon on

can be seen in his sermon on Genesis 3:11, in which Edwards explains the
relationship between Adam and his posterity. Genesis 3:11 is related not
only to the Gospel of John and 1 John 3:8, which reveals the consequence
of Adam's sin, but also to Hebrews 2:14. Moreover, Edwards connects
these verses to Romans 5:14, 1 Corinthians 15:45, and Hebrews, where
the terms "the first Adam" and "the second Adam" come from.[17] By perceiving the covenantal framework in his exegetical perspective, Edwards
attempted to interpret the redemptive-historical nature of salvation
within his wider framework of the doctrinal unity between the Old and
the New Testaments. Thus, one of the most important frameworks for
interpreting the history of redemption is the doctrinal harmony of the
Bible through federal theology.

Further, this doctrinal harmony as an interpretive framework for
understanding the history of redemption is not unrelated to his ecclesiology, since for Edwards, the history of redemption is closely related to
the Christian community. With respect to the covenant of grace, Edwards
states that "the condition of Christ's covenant with his people or of the marriage covenant between him and men, is that they should close with him
and adhere to him."[18] "Closing with" and "adhering to" Christ do not mean
that believers should accomplish the condition by their merit.[19] Rather, the
conditionality of the covenant of grace is focused on a historical realization of this covenant at a point in time in which the redemptive history
of the Bible is fulfilled and the members of Christ "come into being."[20] As
Bogue points out, the covenant of grace for Edwards is completed in time
by Christ's people.[21] In the same light, Reita Yazawa argues, "For Edwards,
the church covenant and the covenant of grace had to be one and the

---

Hebrews 9:13–14 (November 1738), Box 11, F. 823, Beinecke; and Edwards, sermon on Hebrews
12:22–24 (1740), Box 11, F. 837, Beinecke. Information on these materials comes from Douglas
Sweeney's survey. See Douglas Sweeney, *Edwards the Exegete*, 296n15.

17. Edwards, sermon on Genesis 3:11 (February 1739).

18. Edwards, *The "Miscellanies": Entry Nos. 501–832*, WJE 18:148.

19. Edwards says, "If Adam had stood and persevered in obedience, he would have been
made happy by mere bounty (and) goodness; for God was not obliged to reward Adam for
his perfect obedience any otherwise than by covenant, for Adam by standing would not have
merited happiness." See Edwards, *Sermons and Discourses 1720–1723*, WJE 10:392.

20. Edwards, *The "Miscellanies": Entry Nos. 833–1152*, no. 1091, WJE 20:475.

21. Carl W. Bogue, *Jonathan Edwards and the Covenant of Grace* (Cherry Hill, NJ: Mack,
1975), 127.

same."[22] Thus, as Barshinger rightly states, the history of redemption in the view of Edwards has "significant implications for the life of the professing Christian."[23]

Given this, it is not surprising that Edwards presents his federal theology in view of its practical relevance for the Christian community. In rejecting Arminianism and Antinomianism, Edwards changed some points in his view of covenant regarding pastoral ministry.[24] As an example, consider Edwards's change of the sacramental policy of the Northampton church, which followed Solomon Stoddard, who permitted any citizens who professed belief in Christ and maintained an ethical life to partake of the Lord's Supper.[25] (Stoddard even accepted unconverted persons to participate in Communion.[26]) Against this policy, Edwards requested the church to "renew their covenant with God and pursue the life of visible saints at their best."[27] Edwards emphasized the importance of the confession of faith before admission to the sacraments and, by implication, to the covenant. He insists "that it [the profession of true religion] is the duty of God's people thus publicly to own the covenant; and that it was not only a duty in Israel of old, but is so in the Christian church, and to the end of the world; and that it is a duty required of *adult* persons before they come to sacraments."[28] Edwards stresses that without the confession of their true faith before attending sacraments, they "cannot properly be called professing saints."[29]

Edwards relates the doctrine of the covenant of grace to genuine piety. He continues:

---

22. Reita Yazawa, "Federal Theology," in *The Jonathan Edwards Encyclopedia*, ed. Harry S. Stout (Grand Rapids: Eerdmans, 2017), 121.

23. Barshinger, *Jonathan Edwards and the Psalms*, 28.

24. See Michael J. McClymond and Gerald R. McDermott, *The Theology of Jonathan Edwards* (New York: Oxford University Press, 2012), 325; Cornelis van der Knijff and Willem van Vlastuin, "The Development in Jonathan Edwards' Covenant View," *Jonathan Edwards Studies* 3, no. 2 (2013): 270-1, 281. See Edwards, *The "Miscellanies": Entry Nos. a-z, aa-zz, 1–500, WJE* 13:198. For more on this, see Conrad Cherry, *The Theology of Jonathan Edwards: A Reappraisal* (Bloomington: Indiana University Press, 1990), 186–215.

25. McClymond and McDermott, *The Theology of Jonathan Edwards*, 24.

26. McClymond and McDermott, *The Theology of Jonathan Edwards*, 24, 47.

27. Yazawa, "Federal Theology," 121.

28. Edwards, "An Humble Inquiry into the Rules of the Word of God, Concerning the Qualifications Requisite to a Complete Standing and Full Communion in the Visible Christian Church," in *Ecclesiastical Writings, WJE* 12:199.

29. Edwards, "An Humble Inquiry," 199.

None ought to be admitted to the privileges of adult persons in the church of Christ, but such as make a profession of real piety. For the covenant, to be owned or professed, is God's covenant, which he has revealed as the method of our spiritual union with him, and our acceptance as the objects of his eternal favor; which is no other than the covenant of grace; at least it is so, without dispute, in these days of the gospel. To own this covenant, is to profess the consent of our *hearts* to it; and that is the sum and substance of true piety.[30]

Clearly, Edwards taught the connection between "the sum and substance of true piety" and the profession of "the consent of our heart" to the covenant. As Rhys S. Bezzant points out, Edwards used federal theology "to relate vital piety and the benefits of salvation that accrue to the individual believer."[31] Therefore, Edwards's federal theology corresponded to genuine piety. In conclusion, Edwards's federal theology was an attempt to understand the historical aspect of salvation in the revelation of the Bible through the framework of the doctrinal harmony of the Bible.

A REVIEW OF THE LITERATURE

This book focuses on the relationship between Edwards's exegesis and his federal theology. To trace the historiography of the subject, it is essential to explore how Edwards scholars have studied Edwards's biblical exegesis as well as his federal theology. Edwards's federal theology has been frequently mentioned to illustrate either his Calvinism or his deviation from Calvinism. Perry Miller contends that while Edwards abandoned "the whole covenant scheme," his predecessors (the first generation of New Englanders) were advocates of federal theology, which is quite different from Calvin's theology.[32] Since Miller denies that Edwards was a

---

30. Edwards, "An Humble Inquiry," 205.

31. Rhys S. Bezzant, *Jonathan Edwards and the Church* (New York: Oxford University Press, 2014), 63.

32. Perry Miller, "The Marrow of Puritan Divinity," *Errand into the Wilderness* (New York: Harper & Row, 1964), 98; Miller, *Jonathan Edwards* (New York: William Sloan Associates, 1949; reprinted, Amherst: University of Massachusetts Press, 1981), 30–32, 76–78; Miller, "Roger Williams: An Essay in Interpretation," in *The Complete Writings of Roger Williams*, vol. 7 (New York: Russell & Russell, 1963), 5–25.

federal theologian, his work has served as a milestone in Edwards studies among many scholars.

Following Miller, scholars like Peter De Jong, Joseph Haroutunian, Sidney Earl Mead, Sydney Ahlstrom, and William McLoughlin have claimed that federal theology is a departure from Edwards's theology.[33] However, Miller's theological path has been criticized by some scholars, such as John H. Gerstner, Conrad Cherry, Carl Bogue, and Harry S. Stout. In his work *Steps to Salvation*, John H. Gerstner gives some attention to Edwards's covenantal framework (the covenants of redemption, grace, and works).[34] Conrad Cherry, in his work *The Theology of Jonathan Edwards: A Reappraisal*, attempts to replace outmoded stereotypes with new approaches to Puritan studies, offering evidence of the covenant scheme in Edwards's sermons.[35] Carl Bogue's *Jonathan Edwards and the Covenant of Grace* provides an overall exposition of the covenant of grace as the central motif, responding to the question of whether Edwards was a covenant theologian.[36] Harry Stout's article "The Puritans and Edwards" examines the cultural context and acknowledges that Edwards inherited ideas from his Puritan predecessors.[37]

Recent studies of Edwards's federal theology have mainly concentrated on aspects of the relationship between the immanent Trinity and the economic Trinity because federal theology is involved in the doctrine of the Trinity. Amy Plantinga Pauw, Sang Hyun Lee, William J. Danaher, and Ralph Cunnington have insisted that Edwards reformulated a classical

---

33. Peter Y. De Jong, *The Covenant Idea in New England Theology, 1620–1847* (Grand Rapids: Eerdmans, 1945), 138; Joseph Haroutunian, *Piety Versus Moralism: The Passing of the New England Theology* (New York: Harper & Row, 1970), xxii; Sidney Earl Mead, *Nathaniel William Taylor, 1786–1858: A Connecticut Liberal* (Chicago: University of Chicago Press, 1942), ix; Sydney E. Ahlstrom, "Theology in America: A Historical Survey," in *The Shaping of American Religion*, ed. James Ward Smith and A. Leland Jamison (Princeton: Princeton University Press, 1961), 240; William G. McLoughlin, *Revivals, Awakenings, and Reform: An Essay on Religion and Social Change in America, 1607–1977* (Chicago: University of Chicago Press, 1978), 35, 98–122.

34. John H. Gerstner, *Steps to Salvation: The Evangelistic Message of Jonathan Edwards* (Philadelphia: Westminster, 1960), 173–88.

35. Cherry, *The Theology of Jonathan Edwards*, 2–3, 105–23; Cherry, "The Puritan Notion of the Covenant in Jonathan Edwards's Doctrine of Faith," *CH* 34, no. 3 (September 1965): 98, 328–41.

36. Bogue, *Jonathan Edwards and the Covenant of Grace*.

37. Harry S. Stout, "The Puritans and Edwards," in *Jonathan Edwards and the American Experience*, ed. Nathan O. Hatch and Harry S. Stout (New York: Oxford University Press, 1988), 142–57.

Reformed doctrine of the Trinity, using eighteenth-century philosophical idealism.[38] Richard M. Weber, in his essay "The Trinitarian Theology of Jonathan Edwards," claims that while Edwards's Trinitarian position is not "the typical Reformed formulation of the doctrine," it is still "thoroughly consistent with Reformed orthodoxy."[39] Recently, J. V. Fesko, in his work *The Covenant of Redemption: Origins, Development, and Reception*, argues that Edwards's view of the *pactum salutis* departed from Reformed orthodoxy.[40]

Pauw's view was refuted by Steven Studebaker and Robert Caldwell, who contend that Edwards's Trinitarian thought consistently reflects "features of the Augustinian mutual love model" rather than "oscillates between the discordant social and psychological models of the Trinity."[41] In the same light, Reita Yazawa maintains in his dissertation "Covenant of Redemption in the Theology of Jonathan Edwards" that Edwards's view of the covenant of redemption remains within Reformed orthodoxy, further emphasizing the practical significance of the doctrine of the Trinity.[42] Similarly, Jan van Vliet, in a chapter of his book *The Rise of Reformed System*,

---

38. Amy Plantinga Pauw, *The Supreme Harmony of All: The Trinitarian Theology of Jonathan Edwards* (Grand Rapids: Eerdmans, 2002), 11; Pauw, "The Trinity," in *The Princeton Companion to Jonathan Edwards*, ed. Sang Hyun Lee (Princeton: Princeton University Press, 2005), 46–47; Sang Hyun Lee, "Editor's Introduction," in Edwards, *Writings on the Trinity, Grace, and Faith*, WJE 21:26, 27; William J. Danaher, *The Trinitarian Ethics of Jonathan Edwards* (Louisville: Westminster John Knox, 2004), 17; Ralph Cunnington, "A Critical Examination of Jonathan Edwards' Doctrine of the Trinity," *Themelios (Online)* 39, no. 2 (July 2014), 225, http://themelios.thegospelcoalition.org/article/a-critical-examination-of-jonathan-edwardss-doctrine-of-the-trinity. On the debate about whether Edwards's Trinitarian theology belongs to Reformed orthodoxy, see Steven M. Studebaker and Robert W. Caldwell III, *The Trinitarian Theology of Jonathan Edwards: Text, Context, and Application* (Burlington, VT: Ashgate, 2012), 1–18.

39. Richard M. Weber, "The Trinitarian Theology of Jonathan Edwards: An Investigation of Charges against Its Orthodoxy," *JETS* 44, no. 2 (June 2001): 297–318.

40. J. V. Fesko, *The Covenant of Redemption: Origins, Development, and Reception* (Göttingen: Vandenhoeck & Ruprecht, 2016), 122–43.

41. Studebaker and Caldwell, *The Trinitarian Theology of Jonathan Edwards*, 16. Pauw argues that Edwards's Trinitarian thought lurches between the relational and psychological models of the Trinity as well as the atomistic view of personhood in the Trinity, which emphasizes the initiative of an individual. See Pauw, *The Supreme Harmony of All*, 77.

42. In response to contemporary Trinitarian theologies that have a proclivity for criticism of the immanent Trinity, Yazawa argues that the inner-Trinitarian eternal pact between the Father and the Son is the basis for the salvation of the elect, so that the doctrine of the Trinity has practical relevance for the Christian life. In this work, he examines major Reformed thinkers who are considered influences on Edwards with respect to doctrinal and exegetical developments of the covenant of redemption. See Reita Yazawa, "Covenant of Redemption in the Theology of Jonathan Edwards: The Nexus between the Immanent and the Economic Trinity" (PhD diss., Calvin Theological Seminary, 2013).

examines William Ames's influence on Edwards's federal theology, insisting that Edwards's emphasis on Christian practical life is influenced by Ames.[43] Most recently, Adriaan Neele, in his work *Before Jonathan Edwards*, argues that Edwards's "discriminating treatment of the Cocceian and Voetian exposition of the covenant of grace" reflects the thought of federal theologians like Mastricht in particular.[44]

Some scholars have traced developments in Edwards's view of covenant. In a chapter of their pioneering work *The Theology of Jonathan Edwards*, Michael McClymond and Gerald McDermott trace the development of Edwards's view of covenant through three different periods.[45] Offering a corrective to McClymond and McDermott,[46] Cornelis van der Knijff and Willem van Vlastuin's work "The Development in Jonathan Edwards' Covenant View" finds "an increasing focus on redemptive history" in Edwards's view of covenant.[47]

While there has been a growing body of scholarship dealing with Edwards's biblical writings, his exegetical concerns received little attention from his contemporaries. Samuel Hopkins (1721–1803), who was the first biographer of Edwards, states that Edwards "commonly spent thirteen Hours every Day in his Study."[48] Quoting Hopkins's writing, Sereno Dwight,

---

43. Jan van Vliet, "Covenant and Conscience: Amesian Echoes in Jonathan Edwards," in *The Rise of Reformed System: The Intellectual Heritage of William Ames* (Eugene, OR: Wipf & Stock, 2013), 233–65.

44. Adriaan C. Neele, *Before Jonathan Edwards: Sources of New England Theology* (Oxford: Oxford University Press, 2018), 230.

45. The development of Edwards's federal theology is divided into three phases in his career. The first period is found in some "Miscellanies" entries in 1723. The second phase is in 1733, when Edwards began to discuss the covenant between Christ and believers (marriage covenant). The last change appears in 1739, when Edwards distinguished the covenant of redemption from the covenant of grace. See Michael J. McClymond and Gerald R. McDermott, *The Theology of Jonathan Edwards*, 325–27.

46. According to Van der Knijff and Van Vlastuin, Edwards's works on this theme do not reveal "the second transition from a focus on faith as a condition to the distinction between the covenants of redemption and grace" but could reflect "a gradual development." Van der Knijff and Van Vlastuin, "The Development in Jonathan Edwards' Covenant View," 281. In their perspective, McClymond and McDermott's view of the three-phase development of the covenant in Edwards appears not to be correct.

47. Van der Knijff and Van Vlastuin, "The Development in Jonathan Edwards' Covenant View," 281.

48. Samuel Hopkins, *The Life and Character of the Late Reverend Mr. Jonathan Edwards, President of the College of New-Jersey* (Boston: S. Kneeland, 1765), 40. According to Hopkins, Edwards's interest in the Bible is substantial. Although Edwards read "all the Books, especially Books of Divinity," that could help him in his pursuit of knowledge, Edwards "studied

who was one of Edwards's early biographers, points out that Edwards's exceptional acquaintance with the Bible appears in his sermons and treatises.[49] However, Edwards's contemporaries simply indicate the fact that Edwards's attention to the Bible is significant, without undertaking any analysis of his biblical exegesis.

From the mid-twentieth century, scholars began turning to Edwards's biblical writings.[50] Describing Edwards as a biblical preacher in the pastoral ministry, Ralph Turnbull dealt briefly with Edwards's exegetical method.[51] John Gerstner selectively treated Edwards's works to demonstrate the doctrine of the inerrancy of the Bible.[52] Notably, some scholars began to focus on Edwards's soteriology in his biblical writings, alongside the concept of the history of redemption. Stephen Stein found that Edwards's interest in "the Harmony" he projected is "the person and work of Christ," in which "prophecy, typology, and doctrine" converge. With an emphasis on the Christological focus in the view of Edwards, Stein argues that Edwards's view of the Bible text is "pre-critical," which means that he takes Western Christianity's traditional view of the biblical texts.[53] Challenging the prevailing perspective of the division between a pre-critical and a critical era, Robert Brown claims that Edwards is in not the pre-critical camp but that of "hybrid traditionalism," which is "modified in significant ways

---

the Bible more than all other Books, and more than most other Divines do." Edwards drew his "religious Principles" from Scripture rather than "any human system or body of divinity." Edwards's interest in the Bible, according to Hopkins, appears in his sermons and most of his publications, especially in his manuscript notes. See Hopkins, *Life and Character*, 40–41.

49. Sereno E. Dwight, ed., *The Works of President Edwards: With a Memoir of His Life*, vol. 1 (New York: S. Converse, 1829–1830), 600.

50. Barshinger, *Jonathan Edwards and the Psalms*, 15n52.

51. Ralph G. Turnbull, "Jonathan Edwards: Bible Interpreter," *Interpretation* 6 (1952); Turnbull, *Jonathan Edwards: The Preacher* (Grand Rapids: Baker, 1958), 60–78.

52. John H. Gerstner, "The Church's Doctrine of Biblical Inspiration," in *The Foundation of Biblical Authority*, ed. James Montgomery Boice (Grand Rapids: Zondervan, 1978), 23–58. For a discussion of the studies of Edwards's biblical interpretation, see Barshinger, *Jonathan Edwards and the Psalms*, 14–22; Michael J. McClymond and Gerald R. McDermott, *The Theology of Jonathan Edwards*, 167–69.

53. In this view, the meaning of the biblical texts is considered "literally and historically reliable." This means that Edwards was naïve with respect to the critical issues of history in the field of biblical interpretation. See Stephen J. Stein, "The Spirit and the Word: Jonathan Edwards and Scriptural Exegesis," in *Jonathan Edwards and the American Experience*, ed. Nathan O. Hatch and Harry S. Stout (New York: Oxford University Press, 1988), 118, 127.

by accommodation to the new learning."[54] To prove his argument, Brown brings Edwards's view of the history of redemption into the discussion by examining the context of his projected "history of redemption," in which Edwards felt the need to respond to "critical historical approaches to the Bible."[55]

Recent studies of Edwards's biblical writings focus on his exegetical methods. Stephen J. Stein, in an article, examines Edwards's biblical exegesis of Genesis 9:12–17 in his note on the rainbow, no. 348 in "Notes on Scripture," emphasizing that Edwards's hermeneutical approach in this note was "not a basis for the induction of religious truths but rather a convenient and congenial mode for expressing fundamental theological convictions."[56] Glenn Kreider, in his book *Jonathan Edwards's Interpretation of Revelation 4:1–8:1*, examines Edwards's interpretation of Revelation 4–8 in his notebooks, theological treatises, and sermons. In exploring Edwards's use of typology, Kreider finds that Edwards's main method of interpretation is "Christological typology."[57] In their work *The Theology of Jonathan Edwards*, Michael McClymond and Gerald McDermott present the fundamental themes in Edwards's exegetical method.[58] Stephen R. C. Nichols, in his work *Jonathan Edwards's Bible*, gives considerable attention to examining "The Harmony of the Old and New Testament" that Edwards planned to write. In doing so, Nichols asserts that in Edwards's soteriology there is one faith in the Old and New Testaments by which human beings can be saved, and thus, he criticizes the current "dispositional" account of

---

54. Robert E. Brown, *Jonathan Edwards and the Bible* (Bloomington: Indiana University Press, 2002), xvii, xxi, 121. For more information about this, see McClymond and McDermott, *The Theology of Jonathan Edwards*, 170–71; Sweeney, *Edwards the Exegete*, 153.

55. Brown, *Jonathan Edwards and the Bible*, 166.

56. Stephen J. Stein, "Jonathan Edwards and the Rainbow: Biblical Exegesis and Poetic Imagination," *New England Quarterly* 47, no. 3 (September 1974): 454–56.

57. Glenn R. Kreider, *Jonathan Edwards's Interpretation of Revelation 4:1–8:1* (Lanham, MD: University Press of America, 2004), 289.

58. The themes are as follows: "(1) the Old Testament is a massive typological system pointing not only to New Testament truths and events, but also church history and eschatology; (2) all of reality is an expression of the Trinity's desire to communicate its beauty and being to others; and (3) history is a massive story of redemption controlled by Christ and encompassing every atom and moment." See McClymond and McDermott, *The Theology of Jonathan Edwards*, 34–35.

Edwards's soteriology.[59] In his dissertation *Jonathan Edwards and the Psalms*, David P. Barshinger demonstrates that Edwards, when facing the challenges that arose from "new 'enlightened' learning," considered the Psalms "a divinely inspired anchor" to affirm the gospel.[60] Doug Landrum, in his book *Jonathan Edwards' Exegesis of Genesis*, asserts that while Edwards stood in the Puritan hermeneutical tradition, his use of the analogy of faith "placed Edwards beyond the given conservative Puritan boundaries."[61] In doing so, he agrees with Nichols's argument that Stephen Stein was incorrect when he described Edwards as one who "had no typological barriers."[62] Douglas Sweeney's biography of Edwards, *Jonathan Edwards and the Ministry of the Word*, emphasizes Edwards's interest in the Bible for the ministry.[63] More recently,

---

59. According to Nichols, dispositional soteriology means that while justification has to do with God's grace, conversion relates to an epistemological event. According to this position, the regenerate person possesses the inherent good or true saving grace which causes dispositional transformation, resulting in conversion and holy life. This view relates to Anri Morimoto and Gerald R. McDermott and in turn is followed by Steven M. Studebaker, "Jonathan Edwards' Pneumatological Concept of Grace and Dispositional Soteriology: Resources for an Evangelical Inclusivism," *Pro Ecclesia* 14, no. 3 (2005): 339; Anri Morimoto, *Jonathan Edwards and the Catholic Vision of Salvation* (University Park: Pennsylvania State University Press, 1995), 162; Gerald R. McDermott, *Jonathan Edwards Confronts the Gods: Christian Theology, Enlightenment Religion, and Non-Christian Faiths* (New York: Oxford University Press, 2000), 110–29; McDermott, "Jonathan Edwards on Justification by Faith—More Protestant or Catholic?" *Pro Ecclesia* 17, no. 1 (2008): 92–111; McClymond and McDermott, *The Theology of Jonathan Edwards*, 267–68, 361–62. Against Morimoto, McDermott, and Studebaker, Nichols claims that such a dispositional soteriology, which presents a separation of regeneration and conversion, appears to be "a fatal error." Stephen R. C. Nichols, *Jonathan Edwards's Bible*, 11, 14, 142–44, 172–73. For a debate on Edwards's doctrine of justification, see J. V. Fesko, *The Covenant of Redemption: Origins, Development, and Reception* (Göttingen: Vandenhoeck & Ruprecht, 2016), 127n94. For an assessment of the secondary literature that deals with Edwards's doctrine of justification, see Christopher Atwood, "Jonathan Edwards's Doctrine of Justification" (PhD diss., Wheaton College, 2013). For an exegetical work on Edwards's doctrine of justification, see Sweeney, *Edwards the Exegete*, 202–18. In this work, Sweeney asserts that although Edwards uses Catholic language that "sound[s] less protestant" but "remarkably Catholic" in his emphasis on good works, he presents good works "in terms of traditional Calvinism." In Sweeney's words, "Edwards offered little engagement with this Protestant concern in his sermons and biblical manuscripts. He did say, however, that neither holiness nor a regenerate disposition—in themselves—ever justify." See Sweeney, *Edwards the Exegete*, 209, 212, 213.

60. Barshinger, *Jonathan Edwards and the Psalms*, 26.

61. Doug Landrum, *Jonathan Edwards' Exegesis of Genesis: A Puritan Hermeneutic?* (Mustang, OK: Tate, 2015), 146.

62. Landrum, *Jonathan Edwards' Exegesis of Genesis*, 146.

63. Sweeney demonstrates that Edwards's manuscripts indicate his interest in "the doctrinal integrity" of the Bible. See Douglas A. Sweeney, *Jonathan Edwards and the Ministry of the Word* (Downers Grove, IL: InterVarsity, 2009), 89.

Sweeney, in *Edwards the Exegete*, provides a comprehensive outline of Edwards's biblical exegesis, examining Edwards's four main methods: "canonical exegesis," "Christological exegesis," "redemptive-historical exegesis," and "pedagogical exegesis."[64] Thus, Edwards's biblicism is essential to understanding him as an eighteenth-century Reformed Protestant.[65]

Thus far, while there have been substantial discussions of Edwards's view of covenant and biblical exegesis, only a few works have addressed his view of the interrelationship of federal theology and exegesis. Importantly, Nichols is the first to find that Edwards's concept of "redemption history and a covenantal system" is a framework for harmonizing the Old and New Testaments.[66] In a short essay, Garth E. Pauley criticizes Edwards for misunderstanding Deuteronomy 32:35 and using it to construct his particular doctrine.[67] Pauley claims that Edwards's use of federal theology is applied to interpret the text at the expense of understanding its original context.[68] While referring to federal theology's relation to canonical exegesis, Sweeney does not address the aforementioned questions relating to influences on Edwards and the interrelationship of federal theology and exegesis.

A close survey of the works highlighted above suggests that no one has yet written on the relationship between Edwards's federal theology

---

64. For the definitions of these terms, see Sweeney, *Edwards the Exegete*, x.

65. George M. Marsden, *Jonathan Edwards: A Life* (New Haven: Yale University Press, 2003), 5; David W. Kling and Douglas A. Sweeney, eds., *Jonathan Edwards at Home and Abroad: Historical Memories, Cultural Movements, Global Horizons* (Columbia, SC: University of South Carolina Press, 2003), xii; McClymond and McDermott, *The Theology of Jonathan Edwards*, 717. For references to Edwards's interest in exegesis, see Stephen J. Stein, "Edwards as Biblical Exegete," in *The Cambridge Companion to Jonathan Edwards*, ed. Stephen J. Stein (Cambridge: Cambridge University Press, 2007), 193; Stein, "The Spirit and the Word," 123; Stein, "Editor's Introduction," in *Notes on Scripture*, WJE 15:21; Kenneth P. Minkema, "Jonathan Edwards in the Twentieth Century," *JETS* 47, no. 4 (2004): 675.

66. Nichols, *Jonathan Edwards's Bible*, 14, 108.

67. Garth E. Pauley, "Soundly Gathered out of the Text? Biblical Interpretation in 'Sinners in The Hands of an Angry God,'" *TJ* 76 (2014): 95–117.

68. Pauley, "Soundly Gathered out of the Text," 107–9. Pauley's criticism of Edwards's interpretation of Deuteronomy 32:35 is based on the fact that "every modern-day Bible commentary interprets the verse to mean that at some given time Yahweh will destroy the adversaries of Israel that he uses to punish Israel for being unfaithful to the covenant" and the fact that Matthew Henry's and Matthew Poole's Bible commentaries, on which Edwards relied to interpret the text, show the same interpretation as modern-day commentaries.

and his exegesis in a dissertation or a monograph. Moreover, despite the importance of Edwards's view of federal theology for understanding his biblical exegesis, his federal theology has not been properly appreciated in studies of his theology. This book demonstrates that in attempting to understand the historical character of salvation in the revelation of the Bible, Edwards developed his federal theology using biblical exegesis and using his understanding of the doctrinal harmony of the Bible as a framework for interpreting the history of redemption.

METHODOLOGY

Following the introductory chapter, this study is divided into four parts. No account of Edwards's historical theological backdrop would be complete without reference to his Reformed predecessors, those who influenced his view of the covenant and the history of redemption. To this end, part 1 (chapter 2) identifies the definition of redemptive history in Reformed orthodoxy by surveying the views of Edwards's Reformed antecedents on this topic. While Edwards was influenced by a large number of Puritan theologians, the historicized view in his theology comes from Johannes Cocceius, Francis Turretin, Petrus van Mastricht, and Herman Witsius. My intention in this study is to identify Edwards's understanding of the history of redemption by comparing him with these Reformed forebears. Regarding influences on Edwards, my work will consider the following works: *Economy of the Covenants* (Witsius, 1803), *Institutes of Elenctic Theology* (Turretin, 1679–1685), *Theoretico-Practica Theologia* (Mastricht, 1724), and *Summa Doctrinae de Foedere et Testamento Dei* (Cocceius, 1648).

Part 2 (chapters 3, 4, and 5) identifies the definition of redemptive history by which Edwards read the Bible texts in relation to the covenant schema. To understand Edwards's federal theology, one must begin with some analysis of the structure of his covenant system. Thus, these chapters lay out Edwards's federal theology, considering the covenant schema as a summary of redemptive history for Edwards: the covenant of redemption (chapter 3), the covenant of works (chapter 4), and the covenant of grace (chapter 5). I will observe that the redemptive-historical theme plays a crucial role in Edwards's approach to the Bible, and it facilitates the development of his pneumatology, in which he emphasizes the equality among the three persons of the Godhead as covenant members.

The third part of this work (chapters 6, 7, and 8) will reveal the foundation of Edwards's exegetical method as found in his biblical writings, with a focus on the relationship between federal theology and exegesis in accomplishing the harmony of Scripture. This part examines how Edwards defended his federal theology exegetically through the use of multiple exegetical methods. I will show that Edwards developed his federal theology from his comprehensive understanding of the Bible by employing the doctrinal harmony of the Bible as a framework for understanding redemptive history. His key development within the idea of redemptive history lies in perceiving redemptive history within the larger framework of the doctrinal harmony of Scripture.

To examine Edwards's engagement with the relationship between federal theology and biblical exegesis, this book will explore Edwards's diverse writings, including *A History of the Work of Redemption*, "Notes on Scripture," the "Blank Bible," the "Miscellanies," *Typological Writings*, *Apocalyptic Writings*, hundreds of sermons from his extant corpus, *Religious Affections*, *Original Sin*, *The End for Which God Created the World*, and other biblical writings.[69] These are the most significant sources for shedding light on his concept of the history of redemption, on federal theology and its relation to exegesis, and on the nature of the harmony of Scripture. This inquiry will reveal the way in which Edwards read the Bible in trying to harmonize events that occurred in both Scripture and the world.

Part 4 (chapter 9) explores the doctrinal harmony in Edwards's ecclesiology. Specifically, chapter 9 notes how Edwards's view of the doctrinal harmony of the Bible is related to his concern for Christian community.

---

69. Edwards's *Religious Affections*, which was influenced by Turretin, reflects Edwards's biblical exegesis. According to Stein, Edwards's biblical writings can be classified into four categories according to their intended reader. The largest category of exegetical materials consists of "Notes on Scripture" and the "Blank Bible," which represent Edwards's reflections on Scripture. The second largest group of writings is Edwards's sermons, which constitute more than eleven hundred works. The third largest category of materials comprises of Edwards's theological writings, such as *Religious Affections*, *Original Sin*, and *A Dissertation Concerning the End for Which God Created the World*, which are considered the fruit of Edwards's exegetical labors. Last, for his projected works, "A History of the Work of Redemption" and "The Harmony of the Old and New Testaments," there were a number of exegetical writings, such as "notebooks dealing with types, history, and the harmony of the testament," which Edwards used. This classification method is followed by McClymond and McDermott. See Stein, "The Spirit and the Word," 121–22; McClymond and McDermott, *The Theology of Jonathan Edwards*, 167.

Edwards's pastoral concern leads to the question of how federal theology and the church are interrelated. Edwards's interest in the history of redemption can be attributed to his pastoral context, in which he felt the need to define the scriptural concept of redemptive history to his church members. For example, the method Edwards employed in *A History of the Work of Redemption* is "a direct response" against critical-historical approaches to the Bible.[70] Moreover, in rejecting Arminianism and Antinomianism, Edwards changed some points in his view of the conditionality of the covenants, especially the covenants of redemption and grace. This does not mean that his prior view of covenant is in contrast with the latter but rather implies that Edwards developed his own covenant view in terms of his emphasis on redemptive history. Edwards's concern for believers in his ministry is one reason that he attempted to write *A History of the Work of Redemption*. The last reason for Edwards's interest in the redemptive-historical theme can be ascribed to his enthusiastic wish for his congregation to know the glory of God as the ultimate purpose of redemption. In this vein, I will examine the relationship between Edwards's federal theology and his ecclesiology, noting in particular the close relationship between faith and piety. It is through his federal theology that Edwards attempted to develop the Christian's practical engagement with redemptive history.

The concluding chapter (chapter 10) will provide a brief sketch of the relationships among Edwards's understandings of redemptive history, biblical exegesis, and ecclesiology, thus evaluating Edwards's view of the doctrinal harmony of Scripture as an interpretive framework for understanding the history of redemption.

SIGNIFICANCE OF THE STUDY

While many scholars have discussed Edwards's covenantal view and exegetical writings, no one has provided an understanding of the relationship between his federal theology and biblical exegesis. This project proves that federal theology is not antithetical to Edwards's biblical exegesis, nor to the Christian life. This perspective sheds new light on the practical significance of the doctrine of covenant in interpreting the Bible and thus rejects

---

70. Brown, *Jonathan Edwards and the Bible*, 166.

contemporary scholars who argue that scholasticism is dry.[71] Moreover, given that no dissertation or monograph has been published on Edwards's federal theology, with the exceptions of Bogue's book and Yazawa's dissertation, this book will play a formative role in understanding Edwards's federal theology as well as his biblical exegesis, helping scholars who deal with Edwards's biblical writings.

---

71. Richard Muller, "Giving Direction to Theology: The Scholastic Dimension," *JETS* 28, no. 2 (June 1985): 1, 2; Muller, "The Covenant of Works and the Stability of Divine Law, 81; Muller, *Post-Reformation Reformed Dogmatics,* 4 vols. (Grand Rapids: Baker, 1987), 2:525–40; Muller, "'Either Expressly Set Down ... or by Good and Necessary Consequence': Exegesis and Formulation in the Annotations and the Confession," in *Scripture and Worship: Biblical Interpretation and the Directory for Public Worship,* ed. Richard A. Muller and Rowland S. Ward (Phillipsburg, NJ: P&R, 2007), 59–82; Adriaan C. Neele, *Petrus van Mastricht (1630–1706): Reformed Orthodoxy: Method and Piety* (Leiden: Brill, 2009), 1; Yazawa, "Covenant of Redemption in the Theology of Jonathan Edwards," 17–18.

Part 1

—

REDEMPTION *and* HISTORY *in* REFORMED ORTHODOXY

2
—

A SKETCH OF THE HISTORY OF REDEMPTION AMONG EDWARDS'S ANTECEDENTS

INTRODUCTION

When one begins to outline Edwards's view of federal theology and the history of redemption, it becomes difficult to proceed without making frequent reference to his forebears. Furthermore, since this book sets out to explore how Edwards's federal theology relates to that of his Reformed predecessors, it is even more necessary to begin our analysis with a consideration of their definitions and approaches. This will help clarify how the terms "federal theology" and "the history of redemption" developed and came to be understood as part of Reformed orthodoxy.

Federal theology was taught by most of Edwards's principal authorities, including the *Westminster Confession of Faith* (1649), William Ames (1576–1633), Gisbertus Voetius (1589–1676), Johannes Cocceius (1603–1669), Francis Turretin (1623–1687), Petrus van Mastricht (1630–1706), and Herman Witsius (1636–1708).[1] These Reformed theologians influenced each other. For example, most of them were guided by Ames.[2] Van Mastricht was a disciple of Voetius and at the same time was strongly influenced by

---

1. John E. Eusden, "Introduction" in William Ames, *The Marrow of Theology*, ed. and trans. John E. Eusden (Boston: Pilgrim Press, 1968), 65; Carl W. Bogue, *Jonathan Edwards and the Covenant of Grace* (Cherry Hill, NJ: Mack, 1975), 63; Joel R. Beeke, *Puritan Reformed Spirituality* (Grand Rapids: Reformation Heritage, 2004), 138–39. For more on Ames's influence on Edwards's understanding of federal theology, see Jan van Vliet, "Covenant and Conscience: Amesian Echoes in Jonathan Edwards," in *The Rise of Reformed System: The Intellectual Heritage of William Ames* (Eugene, OR: Wipf & Stock, 2013), 233–65.

2. Eusden, "Introduction," 65.

the covenant ideas of both Ames and Cocceius.[3] This denotes a family of approaches within the Reformed tradition.

However, Edwards's Reformed forebears did not consider Ames, or any other single Reformed theologian, the standard representative of their covenantal view. Rather, they sought to synthesize their theological views. For instance, although Cocceius followed the Reformed tradition, he provided this tradition with a new idea in the doctrine of abrogations.[4] Moreover, Cocceius identified only two dispensations within the covenant of grace, but later federal theologians (i.e., Witsius and Heidanus) tended to further divide these categories.[5] Later on, Herman Witsius sought to be "a theologian of synthesis" by defusing the tension between the Voetians and the Cocceians.[6] Likewise, Mastricht incorporated some of the different approaches of his contemporaries into his doctrine of God.[7] This is also

---

3. Eusden, "Introduction" 65.

4. The abrogations of the covenant of works are described by Willem J. Van Asselt as follows: "They are expressions that indicate a once-for-all event; they appear to exclude the idea of gradations or development. Nonetheless, Cocceius also uses terms that do indicate a gradual progression. The abrogation proceeds (*procedit*) by stages (*gradibus*), through which gradually (*paulatim*) and more and more (*magis magisque*) salvation is realized among believers. This suggests a process of deliverance in which one stage is left behind and progress is made toward the next step. This process of deliverance is amenable to description in terms of the covenant of works–covenant of grace schema: the elements of the covenant of works undergo a negative development, going from greater to lesser, while the elements of the covenant of grace undergo a positive development, progressing from lesser to greater." See Willem J. Van Asselt, *The Federal Theology of Johannes Cocceius, 1603–1669*, trans. Raymond A. Blacketer (Leiden: Brill, 2001), 276.

5. According to Van Asselt, Witsius and Heidanus identify more periods within the Old and New Testament economies of salvation. Van Asselt, *The Federal Theology of Johannes Cocceius*, 294–95.

6. Witsius employs the "Cocceian methods while maintaining essentially Voetian theology" in arranging his view of the covenant concept. Beeke, *Puritan Reformed Spirituality*, 339, 355. In the same vein, Mark Beach suggests that Witsius's *Economy* represents his "conciliatory spirit," in that he "sought to bring together the positive strains in both Voetian orthodoxy and Cocceian federalism." J. Mark Beach, "The Doctrine of the *Pactum Salutis* in the Covenant Theology of Herman Witsius," *Mid-America Journal of Theology* 13 (2002): 101–42.

7. Adriaan C. Neele, *Petrus van Mastricht (1630–1706): Reformed Orthodoxy: Method and Piety* (Leiden: Brill, 2009), 219. For more on Mastricht's life and work, see Adriaan C. Neele, "Petrus van Mastricht (1630–1706): Life and Work," in Petrus von Mastricht, *Theoretical-Practical Theology* vol. 1, *Prolegomena*, ed. Joel R. Beeke, trans. Todd M. Rester (Grand Rapids: Reformation Heritage, 2018), xxv–xxxiii.

true of Turretin, who played an important role as a "codifier" of federal theology, which was maintained by "numerous Reformed theologians."[8]

Thus, an exploration of the views of the covenant held by Edwards's predecessors, including Witsius, Mastricht, Cocceius, and Turretin, will further illuminate Edwards's view of federal theology in relation to his understanding of Scripture. For instance, Cocceius's view of salvation history appears akin to Edwards's view of the history of redemption. And the doctrine of covenants for Witsius is "a consistent interpretative procedure yielding a proper understanding of Scripture,"[9] which parallels Edwards's theological approach to Scripture. Moreover, the theology of both Mastricht and Turretin would influence Edwards's constant emphasis on biblical exegesis.[10]

Given the significance of these Reformed scholastics' view of federal theology, it is surprising that Edwards's debt to his predecessors has been largely overlooked in studies about his federal theology. However, investigating each single figure and topic that helped shape his federal theology would exceed the scope of this book. Thus, this chapter seeks to examine and evaluate the formulation of federal theology by Cocceius, Witsius, Mastricht, and Turretin, specifically as these formulations discuss the history of redemption. In this pursuit, this chapter will touch only tangentially on the biblical texts to which these authors refer to provide an exegetical ground for their federal theology. This evaluation will seek to draw out the similarities and differences among the views of the aforementioned Reformed predecessors regarding the redemptive-historical aspect of their federal theology. We begin by turning to Cocceius.

---

8. J. Mark Beach, *Christ and the Covenant: Francis Turretin's Federal Theology as a Defense of the Doctrine of Grace*, Reformed Historical Theology (Göttingen: Vandenhoeck & Ruprecht, 2007), 13. The same is true for Francis Roberts, who "does not merely follow his predecessor [John Ball] but distinguishes himself by establishing his covenant theology more firmly on a scriptural basis." Won Taek Lim, "The Covenant Theology of Francis Roberts" (PhD diss., Calvin Theological Seminary, 2000), 205.

9. Beeke, *Puritan Reformed Spirituality*, 339.

10. Paul Ramsey, "Appendix IV: Infused Virtues in Edwardsean and Calvinistic Context," in *Ethical Writing, WJE* 8:742.

JOHANNES COCCEIUS (1603–1669)

Edwards does not make any direct reference to Cocceius's work throughout his corpus. However, it is nonetheless clear that Edwards's historical
perspective of federal theology was not developed in isolation from the
federal theology of Johannes Cocceius. In fact, Cocceius's federal theology
was somewhat of a landmark in the Reformed theological tradition and
helped shape perspectives for centuries.[11] While aspects of his federal theology can be traced from his Reformed predecessors and contemporaries,
such as William Ames, Cloppenburg, and Olevianus,[12] his historical perspective on covenant appears to be unique.[13]

In fact, many of Cocceius's contemporaries viewed his federal theology
as an innovation that went against the mainstream of Reformed orthodoxy. For example, Cocceian theology was considered "a potential threat
to traditional faith and theology, causing a theological conflict between the
Voetian and Cocceian blocs."[14] Karl Barth opposed Cocceius's historicized
view of theology since he believed that the view could result in "a degra-
dation of the reconciliation accomplished in Christ as covenant history."[15]
Similarly, Charles S. McCoy concluded that Cocceius was an anti-scholastic

---

11. Van Asselt, *The Federal Theology of Johannes Cocceius*, 1, 28; Cornelis van der Knijff and
Willem van Vlastuin, "The Development in Jonathan Edwards' Covenant View," *Jonathan
Edwards Studies* 3, no. 2 (2013): 280.

12. Van Asselt, *The Federal Theology of Johannes Cocceius*, 228; Richard A. Muller, "Toward
the *Pactum Salutis*: Locating the Origins of a Concept," *Mid-America Journal of Theology* 18
(2007): 11–65. It appears that federal theology in the view of Cocceius is closely associated
with those of Cloppenburg and Olevianus. For example, Cocceius, in his "Preface to the
Reader" of the *Summa Doctrinae*, reveals his acquaintance with Olevianus who had already
studied the doctrine of covenant. Heinrich Heppe states, "Olevianus conceives the term of
the covenant of works (from his *foedus legale, foedus naturae,* f. called *creationis*) in contrast to
the covenant of grace (*foedus gratuitum novum*) in the very same way as Cocceius does." See
Heinrich Heppe, *Geschichte des Pietismus und der Mystik in der reformierten Kirche namentlich
in der Niederlande* (Leiden: Brill, 1879), 211n1. German original: "Allerdings fast Olevianus den
Begriff des Werkbunds (von ihm foedus legale, foedus naturae, f. creationis genannt) im
Gegensatz zu dem Gnadenbund (foedus gratuitum novum) schon ganz in derselben Weise auf,
wie Cocceius." For the origin of federal theology, see Muller, "Toward the *Pactum Salutis*," 11–65.

13. For example, Van Asselt claims, "Unlike Voetius, Cocceius did not read the Scripture
as a physics textbook. Cocceius, to a significant extent, left the knowledge of nature to the
realm of reason. The Bible is primarily a history book (*oeconomia temporum*) and a devotional
book." Van Asselt, *The Federal Theology of Johannes Cocceius*, 94, 93, and 106.

14. Van Asselt, *The Federal Theology of Johannes Cocceius*, 25.

15. Van Asselt, *The Federal Theology of Johannes Cocceius*, 9.

theologian.[16] These assessments of Cocceius imply that his view of covenant differed greatly from many Reformed thinkers.

However, as Richard Muller rightly warns, this conclusion depends on thinking that "anachronistically draws a rather strict and narrow line of development from Calvin" and "denominates only what fits in this particular Genevan trajectory as 'orthodoxy.' "[17] As others have argued, Cocceius's theological view can be seen as not only deeply grounded in the Reformed faith and tradition but also not foreign to the scholastic method.[18] For example, Brian J. Lee argues that Cocceius's federal theology is "thoroughly scholastic in its precision and complexity," opposing the claim that "federal theology was 'biblical' and therefore 'anti-scholastic.' "[19] Thus, for Cocceius, "the covenant terminology" provided "the raw materials for constructing a system of thought" in relation to redemption.[20] With this in mind, this section will seek to examine *The Doctrine of the Covenant and Testament of God* (the *Summa Doctrinae*), in which Cocceius describes the structure of his federal theology.[21]

---

16. Charles S. McCoy, "The Covenant Theology of Johannes Cocceius" (PhD diss., Yale University, 1956), 39–40; McCoy, "Johannes Cocceius: Federal Theologian," *Scottish Journal of Theology* 16 (1963): 352–70, 354. Richard Muller provides the definition of Reformed scholasticism as follows: "'Reformed scholasticism' indicates the method characteristic of the classroom and of the more detailed systems of theology developed by the confessionally Reformed branch of the Reformation during its era of orthodoxy. This method, moreover, differed from that of the medieval scholastic by reason of the incorporation of many of the changes in logic and rhetoric brought about by the Renaissance and the Reformation." Richard A. Muller, *After Calvin: Studies in the Development of a Theological Tradition* (Oxford: Oxford University Press, 2003), 36. For another definition of Reformed scholasticism, see James T. Dennison Jr., "The Life and Career of Francis Turretin," in Turretin, *Institutes of Elenctic Theology*, 3 vols., ed. James T. Dennison Jr., trans. George Musgrave Giger (Phillipsburg, NJ: P&R, 1997), 3:647.

17. Richard A. Muller, *Post-Reformation Reformed Dogmatics: The Rise and Development of Reformed Orthodoxy, ca. 1520 to ca. 1725*, vol 1, *Prolegomena to Theology* (Grand Rapids: Baker Academic, 2003), 79.

18. Van Asselt, *The Federal Theology of Johannes Cocceius*, 45; Van Asselt, "Cocceius Anti-Scholasticus." in *Reformation and Scholasticism: An Ecumenical Endeavor*, ed. Willem Van Asselt and Eef Dekker (Grand Rapids: Baker, 2001), 227–52. Cf. Muller, *After Calvin*, 13.

19. Brian J. Lee, "The Covenant Terminology of Johannes Cocceius: The Use of *Foedus, Pactum,* and *Testamentum* in a Mature Federal Theology," *Mid-America Journal of Theology* 14 (2003): 11n11.

20. Lee, "The Covenant Terminology of Johannes Cocceius," 35–36.

21. Van Asselt, *The Federal Theology of Johannes Cocceius*, 37. Van Asselt notes that the literary corpus of Cocceius was colossal. For a detailed explanation of the works of Cocceius, see Van Asselt, *The Federal Theology of Johannes Cocceius*, 31.

To begin, Cocceius seeks to establish the biblical importance of the term "covenant." As Willem Van Asselt states, "By means of the concept of *foedus* (covenant), he [Cocceius] sought to do justice to the historical nature of the biblical narrative."[22] Given his evident enthusiasm for the historical perspective within exegetical research, it is of little surprise that Cocceius employs considerable biblical proof in this regard. In the first chapter of *Doctrine of the Covenant*, Cocceius provides an exegetical analysis of the term covenant (*foedus*), which is based on the Hebrew word ברית and the Greek word διαθήκη. He writes, "The Hebrew word ברית, *berith*, is more commonly and more properly related to ברה, *to choose*, than to ברא, *to cut* (as Grotius thinks)."[23] This makes it clear that Cocceius believed that a central element of the covenant relates to "αἵρεσις (choice) and *selection* of conditions from each party."[24]

He goes on to elaborate on the covenantal choice. He argues that the Scriptures teach that when one party chooses the other contracting party with "love," the relationship between the two parties implies "mutual benevolence and eagerness."[25] To prove his interpretation of covenant as a choice, Cocceius identifies a series of texts, including Genesis 21:32; 26:28–29; Exodus 34:12–13, 15; Deuteronomy 7:2; 1 Samuel 18:3; Isaiah 54:10; Zechariah 11:10; Daniel 9:27; Matthew 26:28; 24:6–8; Job 5:23; Hosea 2:17, 18, and 20; Amos 1:9; and Malachi 2:14.

After defining covenant as a mutual agreement between two parties, Cocceius proceeds to emphasize the unilateral and bilateral character of the divine covenant:

Therefore, the covenant of God with man is μονόπλευρον (one-sided), insofar as it is the design and arrangement of God alone concerning the way of receiving His love and benefits. Indeed, this is very similar to the way in which victors are accustomed to order their vanquished, masters their ἀργυρωνήτοις, slaves, and parents their children. Every covenant of God, however, is not so

22. Van Asselt, *The Federal Theology of Johannes Cocceius*, 38.

23. Johannes Cocceius, *The Doctrine of the Covenant and Testament of God*, trans. Casey Carmichael (Grand Rapids: Reformation Heritage, 2016), 19.

24. Cocceius, *The Doctrine of the Covenant and Testament of God*, 19.

25. Cocceius, *The Doctrine of the Covenant and Testament of God*, 19.

μονόπλευρον (one-sided) that obligation is entirely absent from the other party, as it is for instance when God makes covenant with day and night, obligating Himself by decree that the distinction between day and night would be preserved (Jer 33:20; Gen 8:22).

The covenant of God is δίπλευρον (two-sided) or mutual, when man, clinging to God according to the law of the covenant, obligates himself τῇ ὁμολογίᾳ, by confession, to the force of the divine arrangement, as if to guarantee His love and benefits.[26]

Cocceius's focus on grace, which is seen in this description, is followed by a description of the nature of faith, which reveals the twofold nature of covenant: the covenants of works and grace. He quotes Romans 4:4–5: "To him who works, rewards will not be rewarded according to grace but according to debt. However, the one who does not work but trusts Him who justifies the wicked, his faith is reckoned for righteousness." From this, Cocceius describes faith as follows: "Therefore *faith*, which justifies, is 'not of the one who works' but of the one who confesses that he is guilty and trusts 'God, who justifies the wicked.'"[27] As this phrase suggests, Cocceius focuses on the element of grace even within the covenant of works, as is typical of the Calvinistic understanding of sin. Thus, while Cocceius contrasts the covenant of works and the covenant of grace, he nevertheless understands that the covenant of works is based on the grace of God.

In chapter 2, Cocceius goes on to analyze the covenant of works in detail. According to him, "the covenant of works (*foedus operum*), or friendship with God (*amicita cum Deo*), and the righteousness (*Justitia*) that is from works (*ex operibus*)" can be summarized in two biblical statements, that is, Galatians 3:12 and 10: "The one who will do these things, he will live by them" and "cursed is everyone who does not remain in all things written in the book of the law, that he may do them." In these verses, he finds three elements in the structure of the covenant of works: "*law, promise*, and *threat*."[28]

---

26. Cocceius, *The Doctrine of the Covenant and Testament of God*, 23.

27. Cocceius, *The Doctrine of the Covenant and Testament of God*, 26.

28. Cocceius states, "Indeed, *law, promise*, and *threat* are all included in these pronouncements. For in the offering of the covenant, the word that teaches the way of receiving the love of God is *law*, that which joins to this way the love of God and the benefits is *promise*, and that which excludes every other way to the highest good (*summum bonum*) and indicates the necessary consequence of punishment for sin is *threat*. Obedience to that law is δικαίωμα or

Chapter 3 moves on to his doctrine of abrogations, which is the central argument of his federal theology. According to Cocceius, the covenant of works is gradually abrogated. He argues that since the law in the Old Testament has to do with "wrath," this law is abolished in the era of the New Testament. Cocceius interprets the phrase "we are not under law" in Romans 6:14 as an abolition of the law. Most interesting is that he structures these abrogations in a fivefold manner. He lays out the gradual nullifications of the covenant of works as follows:

> With respect to the possibility of giving life, by sin.
>
> With respect to damnation, by Christ set forth in the promise and received by faith.
>
> With respect to terror, or influence of the fear of death and bondage, by the promulgation of the New Covenant, expiation for sin having been made, whereby those who have been redeemed are under the law of the Redeemer. So that same law, abolished by the Redeemer as the law of sin, becomes the law of the Savior and imputes righteousness to them, who are His own (Gal 2:19; Rom 7:4; 2 Cor 5:15-21).
>
> With respect to the struggle with sin, by the death of the body.
>
> With respect to all created things, by the resurrection of the dead.[29]

For Cocceius, the first abrogation took place when Adam broke the covenant by sin. Adam's failure to participate in "the friendship of God, eternal life, and happiness for man" brought about "a sentence of damnation and of death."[30] Here, he believes various texts from the New Testament come into play, for example, Romans 7:10; 1 Corinthians 15:56; Galatians 3:21; Romans 8:3; and Matthew 19:25-26.[31] Each of these biblical texts reflects the aftermath of sin under the law. Cocceius's New Testament references in his exposition of the fivefold structure of the covenant are largely Pauline, except Matthew 19:25-26. This reflects Cocceius's method as he formulates

---

the cause of righteousness, that is, payment of a right deserved." Cocceius, *The Doctrine of the Covenant and Testament of God*, 28.

29. Cocceius, *The Doctrine of the Covenant and Testament of God*, 58–59.

30. Cocceius, *The Doctrine of the Covenant and Testament of God*, 59.

31. Cocceius, *The Doctrine of the Covenant and Testament of God*, 59.

his doctrine of abrogations. That is, his use of collated biblical texts shows that he maintains a theological understanding of Scripture.

Cocceius asserts that the second abrogation takes place upon "the reception of the sinner into *the covenant of grace*," which implies God's mercy on man in response to the fall.[32] While the condemnation of man took place under the law of the covenant, the acceptance of sinners happens in the context of the covenant of grace. However, in the covenant of grace, God still demands from man "obedience" in accordance with "His lordship."[33] Despite God's judgment upon man, Cocceius argues, God's "wisdom and power" provides "ineffable mercy χάριν (grace)" and χρηστότητα (goodness) in accordance with his "certain indescribable kindness and patience toward the whole human race (Rom 9:22–23; 2:4)." In this regard, Cocceius defines the covenant of grace as "an agreement between God and man the sinner." This covenant of grace grants "*the* good," that is, the "*life*," that was promised in the covenant of works, to those who enter into the covenant of grace by faith in Christ the mediator.[34]

Having provided a detailed exposition of the covenant of grace in subsequent sections and chapters (§78–274), Cocceius turns to the third abrogation. He argues that it occurs "through the promulgation of the New Covenant," which brings about the "expiation of sin." This new covenant grants sinners the power to "claim the goods decreed in the testament as heirs, the suitable mode in that last time." Here, Cocceius distinguishes between the eras of the Old and New Testaments, since there are "a double οἰκονομίαν, economy, and double time." Thus, he believes the third abolition happened first in the Old Testament era, during which believers possessed faith in "the revealed Christ." In this era, faith can be understood as "the *hope* of the future," and Christ is the object of that faith.[35]

In chapter 11, Cocceius makes a clear distinction between the two economies, or two testaments, as far as the covenant of grace is concerned. He argues that those under the era of the first economy did not see "the *Son* of God *given*" nor hear "the word of the gospel about sins having been

---

32. Cocceius, *The Doctrine of the Covenant and Testament of God*, 70.
33. Cocceius, *The Doctrine of the Covenant and Testament of God*, 68.
34. Cocceius, *The Doctrine of the Covenant and Testament of God*, 72.
35. Cocceius, *The Doctrine of the Covenant and Testament of God*, 172–73.

expiated." In this period, "a certain darkness" existed, which he describes as "expectation or less clarity with respect to the little measure of revelation." In the words of Van Asselt, "The whole course of history up to the point of the historical manifestation of the Mediator is characterized by the expectation of the advent of the Mediator."[36] Cocceius maintains that this period is under "wrath and severity" because of "the terror" that the believers at that time experienced. Thus, this dispensation implies "the tolerance of God," based on the "delay of judgment in which God would condemn sin."[37]

For Cocceius, one of the most prominent distinctions between the two economies is found not only in *the manner of teaching* but also in the *judgments*," which reveal "the wickedness of the human disposition." Cocceius first lists the judgments in the historical events of the Bible: "the flood, the confusion of languages, the destruction of Sodom, the plagues of Egypt, ... and chiefly the castigation of the Israelite people, of which was especially the dejection of the ten tribes, the Babylonian captivity, etc."[38] He argues that in the Old Testament, these revelations of the condemnation of sinners were also demonstrated in the manner of teaching. He writes, "And indeed the *old* or *first covenant* that God made with the Israelites added the old law to the promise. The *second* or *new* announces δικαίωμα, merit of righteousness, in Christ Jesus. The former endured through the time παιδαγωίας, of the management of a child. Through the latter διόρθωσις, reformation, was made to the old things (Heb 9:10)."[39]

At first glance, Cocceius seems here to present the dispensation of the Old Testament as inferior to that of the New Testament. However, Cocceius does not draw a sharp distinction between the benefits of the covenant of grace in the old and new economies. Instead, as Brian J. Lee helpfully points out, Cocceius's emphasis upon the unity of the two testaments is maintained, unlike the Anabaptists' and Socinians' denigration of the Old Testament.[40] Thus, Cocceius's view of the difference between the two

---

36. Van Asselt, *The Federal Theology of Johannes Cocceius*, 45.

37. Cocceius, *The Doctrine of the Covenant and Testament of God*, 192–93.

38. Cocceius, *The Doctrine of the Covenant and Testament of God*, 193.

39. Cocceius, *The Doctrine of the Covenant and Testament of God*, 196.

40. Brian J. Lee, "Biblical Exegesis, Johannes Cocceius, and Federal Theology: Developments in the Interpretation of Hebrews 7:1–10:18" (PhD diss., Calvin Theological

dispensations should be understood as a focus on the progressive character of redemptive history. In this respect, Van Asselt rightly notes, "The New Testament, therefore, acknowledges no other blessings than those of the Old Testament, but it proclaims these benefits differently, that is, in their full historical reality."[41] For Cocceius, grace and salvation were already in Christ even during the era of the old dispensation.

Given Cocceius's distinction between the eras of the Old and New Testaments, it is not difficult to see why he, in the next chapter (12), discusses the six benefits he finds offered fully in the New Testament. The first is "the *display of perfect righteousness*" in the Son's obedience to the law. Through this benefit, he argues, believers come to a knowledge of the excellency of God's righteousness that Christ acquired through his obedience to suffering and passion. The second benefit is "the clear notification of the name of God (John 17:26; Isa 52:6; Heb 2:12)," which was revealed through the works of Christ in his "preaching," "obedience," "passion," "resurrection," and "ascension." The third is "'the inscription of the law of God on their hearts' (Heb 8:10 from Jer 31:34)." The fourth is "*absolution of conscience*," which is in opposition to "the more imperfect" offering in the Old Testament. This blessing is described as "consummation," "sanctification," "remission," and "justification (Heb 10:1, 10, 14, 17–18; Rom 3:26; 4:25)." The fifth is "*freedom*," which refers to freedom from "*servitude*" arising from the "*fear of death*" (Heb 2:15). The sixth and final benefit is "*peace* (Ps 72:3; Isa 9:5–6; Zech 6:13; 9:10; Hag 2:13)," which stands in opposition to "the enmity between Israel and the Gentiles," so that now the Gentile is included in the promises.[42]

In chapters 13 and 14, Cocceius deals with the sacraments and the office of bishop in the context of the Old and New Testaments. Here, his focus lies on the intimate relationship of the two testaments. Despite the difference he finds between the old and new dispensations (chapter 11), and by implication the benefits of the two economies (chapter 12), he argues that the sacraments and offices of the New Testament are by no means foreign to those of the Old Testament (chapters 13 and 14). When it comes to

---

Seminary, 2003), abstract.

41. Van Asselt, *The Federal Theology of Johannes Cocceius*, 45.

42. Cocceius, *The Doctrine of the Covenant and Testament of God*, 239–51.

the practice of the sacraments of the Old and New Testaments, Cocceius concludes:

> It appears that one thing must be added about the sacraments of the New Testament, that the sacraments of the Old Testament (when the law of ceremonies ceased to be a bond from the right of the death of Christ) remained for a time ceremonies of freedom and sacraments to be used by Christians, especially those who were converted from the Jews, for the sake of charity, until the whole Israelite people would receive Christ or would not entirely endure Christians or the temple would be destroyed, but they were not to be imposed on the Gentiles.[43]

This makes it clear that Cocceius's description of the sacraments is not limited to those rites practiced by believers and the church. Instead, this comment serves to illuminate his view of the abrogations in which the Bible is revealed through gradual stages.

Last, Cocceius uses chapters 15 and 16 to discuss the fourth and fifth abrogations, which deal with the doctrines of sanctification and eschatology respectively, although these two themes are not separate in both chapters. For the purpose of this discussion, it is enough to point out that the fifth abrogation, although it discusses eschatology, centers on the meaning of the resurrection of the body. The same is true of the fourth abrogation, which entails "the abolishment of the struggle of sin" through "the death of the body."[44]

Cocceius argues that by the death of the body, those who have faith in Christ become "new creatures" that are righteous before Christ. Thus, essential to him is "the benefit of *"sanctification,"* which is deeply related to *"reconciliation,"* *"regeneration,"* and *"justification."*[45] Indeed, it is so important to Cocceius that he provides fifteen reasons why believers should come under the obligation of sanctification, with an emphasis on the necessity of true conversion. Cocceius's interest in the flesh (chapter 15) and the resurrection of the body (chapter 16) is perhaps not surprising, given that his

---

43. Cocceius, *The Doctrine of the Covenant and Testament of God*, 315.

44. Cocceius, *The Doctrine of the Covenant and Testament of God*, 321.

45. Cocceius, *The Doctrine of the Covenant and Testament of God*, 321.

doctrine of abrogations has to do with the death of the body as the result of sin, as already discussed. With respect to his exegetical discussion of sanctification, Cocceius appeals to Romans 6:14 to argue that believers are not under law but "under grace," so that they would not be controlled by sin.[46]

As Van Asselt notes, chapters 3 to 16 of *Summa Doctrinae* follow the "the subsequent structure" of the doctrine of abrogations. Considering the complexity of Cocceius's detailed layout of the doctrine of abrogations, Van Asselt helpfully describes them as follows:

> They are expressions that indicate a once-for-all event; they appear to exclude the idea of gradations or development. Nonetheless, Cocceius also uses terms that do indicate a gradual progression. The abrogation proceeds (*procedit*) by stages (*gradibus*), through which gradually (*paulatim*) and more and more (*magis magisque*) salvation is realized among believers. This suggests a process of deliverance in which one stage is left behind and progress is made toward the next step. This process of deliverance is amenable to description in terms of the covenant of works–covenant of grace schema: the elements of the covenant of works undergo a negative development, going from greater to lesser, while the elements of the covenant of grace undergo a positive development, progressing from lesser to greater.[47]

Thus, it is clear that Cocceius's doctrine of abrogations is historicized.

EVALUATION OF COCCEIUS

Cocceius presents the covenant of works and the covenant of grace in terms of a historical application of the biblical text. His doctrine of abrogations is set forth in the context of biblical history, with a particular focus on sin and the resulting death of the body as well as the manifestation of revelation among believers as the benefit of the covenant of grace. This pattern of the covenant story bears a striking resemblance to the other Puritan theologians' view of covenant. As John von Rohr rightly notes, the

---

46. Cocceius, *The Doctrine of the Covenant and Testament of God*, 325.

47. Van Asselt, *The Federal Theology of Johannes Cocceius*, 276. Note that while the first abrogation is applied to all sinners as a universal, the later abrogations belong to believers only. See Van Asselt, *The Federal Theology of Johannes Cocceius*, 281.

covenantal structure in Puritan thought begins with "a failed covenant" that is followed by a covenant of grace. He writes, "Sin destroyed that covenantal relationship—and the covenant of grace, though actually planned in eternity in a covenant of redemption, constituted God's response to the historical event of the fall. It was an act of God's mercy in repair of human misery."[48]

Second, while Cocceius's view of the covenant involves the order of salvation in the faith of believers, his analysis of the abrogations is heavily historical. When one notes Cocceius's structure of the abrogations, it is difficult to see how he discusses the meaning of *ordo salutis*. However, in Van Asselt's analysis of Cocceius's doctrine of abrogation, he points out that the "salvation-historical phase" in the abrogations "corresponds to a certain state or condition of the believers."[49] If this is true, it means that Cocceius's understanding of the distinction between the old and new dispensations combines "the salvation-historical and the salvation order—or the historical and the existential—elements." Nonetheless, as Van Asselt emphasizes, the abrogation should be considered fundamentally "linear-historical in nature."[50]

Finally, given Cocceius's considerable references to the biblical text, it is difficult to trace which texts take central place in his biblical exegesis of the doctrine of covenant. Nevertheless, a careful survey of his analysis and exegetical explanation of the covenant suggests that he relies heavily on the epistles, especially Romans, Galatians, Hebrews, and the Johannine letters.[51] Moreover, Romans and Galatians play a particularly significant role in his definition of the covenant in the first two chapters of *The Doctrine of the Covenant*. Also, as Cocceius discusses the fivefold nullification of the covenant of works, he cites Romans 6:14, "we are not under law."[52] Thus, it appears that while he refers to numerous Old Testament texts, his formulation of federal theology is based on the New Testament.

---

48. John Von Rohr, *The Covenant of Grace in Puritan Thought* (Atlanta: Scholars Press, 1986), 10.

49. Van Asselt, *The Federal Theology of Johannes Cocceius*, 278.

50. Van Asselt, *The Federal Theology of Johannes Cocceius*, 280–81.

51. See Scripture index of Cocceius, *The Doctrine of the Covenant and Testament of God*, 375–96.

52. Cf. Cocceius, *The Doctrine of the Covenant and Testament of God*, 58, 84, 205, 269, 325.

Further, it seems that the most crucial text in terms of his formulation of the doctrine of the covenant is Romans 6:14.

HERMAN WITSIUS (1636–1708)

In attempting to harmonize the tension[53] between the Voetians and the Cocceians, who were his immediate predecessors, Herman Witsius published *Oeconomia Foederum Dei cum Hominibus* (1677), which has been reprinted several times in English as a multi-volume work entitled *The Economy of the Covenants Between God and Man: Comprehending a Complete Body of Divinity*. Within this work, Witsius employs Cocceius's redemptive-historical method in systematizing his theology.[54] Even though Witsius does not provide an outright definition of redemptive history, the concept shows up in his view of the economy (*oeconomia*) of salvation in Book 3 of *Economy of the Covenants*. In this discussion, he considers the order of salvation (*ordo salutis*) and the administration of the covenant of grace throughout history.

While Book 3 has been said to discuss "the entire field of soteriology,"[55] Witsius particularly focuses on the nature of the covenant of grace. He describes "God's covenant with the elect" in terms of "the contracting parties," "the promises of the covenant," and "the condition in the covenant." Witsius begins by emphasizing the covenant's divine initiative. Witsius identifies the contracting parties, namely, God and the elect, in "the compact between the Father and the Son." He describes God as one who is "truly all-sufficient," "merciful and gracious," "just," and "wise," and then contrasts that description with the elect, who are "sinners," "chosen," and "those for whom Christ engaged or made satisfaction."[56] Here, Witsius

---

53. Gisbertus Voetius (1589–1676) rejected the covenant theology of Johannes Cocceius, which focused on the historical aspect of specific ages and which viewed the Lord's Day as nothing more than ceremonial and thus no longer binding on Christians. Moreover, Voetius criticized Cocceius, who was sympathetic toward Descartes. Beeke, *Puritan Reformed Spirituality*, 335; Van Asselt, *The Federal Theology of Johannes Cocceius*, 72–101. For more works on the debate between Voetian orthodoxy and Cocceian federalism, see Beach, "Doctrine of the *Pactum Salutis* in the Covenant Theology of Herman Witsius," 101n2.

54. Beeke, *Puritan Reformed Spirituality*, 339.

55. Beeke, *Puritan Reformed Spirituality*, 342.

56. Herman Witsius, *The Economy of the Covenants Between God and Man: Comprehending a Complete Body of Divinity*, trans. William Crookshank, 2 vols. (Edinburgh: John Turnbull, 1803), III.i.1–3 (1:285–86).

stresses the gracious character of the covenant of grace by comparing God's attributes with the sinful nature of human beings.

After this emphasis on God's sovereign grace within the covenant, Witsius focuses on the persons of the Trinity. He describes the Father as "the principal author of it [the covenant]," who appointed the elect to be his heirs. The Son is considered the "*Mediator*," "executor of the covenant," and "*the testator*," who established "the testament of grace." The Son is also "the *distributor*" of all the benefits of the covenant of grace. And finally, the Holy Spirit "brings the Elect to Christ, and, in Christ, to the possession of the benefits of the covenant, and intimates to their consciences τὰ ὅσια τοῦ Δαβιδ τα πιστα, the holy pledges, the sure mercies of David, and is the seal and earnest of their complete happiness, 1 Cor. xii. 3, 11, 12. Eph. i. 13, 14."[57] For Witsius, the economy of the Trinity reveals how the elect are appointed as heirs by God's choice from eternity. However, Witsius believes the covenant of grace is accomplished within history through Christ's suffering and crucifixion, as is the benefit of the covenant applied to believers' consciences.

Given Witsius's explanation of the economy of the Trinity, it is not difficult to see that his view of redemptive history focuses on individual faith as it works itself out in the order of salvation (*ordo salutis*). This is observed again in his distinction between "the internal" and the "external" aspects of the covenant of grace. He writes:

> As we restrict this covenant to the Elect, it is evident we are speaking of the internal, mystical and spiritual *communion* of the covenant. For salvation itself, and every thing belonging to it, or inseparably connected with it, are promised in this covenant, all which none but the Elect can attain to. If, in other respects, we consider the *external* economy of the covenant, in the communion of the word and sacraments, in the profession of the true faith, in the participation of many gifts which, though excellent and illustrious, are yet none of the effects of the sanctifying Spirit, nor any earnest of future happiness; it cannot be denied that, in this respect, many are in covenant, whose names, notwithstanding, are not in the testament of God.[58]

---

57. Witsius, *The Economy of the Covenants*, III.1.4 (1:286–87).

58. Witsius, *The Economy of the Covenants*, III.1.5 (1:287).

Thus, the internal, mystical, and spiritual communion of the covenant experienced by the elect is administered through the external economy of the covenant (the word and sacraments). Here, Witsius notes that although the external economy of the covenant, in terms of the communion of the word and sacraments, has many participants, its internal effect relates only to the elect. Furthermore, it appears that while Witsius finds both the internal and external elements important, the former is more essential than the latter.

Witsius then goes on to show how the economy of the covenants relates to historical dispensations. He writes that there exists "a remarkable difference" between the promises of the covenant of works and the covenant of grace. While God promised "life" to man through "perfect obedience" according to the covenant of works, he "did not promise to produce" this obedience in man. However, in the covenant of grace, God established promises that include not only eternal life but also "faith," "repentance," and "perseverance in holiness" through Christ as "the Mediator." As a result, a believer comes to obtain "secure salvation," based on "the suretiship and actual satisfaction of Christ."[59] For Witsius, the promises of the covenant of grace relate to sanctification as an individual component within the order of salvation.

This implies that the covenant of grace includes promises given to an individual in faith. As seen above, Witsius believes these promises contain faith, repentance, and perseverance. This concept is repeated in his view of the conditions of the covenant of grace. For Witsius, these conditions are bound up with the promises of the covenant. For example, a condition of a covenant generally means an "action, which, being performed, gives a man a right to the reward." However, Witsius does not believe this is the case in the covenant of grace, since the condition is involved not in "any action of ours" but in Christ alone.[60] He argues that Christ is in charge of the condition so that the conditions of the covenant are contained in "the universality of the promises" ratified by Christ, who fulfilled the righteousness of the law.[61] Witsius goes on to note two aspects of this condition: "faith

---

59. Witsius, *The Economy of the Covenants*, III.i.7 (1:288).

60. Witsius, *The Economy of the Covenants*, III.i.9 (1:288).

61. Witsius, *The Economy of the Covenants*, III.i.11–13 (1:289–90).

and holiness." On the part of God, faith is called a condition because it is God's "execution of previous promises" and "earnest of future happiness." On the part of man, the performance of holiness is called a condition in terms of its being *"the* assurance" that believers cannot but continue in God's covenant.[62] Witsius believes faith is followed by holiness because both are inseparably related.

This concept of condition serves to underscore the gracious aspect of "the testament of the new covenant." Other elements of redemption Witsius finds in the new covenant include "repentance, faith, and the practice of love to God." He argues that these elements are promised under both "a legal form" as "the rule of our self-examination" and "another form" as "the gift of God," which God himself works in believers so that they can have full hope that eternal life has already begun in them.[63]

As noted, Witsius relates the concept of the condition of the covenant of grace to sanctification and the assurance of faith. He locates the *ordo salutis* within the economy or administration of the covenant through redemptive history. By doing so, he shows that he understands the concept of condition in terms of sanctification. That is, the process of renewal for believers includes faith, repentance, and perseverance in holiness.

Given Witsius's view of the *ordo salutis*, it is clear that the doctrine of the covenants rather than the theme of redemptive history is the interpretive framework through which he reads Scripture.[64] However, this does not mean that the redemptive-historical motif does not play a significant role in revealing the meaning of a series of historical events necessary to the work of redemption. Nevertheless, for Witsius, the application of salvation in an individual's life through the covenantal system is more foundational for his understanding of the biblical text. This becomes even more apparent upon a closer look at his view of the interrelationship between the Old and New Testaments and of the abrogation of the ceremonial law.

In Book 4 of *Economy of the Covenants*, Witsius begins with the narrative of the fall of man. He uses this narrative to draw out a doctrine of salvation in the first age of the world. He describes this first period of grace

---

62. Witsius, *The Economy of the Covenants*, III.i.14 (1:290–91).

63. Witsius, *The Economy of the Covenants*, III.i.15 (1:292).

64. Beeke, *Puritan Reformed Spirituality*, 339.

THE HISTORY OF REDEMPTION AMONG EDWARDS'S ANTECEDENTS

as followed by three eras of grace (Noah to Abraham, Abraham to Moses, and Moses to the prophets). Considering the progressive stages in which God's grace is revealed, Witsius argues that there is a progression of the benefits of the covenant of grace even in the Old Testament.[65]

Witsius then contends that the Old Testament has "some peculiar defects," which are later made up for by the benefits of the New Testament.[66] The first defect he finds is that although representatives such as Noah, Abraham, and Moses knew "the figure of Christ" through grace passed down to them, they did not all realize that "the cause of salvation" means "the satisfaction" and "expiation" of Christ. Second, Witsius maintains that the old economy has "obscurity" in that believers under the Old Testament could only view the word of God at a distance. The third defect he finds is "the greater *rigour* and unrelenting severity" of the old economy caused by "the threatenings of the law" and ambiguous repetition of "the promises of grace." Fourth, the Old Testament is in bondage to "the *elements of the world* (Heb 5:12)." And fifth, he believes it shows "*a more scanty measure of the gifts of grace*" in "*extent* and *degree*."[67]

After enumerating what he sees as the defects of the Old Testament, Witsius turns to the greater blessings in the New Testament. Contrary to the old economy, he finds the New Testament full of the benefits of grace. This is particularly clear in his description of the doctrine of the abrogation of the Old Testament. Witsius uses progressive redemption to describe the abrogation of ceremonial laws in order to find the benefits of the New Testament all the more gracious. According to Witsius, "the progress and the various degrees of this abrogation" parallel the economy of salvation found in the New Testament.

Specifically, Witsius argues that the ceremonial law was abrogated in nine stages. These stages correspond to the New Testament events as follows: (1) the coming of Christ, (2) the death of Christ, (3) the resurrection of Christ, (4) Peter's heavenly vision (Acts 10:11), (5) the "solemn decree of a synod of the apostles" (Acts 15:10, 28, 29), (6) Paul's preaching of freedom in contrast with the moral law (1 Cor 8 and 10), (7) the ruling that ceremonies

---

65. See Witsius, *The Economy of the Covenants*, IV.i.1–xii.78 (2:108–362).

66. Witsius, *The Economy of the Covenants*, IV.xiii.1 (2:362).

67. Witsius, *The Economy of the Covenants*, IV.xiii.1–32 (2:362–78).

might not offend the weak according to the rules of Christian charity (Acts 21), (8) Paul's criticism of Peter's falling back into the use of the ceremonies, and (9) the destruction of Jerusalem.[68] In describing the abrogation of the ceremonial laws, Witsius emphasizes that the benefits of the covenant of grace in the Old Testament era are inferior to those benefits revealed in the New Testament. He notes how the light of the covenant of grace becomes much brighter than that seen during the time of the Old Testament.

For his arguments, Witsius employs texts from the New Testament. He uses passages from Hebrews, Acts, and 1 Corinthians, as seen in the citations above. As Muller points out well, the biblical texts that contributed to both Cocceius's and Witsius's formulation of the covenant come from the New Testament.[69]

Witsius's discussion of the abrogation of the ceremonial law is followed by an analysis of the benefits of the New Testament. He writes, "As the darkness of the night is only dispelled by the beams of the rising morn, so the Old Testament was abrogated only by the introduction of the New."[70] He then lists the benefits of the New Testament in detail. The first benefit Witsius finds is that Christ was "not only exhibited, but also 'made perfect'" through his sufferings and death, thus resulting in "an eternal redemption." Second, "the gospel" promised by the Scriptures was proclaimed to "all nations." Third, the Gentiles were called by the gospel. Fourth, "a more abundant and delightful measure of the Spirit" was poured out on the church. Fifth, "*Christian liberty*" became common to all believers of all ages and New Testament believers.[71] Sixth, there is "the restoration of

---

68. Witsius, *The Economy of the Covenants*, IV.xiv.54 (2: 403–5).

69. Muller, "*Pactum Salutis*," 24.

70. Witsius, *The Economy of the Covenants*, IV.xv.1 (2:405).

71. Witsius distinguishes between liberty common to all believers and liberty common to New Testament believers. With respect to believers in every age, Christian liberty is from (1) the tyranny of the devil, (2) the reigning and condemning power of sin, (3) the rigor of the law, (4) death, and (5) the laws of men. On the other hand, liberty in relation to New Testament believers is (1) "a discharge from the bondage of the elements of the world, or of the ancient ceremonies," (2) "liberty with respect to things indifferent in their own nature, the use of, or abstinence from which was formerly enjoined the Israelites," (3) "immunity from the forensic or judicial laws of the Israelites," and (4) "a clearer and more perfect promulgation, knowledge, and practice of Christian liberty, in all its parts and degrees." See Witsius, *The Economy of the Covenants*, IV.xv.17–19 (2:411–13).

the Israelites." Last, "the riches of the whole church" indicate that "much greater and more extensive benefits shall redound to the Christian church."[72]

Witsius's use of the phrases "the darkness of the night" and "the beams of the rising morn" bear resemblance to Cocceius's description of the doctrine of abrogations; that is, "the elements of the covenant of works undergo a negative development, going from greater to lesser, while the elements of the covenant of grace undergo a positive development, progressing from lesser to greater."[73] In this sense, the economy of salvation for Witsius is historical, the realization of progressive revelation within time. Nevertheless, as Van Asselt points out, Witsius tends to project the economy of salvation into the *ordo salutis*. His distinction of abrogations is focused on the "various salvific phases" found in an individual redemptive experience. This leads Van Asselt to view Witsius's perspective as "a tremendous depreciation" of "the salvation history" and "its abrogation" in the thought of Cocceius.[74] Put simply, Van Asselt believes that Witsius oversimplifies the historical aspect of the covenant.

Moreover, the intrinsic relationship between the Old and New Testaments in Witsius's theology is described in terms of the accomplishment of the promises of the covenant of grace. In other words, the benefits of the New Testament are none other than completing what was left unfinished in the Old Testament. With respect to the dispensation (or economy) of the covenant of grace between the Old and New Testaments, Witsius employs many biblical texts (from Genesis to Revelation) to explain the nature of the covenant of grace. In doing so, Witsius explains how the Old Testament is inferior to the New in relation to the degree of benefits available through the covenant of grace.

EVALUATION OF WITSIUS

Witsius's approach to federal theology suggests that the covenantal lens for him is pivotal to interpreting the Bible. Although the history of redemption plays a role in revealing the relationship between the Old and New Testaments, his focus on the benefits of the covenant of grace lies not

---

72. Witsius, *The Economy of the Covenants*, IV.xv.4-33 (2:406-19).

73. Van Asselt, *The Federal Theology of Johannes Cocceius*, 276.

74. Van Asselt, *The Federal Theology of Johannes Cocceius*, 295n11.

in the Old Testament but in the New. That is, he tends to emphasize the fact that the benefits of the Old Testament are inferior to those of the New Testament. One might even say that Witsius employs the history of redemption to explain how the New Testament excels in the degree and extent of grace compared with the Old Testament. This implies that despite his use of the redemptive-historical method, Witsius's focus on understanding Scripture lies in his covenantal system. It is the lens through which he reads the biblical text. Although his federal theology is firmly grounded upon "biblical exegesis that was passed on from the patristic era,"[75] his view of the history of redemption itself is read in light of individual faith rather than the historical manifestation of redemption. In other words, the order of salvation for individual faith is the driving force behind Witsius's reading of the Bible, which he read through the covenant system. As Beeke points out well, "for Witsius, the doctrine of the covenants is the best way of reading Scripture."[76]

Moreover, his view of the history of redemption also tends to focus on individual faith and sanctification rather than the historical aspect of the divine revelation of salvation history. As Beeke notes, Witsius deals with the *ordo salutis* within the framework of the covenant of grace.[77] In this regard, Witsius is in the same line of thought as William Ames, who argues that stages in salvation history, as the covenant administrations in various time periods, are parallel to a "series of conditions or states of believers."[78] However, as Mark Beach rightly points out, Witsius's federal theology "continues in the line of Voetian Reformed theologians who accented the *ordo salutis*, though neither Witsius's emphasis on the *ordo* nor his doctrine of the *pactum* led him to negate or ignore the texture of redemptive history."[79] Thus, it seems that Witsius concentrates on the description of the individual salvific experience in terms of the application of the covenant of grace to an individual believer.

---

75. Byunghoon Woo, "The *Pactum Salutis* in the Theology of Witsius, Owen, Dickson, Goodwin, and Cocceius" (PhD diss., Calvin Theological Seminary, 2015), abstract.

76. Beeke, *Puritan Reformed Spirituality*, 339.

77. Beeke, *Puritan Reformed Spirituality*, 342.

78. Beeke, *Puritan Reformed Spirituality*, 135.

79. Beach, "The Doctrine of the *Pactum Salutis* in the Covenant Theology of Herman Witsius," 103.

Having examined the theologies of Cocceius and Witsius, let us now turn our attention to Petrus van Mastricht.

PETRUS VAN MASTRICHT (1630-1706)

Petrus van Mastricht, whose former teacher at Leiden University was Cocceius, and who was at the same time a contemporary of Herman Witsius, was Edwards's favorite among his many Reformed forebears.[80] In response to Joseph Bellamy, who asked him about the classic works of Reformed divinity,[81] Edwards writes, "They [Turretin and Mastricht] are both excellent. Turretin is ... better for one that desires only to be thoroughly versed in controversies. But take Mastricht for divinity in general, doctrine, practice, and controversy; or as an universal system of divinity; and it is much better than Turretin or any other book in the world, excepting the Bible."[82] As Adriaan Neele notes, Samuel Hopkins, the first biographer of Edwards, also esteemed Mastricht.[83] Hopkins writes, "That great, learned, and Dutch divine, Van Mastricht, whose body of divinity perhaps excels all others that have yet been written, and is, in my opinion, richly worth the repeated perusal of every one."[84]

However, while many scholars argue that Mastricht is Edwards's favorite theologian, they leave unanswered the question of why in fact Edwards was so fond of Mastricht. Without a doubt, Mastricht's theology had a profound influence on Edwards's federal theology.[85] Edwards scholars have found that Mastricht's progressive view of history bears a considerable resemblance to Edwards's historicized view of covenant. As McDermott argues, Mastricht's view of the covenant of grace indicates "a progressive

---

80. For the implication of Mastricht's influence on Edwards, see Neele, *Petrus van Mastricht*, 8–14.

81. George M. Marsden, *Jonathan Edwards: A Life* (New Haven: Yale University Press, 2003), 318.

82. Jonathan Edwards to the Reverend Joseph Bellamy, January 15, 1747, in Edwards, *Letters and Personal Writings*, WJE 16:217.

83. Neele, *Petrus van Mastricht*, 11.

84. Samuel Hopkins, *The System of Doctrines, Contained in Divine Revelation, Explained and Defended. Showing Their Consistence and Connexion with Each Other. To Which is Added, A Treatise on the Millennium* (Boston: Isaiah Thomas and Ebenezer T. Andrews, 1793), 769.

85. Neele, *Petrus van Mastricht*, 11; Neele, "Appendix VIII: Mastricht and Edwards," in *Petrus van Mastricht*, 316–20. Cf. William S. Morris, *The Young Jonathan Edwards: A Reconstruction* (Brooklyn: Carlson, 1991), 247, 284, 564.

view of history."[86] Cornelis van der Knijff and Willem van Vlastuin contend that Mastricht describes the dispensation of the covenant of grace in "a historical way" and insist that Edwards "worked out the building stones which he found in van Mastricht."[87] Jan van Vliet argues that Mastricht "supplied Jonathan Edwards with a highly-articulated structure of the administration of the covenant of grace through time."[88] Neele finds that Mastricht's eschatology, which deals in depth with "progressive dispensational history of the sacred and secular," echoes Edwards's *history* project.[89] The influence flowing from Mastricht to Edwards prompts a deeper investigation into how Mastricht's theology may have impacted Edwards's federalism.

As far as the particulars of Mastricht's theology, Neele notes that aspects of Edwards's doctrine of the covenant of grace reflect Mastricht's thoughts in *Theoretico-practica Theologia* (hereafter cited as *TPT*) on "the Sabbath," "fall," "supralapsarianism," the "Trinity," and "ascension."[90] All of these references appear to be consistent with Edwards's view of the covenant of grace and the Trinity.[91] While Mastricht's view of covenant is found throughout the references mentioned above as well as in various places in *TPT*,[92] it is the chapters on the covenants of nature and grace (III.12 to

---

86. Gerald R. McDermott, *One Holy and Happy Society: The Public Theology of Jonathan Edwards* (University Park: Pennsylvania State University Press, 1992), 79.

87. Van der Knijff and Van Vlastuin, "The Development in Jonathan Edwards' Covenant View," 280.

88. Jan van Vliet, "Covenant and Conscience: Amesian Echoes in Jonathan Edwards," in *The Rise of Reformed System: The Intellectual Heritage of William Ames* (Eugene, OR: Wipf & Stock, 2013), 233–65.

89. Adriaan C. Neele, *Before Jonathan Edwards: Sources of New England Theology* (Oxford: Oxford University Press, 2018), 219.

90. Neele, *Petrus van Mastricht*, 10–11. Recently, book 1 of Mastricht's *Theoretico-practica Theologia* (hereafter *TPT*), which consists of three chapters, has been translated into English. For a brief comment on its structure, see Joel R. Beeke, "Editor's Preface," in Mastricht, *Theoretical-Practical Theology* vol 1, *Prolegomena*, xi–xiv.

91. Neele, *Petrus van Mastricht*, 11.

92. Jan van Vliet, in his dissertation, argues that Mastricht's "entire theological system is structured around the concept of covenant theology." Neele suggests that Van Vliet is wrong. See Jan van Vliet, "William Ames: Marrow of the Theology and Piety of the Reformed Tradition" (PhD diss., Westminster Theological Seminary, 2002), 365; Neele, *Petrus van Mastricht*, 110n24. Nevertheless, Mastricht's doctrine of covenant is interrelated with his doctrine of the Trinity. See Neele, *Petrus van Mastricht*, 251. With respect to the theological structure, *TPT* has a fourfold structure: Exegesis, Doctrine, Elenctic, and Praxis. Muller writes, "Mastricht (1630–1706) began each division of his system with an exegetical study of a key Scriptural text relating to the doctrine about to be presented. Mastricht analyzes the

book V.1 and 2; book VIII.1 to 4) in which Mastricht lays out his federal theology as it concerns the definition and historical aspects of the covenant.

But before analyzing Mastricht's federal theology, one should first note that Mastricht understands federal theology within the context of divine providence. This is clear from the structure of *TPT* from books II to VIII. These books are entitled "faith in the triune God" (book II), "the operation of God" (book III), "human apostasy from God" (book IV), "the redemption of Christ" (book V), "the application of redemption" (book VI), "the church and ecclesiastics" (book VII), and "dispensation of the covenant of grace" (book VIII). Particularly, book III is structured in eight chapters, and the last three chapters consist of the doctrines of "general providence of God" (chapter 10), "special providence" (chapter 11), and "the covenant of nature" (chapter 12).

In this framework, Mastricht's federal theology unfolds according to explicitly providential history. He writes:

From general providence, by which God is taken up with anything, and from special providence, by which he is particularly engaged with the rational creature, it finally follows that the most special thing about humans, as long as they form the church, is found in the covenant [*confoederatione*], by which God stipulates obligation or supplication and promises blessing. They accept the stipulation and expect blessing, and the ὁμολογία or agreement of both parties produces a pact [*foedus*] and mutual obligation. God gave this covenant's first sign with the entire human race in Genesis 2:16–17. For although no covenant is mentioned in this same passage, nevertheless, it is mentioned elsewhere—in Hosea 6:7—and the thing

---

original language of the passage, comparing difficult terms with other places in Scripture. Only after having established the meaning of the text does he move on to his formulation of positive doctrine. Next, Mastricht enters critical debate with the historical adversaries of orthodox and Reformed teaching, and finally he deals at length with the practical application of each doctrine. This pattern is followed throughout the system." This, according to Muller, is a great example of "the perfect balance of Mastricht's scholasticism: exegetical, dogmatic, historico-polemical and practical." See Richard A. Muller, "Giving Direction to Theology: The Scholastic Dimension," *JETS* 28, no. 2 (1985), 184–85, 191. Cf. Neele, *Petrus van Mastricht*, 139.

itself makes a pact. For when there are two contracting parties and agreement about the contracting, there is a pact.[93]

Here, Mastricht begins his discussion of the covenant of nature between God and men with an emphasis on the initiative of God and his goodness in covenanting. This is understandable when one notes that for the classical Reformed tradition, the concept of covenant and the doctrine of providence are inseparably connected.[94] Mastricht believes that covenant involves promises, the agreement of two parties, and mutual obligation by confederation.

With this basic definition in view, Mastricht proceeds to an exegetical consideration of the covenant by providing an exposition of Genesis 2:16–17. Mastricht uses this text to discuss the meaning of (1) contracting parties ("Contrahentes *partes, seu confeoderandi*"), (2) contract ("Contractus, *seu actus confoederationis*"), (3) contracting ("Contrahenda, *seu argumentum confoederationis*"), and (4) agreement ("Consensus *foederalis partium contrahentium*").[95] In this discussion, Mastricht explores various biblical texts from both the Old and New Testaments that relate to these covenantal terms. Notably, in the original language of these biblical texts, references are made first to the ברית (covenant) of Elohim, which implies "*trinus personis, Pater, Filius, & Spiritus*" ("three persons, Father, Son, and Holy Spirit") and second to האדם as the human party of the covenant. Also, the text includes ומעץ הדעת טוב ורע לא תעכל ממנו ("and from the tree of the knowledge

---

93. Mastricht, *Theoretico-practica theologia: qua, per singula capita theologica, pars exegetica, dogmatica, elenchtica & practica, perpetua successione conjugantur*, 3rd ed. (Utrecht: Apud W. van de Water, 1724), III.12.i (413). Latin original: "Providentiae generali, qua circa quodvis Deus occupatur, & providentiae *speciali*, qua circa creaturam *rationalem* peculiariter distinetur, succedit tandem *specialissima*, qua circa *homines*, quatenus illi *Ecclesiam* sibi efformant, versatur *confoederatione*; ubi ab ipsis Deus stipulator officium aut supplicium, & *promittis* beneficium: *illi recipiunt* stipulatum, & *exspectant* beneficium; & utriusque partis ὁμελεγια seu consensus producit *foedus, &* mutuam obligationem. Confoederationis huius primum specimen, cum universe genere humano, Deus praestitit in Paradiso Gen. ii. 16. 17. Quamvis enim nullius foederis, ibidem exserta fiat mentio; fit tamen alibi Hos. Vi. 7. & res ipsa foedus praestat: ubi enim sunt *partes* contrahentes, & contrahentium *consensus* in idem, ibi *foedus* est:"

94. Michael Horton argues that the concept of covenant "helps us to see in our doctrine of providence the inseparable relation of God's sovereignty and human freedom—indeed, creaturely freedom in general." Michael S. Horton, *God of Promise: Introducing Covenant Theology* (Grand Rapids: Baker, 2006), 111.

95. Mastricht, *TPT*, III.12.ii, 413–15.

of good and evil you must not eat"), referring to the prohibition (Gen 2:17), and to בְּיוֹם as the day of death.

In his exegesis, Mastricht's language comes close to a theological appropriation of covenant language. For instance, concerning the last aspect, or "*consensus*," of covenant, Mastricht writes:

> The agreement of the contracting parties of the covenant is, as it were, the form of the covenant [*confoederationis*], without which there is no covenant [*foedus*]. Indeed this is designated clearly enough on God's behalf—by the very prohibition and threat; on the human's behalf it is not explicitly stated in the text. Nevertheless, it is intimated adequately, because he is silent and does not contradict anything. Whoever keeps silent is assumed to consent, and it is also signified more clearly in Genesis 3. When Eve first refused to obey because of Satan's temptation, the reason was added in verse 3: " 'But concerning the fruit of the tree which is in the middle of the garden,' God said, 'of it you shall never eat.' "[96]

Mastricht argues that the agreement of the human party of the covenant is implied by God's prohibition and threat. Although no direct reference to the human consent appears in the text, it is nevertheless implied since "not speaking" means consent. For Mastricht, human consent to the covenant is something inferred, not something observed.

After establishing the implied human agreement necessary to covenant, Mastricht turns again to the subject of God's sovereignty and goodness. He argues that in the covenant of nature, God "takes to guide his own [people] by confederations."[97] This is consistent with Mastricht's understanding of covenant in general, in which covenant "denotes agreement between God and his own people, by which God promises blessedness."[98] Thus, in

---

96. Mastricht, *TPT*, III.12.ii, 415. "Consensus foederalis partium contrahentium: Qui est quasi forma confoederationis, absque quo foedus nullum est. Hic quidem ex parte Dei, satis clare designatur, ipsa prohibitione & comminatione: ex parte hominis, non quidem exprimitur in textu; satis tamen innuitur, eo quod tacuerit, nec quicquam contradixerit: consentire enim censetur, qui tacet, & clarius etiam significatur Ge. III. Quando primum renuebat Eva, auscultare tentationi Satane, addita hac ratione vers. 3. Sed de fructu arboris, quae est in medio horti, Deus dixit, de eo nequaquam comedetis."

97. Mastricht, *TPT*, III.12.iii, 415.

98. Mastricht, *TPT*, III.12.iii, 416.

covenant, God enters into a bond with the "whole human race," as "author of the covenant" as well as a "party" of it. God offers and humanity receives: "Deus *offert*, homo *accipit*." While God "offers office" and "promises gift," humanity "accepts office with the most duty."[99]

Mastricht follows these statements on the covenant of nature with a description of the human violation of the covenant of grace (books IV and V). His emphases on God's sovereignty and goodness reappear in his focus on Christ's redemption offered in the covenant of grace. He writes:

> Both [redemption and its application], as a rule, acknowledge the covenant of grace as a substitute after the violation of the covenant of works. In book five we will discuss redemption ξὺν θεῷ; its application in book six. Therefore we will speak first about the covenant of grace, then about is Mediator or Redeemer, and finally about redemption. We will unfold the covenant of grace in the first promise—made to the first man and sinner immediately after the violation of the covenant of works—which is found in Genesis 3:15.[100]

Mastricht's soteriological concern comes to the fore in his exegetical and theological expositions of the covenant of grace. He focuses on the mediator as redeemer and how this affects believers' faith. It is perhaps then unsurprising that Mastricht devotes a great deal of space to an in-depth discussion on the mediator himself, his works, and the application of redemption to believers.[101]

After having explored the application of redemption through such topics as "nature, limit, benefit, object, and means" in book VI,[102] Mastricht turns to the topic of book VIII, "about the dispensation of the covenant of grace." It is here that he lays out three historical periods he finds in Scripture. These eras are from the time of the patriarchs to Moses, from

---

99. Mastricht, *TPT*, III.12.iii, 417.

100. Mastricht, *TPT*, V.1.i, 489. "Utraque velut pro norma agnoscit *foedus gratia*, substitutum violato foederi operum. *Redemptionem* libro *quinto* expediemus ξὺν θεῷ; eius *applicationem* libro *sexto*. Dicendum igitur primo de foedere gratia, dein de *Mediatore* eius, seu Redemptore, denique de *redemptione*. Foedus gratiae pandemus in prima promissione, protoplastis *peccatoribus*, immediate post violationem foederis operum, facta; quae prostat Gen. III. 15."

101. Mastricht deals with the themes of mediator and the application of redemption to believers in books 5 and 6, which comprise about 330 pages.

102. Mastricht, *TPT*, VIII.1.i, 963.

Moses to Christ, and from Christ to eternity. He insists that "the covenant of grace is renewed and developed" in each of these three periods.[103] He writes, "God has dispensed the covenant of grace in diverse ways, according to diverse ages of times."[104]

This raises the question, how does Mastricht's view of the covenant of grace reflect a progressive history of revelation? That is, in what way has salvation history been increasingly revealed as time has passed? To answer this question, a brief examination of Mastricht's doctrinal sections on the covenant of grace is necessary.

In the doctrinal section of book VIII chapter 1, Mastricht begins by discussing each of the dispensations of the covenant and how they influenced theology and the status of the church. He continues throughout book VIII to examine the complex biblical texts and historical events that describe theological progress and the history of the church. He writes, "According to the different ages, even until the fullness of time, God has proclaimed the mystery of the covenant of grace in the church and dispensed his benefits in various ways."[105]

Mastricht then subdivides the first dispensational phase (from the time of the patriarchs to Moses) into three periods. These sub-periods are: "protoevangelium [Genesis 3:15] to Noah," "Noah to Abraham," and "Abraham to Moses." He describes the first sub-period as the "foundation of the church," the "corruption of the church," "the first restoration of the corruption of the church," and a period that contains the "constitution & promulgation of the covenant of grace." In this section, Mastricht analyzes a series of patriarchs, including Adam, Abel, Seth, Enosh, Kenan, Mahalalel, Jared, Enoch, Methuselah, Lamech, and Noah. In his analysis, he also lays out the historical events described in the Bible.[106]

In his discussion of the next sub-period, the time from Noah to Abraham, Mastricht focuses on the split of the church. He finds there the division of "especially the Sethite & the Cainite" through the flood and that of "generally

---

103. Mastricht, *TPT*, VIII.1.i, 963.

104. Mastricht, *TPT*, VIII.1.iii, 965.

105. Mastricht, *TPT*, VIII.1.iii, 965. "quod Deus, pro diversa temporum aetate, usque ad eius πλήρωμα, mysterium foederis gratiae, in Ecclesia promulgaverit, eius beneficia diversimode dispensaverit."

106. Mastricht, *TPT*, VIII.1.xv, 969–71.

the seed of the woman & the serpent,"[107] from which "all apostasy, heresy, schism, hatred, and persecution of all worse time drew origin."[108]

He then discusses the third sub-period, the time which "flows forth from Abraham to the birth of Moses."[109] Mastricht considers this dispensation of the covenant exegetically, extrapolating the history of the patriarchs including Abraham, Isaac, Jacob, Levi, Joseph, Kohath, and Amram.[110] After providing a detailed exegesis of the Genesis text, Mastricht explains the process of the transmission of theology. He asserts, "Just as Adam received his theology directly from God, and Shem and all the rest from Methuselah, so Abraham, Isaac, and Jacob were able to receive [their theology] from Shem and Eber."[111] He believes the theology they inherited was "excellently strengthened" by the divine command given to Abraham and his descendants that they should stay where God told them to live (Gen 26:2–6).[112] Mastricht believes the church also experienced a dispensation of the covenant during this sub-period. Incidentally, this is also when the schisms of "Ishmael" and "Edom" and "persecutions" took place.[113] In any event, it appears that Mastricht reads the biblical texts regarding his doctrine of the covenant of grace canonically, through the lens of the providential history of God. In doing so, he understands the history of redemption in terms of the transmission and development of salvific knowledge.[114]

For Mastricht, the second major dispensational period "flows from Moses to Messiah." Mastricht further subdivides this period into three sub-periods: (1) "Moses to David," (2) "to the Babylonian captivity," and (3) "to Messiah." He concedes that while "the dispensation of the covenant of grace would be the same, and hence the same testament," there still was

---

107. Mastricht, *TPT*, VIII.1.xxii, 978.

108. Mastricht, *TPT*, VIII.1.xvii, 973.

109. Mastricht, *TPT*, VIII.1.xxvii, 980–84.

110. Mastricht, *TPT*, VIII.1.xxiii, 979.

111. Mastricht, *TPT*, VIII.1.xxxii, 984. "sicut Adamus suam Theologiam accepit immediate a Deo, & Semus cum caeteris, à Methusalacho: ita Abrahamus, Isaacus & Jacobus, eam traditione Potuerunt habere à Semo & Hebero."

112. Mastricht, *TPT*, VIII.1.xxxii, 984.

113. Mastricht, *TPT*, VIII.1.xxxiii, 986–87.

114. The development of theology in history is also discussed by other figures in Reformed orthodoxy, such as John Owen. See Adriaan Neele, *Before Jonathan Edwards*, 217–18.

a "more solemn renovation, illustration, and application" of the covenant that warrants its description as a separate dispensational era.[115] For this argument, Mastricht provides a brief biblical exegesis of Deuteronomy 5:2 and then a description of what he calls a renewal of the covenant of grace. He says, "When God had moved Israel from Egypt to the mountain Sinai through the Red Sea, he renewed the covenant with him, promulgating the law solemnly." He continues, "God would have promulgated moral laws which may oblige Israelites as human beings, ceremonial laws which may oblige them as members of the church, and forensic laws which may oblige them as citizens of the state." Thus, Mastricht identifies a threefold renewal of the covenant of grace that includes "judicial," "moral," and "ceremonial" laws. He relates the judicial law to "national" law, the moral law to "nature" or "work," and the ceremonial law to "favored" or "evangelical" law, which implies grace.[116] "Under this dispensation," he insists, "the Israelite Church remained unchanged, without any essential variation even until the revelation of the Messiah, for about fifteen hundred years."[117]

Mastricht then turns to the second sub-period, which runs from Moses to the Babylonian captivity and includes Moses, Joshua, Othniel, Ehud, Deborah, Gideon, Abimelech, Tola, Jair, Jephthah, Ibzan, Elon, Abdon, Samson, Eli, and Samuel.[118] In his discussion of these figures, it is clear that Mastricht's understanding of the biblical texts is not limited to literary approaches to biblical narrative nor to the historiography of the Old Testament accounts, acknowledging that the authors of the Bible sought to describe real events. Still, while Mastricht provides a detailed biblical exposition following the order of the biblical record, his description of the dispensation of the covenant of grace is focused on movement toward the Messiah and his salvific work. Mastricht thus invites his readers to envisage the wider picture of salvation history.

---

115. Mastricht, *TPT*, VIII.2.i, 992.

116. Mastricht, *TPT*, VIII.2.ii, iii–xix, 993–95. Mastricht then begins to provide evidences of "confederation" between God and Israel. For example, God promised to be their God (Deut 4:13; 5:2, 5, and 6; Lev 26:3–12). He also promised to "give Messiah, Prophet, Mediator" to them. God's promise is found in his plan to "circumcise Israel's heart through his Spirit." Moreover, God promised "external and temporary blessings for them." See Mastricht, *TPT*, VIII.2.xx, 997.

117. Mastricht, *TPT*, VIII.2.xx, 997.

118. Mastricht, *TPT*, VIII.2.xxii–xxiii, 997–1003.

Similar to the pattern of his descriptions of the previous periods, Mastricht continues to describe the development of both theology and the church in the dispensations from Moses to Christ and from Christ to eternity.[119] It would be tedious to recount in detail his biblical and doctrinal expositions, which include a complex analysis of the original Hebrew and Greek, various Christian doctrines and histories, and meticulous subdivisions of the dispensational periods in support of his view of progressive revelation. However, it is worth noting that Mastricht devotes a good deal of time to his exposition of the dispensation from Christ to eternity. For example, the period of the New Testament under Christ is further divided into seven periods, and in each, Mastricht discusses historical, theological, and ecclesiastical developments at length. In doing so, he deals with various themes, including "theology, sacred and secular history, typology and shadows, confessions and creeds, heresies, persecutions, schisms, [and] the rise and fall of the antichrist," which points to "the institutions and theologies of Roman Catholicism in the West and Islam in the East."[120] Compared with chapters 1, 2, and 4 of book VIII, which deal with the histories of the patriarchs until Moses, the number of pages devoted to addressing the period from Christ until eternity is overwhelming.[121]

This implies that Mastricht's understanding of the covenant of grace is Christocentric. Furthermore, in this last dispensational phase, he describes how Christian theology has been persecuted by heresies such as the "Anabaptists," "Enthusiasts," "Socinians," "Jesuits," "Lutherans," and "Arminians."[122] That is, he discusses the status of the church and Christian theology by examining the recent history of the church at that time.[123] Mastricht's view of the history of the church, which merges "the history

---

119. Mastricht, *TPT*, VIII.2.xxiv–xxv, 1003–8.

120. Neele, *Before Jonathan Edwards*, 224.

121. See Mastricht, *TPT*, VIII.3.i–3.lii, 1039–1190.

122. Mastricht, *TPT*, VIII.3.xliii, 1149–53.

123. Mastricht tends to emphasize God's protection of the church against various heresies. This viewpoint could be in line with the Reformed doctrine of the perpetuity of the true church in the secular world. According to John T. McNeill, "the perpetuity of the true church" appears to be "a consistent element in the Reformed doctrine of the church," as seen in Calvin. See Calvin, *Institutes*, 497n10. For more information, see Heinrich Heppe, *Reformed Dogmatics: Set out and Illustrated from the Sources*, ed. Ernst Bizer, trans. G. T. Thomson (London: Allen & Unwin, 1950), 664; John T. McNeill, "The Church in Post-Reformation Reformed Theology," *Journal of Religion* 24 (1944): 102–7.

of the church, and the covenant of grace with sacred and world history concurrently," makes it possible for Neele to assert that one of greatest influences on Edwards's *history* project may be found in *TPT*.[124]

While Mastricht lays out the dispensations of the covenant of grace and in doing so refers to the historical developments of both theology and the church, his emphasis lies on the unity of the covenant in the Old and New Testaments rather than on the progressive development of redemptive history. As a result, Mastricht's historical survey of the covenant of grace focuses on the "one single covenant form" of the covenant, as seen in Aza Goudriaan's analysis.[125] This point of view is further supported by the centrality of faith in Mastricht's theology. According to Neele, Mastricht in *TPT* begins the doctrine of God with "an exposition on saving faith." This point makes Mastricht "unique" among his Reformed contemporaries.[126] Neele's helpful summary of Mastricht's view of the *locus* of faith notes Mastricht's centrality of faith before discussing his thoroughgoing theological aspects in *TPT*.[127] He asserts:

> For Mastricht, then, faith is an entry point for (1) the covenant of grace, (2) the doctrine of God, and (3) the remainder of the system of doctrine. Therefore, the art of living to God, through Christ and regulated by Scripture, gets here an additional dimension: faith. Mastricht, then, was also concerned with a living to God through faith. Other seventeenth-century Reformed theologians held, of course, to the centrality of faith, but Mastricht returned explicitly to this early protestant concept. These organizational principles, then—the division of theology and the centrality of faith—may have contributed to the location of *De Fide Salvifica*.[128]

Thus, Neele contends in his concluding chapter that Mastricht differs from "most of his contemporaries, who located the discussion of faith in the context of the *ordo salutis*." Yet for Mastricht, "the essence of faith" is defined

---

124. Neele, *Before Jonathan Edwards*, 218, 219.

125. Aza Goudriaan, *Reformed Orthodoxy and Philosophy, 1625–1750: Gisbertus Voetius, Petrus van Mastricht, and Anthonius Driessen* (Leiden: Brill, 2006), 222, 223.

126. Neele, *Petrus van Mastricht*, 106.

127. Neele, *Petrus van Mastricht*, 106–11.

128. Neele, *Petrus van Mastricht*, 110.

as "the union and communion with Christ, thereby receiving God as highest end," since this faith is "habitual" and "directed to God."[129] In this regard,
Neele asserts that Mastricht's "lesser attention to the marks of faith and the
inward concerns of the believer" led him to split paths from his contemporaries.[130] Thus, for Mastricht, the unity of the covenant of grace in the Old
and New Testaments is deeply involved in the nature of faith toward union
with Christ. In other words, Mastricht's view of the unity of the covenant in
the Old and New Testaments is inseparably connected with his doctrine of
faith, which focuses on a person's participation in union with Christ, rather
than with his interest in the historical character of salvation history.

Much more could be said about Mastricht's approach to the federal
scheme, particularly the overall trajectory of the complex argument by
which he comes to a conclusion about the nature of the history of redemption based on his biblical exposition. Yet for the purpose of this book, it
is enough to discuss in more detail Mastricht's view of the final period of
the dispensation of the covenant. A representative example of his view of
the subject can be found in his summary of the "epilogue to the universal
ecclesiastical history" and his reference to the "status of the church under
eternity."[131] He writes:

> We have examined the dispensations of the covenant of grace
> under the Patriarchs, under Moses, and under Christ. Now noth-
> ing remains but to proceed to the dispensation of the same covenant
> under eternity, which will indeed be begun in this life, but it will
> be continued and consummated after this life through seven steps,
> as it were. It happens this way:

---

129. The nature of faith as habitual is related to Mastricht's concern regarding the nature
of theology. Neele summarizes the habitual character of theology as follows: "The term theology carried from the patristic fathers onwards the basic idea of a *habitus*, or inward disposition,
which permitted for a dual significance. The primary meaning, termed as practical *habitus*,
referred to, in so far as it concerned practical salvation-oriented knowledge of God united to
the life of faith and the longing for God, whose end is eternal happiness with God. The other
connotation, termed as cognitive *habitus*, referred to, in so far as it concerned self-conscious
scholarly quest, a discipline whose *locus* was usually a pedagogical setting." In this vein, he
argues that faith and theology are "eminently related." Neele, *Petrus van Mastricht*, 94, 110.
For Mastricht on the *locus* of theology and faith, see *Petrus van Mastricht*, 95–111. For more
information on the terminology of *habitus*, see Victor Babajide Cole, *Training of the Ministry*
(Bangalore, India: Theological Book Trust, 2001), 5–10.

130. Neele, *Petrus van Mastricht*, 281.

131. Mastricht, *TPT*, VIII.4.xlv, 1186.

1. The return of Christ
2. The abolition of the antichrist
3. The resurrection of the dead
4. The final judgment
5. The justification and condemnation of human beings
6. The consummation of the ages and the handing over of the kingdom
7. Eternal life

All these things, even if they are not clearly described, they are intimated well enough with the opening of the seventh seal, which is set forth in Revelation 7–11. Reader, you should not expect us to untangle those chapters one by one and show these seven steps in the very same order. For they are hidden here and there throughout the whole structure. But many passages clearly explain the status of the church in eternity. For example, Revelation 7:9[–12]: Martyrs in this age are said to stand before the throne of God and before the Lamb, clothed in white robes, with palm branches of victory in their hands, praising God and the Lamb, with angels all around the throne of God, with the elders and the four living creatures, which truly observe the status of eternity. Similarly, Revelation 10:6, it is said that after this there would be no delay when the mystery of God would be fulfilled.[132]

For Mastricht, the end of the dispensation of the covenant of grace comes when the mystery of God has been revealed, which will occur at the end of the world. Having examined his view of the history of redemption, it is easy to conclude that his understanding of the dispensations of the

---

132. Mastricht, *TPT*, VIII.4.i, 1191. "Examinavimus dispensationes foederis gratiae, sub Patriarchis, sub Mose & sub Christo: jam non restat, nisi ut progrediamur ad dispensationem ejusdem foederis sub *aeternitate*. Quae inchoabitur quidem in *hac vita*; sed continuabitur et consummabitur post hanc vitam per septem hos quasi passus; occurret enim 1. Reditus Christi. 2. Abolitio Antichristi. 3. Resuscitatio mortuorum. 4. Extremum judicium. 5. Justificatio & condemnation hominum. 6. Consummatio seculorum & tradition regni. 7. Vita aeterna. Ista omnia, si non diserte narrantur; saltem innuuntur apud aperturam *septimi sigilli*, quae explicatur à Johanne Apoc. cap. vii. usque ad cap. xi. inclusive. Non exspectabis à nobis Lector, ut ista capita singulatim resolvamus, & septem illos passus eo ordine ex ipsis repraesentemus; latent enim disperse per totum contextum. Explicari autem statum Ecclesiae sub *aeternitate*, patet ex multis; quando i. cap. vii. 9. Martyres sub hac aetate dicuntur substitisse coram Throno Dei, & coram agno, vestiti stolis albis, gestantes manibus suis *palmas* victoriae, celebrantes Deum & Agnum, juxta cum Aangelis circa thronum Dei, cum Senioribus & quatuor Animalibus, quae sane spectant ad statum aeternitatis: quando item cap. x. 6—dicitur jurasse, quod post haec non sint futura tempora, quando mysterium Dei sit complendum." For a detailed summary of the dispensation of the covenant of redemption from Moses to Christ, see Mastricht, *TPT*, VIII.3.xlv, 1186–87.

covenant of grace plays a pivotal role in how he sees the covenant reno-
vated and amplified throughout time.

EVALUATION OF MASTRICHT

An examination of the exegetical and doctrinal aspects of Mastricht's discussion of the covenant of grace shows that he follows the order of the
biblical canon. His methods to prove the federal scheme do not seem creative but rather fall in line with biblical history. However, his biblical exegesis provides a detailed and complex analysis of the original languages,
inter-textual interpretations, and biblical context. Moreover, his doctrinal exposition not only presents the concept of the history of redemption
in a systematic way but also considers it via a deeply exegetical approach.
These exegetical and theological considerations are significant as he lays
out his doctrine of the covenant.

Mastricht attempts to approach redemptive history from a comprehensive understanding of the Bible and not merely his own systematic
methods. This approach is not unique. As Muller notes, this line of theological reflection is also found in seventeenth-century orthodoxy's theological method.[133] And as Neele remarks, "Old Testament exegesis was for
Mastricht not only a philosophical and etymological quest but also a careful
listening to and standing in a rabbinic exegetical trajectory before arriving
at the results of biblical exegesis as foundation for doctrine and practice."[134]
In this vein, Marsden is mistaken when he critiques Mastricht for being
more systematic and less biblical.[135]

While Mastricht's exposition of the covenant of grace is complex and
detailed, as echoed in Reformed scholastic orthodoxy, there is one view that
sets him apart from his peers and predecessors. His theological framework

---

133. Muller writes, "At virtually no point in the development of the older Protestant
dogmatics can one find a case of 'proof texting' in the negative sense of the term: the older
dogmatics consistently folded the best exegesis of its day into its pattern and method of formulation. That exegesis, moreover, was not only linguistically and textually sophisticated,
it also was rooted in—and frequently explicitly cognizant of—the older Christian exegetical
tradition and its theological results." Richard A. Muller, "The Covenant of Works and the
Stability of Divine Law in Seventeenth-Century Reformed Orthodoxy: A Study in the Theology
of Herman Witsius and Wilhelmus à Brakel," *Calvin Theological Journal* 29, no. 1 (1994): 81. Cf.
Muller, *Post-Reformation Reformed Dogmatics*, 4 vols. (Grand Rapids: Baker, 1987), 2:525–40.

134. Neele, *Petrus van Mastricht*, 279.

135. Marsden, *Jonathan Edwards: A Life*, 488.

appears to be focused on the redemptive knowledge of Christ as Messiah. As seen in his view of the history of the Old and New Testaments in terms of the developments of theology and the church, Mastricht approaches biblical history in terms of the transmission, renovation, and amplification of redemptive knowledge from the periods of Moses to Christ and Christ to eternity. "While Mastricht's work is concerned with doctrinal engagement, he was concerned with preservation and transmission of truth about God and salvation," asserts Todd Rester.[136]

As Goudriaan argues, for Mastricht, "the history from the time of the patriarchs to Moses and then to Christ" has to do with "theological progress."[137] That is why Mastricht presents "the most important developments of the Church on earth" in a history of three main dispensations.[138] Mastricht's understanding of the developments of theology and the church points to the renovation and amplification of salvific knowledge, which is directed to Christ as mediator in the providential history of God. Therefore, the overall picture is that Mastricht understands the history of redemption as centered in the development of the theological knowledge of salvation, with a focus on how God protects the saving knowledge of Christ throughout history.

FRANCIS TURRETIN (1623–1687)

Francis Turretin's *Institutes of Elenctic Theology* was also a significant source for Edwards. By way of reminder, Edwards, when writing to Joseph Bellamy, compares Mastricht (*Theoretico-practica Theologia*) and Turretin (*Institutio Theologiae Elencticae*). He notes that Turretin is better for one who "desires only to be thoroughly versed in controversies." Although Edwards clearly prefers Mastricht to Turretin, he still states that the writings of both are "excellent."[139] Thus, James T. Dennison and Paul Ramsey argue that Edwards

---

136. Todd M. Rester, "Translator's Preface," in Mastricht, *Theoretical-Practical Theology* vol 1, *Prolegomena*, xix.

137. Goudriaan, *Reformed Orthodoxy and Philosophy, 1625–1750*, 222.

138. Goudriaan, *Reformed Orthodoxy and Philosophy, 1625–1750*, 222.

139. Jonathan Edwards to the Reverend Joseph Bellamy, January 15, 1747, in Edwards, *Letters and Personal Writings*, 217. While the term "Elenctic" in the title of the *Institutes* of Turretin suggests that this work tends to be polemic, it is not restricted to polemic theology. Throughout his work, Turretin intends to lay out Reformed foundational theology. In this vein, Dennison. argues: "Elenctic theology is thus polemic theology, since it is devoted to refutation

describes Turretin as "the great."[140] They maintain that Edwards's theology "was demonstrably dependent upon the writings of Francis Turretin (1623–1687) and Petrus van Mastricht (1630–1706)."[141]

As far as Turretin's place in the Reformed landscape, Adriaan Neele and B. Loonstra contend that Turretin belongs to the same category of covenant theologians as Witsius and Mastricht since they were all influenced by Johannes Cloppenburg's covenant theology.[142] Although Turretin was not influenced by Cloppenburg's federal theology to the same degree as the others, his federal theology does focus on the historical process of divine revelation. Wilson writes that Turretin emphasizes "the progressive disclosure of divine intention" throughout history. That is why Wilson insists that Turretin's "three ages of the Old Testament were in effect stages moving toward the perfect manifestation of the messiah."[143]

An attentive reader also will also note that Turretin's federal theology, as drawn out by Wilson, gives centrality to the idea of Christ as Messiah. That this Christological aspect plays a crucial role in his approach to federal theology is beyond doubt. As J. Mark Beach points out, for Turretin, "Christ as the promised Messiah" is "the center of the covenant of grace." Furthermore, Beach convincingly supports his argument that Turretin's federal theology is that of "divine grace."[144]

What about Turretin's understanding of history in the context of the covenant of grace? To answer this question, it seems fitting to focus on the second volume of Turretin's *Institutio Theologiae Elencticae*, the twelfth

---

of errors. But it should be noted that Turretin is not content only with refutation of error. He is positively concerned with the statement of the truth as well." See James T. Dennison Jr., "The Life and Career of Francis Turretin," in Turretin, *Institutes of Elenctic Theology*, 3:647.

140. Dennison, "The Life and Career of Francis Turretin," 657n110; Ramsey, "Appendix IV," 742. See Edwards, *Religious Affections*, WJE 2:289.

141. Ramsey, "Appendix IV," 743. Cf. Dennison, "The Life and Career of Francis Turretin," 648.

142. Neele, *Petrus van Mastricht*, 6n19. Cf. B. Loonstra, *verkezing, verzoening, verbond: beschrijving en beoordeling van de leer van het pactum salutis in de gereformeerde theologie* (Gravenhage: Boekencentrum, 1990), 109.

143. John F. Wilson, "Editor's Introduction," in Edwards, *A History of the Work of Redemption* WJE 9:46. The three ages of history comprise Adam to Abraham, Abraham to Moses, and Moses to Christ. See Turretin, *Institutes of Elenctic Theology*, XII.vii.7 (2:218).

144. Beach, *Christ and the Covenant*, 13.

topic, entitled "The Covenant of Grace and Its Twofold Economy in the Old and New Testaments."

As with some of the other theologians studied here, Turretin argues that there are dispensations of the covenant of grace. Yet to truly understand his emphasis on these dispensations, it is helpful to be familiar with the context in which his theology was written.

Turretin lived and wrote amid polemical debates involving the Socinians, the Remonstrants, and the Anabaptists. These groups believed the old covenant (the covenant of grace under the dispensations of the Old Testament) was inferior to the new covenant given in Christ.[145] Turretin's view of dispensations is formed largely as a response. He tends to emphasize the unity of the covenant of grace.

Before laying out Turretin's view of redemptive history, a brief examination of the structure of his federal theology will be helpful. Specifically, this section will examine (1) his definition of federal theology, (2) the centrality of Christ in the federal structure, and (3) the unity of the covenant of grace. After that, this section will seek to provide an overview of Turretin's view of the dispensations of the covenant of grace with the aim of exposing his understanding of the historical aspect of the covenant.

At the beginning of his analysis of the covenant of grace, Turretin provides the origin and meanings of the biblical terms "berith," "diatheke," "foedus," and "evangelium."[146] Turretin especially draws attention to the significance of the term *diathēkē*, which means not only "a testament" but also "covenant." His writing on the topic reveals a careful examination of the biblical texts. He asserts:

If the passages in the New Testament where the word *diathēkēs* occurs are carefully examined, they not only do not exclude the signification of a covenant (*synthēkēs*), but also often necessarily demand it. In Lk. 1:72 and Acts 3:25 mention is made of a *diathēkēs* made with the fathers in Abraham. From Gen. 17:10, 11, it cannot be denied to have had the relation of a covenant. Hence the covenant sealed by that sacrament is called "the covenant of circumcision"

---

145. Turretin, *Institutes of Elenctic Theology*, XII.iv.2–4 (2:192–93). With respect to the polemical concerns, see Beach, *Christ and the Covenant*, 215.

146. Turretin, *Institutes of Elenctic Theology*, XII.i.1–12 (2:169–74).

(diathēkēs peritomēs, Acts 7:8). In Rom. 9:4, diathēkai are said to belong to the Jews, surely not testaments (which were not many), but covenants (which are often renewed). In Gal. 4:24, "these are the two diathēkai" ("covenants," to wit, the legal and evangelical). The proof that it does treat of these will be given hereafter. And as often as Christ is called the Mediator of diathēkēs in Hebrews (chaps. 8 and 9) and his blood the blood diathēkēs, although the testamental relation is connoted, the federal relation (schesis) cannot and ought not to be excluded because there are properly no sureties of testaments; but between adverse parties a mediator is appointed to reconcile them and to unite them with each other by a covenant.[147]

The etymological approach to the covenantal terms that is seen here is not a novelty. It is employed by Reformed theologians such as Cocceius, Anthony Burgess, Herman Witsius, Wilhelmus à Brakel, and William Strong, all of whom use a strikingly similar paradigm in their analysis of the federal scheme. As seen above, Cocceius provides an exegetical analysis of the covenant term foedus, whose scriptural originals are ברית and διαθήκη. And as Muller points out, Witsius and à Brakel find their federal terms, such as "promise, oath, pledge, and command," in their exegetical consideration of the biblical words berith and diatheke.[148] This is also true for Anthony Burgess and William Strong, both of whom explore the origins and meanings of the words "consent," "agreement," "stipulation," and "promise."[149]

However, as far as his formulation of federalism, Turretin is very brief compared with Cocceius, Witsius, and Mastricht. He makes use of a simpler binary structural theology. He argues simply that promise in the covenant and its fulfillment is through Christ as mediator. For Turretin, Christ is the center of the federal scheme. This is something Turretin

---

147. Turretin, Institutes of Elenctic Theology, XII.i.5 (2:171).

148. Muller, "The Covenant of Works and the Stability of Divine Law in Seventeenth-century Reformed Orthodoxy," 81–83.

149. See Anthony Burgess, Vindiciae Legis: or, A Vindication of the Morall Law and the Covenants, From the Errours of Papists, Arminians, Socinians, and More Especially Antinomians (London: James Young, 1646), 121; William Strong, A Discourse of the Two Covenants: Wherein the nature, differences, and effects of the covenant of works and of grace are … discussed (London: J.M., 1678), 241.

continually stresses as he writes about the promise and fulfillment sides of the covenant.

Turretin approaches the nature of the covenant of grace with three questions: "Who were the contracting parties; who is the mediator; what are the clauses of the covenant—both on God's part and on man's?"[150] In his answers to each of these questions, Turretin turns to the centrality of Christ as the covenant mediator. First, the covenant of grace is "a gratuitous pact entered into in Christ between God offended and man offending." Second, God promises to give "remission of sins and salvation to man" based on Christ's saving work. Third, man in turn becomes involved in faith and obedience coming from "the same grace." He believes the first and original cause of the covenant is God's "mere goodness and free good will (*eudokia*)."[151]

Turretin then describes the covenant of grace as "the pact between the Father and the Son." He bases this claim on Scriptural proofs that relate to the will of the Father to stipulate "the obedience of his Son," Christ's "faithful and constant performance of the duty," and "the kingdom and glory promised" to Christ. Some of the texts Turretin cites include Luke 22:29, "I appoint unto you a kingdom, as my father hath appointed unto me"; Isaiah 42:1, "I uphold; mine elect, in whom my soul delighteth"; Isaiah 49:6, 8, "I give thee for a covenant of the people, that thou mayest be my salvation unto the end of the earth"; and others (e.g., Ps 110:4; 2:8; Isa 61:2; 42:6, 7; 49:1-6, 8; 53:10; Heb 10:5, 7; Gal 4:4; John 10:18; 17:4, 5, 11, 17).[152]

Following his overview of the structure of the federal scheme, Turretin turns to a description of the covenantal pattern of Christ's works in redemptive history. He argues that there are three periods of the covenant of grace. These periods correspond to the ideas of "destination," "the promise," and "execution." The first period, which relates to "destination," is when Christ was appointed as "a sponsor and Mediator" of the church, in accordance with "the counsel of the most holy Trinity." This is proved by scriptural texts such as Proverbs 8:23, 1 Peter 1:20, and Psalm 2:7-8. These verses indicate that Christ was appointed before the creation of the world

150. Turretin, *Institutes of Elenctic Theology*, XII.ii.1 (2:174).
151. Turretin, *Institutes of Elenctic Theology*, XII.ii.5-6 (2:175).
152. Turretin, *Institutes of Elenctic Theology*, XII.ii.13-14 (2:177-78).

and that he was assured of receiving the promises from the Father in eternity. In Turretin's understanding, this period focuses on Christ in his own eternal destination.

The second period relates to the promise. Turretin writes that after the fall, God provided "himself for the actual performance of those things which he had promised from eternity." Thus, Christ "began to do many things pertaining to the office of Mediator," with respect to "prophecy," "his kingdom," and "the priesthood."[153]

The last period relates to the execution of God's plan to fulfill his promise. Turretin argues that the covenant of grace during this era is found in Christ's incarnation, through which he would fulfill "the work of our salvation."[154] Thus, in each dispensation, it is apparent that Turretin regards that Christ as mediator is central to the doctrine of the covenant of grace.

Through this emphasis on Christ as mediator, Turretin responds to the Socinians, Remonstrants, and Anabaptists, whom he describes as "modern Pelagians."[155] He writes:

> This most important controversy is waged by us with the ancient and modern Pelagians (to wit, the Socinians, Remonstrants, Anabaptists and others who deny the identity of the gratuitous covenant). They hold that the fathers of the Old Testament were not saved by the gratuitous mercy of God in Christ, the Mediator (God-man, *theanthrōpō*) through faith in him about to come.[156]

He continues his response to what he sees as a Pelagian tendency:

> The gospel (meaning the doctrine of the grace of God in Christ) is used in two ways: either for the gospel promised or *epangleia*; or for *euangelismō* or the gospel completed and manifested. In the former sense, it was under the Old Testament; in the latter only in the New. In this respect, it is said to have been "kept" secret in preceding ages (Rom 16:25), not absolutely and simply, since in the same book it is said to have been promised and manifested by

---

153. Turretin, *Institutes of Elenctic Theology*, XII.ii.15 (2:178).

154. Turretin, *Institutes of Elenctic Theology*, XII.ii.15 (2:178).

155. Turretin, Institutes of Elenctic Theology, XII.v.1 (2:192).

156. Turretin, *Institutes of Elenctic Theology*, XII.v.1 (2:192).

the prophetic Scripture (Rom 1:12), but relatively: (1) as to natural knowledge because flesh and blood does not reveal this; (2) as to its promulgation among the Gentiles because God permitted them to walk in their own ways and made known to them nothing about Christ; (3) as to its fulfillment among the Jews because he reserved its fulfillment not for their times, but for ours. The apostle, therefore, does not mean that the gospel was altogether unknown under the Old Testament, but when compared with the light of the New Testament, by which he made it more clearly known and to more persons (Eph 3:5).[157]

Here, Turretin says that the gospel under the Old Testament is something promised, while under the New Testament, the gospel is something accomplished.

Turretin means to imply not that there are two kinds of covenant but rather that there is a twofold economy of the one covenant of grace. In this twofold economy, the gospel comes to be more clearly made known. This carries an echo of Cocceius's federal formula, which attempts to account for the relationship between revelation and history. As Van Asselt notes about Cocceius's understanding, "The various stages in the abrogations are components of a movement in which a comparative element can be discerned: it is a movement from lesser to greater."[158]

The analysis presented in this section thus far suggests that Turretin's positive approach to federal theology eventually gave way to his vigorous denials of the theology of the Socinians, Remonstrants, Anabaptists, and Arminians. However, it is also possible to ascertain his perspective on the history of redemption by examining the basic structure of his federal theology. In fact, in attempting to refute his opponents, Turretin raises a question: "Why did God dispense the single covenant of grace in different ways?" In his answer to this question we find our answer as well. Turretin turns to a twofold economy of the covenant of grace: the Old Testament and the New Testament.

---

157. Turretin, *Institutes of Elenctic Theology*, XII.v.24 (2:201).

158. Van Asselt, *The Federal Theology of Johannes Cocceius*, 281.

According to Turretin, the "economical diversity" of the covenant has to do with "the mystery of Christ" that was destined to be revealed "at first somewhat obscurely and then more clearly." While the Old Testament, or old dispensation, "promised Christ about to come," the New Testament, or new dispensation, "announces Christ as manifested and incarnate and dead." "In the former," Turretin argues with a reference to Hebrews 1:2, "God spoke to the fathers at sundry times and in divers[e] manners (*polymerōs kai polytropōs*). In the latter, however, he hath spoken unto us by his Son (Heb 1:2)."[159]

In light of this twofold understanding, Turretin continues to distinguish between the two dispensations. While the history of the Old Testament stretches from Adam to Christ, the New Testament "extends from Christ to the end of the world." Turretin then increases the complexity of his argument when he recognizes "a threefold division" of all of history. He believes this "threefold division" can be superimposed over the twofold dispensation described above. These three divisions include (1) all of time "under the promise before the law," (2) the period "under the law, from Moses to Christ," and (3) the era "under the gospel, where the New begins."[160] Nevertheless, Turretin makes it clear that the twofold distinction runs parallel with the distinction between promise and fulfillment since he believes that the promise in the scriptural usage "is extended to all the ages following the law until Christ."[161] Ever present in this account of the twofold economy is the theme of the progressive revelation of the covenant of grace, by which God's promise has been accomplished from lesser to greater.

Regarding the Old Testament, Turretin maintains that the covenant of grace "under the bare promise made to Adam" received not only "more federal relation (*schesin*)" in the era of Abraham but also "a more perfect character of a testamentary disposition in the time of Moses." He believes that during this period, when the law is given, "the progress of the revelation of the covenant of grace is marked." He argues that before the law, the covenant of grace was in a state of "the infancy and rudiments," compared

---

159. Turretin, *Institutes of Elenctic Theology*, XII.vii.1 (2:216–17).
160. Turretin, *Institutes of Elenctic Theology*, XII.vii.7 (2:218).
161. Turretin, *Institutes of Elenctic Theology*, XII.vii.7 (2:218).

with its later "more perfect constitution."[162] Thus, Turretin distinguishes between the Old and New Testaments according to his understanding of the promise-fulfillment structure of the covenant.

Although Turretin's view of the dispensations of the covenant appears to be simple, especially when compared with the aforementioned Reformed scholastics, he nonetheless subdivides the Old Testament into three stages (from Adam to Abraham, to Moses, and to Christ). He is not afraid to spiritualize these stages. Concerning the first stage, Turretin focuses on "the seed of the woman," which he believes refers to Christ (an idea also seen in Mastricht).[163] Turretin concludes that "the primeval promise" given to the "first parents" included "the principal parts of the covenant of grace and of the gospel" in "a compendium." This provided humanity with "a manifestation of the obligation of the worship and obedience" of God and revealed that "the promise on God's part" requires "faith on man's part."[164]

After the creation narrative, Turretin turns his attention to the covenant during the time of Abraham. During this period, he argues, God's promise given to the first parents was "almost obliterated in the minds of men." Moreover, during this time, "the holy race of Shem and the family of Terah (Josh 24:2)" were contaminated by "the contagion of idolatry." As a result, God "selected and called Abraham" to renew the "covenant with him and his seed." Turretin believes that this was God affirming that "the Messiah should be born of [Abraham's] posterity and demanding faith and obedience in turn from [Abraham] (Gen 22:18; 17:1, 2)."[165]

During the third stage of the covenant, from Moses to Christ, Turretin believes that the covenant of grace was not confined to "certain persons and families" but rather "enlarged" to "an entire and numerous nation." During this period, God reveals himself not only as "'l shdy (Gen 17:1, as omnipotent and self-sufficient)" but also as "yhvh (Ex 6:2, 3)," who has "eternity and immutability of essence, so that he would be 'faithful' for 'his promise' to deliver the Israelites from 'the Egyptian captivity.' "[166] Thus, Turretin maintains that the whole course of history reflects redemptive

---

162. Turretin, *Institutes of Elenctic Theology*, XII.vii.7 (2:218).
163. Turretin, *Institutes of Elenctic Theology*, XII.vii.11 (2:220).
164. Turretin, *Institutes of Elenctic Theology*, XII.vii.17 (2:222).
165. Turretin, *Institutes of Elenctic Theology*, XII.vii.17 (2:222).
166. Turretin, *Institutes of Elenctic Theology*, XII.vii.18–24 (2:222–25).

progress, in which the divine promise is revealed, renewed, and fulfilled. As Beach notes, for Turretin, the second stage from Abraham to Moses "is more appropriated under the economy of a promise."[167]

Turretin then turns his attention to how the covenant of grace in the Old Testament relates to that same covenant administered in the New Testament. He argues there is a "twofold relation." One is a "legal relation," in which the law functions as "the letter that kills" (2 Cor 3:6). The other is an "evangelical" relation, in terms of which the law functions as "a schoolmaster unto Christ (Gal 3:24)," which brings about "joy" over against "the former relation."[168] Thus, he believes that the administration of the covenant in the Old Testament can be seen "either as to the external economy of legal teaching or as to the internal truth of the gospel promise lying under it." The "marks" and "effects" of the external economy of the covenant consist of the following terms and phrases: the "Messiah's coming," "obscurity," "bondage," "rigor and severity," and "purity of flesh." On the other hand, the internal dispensation contains "Christ and promises temporal and spiritual." By "temporal," Turretin means that since the Israelite people's "disposition" was still like "children," so that they were "more affected by carnal than spiritual things," the "inheritance of the land of Canaan and the earthly blessings" were promised to "the faithful worshippers of God." Meanwhile, the spiritual blessings indicate "the substance of the covenant of grace … primarily and principally, as absolutely necessary to salvation." By this distinction, Turretin finds the *ordo salutis* in the covenant, namely, (1) the "remission of sins and justification," (2) "adoption," (3) "sanctification," (4) "the gift of the Spirit," (5) "the resurrection of the dead," and (6) "eternal life."[169]

While Turretin discusses the covenant in the Old Testament in great detail, he touches on the New Testament only briefly. However, although his attention to the new dispensation is somewhat cursory, his emphasis upon the centrality of Christ is nonetheless significant. He defines the new dispensation as follows:

---

167. Beach, *Christ and the Covenant*, 248.

168. Turretin, *Institutes of Elenctic Theology*, XII.vii.31 (2:227).

169. Turretin, *Institutes of Elenctic Theology*, XII.vii.32–45 (2:227–32).

Thus far the old dispensation; the new succeeds, the administration of the covenant without the law and ceremonies after the appearance of Christ. It is called "new" not as to the substance of the covenant (which is the same in both) but: (1) as to the circumstances and mode being manifested without a veil and the law (in which way that covenant appeared as if new or renewed), also because it sets forth Christ not to be exhibited but as exhibited, in which way it can be called new both intensively as to degree of light and extensively as to amplitude, extending itself indiscriminately to all nations; (2) as to the excellence and glory of this dispensation which far surpasses the old (2 Cor 3:9, 10), as new is elsewhere taken for what is remarkable and superior (Rev 5:9; Ps 33:3); (3) as to perpetual duration, by which it happens that it is as it were always new, while those things which ought to cease are called old.[170]

Turretin stresses that the new dispensation does not need to be renewed since it is the reality of the shadow in the law. As for the difference between the covenant of grace in the Old and New Testaments, the former is a "thin shadow and rude outline," while the latter is "a living and express image."[171]

His view of the relationship between the Old and New Testaments appears to parallel his understanding of the relationship between the covenant of works and the covenant of grace. He asserts that the covenant of grace is called "'new' not only because it succeeded the old covenant of works and because in a far more illustrious manner it was renewed in Christ under the New Testament, but also because it is eternal, immutable and never to be abrogated (Heb 8; Jer 31, 32)."[172] Turretin thus does not focus on the negative progress of the covenant of works. At this point, he differs from Coccejus, who held that "the elements of the covenant of works undergo a negative development, going from greater to lesser, while the elements of the covenant of grace undergo a positive development, progressing from lesser to greater."[173]

---

170. Turretin, *Institutes of Elenctic Theology*, XII.vii.46 (2:232).

171. Turretin, *Institutes of Elenctic Theology*, XII.viii.22 (2:239).

172. Turretin, *Institutes of Elenctic Theology*, XII.i.9 (2:172).

173. Van Asselt, *The Federal Theology of Johannes Coccejus*, 276.

EVALUATION OF TURRETIN

Turretin's dogmatic works on the covenant bear a striking similarity to those of the Reformed scholastics mentioned above. An example of this is found in his twofold understanding of the nature of the history of redemption. In one approach, he understands salvation as being progressively revealed. In another approach, he seeks to understand how salvation history is applied to individual faith. Moreover, like his contemporaries, Turretin employs various terms and distinctions, such as a threefold law that is "moral, ceremonial, and forensic"; "abrogations" of the law; the order of salvation; the old and new dispensations; schoolmaster; the analogy of child and adult; and so forth.[174] Thus, certain aspects of Turretin's conception of the covenant of grace seem to be shared by the Reformed scholastics Cocceius, Witsius, and Mastricht.

Nevertheless, his view of the history of redemption is distinct in that he focuses on the twofold structure of promise and fulfillment. He believes that the covenant of grace is that Christ is revealed in a manner that displays the divine promise in both design and execution. In other words, Turretin's understanding of the history of redemption hinges on a certain view of the promise-fulfillment structure. Given this, it is not surprising that compared with his contemporaries, his analysis of federal theology comprises a simpler and clearer structure of the covenant scheme.

Moreover, as noted above, Turretin does not deal in depth with the stage of redemptive history revealed in the New Testament. Yet this is perhaps not surprising. Considering his promise-fulfillment structure, it seems most likely that Turretin did not feel any need to write a detailed analysis of the new dispensation since the New Testament represents the utter fulfillment of the covenant of grace. It is as if he believed that the covenant of grace did not need a renewal in the New Testament but was simply revealed in a fuller way. This may provide some insight into why he does not subdivide the stages of the new dispensation in detail but feels the need to do so with the time recorded in the Old Testament.

Compared with the other theologians mentioned in this chapter, Turretin's federal theology appears to be more systematic and less exegetical. That is not to say, however, that he makes less use of the biblical

---

174. Turretin, *Institutes of Elenctic Theology*, XII.vii.32–45 (2:227–32).

proof texts than others nor that his approach to federal theology is reached by reflection grounded on reason without biblical consideration. Rather, Turretin lays out his federal theology systematically, with an emphasis on the unity of the covenant. This is largely due to his desire to refute the "Pelagian tendency" he believed was being put forth by the Socinians, Anabaptists, and Arminians. Given this context, it is understandable that the centrality of Christ as mediator comes to the fore in his understanding of the covenant. In fact, this motif plays a crucial role in his approach to federal theology as a whole. As Beach helpfully points out, "Turretin's work as a theologian is in the role of codifier and defender of the faith."[175]

CONCLUSION

This chapter showed that there are large overlaps in the views of Cocceius, Witsius, Mastricht, and Turretin. They use similar terminology, make similar claims about salvation, and seek to understand divine grace using biblical exegesis, theology, and history. Yet there are also differences. While Mastricht and Cocceius stress how salvation is revealed with increasing clarity in historical stages, Witsius focuses on the *ordo salutis*, or steps in which a person experiences salvation. And Turretin, in an attempt to refute a sharp distinction between the Old and New Testaments, is the most vigorous defender of the unity of the covenant of grace. Thus, it is correct to view "federal theology" as a family of approaches rather than a specific method or set of ideas. A unifying factor for these Reformed theologians is a rejection of what they see as the Pelagian view of the relationship between the Old and New Testaments.[176]

As chapter 3 will argue, many aspects of Edwards's approach to federal theology echo those of the Reformed scholastics before him. However, his historical approach tends to follow the biblical narratives and is far less systematic than his Reformed forebears.

---

175. Beach, *Christ and the Covenant*, 13.
176. See Van Asselt, *The Federal Theology of Johannes Cocceius*, 228.

Part 2

—

REDEMPTIVE HISTORY *in* JONATHAN EDWARDS

3

—

THE DOCTRINE OF
THE COVENANT OF REDEMPTION
AND THE HISTORY OF REDEMPTION

INTRODUCTION

THE STATE OF EDWARDS'S *HISTORY* PROJECT

As explained above, some of the major players in seventeenth-century federal theology include Cocceius, Witsius, Mastricht, and Turretin. It was argued that Edwards's federal theology should be read with this backdrop in mind. However, this does not mean that Edwards's view of redemptive history completely aligns with those of his Reformed predecessors. On the contrary, echoes of Reformed themes can be found in Edwards's view of redemptive history and his federal theology, for that matter, but these are not exact replicas. Although Edwards consciously locates himself as a son of the Reformation, he does not abstain from a creative exposition of the covenantal view. With this in mind, this section now turns to Edwards's understanding of the history of redemption.

Our investigation begins with a letter Edwards wrote to the trustees of the College of New Jersey. In it, he introduces the *history* project as "a body of divinity in an entire new method, being thrown into the form of a history."[1] This description raises many questions, some of which have arisen among Edwards scholars. As William J. Scheick points out:

---

1. Jonathan Edwards to the Trustees of the College of New Jersey, October 19, 1757, in Edwards, *Letters and Personal Writings*, WJE 16:727.

The *History* proved troublesome to many of Edwards' critics. The major difficulty has been to discover what Edwards could have meant by his claim to "an entire new method." One critic, in despair proclaims the study to be "a thoroughly traditional book." Others try to exonerate Edwards, noting that he had not had a chance to perfect the work or that he had set himself a task beyond realization.[2]

Given the difficulty in understanding the "entire new method" Edwards envisioned, it comes as no surprise that the nature of this intended work has been debated among a series of scholars. The varying views on the subject fall largely into two different perspectives regarding the degree of continuity (or discontinuity) between Edwards and his New England Puritan contemporaries and/or Reformed predecessors. All the views seek to answer the question of the degree of innovation found in Edwards's view of history.

Scheick, after reviewing various scholarly works on the subject, finds Edwards's view "innovative." Scheick argues that Edwards's uniqueness stems from his understanding of history as "an allegory of the conversion experience."[3] This leads Scheick to conclude that there is "nothing else quite like" Edwards's method in New England Puritan literature.[4]

Patricia Wilson-Kastner also argues that Edwards's view of history differs from his Puritan forebears. She maintains that before Edwards, the Puritans had modified Luther's and Calvin's notion of grace into the belief that "the individual's justification by God is one temporal act" that brings about "sanctifying grace." In this understanding, the one who receives sanctifying grace can be a "real participant" in salvation by "doing good works" that "are meritorious before God." Thus, human beings "could change the course of history with its human benefits or curses." By contrast, she believes Edwards "defined history purely in terms of the action

---

2. William J. Scheick, "The Grand Design: Jonathan Edwards' History of Redemption," *Eighteenth-Century Studies* 8, no. 3 (Spring, 1975): 300.

3. As an "individual soul" experiences "the regenerative process," it is as if "history evinces a symbolic representation of the spiritual progress of the saint." He writes: "As the soul grows in grace and as history approaches eternity, both by means of *a posteriori* phases, the more luminous they become." Scheick, "The Grand Design," 301, 313.

4. Scheick, "The Grand Design," 313.

of God's Spirit," so that there is no room for "human initiative or novelty; God was the sole agent of history."[5]

Perry Miller and Peter Gay attempt to assess Edwards's *history* project in light of new history that emerged from eighteenth-century figures including Locke, Newton, William Robertson, Edward Gibbon, etc.[6] For Miller, if Edwards's *History of the Work of Redemption* is read as a history that does not merely consider an accumulation of historical data but rather focuses on the idea or the mind that determines the coherence of history, it "becomes a pioneer work in American historiography."[7] However, Gay, who initially agrees with Miller in his assessment of Edwards as a historical thinker,[8] goes on to claim that Edwards, in his historical method, is "far from being the first modern American."[9] Instead, he concludes that Edwards's *History*

---

5. Patricia Wilson-Kastner, "Jonathan Edwards: History and the Covenant," *Andrews University Seminary Studies*, 15 (1977): 206–7.

6. Peter Gay, *A Loss of Mastery: Puritan Historians in Colonial America* (Berkley: University of California Press, 1966), 93; 104; Perry Miller, *Jonathan Edwards* (New York: William Sloan Associates, 1949; reprinted, Amherst: University of Massachusetts Press, 1981), 312–13.

7. Miller, *Jonathan Edwards*, 311. Miller tends to see Edwards's work as innovative. He argues that Edwards does not consider history to be merely an accumulation of historical data. He suggests, "If Edwards' book be read as a study of this problem, and the superficial narrative be stripped from the philosophical thesis, it becomes a pioneer work in American historiography. His tentative effort, arrived at in solitude, when none among his contemporaries, or for that matter among his disciples, neither Erskine nor his own son, could grasp what he was after, is an achievement truly staggering. For a mind imbued with Newtonianism to break away from the reigning conception of space toward an appreciation of time, to subordinate the idea of an eternal and immutable, or at best a cyclical, pattern of the past to a vision of a dynamic process of realization within temporal existence—this was such a metaphysical excursion as his contemporaries could not begin to comprehend. In its divination of the methodology to which our culture has been more and more committed, the *History of Redemption* is a prophetic book." Miller, *Jonathan Edwards*, 311. Miller argues later: "For Edwards the essential conception was clear, that what men call history is the idea they have of the past, not the actual events which they never witnessed." Considering the relationship between Edwards's *history* project and his sermon series of 1739, Miller claims that Edwards's concept of history relates to his doctrine of cause. He writes, "The idea which determines the coherence of history is not just a whimsical notion of the historian: it would indeed be just that were it a supine induction from evidences (if one surrenders his mind to his footnotes, he can write untold monographs, and call them history!): 'In order to see how a design is carried on, we must first know what the design is.'" History for Edwards is "a grand conception, a design, a chain of events within a scheme of causation." Miller, *Jonathan Edwards*, 312–13.

8. Robert E. Brown, *Jonathan Edwards and the Bible* (Bloomington: Indiana University Press, 2002), 170.

9. Gay, *A Loss of Mastery*, 116.

of the Work of Redemption is "a thoroughly traditional book" and rooted in the Augustinian tradition.[10]

George Marsden claims that Edwards's *history* project imitates the Bible itself rather than "the forms" which were used by "Thomas Aquinas or even the Reformed systematizers such as Francis Turretin or Peter van Mastricht."[11] Similarly, Robert E. Brown argues that Edwards's "new method of divinity" sought to be different from "the prevailing *loci* model of Reformed divinity that treated critical and philosophical issues within the doctrine of Scripture."[12] Michael McClymond and Gerald McDermott believe Edwards's intention was to "translate the content of traditional dogmatic theology into historical or narrative form."[13] In their view, Edwards's phrase "entire new method" implies that Edwards "is going to do something unprecedented."[14]

On the other hand, John F. Wilson claims that the manner Edwards uses in *A History of the Work of Redemption* is "derived from that of the conventional Puritan plain-style sermon." In his analysis of "Miscellanies" pertaining to the redemption motif, Wilson identifies the Redemption Discourse as "a systematic elaboration of a grand theme that appears at a remarkable number of places and times and under many different headings in the storehouse of his essays."[15] In this appraisal, Edwards's intended work is identified as an expansion of the Redemption Discourse, though without any novelty.[16] Thus, Wilson assesses the sermon series of 1739 as

---

10. Gay, *A Loss of Mastery*, 94.

11. George M. Marsden, *Jonathan Edwards: A Life* (New Haven: Yale University Press, 2003), 488.

12. Brown, *Jonathan Edwards and the Bible*, 183.

13. Michael J. McClymond and Gerald R. McDermott, *The Theology of Jonathan Edwards* (New York: Oxford University Press, 2012), 184–85. For more explanation of the nature of the project, see John F. Wilson, "Jonathan Edwards' Notebooks for 'A History of the Work of Redemption,'" in *Reformation, Conformity and Dissent: Essays in Honour of Geoffrey Nuttall*, ed. R. Buick Knox (London: Epworth, 1977), 239–54; Brown, *Jonathan Edwards and the Bible*, xvii, 169–78.

14. McClymond and McDermott, *The Theology of Jonathan Edwards*, 185.

15. John F. Wilson, "Editor's Introduction," in Edwards, *A History of the Work of Redemption*, *WJE* 9:13. Wilson still agrees with Miller and Gay somewhat in his assessment of Edwards's *History of the Work of Redemption* that Edwards's historical method does not match the Enlightenment-influenced history writing that took "shape in Europe at the end of Edwards' life." John F. Wilson, "Jonathan Edwards as Historian," *CH* 46, no. 1 (1977): 12.

16. See Brown, *Jonathan Edwards and the Bible*, 171. When it comes to the character of the divinity Edwards had in mind, remember that Edwards's *history* project had already been

"a part of the broad stream of Puritan interpretation" of redemption, a conclusion also reached by Robert Brown.[17]

More recently, Sean Michael Lucas attempted to refute Miller and Gay by suggesting that Edwards's historical work goes beyond just providing "'a story book for fundamentalists' or replicating other attempts at universal history for Christian epic." He contends that the new method of Edwards can be found in his focus on redemptive history. "Unlike other chroniclers of his day who focused on the providential founding of New England or on the harmonization of 'sacred' with 'profane' history," asserts Lucas, "Edwards repeatedly demonstrated in *A History of the Work of Redemption* how biblical history was organically and chronologically unfolding Christ's work of redemption."[18] In this sense, he argues that it is Edwards's redemptive-historical focus that is the revolutionary aspect of his method, especially compared with his contemporaries. Nevertheless, he concedes that Edwards's approach to redemptive history derives from classic Reformed thought that focused on the intra-Trinitarian covenant made to accomplish the design of glorifying God.[19]

Douglas Sweeney considers the new methods as something familiar to the early-modern Calvinists. "He employed it elsewhere too, though,

---

begun even before his response to the invitation of the trustees of the College of New Jersey. As seen in his letter to the trustees, Edwards began the great work "long ago, not with any view to publication." According to Miller, Edwards's response to the trustees implies that Edwards has reflected "a series of sermons on the idea." Wilson points out that the Scottish clergyman John Erskine's letter of September 6, 1754, to Joseph Bellamy indicates Edwards's intention of the development of the Redemptive Discourse of 1739. Erskine writes, "Tho' I long to see Mr. Edwards' refutation of the several branches of Arminianism, yet I more long to see his intended history of Man's Redemption. From such a pen, upon such a subject, something highly valuable may be expected." Edwards to the Trustees of the College of New Jersey, October 19, 1757, Letters and Personal Writings, 727; Miller, *Jonathan Edwards*, 307; John Erskine, "Unpublished Letters of the late Rev. Dr. Erskine," *Church of Scotland Magazine and Review* (USA: Palala Press, 2015), 332. For more on the controversy surrounding the nature of the *history* project, see Wilson, "Jonathan Edwards as Historian," 5–18.

17. Brown, *Jonathan Edwards and the Bible*, 171.

18. Sean Michael Lucas, "A History of the Work of Redemption," in *A Reader's Guide to the Major Writings of Jonathan Edwards*, ed. Nathan A. Finn and Jeremy M. Kimble (Wheaton, IL: Crossway, 2017), 179–80.

19. Lucas, "A History of the Work of Redemption," 180. For more discussion on Edwards's view of the nature of "divinity in an entire new method," see Wilson, "Jonathan Edwards as Historian," 12; Stephen M. Clark, "Jonathan Edwards: The History of the Work of Redemption," *WTJ* 56, no. 1 (1994): 47; Michael McClymond, *Encounters with God: An Approach to the Theology of Jonathan Edwards*, Religion in America (New York: Oxford University Press, 1998), 66.

and surely understood," asserts Sweeney, "that its most prominent components had been tested long before." Sweeney goes on to say, "Other early-modern Calvinists had structured their theologies according to the progress of redemption in the Bible."[20] Most recently, Adriaan Neele rejected McClymond's argument that Edwards's structuring of Christian theology as a history of redemption is not innovative. However, he does grant that Edwards's view of "all parts of divinity" (to which he referred in his letter to the Princeton trustees) would have resonated with "many Post-reformation works whose authors were known in early New England." Considering Mastricht's *De dispensationis foederis gratiae* as a background to Edwards's envisioned body of divinity, he finds Edward's new method non-original.[21]

However, this section neither directly addresses the debate over the character of *A History of the Work of Redemption* nor attempts to provide a sketch of the context in which Edwards planned to write it. Rather, the purpose of this part is to identify his covenant scheme as a summary of his view of redemptive history. For this purpose, this part consists of three chapters divided according to Edwards's federal schema, the covenants of redemption, works, and grace.

INTRODUCTION TO THE COVENANT OF REDEMPTION

Edwards's doctrine of the covenant of redemption as the inner-Trinitarian eternal pact between the Father and the Son is part of his doctrine of the Trinity.[22] Accordingly, scholarly works on Edwards's understanding of the covenant of redemption have mainly concentrated on aspects of the relationship between the immanent Trinity and the economic Trinity.[23] In this

---

20. Sweeney, *Edwards the Exegete*, 139.

21. Adriaan C. Neele, *Before Jonathan Edwards: Sources of New England Theology* (Oxford: Oxford University Press, 2018), 219.

22. Lucas notes that the covenant of redemption for Edwards implies two elements: "pre-temporal" and "intra-Trinitarian," that is, Christ's covenant with the two members of the Godhead before the creation of the world. See Sean Michael Lucas, *God's Grand Design: The Theological Vision of Jonathan Edwards* (Wheaton, IL: Crossway, 2011), 27–28.

23. On the debate about whether or not Edwards's Trinitarian theology belongs to Reformed orthodoxy, see Amy Plantinga Pauw, *The Supreme Harmony of All: The Trinitarian Theology of Jonathan Edwards* (Grand Rapids: Eerdmans, 2002); Steven M. Studebaker and Robert W. Caldwell III, *The Trinitarian Theology of Jonathan Edwards: Text, Context, and Application* (Burlington, VT: Ashgate, 2012); Richard M. Weber, "The Trinitarian Theology of Jonathan Edwards: An Investigation of Charges against Its Orthodoxy," *JETS* 44, no. 2 (June 2001): 297–318; William J. Danaher, *The Trinitarian Ethics of Jonathan Edwards* (Louisville: Westminster John Knox, 2004); Reita Yazawa, *Reita Yazawa, "Covenant of Redemption in the*

regard, Amy Plantinga Pauw asserts that Edwards employed "two distinct models of the immanent Trinity": (1) the Augustinian view that portrays "the Son and Spirit as the Wisdom and Love of the one God" and (2) a social model that "depicts the Godhead as a society or family of persons."[24] From this, she argues that Edwards's Trinitarianism provides "largely untapped resources for understanding the complex issues of Christian practice and communal life."[25] In her view, Edwards's use of the social model of the Trinity provides an example for Christian community.

Maintaining Pauw's view, Sang Hyun Lee insists that Edwards's depiction of the three persons of the Trinity departs from both Augustine and "the Western church's traditional tendency to see God's unity in the singularity of divine substance."[26] Following Pauw, William J. Danaher argues that Edwards reinterprets the Trinity through the lens of his own philosophical

Theology of Jonathan Edwards: The Nexus between the Immanent and the Economic Trinity" (PhD diss., Calvin Theological Seminary, 2013); Ralph Cunnington, "A Critical Examination of Jonathan Edwards' Doctrine of the Trinity," Themelios (Online) 39, no. 2 (July 2014): 224–40, http://themelios.thegospelcoalition.org/article/a-critical-examination-of-jonathan-edwardss-doctrine-of-the-trinity. On the various studies of Edwards's Trinitarian theology, see Herbert W. Richardson, "The Glory of God in the Theology of Jonathan Edwards: A Study in the Doctrine of the Trinity" (PhD diss., Harvard University, 1962); Krister Sairsingh, "Jonathan Edwards and the Idea of Divine Glory: His Foundational Trinitarianism and Its Ecclesial Import" (PhD diss., Harvard University, 1986); Rachel S. Stahle, "The Trinitarian Spirit of Jonathan Edwards' Theology" (PhD diss., Boston University, 1999); Robert W. Caldwell III, Communion in the Spirit: The Holy Spirit as the Bond of Union in the Theology of Jonathan Edwards (Eugene, OR: Wipf & Stock, 2007); M. X. Lesser, Reading Jonathan Edwards: An Annotated Bibliography in Three Parts, 1729–2005 (Grand Rapids: Eerdmans, 2008). For brief descriptions of these works, see Studebaker and Caldwell, The Trinitarian Theology of Jonathan Edwards, 1–18. For a critic of the social model of the Trinity, i.e., Social Trinitarianism, see Stephen R. Holmes, "Three Versus One? Some Problems of Social Trinitarianism," Journal of Reformed Theology 3 (2009): 77–89.

24. Pauw, The Supreme Harmony of All, 11; Sang Hyun Lee, ed., The Princeton Companion to Jonathan Edwards (Princeton: Princeton University Press, 2005), 46–47. According to Lee, while the first model emphasizes "divine unity," the other model focuses on "relationality" within the Trinity. Edwards "was willing to live with the theological tension between these two models for the Trinity" (Pauw, The Supreme Harmony of All, 11).

25. Pauw, The Supreme Harmony of All, 16.

26. Sang Hyun Lee, "Editor's Introduction," in Writings on the Trinity, Grace, and Faith, WJE 21:27, 26. Here, Lee argues that traditional western theology focuses on God's simplicity alone that indicates "God's unity in the singularity of divine substance." This view, he argues, makes it "difficult to explain how such an impassible God is capable of activities such as creation and incarnation." See Lee, "Introduction," in The Princeton Companion, ed. Sang Hyun Lee, xiii. For some critics of Sang Hyun Lee's interpretation, see Stephen R. Holmes, "Does Jonathan Edwards Use a Dispositional Ontology? A Response to Sang Hyun Lee," in Jonathan Edwards: Philosophical Theologian, ed. Paul Helm and Oliver D. Crisp (Burlington, VT: Ashgate, 2003), 99–114; Oliver D. Crisp, "Jonathan Edwards on the Divine Nature," Journal of Reformed Theology 3 (2009): 175–201.

idealism in the context of the eighteenth century.[27] Ralph Cunnington holds an adapted version of this view, maintaining that Edwards's use of the "tools of eighteenth-century philosophy" reveals that his doctrine of the Trinity is "innovative," despite "its remaining within the bounds of Western orthodoxy."[28] Most recently, Obbie Tyler Todd has claimed that there is "an abiding tension" in "the distinction between the individual agency and the relational community in God's personhood."[29] In this line of thought, Edwards is considered to have reformulated a classical Reformed doctrine of the Trinity using eighteenth-century philosophical idealism.

However, Pauw's view is refuted by Steven Studebaker and Robert Caldwell, who contend that Edwards's Trinitarian thought consistently reflects "features of the Augustinian mutual love model" rather than "oscillates between the discordant social and psychological models of the Trinity."[30] In the same vein, Reita Yazawa claims that Pauw's argument about the two models in Edwards may be "anachronistic," since "the dichotomy of the social and psychological models" derives from French theologian Théodore de Régnon (1831–1893).[31]

However, Pauw argues that in the 1740s Edwards shifted away from rational arguments about the Trinity to a historical consideration of God's redemptive activity.[32] This, according to her, echoes Edwards's

---

27. Danaher, *The Trinitarian Ethics of Jonathan Edwards*, 17.

28. Cunnington, "A Critical Examination of Jonathan Edwards' Doctrine of the Trinity," 225.

29. Obbie Tyler Todd, "What is A Person? Three Essential Criteria for Jonathan Edwards's Doctrine of Personhood," *JETS* 61, no. 1 (2018): 127.

30. Pauw argues that Edwards's Trinitarian thought lurches between the relational and psychological models of the Trinity as well as the atomistic view of personhood in the Trinity which emphasizes the initiative of an individual. See Pauw, *The Supreme Harmony of All*, 77; Studebaker and Caldwell, *The Trinitarian Theology of Jonathan Edwards*, 16.

31. Yazawa, "Covenant of Redemption in the Theology of Jonathan Edwards," 20. The following materials are indebted to Yazawa: Steven M. Studebaker, *Jonathan Edwards' Social Augustinian Trinitarianism in Historical and Contemporary Perspectives* (Piscataway, NJ: Gorgias, 2008), 78; Théodore de Régnon, *Études de théologie positive sur la Sainte Trinité*, 4 vols. (Paris: Victor Retaux, 1892–1898); Michael René Barnes, "De Régnon Reconsidered," *Augustinian Studies* 26, no. 2 (1995): 51–79; Barnes, "Augustine in Contemporary Trinitarian Theology," *Theological Studies* 56 (1995): 237–50. For a brief review of the difference between the Trinitarian views of East and West, see Robert Letham, "The Trinity between East and West," *Journal of Reformed Theology* 3 (2009): 42–56.

32. Pauw, *The Supreme Harmony of All*, 10; Lee, "Introduction," *The Princeton Companion to Jonathan Edwards*, xiii. Pauw states in her introduction to *WJE*, vol. 20, "During his last years at Northampton, Edwards took up again the question of the Trinity, a subject to which he had devoted concentrated attention in the 1720s and early 1730. Whereas his earlier 'Miscellanies'

"decision to abandon" his projected work entitled "A Rational Account of the Principles and Main Doctrines of the Christian Religion" and instead employ "an entire new method, being thrown in the form of an history," using Edwards's own words.[33] However, Pauw mistakenly believes that Edwards's explanation of the Trinity through his use of reason would have been quite different from the historical perspective that would be seen in *A History of the Work of Redemption*.

There is no doubt that Edwards's use of reason resulted from his attempt to demonstrate the reasonableness of the Trinity, which was being challenged by British deists under the influence of the English Enlightenment.[34] Moreover, for Edwards, there is no "gap" between the doctrine of the Trinity and the Christian life.[35] However, these facts cannot confirm that reason itself is a driving force in Edwards's understanding of the Trinity, nor do they signify that Edwards's view of the Trinity rests on "his conviction of the Trinity's profound practical value for Christian faith and life," as Pauw argues.[36] Rather, as Sweeney rightly notes, "in opposition to their (deists) call for a modern religion of nature and reason, Edwards insisted late in his life on the necessity of transcendent, supernatural revelation."[37] Although Edwards echoed the Calvinist dictum of the importance of both the "book of nature" and the "book of Scripture," he placed an emphasis on the priority of the Bible rather than reason.[38] Moreover, even before Edwards planned to write *A History of the Work of Redemption* in the 1740s,

---

entries on the Trinity explore the doctrine's connections to his philosophical idealism and notions of consent and excellency, Edwards' approach in the 1740s reflects new apologetic strategies. Since the beginning of the century, the classical doctrine of the Trinity had come under wide attack as a prime example of metaphysical abstruseness and irrationality by both deists and more moderate critics of Christian tradition, including Samuel Clarke, Edwards' favorite source for arguments from the ancients. Starting in this period, and continuing to the end of his life, Edwards brought a new theological urgency to defending the doctrine's reasonableness." See Pauw, "Editor's Introduction," in The "Miscellanies": Entry Nos. 833–1152, *WJE* 20:29–30.

33. Pauw, *The Supreme Harmony of All*, 10; Edwards, *Letters and Personal Writings*, 727. See Adriaan C. Neele, "The Reception of Edwards's *A History of the Work of Redemption* in Nineteenth-century Basutoland," *Journal of Religion in Africa* 45 (2015): 70.

34. Ava Chamberlain, "Editor's Introduction," in The "Miscellanies,": Entry Nos. 501–832, *WJE* 18:27.

35. Sang Hyun Lee, "Editor's Introduction," in *Writings on the Trinity, Grace, and Faith*, 4.

36. Pauw, *The Supreme Harmony of All*, 11.

37. Douglas A. Sweeney, *Jonathan Edwards and the Ministry of the Word: A Model of Faith and Thought* (Downers Grove, IL: IVP Academic, 2009), 92.

38. Sweeney, *Jonathan Edwards and the Ministry of the Word*, 91.

he explained his view of the Trinity and the covenant of redemption in terms of the history of redemption. This is clear in his *Discourse on the Trinity*, in which Edwards employs rationality and exegetical considerations using the history of redemption as an interpretive framework by which the doctrine of the covenant becomes the uniting system of the whole Bible.

A close survey of the aforementioned scholars' works reveals an emphasis on the historical and cultural contexts that may have played into Edwards's understanding of the role of the covenant of redemption in his doctrine of Trinity. However, no study has fully explored Edwards's view of the covenant of redemption and its relation to his interpretive framework, the history of redemption.[39] This book attempts to consider that question. To do so, this chapter investigates Edwards's Trinitarian texts, including *Discourse on the Trinity* and the *Treatise on Grace* as essential sources,[40] as well as other sources, including the "Blank Bible," "Notes on Scripture," "Miscellanies," sermons, and several other publications, which are considered important for Edwards's understanding of the covenant of redemption.

This chapter demonstrates that Edwards's doctrines of the Trinity and the covenant of redemption proceed from his understanding of the history of redemption. The first section explores Edwards's Trinitarian writings and thus considers his view of the immanent Trinity, which involves the nature of the covenant of redemption as part of the eternal counsel of the triune God. The following section discusses Edwards's view of the relationship between the immanent Trinity and the economic Trinity. The last section examines the distinction of the economy of the persons of the Godhead and the covenant of redemption, so that the roles of the three persons (the Father, the Son, and the Holy Spirit) come into focus. This paper concludes that Edwards's understanding of the covenant of redemption is located within the essential theme of the history of redemption as his interpretive framework.

---

39. While Carl Bogue deals with redemptive-historical theme in the covenant of redemption, its focus is on the covenant of grace rather than the covenant of redemption. See Carl W. Bogue, *Jonathan Edwards and the Covenant of Grace* (Cherry Hill, NJ: Mack, 1975), 95–113.

40. Scholars agree that *Discourse on the Trinity* reflects Edwards's mature Trinitarian view. See Caldwell, *Communion in the Spirit*, 28; Cunnington, "A Critical Examination of Jonathan Edwards' Doctrine of the Trinity," 225; Kyle Strobel, *Jonathan Edwards' Theology: A Reinterpretation* (London: Bloomsbury T&T Clark, 2013), 35.

THE IMMANENT TRINITY

What is the purpose of the covenant of redemption? Where does it come from? Who are the parties of the covenant? How do the covenantal parties relate to each other? These questions are answered in Edwards's brief description of the covenant of redemption in *A History of the Work of Redemption*. He writes:

> There were many things done in order to the Work of Redemption before that. Some things were done before the world was created, yea from all eternity. The persons of the Trinity were as it were confederated in a design and a covenant of redemption, in which covenant the Father appointed the Son and the Son had undertaken their work, and all things to be accomplished in their work were stipulated and agreed.[41]

The covenant of redemption is an eternal pact, formed by an agreement between the Father and the Son before the creation of the world, in which the Father appoints Christ to the office of mediator for his elected people. As seen in this brief definition, Edwards's understanding of the covenant of redemption rests on his doctrine of the immanent Trinity and the economic Trinity. Thus, the nature of the Godhead in the immanent Trinity is a proper place to start a discussion of the covenant of redemption.

In *Discourse on the Trinity*, Edwards begins his discussion of the Trinity with the concept of the "idea" of God himself, which generates an infinite "happiness" in God. The conception of "idea" is, in Edwards's view, compatible with an understanding of the nature of the Trinity. For instance, while "the manner of the divine understanding" is not available in human words, human beings, as made in the "image of God," have the same kind of "understanding," "will," "idea," and "love" as God, excepting "a distinction of the 'perfection of degree and manner' to understand oneself." This implies that the possibility of humans understanding themselves originates with God, who created human beings in accordance with his own image. In the same way, the divine nature can be understood only by God himself

---

41. Edwards, *A History of the Work of Redemption*, WJE 9:118. A similar definition is found in his sermon on 1 Corinthians 13:1–10. See Edwards, "470. Sermon on 1 Cor. 13:1–10 (b) (Apr. 1738)," in *Sermons, Series II, 1738, and undated, 1734–1738, WJEO* 53.

through his "mere perception or unvaried presence of his infinitely perfect idea."[42] Thus, God's understanding of himself comes to pass through his perception of his perfect idea.

Edwards notes two facets of the very same essence in God's being: God's self-understanding in "his having a perfect idea of himself" leads to the sum of God's "inclination, love, and joy." Thus, the perfect understanding in the perception of his perfect idea of himself generates "God's love to himself." That God loves himself means that "he [God] must become his own object." Since God has "delight and joy" in his understanding of himself, there must be a "duplicity"—"God and the idea of God."[43] Edwards therefore defines "the Deity" as follows: "And I do suppose the Deity to be truly and properly repeated by God's thus having an idea of himself; and that this idea of God is a substantial ideal and has the very essence of God, is truly God, to all intents and purposes, and that by this means the Godhead is really generated and repeated."[44] Here, the repetitions and generations of the Godhead eternally take place in God himself through his reflection on himself.

This self-generation of the Godhead in turn relates to the concept of the "image" of God. Edwards writes:

God's idea of himself is absolutely perfect, and therefore is an express and perfect image of him, exactly like him in every respect. There is nothing in the pattern but what is in the representation— substance, life, power, nor anything else—and that in a most absolute perfection of similitude; otherwise it is not a perfect idea. But that which is the express perfect image of God, and in every respect like him, is God to all intents and purposes, because there is nothing wanting; there is nothing in the Deity that renders it the Deity but what has something exactly answering of it in this image, which will therefore also render that the Deity.[45]

---

42. Edwards, "Discourse on the Trinity," in *Writings on the Trinity, Grace, and Faith, WJE* 21:113.

43. Edwards, "Discourse on the Trinity," 114.

44. Edwards, "Discourse on the Trinity," 114.

45. Edwards, "Discourse on the Trinity," 114.

Edwards emphasizes the perfection of God's understanding of himself. This view plays a pivotal role in his understanding of the nature of the second person, for God's perfection of self-understanding offers the same divine nature and essence to the second person in the Trinity. He writes:

> Therefore, as God with perfect clearness, fullness and strength understands himself, views his own essence (in which there is no distinction of substance and act, but it is wholly substance and wholly act), that idea which God hath of himself is absolutely himself. This representation of the divine nature and essence is the divine nature and essence again. So that by God's thinking of the Deity, [the Deity] must certainly be generated. Hereby there is another person begotten; there is another infinite, eternal, almighty, and most holy and the same God, the very same divine nature.[46]

For Edwards, the Son is none other than "God's own perfect idea of himself."[47] As seen in his exposition of the first person of the Trinity, God's self-loving and generation presumes that the second person is "the only begotten and dearly beloved Son of God."[48] Having established consubstantiality in the second person of the Godhead, Edwards moves on to a fuller exposition of the Son of God.

He describes the nature of the second person in five aspects, all of which rely on the concept of *idea*. First, the Son of God is "the divine idea of himself." As "images" bring about an "idea," which is "the most immediate representation," Christ as the image of God is the "most immediate representation of Godhead, viz. the idea of God." Second, the Son is "the object of God's eternal and infinite love," since God possesses "perfect joy and happiness" in his understanding of his own "glorious essence [the Son]." Thus, Edwards identifies God's own idea with the Son. Third, Christ is "the face of God," which signifies the "appearance" or "presence" of God that God sees when he looks at himself, as a man looks at his own face reflected in a mirror. Fourth, Christ is the "brightness, effulgence or shining forth of God's glory" in two respects: (1) although there is the glory of God in

---

46. Edwards, "Discourse on the Trinity," 116.

47. Edwards, The "Miscellanies," no. 446, WJE 13:494.

48. Edwards, "Discourse on the Trinity," 117.

himself, it was not until "his idea of himself" that God's glory shines and appears to himself, and (2) God is "well represented by the luminary and his idea to the light." In other words, God's glory is revealed to himself by the light. Fifth, "the Son of God is God's own eternal and perfect idea," for the Son of God is called "the wisdom," "the logos," and "the Amen," which means "truth" in Hebrew.[49]

While Edwards uses "idea" to understand the Son, he considers the love between the Father and the Son to be the Holy Spirit. In *Treatise on Grace*, Edwards argues that the Holy Spirit is "in a peculiar manner called by the name of love."[50] First John 4:8 evidences that "God is love." Thus, Edwards argues that love indicates "the Godhead" or "the divine essence." Thus, the divine essence is called "in a peculiar manner as breathed forth and subsisting in the holy Spirit."[51]

For Edwards, there is a subtle distinction between the *divine nature* and *essence*. This means not that he believes the three persons have their own essences but rather that Edwards finds a distinct place for the role of the Holy Spirit. For example, in *Discourse on the Trinity*, Edwards argues that it is not until the rise of the Holy Spirit, who is a "most pure act" and an "infinitely holy and sweet energy," that the Deity comes into action.[52] For Edwards, the divine nature tends to point to the state of the Godhead, while the divine essence includes the actions within the Godhead. Edwards writes:

> This is the eternal and most perfect and essential act of the divine nature, wherein the Godhead acts to an infinite degree and in the most perfect manner possible. The Deity becomes all act: the divine essence itself flows out and is as it were breathed forth in love and joy. So that the Godhead therein stands forth in yet another manner of subsistence, and there proceeds the third person in the Trinity, the Holy Spirit, viz. the Deity in act: for there is no other act but the act of the will.[53]

---

49. Edwards, "Discourse on the Trinity," 117–20.
50. Edwards, "Treatise on Grace," in *Writings on the Trinity, Grace, and Faith*, 181.
51. Edwards, "Treatise on Grace," 181.
52. Edwards, "Discourse on the Trinity," 121.
53. Edwards, "Discourse on the Trinity," 121.

Edwards considers the divine essence the distinct domain of the Holy Spirit, in terms that it refers to actions flowing out of the Trinity. The divine nature, on the other hand, is distinguished from this action. This becomes even clearer in Edwards's summary of the Trinity in his conclusion, which follows:

> The Father is the Deity subsisting in the prime, unoriginated and most absolute manner, or the Deity in its direct existence. The Son is the Deity generated by God's understanding, or having an idea of himself, and subsisting in that idea. The Holy Ghost is the Deity subsisting in act, or the divine essence flowing out and breathed forth, in God's infinite love to and delight in himself. And I believe the whole divine essence does truly and distinctly subsist both in the divine idea and divine love, and that therefore each of them are properly distinct persons.[54]

The Father is Deity in its primal state. The Deity generated by God's self-understanding is the Son. The Holy Spirit is the "Deity" or "the divine essence" flowing out as the love between the persons of the Trinity. Thus, the "whole divine essence" points to the Deity that loves each other in the Trinity. The same argument is found in Edwards's "Blank Bible." He writes, "Holy Ghost is only divine love, or the essence of God flowing out in love and joy."[55] The Spirit subsists in the love of the Trinity.[56] In this way, Edwards assigns the Holy Spirit a distinct place within the Trinity.

Edwards's description of the distinctive character of the Holy Spirit is closely related to his interest in the equality of the three persons. "In several places," Studebaker writes, "Edwards gave extended thought to the nature of their equality and both of these sections reveal his particular interest in the full equality of the Holy Spirit."[57] This is confirmed by *Discourse on the Trinity*, in which Edwards finds that the Holy Spirit, as love, shares the understanding of the other two persons. He writes:

---

54. Edwards, "Discourse on the Trinity," 131.
55. Edwards, "Romans," in *The "Blank Bible," WJE* 24:997.
56. Edwards, "Discourse on the Trinity," 121.
57. Studebaker and Caldwell, *The Trinitarian Theology of Jonathan Edwards*, 79.

The whole divine essence is supposed truly and properly to subsist in each of these three—viz. God, and his understanding, and love—and that there is such a wonderful union between them that they are after an ineffable and inconceivable manner one in another; so that one hath another, and they have communion in one another, and are as it were predicable one of another.[58]

The Holy Spirit has the same understanding of the other persons due to the "communion" among the persons by which the three persons belong to each other. Edwards writes elsewhere, "God loves the understanding and the understanding also flows out in love, so that the divine understanding is in the Deity subsisting in love."[59] In other words, the persons of the Godhead subsist in love and thereby possess the same understanding.

A similar emphasis appears in *On the Equality of the Persons of the Trinity*. Edwards writes, "The Holy Ghost is the last that proceeds from both the other two, yet the Holy Ghost has this peculiar dignity: that he is as it were the end of the other two, the good that they enjoy, the end of all procession." He also contends that the Holy Spirit has "superiority." He writes, "the Holy Ghost, that is, divine love, has the superiority, as that is the principle that as it were reigns over the Godhead and governs his heart, and wholly influences both the Father and the Son in all they do."[60]

Edwards's approach to the immanent Trinity focuses on the distinct characteristics of the three persons while maintaining their equality. Moreover, he describes the nature of the immanent Trinity in terms of the inner order and the manner of their existence. The following section thus considers the relationship between the immanent Trinity and the economic Trinity in an attempt to shed light on Edwards's interpretive framework.

THE ECONOMIC TRINITY

Edwards's view of the economic Trinity flows out of his view of the immanent Trinity. Moreover, his understanding of the economic Trinity plays a pivotal role in his view of the covenant of redemption. That is, the economic

---

58. Edwards, "Discourse on the Trinity," 133.

59. Edwards, "Discourse on the Trinity," 133.

60. Edwards, "On the Equality of the Persons of the Trinity," in *Writings on the Trinity, Grace, and Faith*, 147.

Trinity can be described in terms of the immanent Trinity as well as the covenant of redemption. Thus, this section is divided into two descriptive subsections. The first explores how the immanent Trinity relates to the economic Trinity, and the second considers how the economic Trinity relates to the covenant of redemption.

THE IMMANENT AND THE ECONOMIC TRINITY:
AD INTRA AND AD EXTRA

For Edwards, the relationship between the immanent Trinity and the economic Trinity can be explained by the phrases *ad intra* and *ad extra*. According to Richard Muller, *ad intra* indicates "absolute and necessary knowledge concerning creation, providence, and salvation that God alone can know," while *ad extra* points to "the relative and accommodated" knowledge.[61] Since the *ad intra–ad extra* language "offers considerable insight into the nature and character of the older Reformed approach to the questions of divine absoluteness and divine relationality,"[62] the term is also crucial for understanding Edwards's view of God's existence and actions.

First, Edwards insists that God's interactions with the world (*ad extra*) flow out of the "proceedings of the divinity *ad intra*."[63] As far as God's internal proceedings (*ad intra*), Edwards identifies two categories: "the proceeding and generation of the Son" and "the proceeding and breathing forth of the Holy Spirit."[64] This is seen in Miscellany no. 448, in which Edwards schematizes *ad intra* by arguing that God is glorified within himself in these two ways: (1) by appearing or being manifested to himself in his own perfect idea, or in his Son, who is the brightness of his glory and (2) by enjoying and delighting in himself, by flowing forth in infinite love and delight toward himself, or in his Holy Spirit.[65] From these two categories of

---

61. Richard A. Muller, "God as Absolute and Relative, Necessary, Free, and Contingent," *Always Reformed: Essays in Honor of W. Robert Godfrey*, ed. R. Scott Clark and Joel E. Kim, (Escondido, CA: Westminster Seminary California, 2010), 57–58. For a fuller summary of the *ad intra*, the *ad intra–ad extra*, and the *extra* distinctions, see Muller, *Post-Reformation Reformed Dogmatics: The Rise and Development of Reformed Orthodoxy, ca. 1520 to ca. 1725*, vol. 3, *The Divine Essence and Attributes*, 453–75.

62. Muller, "God as Absolute and Relative, Necessary, Free, and Contingent," 57.

63. Edwards, *The "Miscellanies,"* no. 1151, WJE 20:525.

64. Edwards, *The "Miscellanies,"* no. 1082, WJE 20:466.

65. Edwards, *The "Miscellanies,"* no. 448, WJE 13:495.

ad intra, it follows that the purpose of creation *ad extra* is also twofold: the manifestation of God's name and the communication of his love to the elect, that is, considered in general, not yet as created individuals.[66] Edwards insists, "God glorifies himself towards the creatures also two ways: (1) by appearing to them, being manifested to their understandings; (2) in communicating himself to their hearts, and in their rejoicing and delighting in, and enjoying the manifestations which he makes of himself."[67]

When it comes to creation, the purpose of the proceeding and generation of the Son is to manifest God's name, including "truth," "majesty," and "beauty," through glorifying himself.[68] Meanwhile, the aim of the proceeding and breathing forth of the Holy Spirit is to communicate "his infinite happiness" to the creatures, making them happy.[69] While manifestation refers to "truth," communication points to "grace."[70] Therefore, the *ad intra* operation of the immanent Trinity is a divine archetype for the *ad extra* actions of the economic Trinity regarding God's relationship to creation.[71]

The relationship between *ad intra* and *ad extra* further implies that Edwards maintains both the unity of and distinction among the three persons of the Godhead.[72] As Richard Muller argues, "A similar *ad intra–ad extra* model … can be identified in the Reformed appropriation of the traditional Trinitarian rule that all essential acts of the Godhead are acts of the three persons operating as the one God, which nonetheless (as is clear in incarnation and sanctification) terminate on one of the divine persons."[73] Just as there is unity and distinction of the persons of the Godhead in the immanent Trinity, so there is unity and distinction in the economic Trinity. This means that the three persons of the Godhead play distinct roles in the history of redemption.

Thus, it is helpful to examine the distinction of the persons of the Godhead as it relates to the economic Trinity and the covenant of

---

66. Edwards, *The "Miscellanies,"* no. 1084, *WJE* 20:467.

67. Edwards, *The "Miscellanies,"* no.. 448, 495.

68. Edwards, *The "Miscellanies,"* nos. 1082 and 1066, *WJE* 20:465, 446.

69. Edwards, *The "Miscellanies,"* no. 1066, 446.

70. Edwards, *The "Miscellanies,"* no. 1094, *WJE* 20:483.

71. Muller, *God as Absolute and Relative, Necessary, Free, and Contingen*, 57.

72. Lee, "Editor's Introduction," in *Writings on the Trinity, Grace, and Faith* 21:4.

73. Muller, *God as Absolute and Relative, Necessary, Free, and Contingen*, 61.

redemption. Among Edwards's various works, it is Miscellany no. 1062 that discusses the covenant of redemption in greatest depth.[74] Here, Edwards emphasizes God's initiative and unchangeable grace in the covenant of redemption through the unity and distinction of the persons of the economic Trinity.

THE DISTINCTION OF PERSONS OF THE TRINITY

Edwards begins his discussion of the "Economy of the Trinity and Covenant of Redemption" with an affirmation of the unity and distinction of the persons in the Godhead. In his exposition of this subject, the concept of subordination is pivotal. In this regard, Edwards's view aligns with the Puritan reformed *ad intra–ad extra* model. Edwards's *ad intra–ad extra* understanding appears in the "Reformed language of the trinitarian nature of the decree and the subordination of the Mediator to his own divinely decreed work."[75]

Moreover, regarding the history of redemption, Edwards distinguishes between the economic Trinity *ad extra* and the covenant of redemption and between the beginning of the covenant of redemption and its establishment. In other words, there are subtle distinctions within Edwards's concept of the covenant of redemption concerning the roles of the divine persons. However, for Edwards, the immanent Trinity, the economic Trinity, and the covenant of redemption are interwoven with each other under the grand design, the history of the work of redemption. Therefore, not only does Edwards pay attention to the elaborate plan of redemption within the Trinity and God's initiative of grace, but also, Edwards's description of the Trinity is woven into his concept of the history of redemption.

Edwards notes that while there is "a subordination" among the three persons of the Trinity, no one person is inferior to another. When it comes to their actions concerning "the creature," the persons of the Godhead are subject to themselves. For example, the Father functions as the "Head of the Trinity," the Son as one who acts under the Father, and the Holy Spirit

---

74. Yazawa, "Covenant of Redemption in the Theology of Jonathan Edwards," 76; Lee, "Editor's Introduction to 'Discourse on the Equality of the Persons of the Trinity,'" in *Writings on the Trinity, Grace, and Faith, WJE* 21:145.

75. Muller, *God as Absolute and Relative, Necessary, Free, and Contingen*, 61.

as one who acts under both the Father and the Son. Edwards's idea of this subordination is summarized well in his sermon on John 10:15. He writes,

> Indeed there is an Oeconomical subordination in the Trinity tho there be no difference of degree of Glory or excellency Yet there is order in the Trin[ity] the three persons of the Trinity may be looked upon as a soci[ety,] a kind of family so there is Oeconomical order thus the Father tho he be no Greater than the son Or the Holy Ghost yet he is first in order the son next the Holy Ghost Last.[76]

This makes it clear that, for Edwards, the nature of subordination relates to the inner order of the Trinity and not to inferiority. Rather, the persons are the same in "glory and excellency of nature."[77] To illustrate this, Edwards argues that the Son is "the brightness of his [God's] glory," "the very image of the Father," and "the express and perfect image of his [God's] person," in whom there is the "Father's infinite happiness." Of course, the Son submits to the Father, in that his "subsistence" comes from the Father: the Son is begotten by the Father. Edwards makes it clear, however, that this dependence does not include an "inferiority of Deity," since "everything in the Father" is continuously "repeated or expressed."[78] The Son, as the idea of God, has the very essence of God in the repetition of God's having an idea of himself, and the persons of the Trinity are equal in nature.

Edwards contends that subordination is not a reference to any "natural subjection" but to "mutual free agreement," which the persons made by their own will to manifest the glory of the Deity and communicate "its fullness." The economy, which is established by mutual agreement among the persons of the Trinity, originates from "the mere pleasure of the members of this society."[79]

Having sought to establish the concept of subordination and unity, Edwards notes a distinction among the persons of the economic Trinity in terms of their subsistence and actions. He argues that there exists "a

---

76. Edwards, "John 15:10 (Mar. 1736)," in *Sermons and Discourses, 1731–1732, WJEO* 46:L. 3r–L. 3v.

77. Edwards, *The "Miscellanies," no. 1062, WJE* 20:430.

78. Edwards, *The "Miscellanies," no. 1062, WJE* 20:430.

79. Edwards, *The "Miscellanies," no. 1062, WJE* 20:431.

natural decency" or "fitness" in the established economy.[80] This means that the actions of the persons of the Trinity are ordered in accordance with the order of their subsistence. Edwards writes:

> As the Father is first in the order of subsisting, so he should be first in the order of acting; that as the other two persons are from the Father in their subsistence, and as to their subsistence naturally originated from him and dependent on him, so that, in all that they act, they should originate from him, act from him and in a dependence on him; that as the Father, with respect to the subsistence, is the fountain of the Deity, wholly and entirely so, so he should be the fountain in all the acts of the Deity. This is fit and decent in itself. Though it is not proper to say decency *obliges* the persons of the Trinity to come into this order and economy, yet it may be said that decency requires it, and that therefore the persons of the Trinity all consent to this order, and establish it by agreement, as they all naturally delight in what is in itself fit, suitable and beautiful.[81]

That is, before entering into the covenant of redemption, each person in the Trinity willingly agreed about the order establishing the economy. Therefore, "the order or the economy" of the three persons of the Trinity in their actions involving creation *ad extra* precedes the covenant of redemption.[82]

From this, a question arises: Why does Edwards distinguish between the voluntary divine will that brought order to the Trinity's actions *ad extra* and the formation of the covenant of redemption? Edwards contends that the Father takes initiative with the other persons with respect to the "determination to glorify and communicate himself."[83] In other words, the economy or order *ad extra* originates from the Father's "natural disposition" or "inclination," even though it was established by the voluntary agreement of the three persons of the Godhead.[84] Edwards writes, "We must conceive of God's natural inclination as being exercised before wisdom

---

80. Edwards, *The "Miscellanies,"* no. 1062, *WJE* 20:431.
81. Edwards, *The "Miscellanies,"* no. 1062, *WJE* 20:431.
82. Edwards, *The "Miscellanies,"* no. 1062, *WJE* 20:431–32.
83. Edwards, *The "Miscellanies,"* no. 1062, *WJE* 20:432.
84. Edwards, *The "Miscellanies,"* no. 1062, *WJE* 20:432.

is set to work to find out a particular, excellent method to gratify that natural inclination."[85] The Father's disposition is for Edwards the original causation of the economy. Therefore, the economy of the Trinity, which is "an establishment" found in "the natural order" of the subsistence of the persons of the Trinity, is distinguished from the covenant of redemption as "an establishment of wisdom," which conceives "a particular method" for the end of the creation.[86]

THE ROLES OF THE PERSONS OF THE TRINITY

Since their roles in the Trinity, as Lee notes, "are laid out" according to the covenant,[87] the covenant of redemption is involved both in the inner-Trinitarian subsistence and the loving action among the persons of the Trinity. Edwards's view is representative of other Reformed scholars. For example, Cocceius also emphasizes the roles of the three persons in the covenant of redemption. And as Willem J. Van Asselt argues, "It [the pact between the Father and the Son] is a relationship within God himself, and it is the eternal basis for God's relationship to the elect in time."[88] Similarly, when examining the ramifications of the covenant of redemption for Christian practice, Yazawa finds that for Reformed scholastics, "God's work of salvation" has "its seminal form within the immanent Trinity."[89] These views underscore the point that the covenant of redemption is best described in terms of the work of God in the inner-Trinitarian mind. It is in this way that sovereign grace comes to the fore in redemptive history.

For Edwards, history before creation and after the end of the world is consistent with this redemptive history. In *A History of the Work of Redemption*, Edwards contends, "As things that were in order to this work, as God's electing love and the covenant of redemption never had a beginning, so the fruits of this work [the work of redemption] that shall be after the end of the work never will have an end."[90] This reflects Edwards's belief

---

85. Edwards, *The "Miscellanies,"* no. 1062, WJE 20:432.

86. Edwards, *The "Miscellanies,"* no. 1062, WJE 20:432.

87. Sang Hyun Lee, "Editor's Introduction," in *Writings on the Trinity, Grace, and Faith*, 39.

88. Willem J. Van Asselt, *The Federal Theology of Johannes Cocceius, 1603–1669*, trans. Raymond A. Blacketer (Leiden: Brill, 2001), 230.

89. Yazawa, "Covenant of Redemption in the Theology of Jonathan Edwards," 62–63.

90. Edwards, *A History of the Work of Redemption*, 119.

that God's love and eternal pact have no beginning, since they originate from the eternal God. Moreover, although the work of redemption is not "an eternal work," since it will be fully accomplished, the fruit obtained by the work of redemption is eternal.[91] Thus, the history of redemption is a realization of the inner-Trinitarian redemptive plan.

THE FATHER

Given the relationship between the covenant of redemption and the inner-Trinitarian subsistence, the distinction between the economy of the Trinity *ad extra* and the covenant of redemption is particularly important for understanding the roles of the persons of the Trinity. Edwards goes on to say that the economy of the persons of the Trinity is distinguished from the covenant of redemption itself. Prior to the covenant of redemption, it is the Father's "will and determination" whether to forgive sinners and provide redemption for them. Thus, the Father plays the role of the "head of the society of the Trinity."[92]

Edwards argues that once the economy of the persons of the Trinity is established, the Father "begins that great transaction of the eternal covenant of redemption." By "virtue of his economical prerogative," the Father becomes "the first mover" in the transaction, in which the determination of "redemption" and "Redeemer" come about. The Father offers the Son "matter," "authority for the office," redemptive "works" to do, "the reward," and "success." All these things take place in response to "the capacity" of the Father as the head.[93]

However, Edwards does not limit the Father's capacity to his economic prerogative as the head of the Trinity. Rather, he contends that the Father acquires "a new right" to do the work of redemption by the "new establishment, a free covenant." The Father, as the instigator of the covenant of redemption, is restrained to "direct and prescribe" to the other persons something that does not belong to the economy of the persons of the Trinity. That is because the Father cannot prescribe to the other persons those things which are contained in the persons' "oeconomical divine character."

---

91. Edwards, *A History of the Work of Redemption*, 119.
92. Edwards, *The "Miscellanies,"* no. 1062, WJE 20:432.
93. Edwards, *The "Miscellanies,"* no. 1062, WJE 20:435–36.

However, when the Son is engaged in the covenant with his free will, so that he agrees with the stipulations, such as "coming into the world in such a state of humiliation" and "suffering," the Father then has a right to prescribe to the Son those things belonging to "the infinite majesty and glory of divine persons." By virtue of the Son freely entering into the covenant, "the Father acquires a new right of headship and authority over the Son, to command him and prescribe to him and rule over him as his proper lawgiver and judge."[94] In this sense, the beginning of the covenant of redemption is distinguished from the Father's and the Son's entering into the covenant.

As seen above, the nature and order of the persons in the economy of the Trinity corresponds to the order of the immanent Trinity, which in turn is in concert with the roles of the persons within the covenant of redemption. Although the subordination of the covenant of redemption is considered "new in kind," its order follows the economic order of the Trinity, since the Father now has a new right to prescribe to the Son the same economic divine character.[95]

THE SON

Having described the role of the Father, Edwards proceeds to explain the obedience of the Son within the covenant of redemption using the concept of humiliation. He claims, "No other subjection or obedience of the Son to the Father arises properly from the covenant of redemption, but only that which implies humiliation."[96] Edwards continues:

> If there were any such thing as a way of redemption without the humiliation of any divine person, the persons would act in man's redemption in their proper subordination, without any covenant of redemption or any new establishment, as they do in the affair of rewarding the elect angels. 'Tis true that if there were no humiliation of any divine person required in order to man's redemption, the determination that there should be a redemption would be a determination not implied in the establishment of the economy of

---

94. Edwards, The "Miscellanies," no. 1062, WJE 20:436–37.
95. Edwards, The "Miscellanies," no. 1062, WJE 20:437.
96. Edwards, The "Miscellanies," no. 1062, WJE 20:437.

the Trinity, as indeed the determination of no particular work is implied in that establishment.[97]

Edwards believes the Son's humiliation derives not from the covenant of redemption but from his own economic office. Edwards then classifies the humiliation of the Son into four categories. First, there are two kinds of obedience that are rooted in the Son's economic office: his obedience to the Father as Redeemer before his humiliation and his obedience as "God-man" after his humiliation. Then, there is a third kind of obedience performed "under the law" and "in the form of a servant." Edwards refers to this obedience as "new in kind."[98] While the first two kinds of obedience reflect "humiliation below his proper divine glory," the latter is obedience "under law" and "in the form of a servant" that justifies sinners. Thus, the obedience of the Son before and after his humiliation does not merit for sinners, nor is it imputed to sinners.[99] Last, there is the Son's subjection that is not entailed in his economic character. This subjection occurs through the Son's covenant engagement. The Son promises to obey the Father in the covenant of redemption, by which the Son receives "rules," "authority," and "what the Father promises."[100]

For Edwards, the reward the Son receives is none other than the Son's "vicarious dominion." That is, the Son is enthroned to rule as God's "vicegerent" by the Father as the "King of heaven and earth" and "Lawgiver" in his economy. Edwards goes on to say, "This the Father promised him in the covenant of redemption, as reward for the forementioned subjection and obedience that he engaged in that covenant." Further, in order to acquire the "success of his labors and sufferings in the work of redemption," the Son's office as the vicegerent of the Father continues to the end of the world. However, when the purpose of the covenant of redemption is fulfilled, all the things "return to be administered by the Trinity."[101] As we will consider later, words such as "Lawgiver," "Judge," "reward," "return,"

---

97. Edwards, *The "Miscellanies,"* no. 1062, *WJE* 20:437–38.
98. Edwards, *The "Miscellanies,"* no. 1062, *WJE* 20:441.
99. Edwards, *The "Miscellanies,"* no. 1062, *WJE* 20:438.
100. Edwards, *The "Miscellanies,"* no. 1062, *WJE* 20:438–39.
101. Edwards, *The "Miscellanies,"* no. 1062, *WJE* 20:439.

and so on are rooted in the Bible, although Edwards does not refer to any biblical texts directly.

THE HOLY SPIRIT

Given the importance of subordination in the unity and distinction of the persons of the Trinity, it is not difficult to see why Edwards pursues this subject with regard to the Holy Spirit. He argues that the Holy Spirit's subjection to the Son is twofold. First, the Holy Spirit's acts are under the control of the Son as "the Father's vicegerent" until the Son's "vicarious dominion and authority" ends.[102] This means that there will be no subjection of the Holy Spirit to the Son at the end of the world, after the purpose of the covenant of redemption has been accomplished. Second, the Holy Spirit is put under the Son as "God-man," which means that the Holy Spirit is subject to the Son in his nature as God and the Son in his nature as man. Edwards contends that these natures correspond to the Son as both "the husband and vital head of the church." In this sense, Edwards argues that the Holy Spirit is the "inheritance that Christ as God-man purchased for himself and his church."[103]

However, Edwards distinguishes between the subjection of the Holy Spirit and the subjection of the Son. He argues that the Holy Spirit's subjection to the Son in the covenant of redemption is not "a new kind of subjection," as was the Son's subjection under the law which led to humiliation. In contrast, the Holy Spirit's subjection to the Son as God-man does not involve "abasement" since his subjection results from "the economy of the Trinity." In other words, the subjection of the Holy Spirit to the Son arises not from the establishment of the covenant of redemption but from the economy of the Father. Thus, the Holy Spirit is subject to the Son not in terms of "abasement" but in terms of "the gift by the Father" because

---

102. Edwards, The "Miscellanies," no. 1062, WJE 20:440.

103. Through the Holy Spirit's twofold subjection to the Son, Edwards finds that the Son has a twofold dominion over the world. He states, "He [Christ] was invested with a twofold dominion over the world: one vicarious, or as the Father's vicegerent, which shall be resigned at the end of the world; the other as Christ God-man, and head and husband of the church. And in this latter respect he will never resign his dominion, but will reign forever and ever, as is said of the saints in the new Jerusalem, after the end of the world, Rev. 22:5." See Edwards, The "Miscellanies," no. 1062, WJE 20:440.

of his "economical character."[104] Therefore, for Edwards, the roles of the persons in the Trinity in the covenant of redemption are interconnected with their offices and roles in the economy of the Trinity.

Moreover, Edwards uses the word "gift" to refer to the Holy Spirit. In Miscellany no. 220, Edwards writes, "All Gospel righteousness, virtue and holiness is called grace, not only because 'tis [it's] entirely the free gift of God, but because 'tis the Holy Spirit in man; which, as we said, is grace or love."[105] Here, grace means the free gift of God, that is, the Holy Spirit. For Edwards, the Holy Spirit is not simply an applicator of the benefits of salvation but rather the grace and benefit itself. Thus, in *Treatise on Grace*, Edwards asserts that "when the sacred Scriptures call grace spirit, the Spirit of God is intended; and that grace is called 'Spirit' no otherwise than as the name of the Holy Ghost, the third person in the Trinity, is ascribed to it."[106]

Why does Edwards focus on the Holy Spirit as grace or gift? It appears it is an attempt to address at least two concerns. First, as Lee points out, Edwards criticizes "a general tendency in Puritan theology to see the Holy Spirit as the one who applies what the Father and the Son have accomplished."[107] For Edwards, this understanding falls short of reality since ascribing these works to the Holy Spirit does not ascribe "equal glory" to him compared with the other persons of the Trinity. Thus, Edwards defines the Holy Spirit as "the thing purchased," that is, Christ's inheritance: "But according to this, there is an equality. To be the love of God to the world is as much as for the Father and the Son to do so much from love to the world; and to be [the] thing purchased was as much as to be the price, and the thing bought with that price, are equal."[108] Edwards argues that the Holy Spirit is not only the one who applies the benefits of Christ but "the thing purchased" itself. This establishes the Holy Spirit's equality with the other persons of the Trinity.

A second consideration is Edwards's controversy with the Arminians about grace. In the "Efficacious Grace" section of the "Controversies"

---

104. Edwards, The "Miscellanies," no. 1062, WJE 20:441.
105. Edwards, The "Miscellanies," no. 220, WJE 13:345.
106. Edwards, "Treatise on Grace," 192.
107. Lee, "Editor's Introduction," in *Writings on the Trinity, Grace, and Faith*, 39.
108. Edwards, "Discourse on the Trinity," 137–38.

notebook that lays out his view against the tenets of Arminianism promoted by Daniel Whitby and George Turnbull, Edwards affirms that true grace is obtained not through human power but through a supernatural act of God. He begins the note with a mention of the Holy Spirit as follows:

> According to Dr. Whitby's notion of the assistance of the Spirit, the Spirit of God does nothing in the hearts or minds of men beyond the power of the DEVIL, nothing but what the devil can [do] and nothing showing any greater power in any respect than the devil shows and exercises in his temptations. For he supposes that all the Spirit of God does is to bring moral maxims and inducements to mind, and to set [th]em before the understanding, etc.[109]

Edwards's concern is that the Arminian view of grace reduces the role of the Holy Spirit in human salvation to bringing to mind "moral maxims and inducements." In contrast, Edwards asserts that it is not "the laws of nature" but "the grace of God" that is supremely authoritative in giving human beings "saving virtue."[110] That is, "saving virtue" is obtained by "a supernatural and sovereign operation of the Spirit of God."[111] For Edwards, the Holy Spirit is not just the deliverer of the benefit but rather the divine influence itself. The same argument is found in Miscellany no. 1263, in which Edwards states, "These are infinitely greater effects .... the great degrees in which the miraculous influences of the Spirit of [God] was given to Christ and to his apostles, and the great degrees in which a spirit of saving grace was given, which is properly supernatural and in many respects arbitrary in its operation."[112] Edwards argues that the Holy Spirit himself exerts his own miraculous influences on the human mind. While it is true that Edwards attributes "saving virtue" to the persons of the Trinity, he nevertheless tends to equate grace with the Holy Spirit.

109. Edwards, "'Controversies' Notebook: Efficacious Grace," in *Writings on the Trinity, Grace, and Faith*, 294.

110. Edwards, "'Controversies' Notebook: Efficacious Grace," 300.

111. Edwards, "'Controversies' Notebook: Efficacious Grace," 300.

112. Edwards, *The "Miscellanies": Entry Nos. 1153–1360*, WJE 23:211.

CONCLUSION

As demonstrated in this chapter, Edwards approaches the doctrine of the Trinity from the perspective of redemptive history. Of the immanent Trinity, Edwards argues that God understands himself through his perfect idea, that is, the Son. That perfect idea brings about God's love of himself, which is the Holy Spirit. In this description, Edwards is preoccupied with equality of the persons of the Trinity. As to the economic Trinity, Edwards argues that the roles flow forth from this inner order. This means that the redemptive work of God has its seminal form within the immanent Trinity.

Edwards describes the Trinitarian roles in the covenant of redemption as follows. The Father assumes headship so that he may acquire the right to appoint the Son as mediator; the Son voluntarily enters into the covenant, which involves humiliation but also becoming the Father's viceregent and God-man; and the Holy Spirit becomes subject to the Son. However, Edward notes that the Holy Spirit's subservience to the Son does not include abasement because his subjection belongs to "the economy of the Trinity" and not to the covenant of redemption itself. In this sense, Edwards argues that the Holy Spirit is the gift since he is the divine influencer who exerts his own miraculous saving grace on human beings.

Therefore, Pauw and Lee are misled when they argue that Edwards's doctrines of the Trinity arise from an interest in Christian society. They fail to account for the relationality involved in older Reformed language about God that predates Edwards. They also do not take into consideration his interpretive framework: the history of redemption.

4

—

THE DOCTRINE OF THE COVENANT OF WORKS AND THE HISTORY OF REDEMPTION

INTRODUCTION

As seen in the previous chapter, Edwards's understanding of the covenant of redemption includes the view that the immanent Trinity, the economic Trinity, and the roles of the Godhead are interconnected within the framework of the history of redemption. This holds true in his doctrine of the covenant of works, which involves the relationship between the federal heads, God and Adam. However, among the scholarly works on Edwards's federal theology, the dearth of writing on Edwards's view of the covenant of works is apparent.[1]

Perhaps one reason for this lack of scholarly interest is the generally understood fact that Edwards neither wrote about his view of the covenant of works in a systematic manner nor discussed the doctrine at length. However, these facts should not be taken to imply that the covenant of

---

1. While scholars have probed Edwards's view of the covenants of redemption and grace, relatively little has been said about the covenant of works. From the mid-1970s to the present, only two dissertations have been written regarding the covenants of redemption and grace. The first, written by Carl Bogue, is entitled "Jonathan Edwards and the Covenant of Grace." In it, Bogue seeks to provide an overall exposition of the covenant of grace as the central motif in Edwardsian theology. The second is Reita Yazawa's "Covenant of Redemption in the Theology of Jonathan Edwards." Here, Yazawa explores the practical implications of Edwards's doctrine of the covenant of redemption. However, no monograph or dissertation exists examining Edwards's writings on the covenant of works. See Carl W. Bogue, *Jonathan Edwards and the Covenant of Grace* (Cherry Hill, NJ: Mack, 1975); Reita Yazawa, "Covenant of Redemption in the Theology of Jonathan Edwards: The Nexus between the Immanent and the Economic Trinity" (PhD diss., Calvin Theological Seminary, 2013).

works is less important than other doctrines for Edwards. Rather, the doctrine of the covenant of works assumes a significant role in his understanding of the Trinity, justification, imputation, and how Christians ought to live (even though Edwards does not refer directly to the covenant of works in his expositions of these doctrines). As Muller points out, the significance of the covenant of works could be involved in theological issues including "the relationship of Adam and Christ, the *imago Dei*, original righteousness and original sin, the history of salvation recorded in Scripture, and the distinction of law and gospel."[2]

One of the most distinct themes of federalism, as Karlberg points out, is "the use of the law-gospel distinction." He argues that the law-gospel parallel evinces the "Pauline teaching on the two Adams in Romans 5."[3] Michael Horton notes that Calvin and his successors first developed the "covenant of works-grace scheme" as a result of their "commitment to the distinction between law and gospel."[4] According to Horton, both Zacharias Ursinus, who was a primary author of the Heidelberg Catechism, and Theodore Beza, who was Calvin's successor in Geneva, noticed the importance of the distinction between law and gospel in relation to the covenant scheme. This is also true of William Perkins, a leader of the Puritan movement in the Church of England during the Elizabethan era, who emphasized the need for this distinction, considering their different functions.[5] In an attempt to avoid the polarization of legalism on the one hand and antinomianism on the other, the classical Reformed tradition sought an essential harmony between the law and the gospel.[6]

---

2. Richard A. Muller, "The Covenant of Works and the Stability of Divine Law in Seventeenth-Century Reformed Orthodoxy: A Study in the Theology of Herman Witsius and Wilhelmus à Brakel," *Calvin Theological Journal* 29, no. 1 (1994): 80.

3. Mark W. Karlberg, "Reformed Interpretation of the Mosaic Covenant," *WTJ* 43 (Fall 1980): 2; Karlberg, "The Original State of Adam: Tensions within Reformed Theology," *EQ* 87 (1987): 291–309; Karlberg, "The Mosaic Covenant and the Concept of Works in Reformed Hermeneutics" (PhD diss., Westminster Theological Seminary, 1980).

4. Michael S. Horton, *God of Promise: Introducing Covenant Theology* (Grand Rapids: Baker, 2006), 85.

5. Horton, *God of Promise*, 85–86.

6. For the Puritans' view of the relationship between law and gospel and the debate on this matter, see Joel R. Beeke and Mark Jones, "The Puritans on Law and Gospel," *A Puritan Theology: Doctrine for Life* (Grand Rapids: Reformation Heritage, 2012), 321–33.

A similar view of the relationship between the law and the gospel is also found in Edwards, who opposed the two poles of Arminianism and antinomianism. Edwards's understanding of the covenant of works is focused not only on the federal heads, God and Adam but also on the law and gospel parallel. Thus, one would expect Edwards's doctrine of the covenant of works to be significant in his own handling of the pre-fall state of the created reality of human beings and the relationship between the law and the gospel.

It is still somewhat unsurprising that Edwards would provide a different exposition of the covenant view, albeit with a considerably similar appropriation of the doctrine of the covenant of works. For example, not only does the covenant of works for Edwards precede the covenant of grace in terms of "the chronology of historical revelation,"[7] but there is also a sense in which the covenant of works exists conceptually in eternity.[8] Moreover, Edwards sees the Mosaic dispensation of the covenant of grace as a second promulgation of the covenant of works. "It stands," Edwards writes, "in full force to all eternity without the failing of one tittle."[9] Although it is unjust to call Edwards's viewpoint completely novel and innovative,[10] it is nonetheless clear that his view looks different from

---

7. Carl W. Bogue, *Jonathan Edwards and the Covenant of Grace*, 144.

8. According to Gerstner, the origin of the covenant of works for Edwards is found in the covenant with the angels. Quoting Edwards's writing, he argues that the covenant of works precedes the covenant of redemption in terms that humanity "must be lost before they are redeemed." He writes, "Though some angels stood and some fell by their 'covenant of works,' Christ was involved both in the falling of some and the standing of others. There was a sense in which the angels who successfully met their covenant of works were saved nevertheless by the grace of Jesus Christ. It was the fallen angel, Satan, who brought on the fall of man under the Covenant of Works." John H. Gerstner, *The Rational Biblical Theology of Jonathan Edwards*, vol. 2 (Powhatan, VA: Berea, 1991), 94. For Edwards's work cited by Gerstner, see *The "Miscellanies": Entry Nos. a-z, aa-zz, 1-500*, WJE 13:437-38.

9. Edwards, *The "Miscellanies": Entry Nos. a-z, aa-zz, 1-500*, 217.

10. The view of the Mosaic covenant as a republication of the covenant of works has been debated by Reformed theologians. While a review of the secondary literature on the Mosaic covenant exhibits a significant diversity of claims, the debated issue is primarily whether the Mosaic covenant is to be seen as the covenant of works or the covenant of grace. On one hand, in an attempt to guard the Reformed doctrine of justification on the basis of the sacrifice of Christ alone, the advocates of republication assert that the covenant of works in the Mosaic dispensation was to convict Israel of their sin and inability to be saved. In this vein, they tend to reject the idea of grace in the Mosaic covenant. For the works of these scholars, see Meredith G. Kline, *Treaty of the Great King: The Covenant Structure of Deuteronomy: Studies and Commentary* (Grand Rapids: Eerdmans, 1963); Kline, *By Oath Consigned: A Reinterpretation of the Covenant Signs of Circumcision and Baptism* (Grand Rapids: Eerdmans, 1968); Kline, *Kingdom*

his Reformed forebears regarding the abrogation of the covenant. Also, Edwards regards the covenant with Israel as "a further revelation of the covenant of works."[11] The significance of this can scarcely be overemphasized in developing a reading of Edwards's federal theology.

Prologue: Genesis Foundations for a Covenantal Worldview (Overland Park, KS: Two Age, 2000); Kline, "Gospel until the Law: Rom. 5:13-14 and the Old Covenant," *JETS* 34 (1991): 433-46; Kline, "Covenant Theology Under Attack," *New Horizons* 15 (February 1994): 3-5; Mark W. Karlberg, "The Mosaic Covenant and the Concept of Works in Reformed Hermeneutics"; Karlberg, "Reformed Interpretation of the Mosaic Covenant"; Karlberg, "Justification in Redemptive History," *WTJ* 43 (1981): 213-46; Karlberg, "Moses and Christ—The Place of Law in Seventeenth-Century Puritanism," *TJ* 10, no. 1 (Spring 1989): 11-32; Karlberg, "The Original State of Adam: Tensions within Reformed Theology"; Karlberg, "The Search for an Evangelical Consensus on Paul and the Law," *JETS* 40 (1997): 563-79; Karlberg, "Recovering the Mosaic Covenant as Law and Gospel: J. Mark Beach, John H. Sailhamer, and Jason C. Meyer as Representative Expositors," *EQ* 83, no. 3 (2011): 233-50; Brenton C. Ferry, "Cross-Examining Moses' Defense: An Answer to Ramsey's Critique of Kline and Karlberg," *WTJ* 67 (2005): 163-38; Ferry, "Works in the Mosaic Covenant: Reformed Taxonomy," in *The Law is Not of Faith: Essays on Works and Grace in the Mosaic Covenant*, ed. Bryan D. Estelle, J. V. Fesko, and David Van Drunen (Phillipsburg, NJ: P&R, 2009): 76-103; Michael S. Horton, *Covenant and Salvation: Union with Christ* (Louisville: Westminster John Knox, 2007); Horton, "Obedience Is Better than Sacrifice," in *The Law is Not of Faith: Essays on Works and Grace in the Mosaic Covenant*, 315-36; David Van Drunen, "Natural Law and the Works Principle under Adam and Moses," in *The Law is Not of Faith: Essays on Works and Grace in the Mosaic Covenant*, 283-314; Van Drunen, "Israel's Recapitulation of Adam's Probation under the Law of Moses," *WTJ* 73 (2011): 303-24. However, the theory of republication has been challenged by the following scholars: Ernest F. Kevan, *The Grace of Law: A Study in Puritan Theology* (Grand Rapids: Baker, 1965); Sinclair Ferguson, *John Owen on the Christian Life* (Carlisle, PA: Banner of Truth, 1987); Jan Rohls, *Reformed Confessions: Theology from Zurich to Barmen*, trans. John Hoffmeyer (Louisville: Westminster John Knox, 1998); D. Patrick Ramsey, "In Defense of Moses: A Confessional Critique of Kline and Karlberg," *WTJ* 66 (2004): 373-400; Cornelis P. Venema, "The Mosaic Covenant: A 'Republication' of the Covenant of Works?," *Mid-America Journal of Theology* 21 (2010): 35-101; Robert Letham, "Not a Covenant of Works in Disguise," *Mid-America Journal of Theology* 24 (2013): 143-77. Considering the *Westminster Confession of Faith* as the best standard for determining the character of the covenant of works, these scholars emphasize that the *Westminster Confession* opposes such an idea of republication of the covenant of works in the Mosaic dispensation. Kevan's summary is helpful for understanding the nature of the debate: "It is not possible to make an accurate classification of the Puritans on the basis of their views about the Mosaic Covenant, because many of them held several of the different views in varying combinations. On the whole, however, they can be divided into two groups on this subject; those who regarded the Mosaic Covenant as a Covenant of Works, and those who regarded it as a Covenant of Grace." According to Kevan, while there are different interpretations of the Mosaic covenant in the thoughts of the Reformed orthodox, "the outcome of the Puritan debate indicates that the Mosaic Covenant was a form of the Covenant of Grace; and this view was embodied in the *Confession of Faith*." Kevan, *The Grace of the Law*, 113-14, 117. For more discussion of the classification of the different positions in Reformed orthodoxy, see Stephen J. Casselli, *Divine Rule Maintained: Anthony Burgess, Covenant Theology, and the Place of the Law in Reformed Scholasticism* (Grand Rapids: Reformation Heritage, 2016), 91-93.

11. Van der Knijff and Van Vlastuin, "The Development in Jonathan Edwards' Covenant View," 279.

Again, Edwards does not refer to the covenant of works at length. This makes it all the more necessary to begin with a historical survey of the idea of the covenant of works among Edwards's Reformed forebears, without which an analysis of Edwards's exposition of the covenant of works would prove considerably difficult. Thus, this chapter aims to provide a review of the secondary literature on the doctrine of the covenant of works and then to analyze Edwards's own view on the subject. Particular attention will be paid to Edwards's understanding of Adam as the federal head of the covenant of works, the antithesis of the law and the gospel, and the Mosaic covenant as the promulgation of the covenant of works (which reveals the nature of the historical dispensation of the covenant of works).

THE STATE OF THE DOCTRINE OF
THE COVENANT OF WORKS

The doctrine of the covenant of works describes the relationship between the federal heads, God and man, in Eden and implies both an eternal life of rewards for obedience and the threat of punishment for disobedience. When the doctrine of the covenant of works reached confessional status in the *Westminster Confession of Faith*, which distinguished between the covenant of works and the covenant of grace, it raised a number of exegetical and theological questions.[12] While it quickly became a theological commonplace in Reformed orthodoxy,[13] many scholars have questioned the origin and the nature of the covenant of works because, in their view,

---

12. *The Confession of Faith and Catechisms, Agreed upon by the Assembly of Divines at Westminster: Together with Their Humble Advice Concerning Church Government and Ordination of Ministers* (London: The Sign of the Kings Head, 1649), 13. Note that the *Westminster Confession* distinguishes between the covenant of works and the covenant of grace. Because of this distinction, the doctrine of the covenant of works not only played a foundational role in covenant theology but also provided a distinctive principle of Reformed hermeneutics of Holy Scripture. See I. John Hesselink, *On Being Reformed: Distinctive Characteristics and Common Misunderstandings* (Ann Arbor: Servant, 1983), 102; Lyle D. Bierma, *German Calvinism in the Confessional Age: The Covenant Theology of Caspar Olevianus* (Grand Rapids: Baker, 1996), 11; Anthony T. Selvaggio, "Unity or Disunity? Covenant Theology from Calvin to Westminster," in *The Faith Once Delivered: Essays in Honor of Dr. Wayne Spear*, ed. Anthony T. Selvaggio (Phillipsburg, NJ: P&R, 2007): 217–45; Beeke and Jones, "The Puritans on the Covenant of Works," 217.

13. Mark W. Karlberg, *Federalism and the Westminster Tradition: Reformed Orthodoxy at the Crossroads* (Eugene, OR: Wipf & Stock, 2006), 1.

neither Scripture nor earlier reformers referred to the existence of such a covenant with Adam.[14]

On this ground, one criticism arose from neo-orthodox scholars who argued for discontinuities between Calvin and later Calvinists.[15] Karl Barth contended that federal theology "did not allow itself to be bound to Scripture and confined to the event attested in Scripture in accordance with its reformation inheritance."[16] According to Barth, there is only one covenant of grace in Calvin: "the *foedus evangelii*." However, in contrast to the concept of *foedus* in the writings of Zwingli, Bullinger, and Calvin, Barth claims that "the concept of the foedus is suddenly divided into that of a *foedus generale* ... and the eternal *foedus speciale*."[17] Following Barth, R. Sherman Isbell argues that "the covenant of works is a devise [sic] to set forth the legal order which lies behind justification and in terms of which the work of Christ is in part understood."[18] Michael McGiffert emphasizes that "the covenant of works, unlike the covenant of grace, became distinctive as a contract with the conditions of a legal *quid pro quo* relationship."[19]

---

14. Kevan, *The Grace of Law*, 112. For various discussions, see Muller, "The Covenant of Works and the Stability of Divine Law in Seventeenth-Century Reformed Orthodoxy," 75–100; J. Mark Beach, *Christ and the Covenant: Francis Turretin's Federal Theology as a Defense of the Doctrine of Grace* (Göttingen: Vandenhoeck & Ruprecht, 2007).

15. Karl Barth, *Church Dogmatics*, vol. IV: *The Doctrine of Reconciliation*, part 1, trans. G. W. Bromiley (Edinburgh: T. & T. Clark, 1956); Holmes Rolston III, *John Calvin Versus the Westminster Confession* (Richmond, VA: John Knox, 1972); Rolston, "Responsible Man in Reformed Theology," *Scottish Journal of Theology* 23, no. 2 (1970), 129–56; James B. Torrance, "Covenant or Contract : A Study of the Theological Background of Worship in Seventeenth-Century Scotland," *Scottish Journal of Theology* 23, no. 1 (1970): 51–76; Torrance, "The Covenant Concept in Scottish Theology and Politics," in *The Covenant Connection: From Federal Theology to Modern Federalism*, ed. Daniel J. Elazar and John Kincaid (Lanham, MD: Lexington, 2000): 143–62; Torrance, "Strengths and Weaknesses of the Westminster Theology," in *The Westminster Confession: The Westminster Confession in the Church Today: Papers Prepared for the Church of Scotland Panel on Doctrine*, ed. Alisdair I. C. Heron (Edinburgh: Saint Andrews Press, 1982), 40–53; Torrance, "Calvin and Puritanism in England and Scotland: Some Basic Concepts in the Development of 'Federal Theology,' " in *Calvinus Reformator*, ed. B. J. van der Walt (Potchefstroom: Potchefstroom University for Christian Higher Education, 1982): 264–77; David N. J. Poole, *The History of the Covenant Concept from the Bible to Johannes Cloppenburg: De Foedere Dei* (San Francisco: Mellen Research University Press, 1992); Michael McGiffert, "Grace and Works: The Rise and Division of Covenant Divinity in Elizabethan Puritanism," *Harvard Theological Review* 75, no. 4 (1982): 463–502; McGiffert, "From Moses to Adam: The Making of the Covenant of Works," *Sixteenth Century Journal* 19, no. 2 (1988): 131–55; R. Sherman Isbell, "The Origin of the Concept of the Covenant of Works," (Master's thesis, Westminster Theological Seminary, 1976).

16. Barth, *Church Dogmatics*, IV:56.

17. Barth, *Church Dogmatics*, IV:58.

18. Isbell, "The Origin of the Concept of the Covenant of Works," 6.

19. McGiffert, "Grace and Works," 464.

The same is true for James B. Torrance, Holmes Rolston III, and David N. J. Poole, who argue that the covenant of works is a legal covenant in contrast to an evangelical one.[20] In this view, the federal covenant made "a radical dichotomy" between the law and grace.[21]

However, the view of neo-orthodoxy has not gone uncontested. Rejecting neo-orthodoxy's presuppositions, Cornelis P. Venema argues that one must guard against "jettisoning the doctrine of the covenant of works."[22] Considering the biblical legitimacy of the doctrine, Richard Muller points out that the covenant of works is an example of "a consequent doctrine," which means a doctrinal construct "drawn as a conclusion from the examination and comparison of a series of biblical loci or *sedes doctrinae*."[23] This position was supported by many Reformed theologians in the seventeenth century.[24]

With respect to the Reformation inheritance, Peter Lillback found the doctrine of the covenant of works implicit in Calvin.[25] Lyle D. Bierma discovered that the term *ius creationis*, which is used by Calvin, may imply that "the roots of prelapsarian covenant doctrine (the covenant of works) go deeper than even Ursinus (1534–1583)."[26] In his dissertation on seventeenth-century reformed scholasticism, Stephen J. Casselli demonstrates that covenant theologians in no way departed from their Reformation forebears.[27] Similarly, using the example of federal theology, Michael Horton demonstrates that Calvin's theological successors like Zacharias

---

20. Torrance, "Covenant or Contract," 52; Rolston, *John Calvin Versus the Westminster Confession*, 16; Poole, *The History of the Covenant Concept from the Bible to Johannes Cloppenburg*, 180.

21. Torrance, "Covenant or Contract," 67; Poole, *The History of the Covenant Concept from the Bible to Johannes Cloppenburg*, 164.

22. Cornelis P. Venema, "Recent Criticisms of the 'The Covenant of Works' in the Westminster Confession of Faith," *Mid-America Journal of Theology* 9, no. 2 (1993): 165–98.

23. Muller, "The Covenant of Works and the Stability of Divine Law," 75.

24. See Beeke and Jones, "The Puritans on the Covenant of Works", 218–19.

25. Peter A. Lillback, *The Binding of God: Calvin's Role in the Development of Covenant Theology* (Grand Rapids: Baker, 2001), 287.

26. Lyle D. Bierma, review of *The Origins of the Federal Theology in 16th Century Reformation Thought* by David A. Weir, *Calvin Theological Journal* 26, no. 2 (1991): 484.

27. Stephen J Casselli, "Anthony Burgess' *Vindiciae Legis* and the 'Fable of Unprofitable Scholasticism': A Case Study in the Reappraisal of Seventeenth Century Reformed Scholasticism" (PhD diss., Westminster Theological Seminary, 2007), iv.

Ursinus, Theodore Beza, William Perkins, Louis Berkhof, and Geerhardus Vos refined and developed Calvin's theology.[28]

Moreover, the covenant of works does not imply works-righteousness that becomes a meritorious cause of salvation. Ernest F. Kevan finds that "all the Puritans concurred in the view that whatever good Adam would have received by his obedience was of Grace."[29] Everett H. Emerson confirms that "covenant theologians make clear that man is able to enter into the agreement with God only when God supplies the means."[30] Rejecting the antinomians' view of the covenant, John Von Rohr demonstrates that "Puritans, in affirming contingency but in denying meritoriousness, avoided all charges of work-righteousness and yet saved the conditionality of the covenant."[31]

Indeed, Reformed orthodox theologians emphasized the gracious character of the covenant of works. For example, Anthony Burgess believed that Adam's obedience would acquire the covenant promises given through the sovereignty and grace of God. He writes:

> If God can give good things to man, he may also promise to give them: and therefore both to give, and to promise to give, are acts of liberality and dominion, and so not repugning to the majesty of God: nor does God by promising to give, lose his dominion, no more than he does by giving. It is true, a promise does induce an obligation, and so in man it is with some imperfection, but in God it is not, because he does not hereby become obliged to us, but to his ownself: so that we have not a right of justice to the things, because God has promised it to us, but only God cannot deny himself nor his word, and therefore we are confident.[32]

---

28. Horton, *God of Promise*, 86.

29. Kevan, *The Grace of Law*, 112.

30. Everett H. Emerson, "Calvin and Covenant Theology," *CH* 25, no. 2 (June 1, 1956): 137.

31. John Von Rohr, *The Covenant of Grace in Puritan Thought*, (Atlanta: Scholars Press, 1986), 54. For more on the historiographical survey of Puritan covenant theology, see Won Taek Lim, "The Covenant Theology of Francis Roberts" (PhD diss., Calvin Theological Seminary, 2000), 1–28.

32. Anthony Burgess, *Vindiciae Legis, Or, A Vindication of the Morall Law and the Covenants, from the Errours of Papists, Arminians, Socinians, and More Especially Antinomians.* 123.

As noted, the freedom and majesty of God are maintained in the covenant of works. Adam's obedience could not merit the happiness and goods that God would grant him. Similarly, William Strong (d. 1654) argued that even in the state of innocence, Adam had nothing in himself to satisfy "the holiness of God." God instituted the covenant of works, in which "a promise" and "threatening" were added in order that Adam keep the law. Thus, the covenant of works is based on God's love to "try the obedience of the best of his creatures, to give them matter and occasion to exercise the graces that he has given them."[33]

Further, Reformed orthodoxy maintained that although the covenant of works was abrogated, the law as a rule remains adapted in the covenant of grace. Or, better, the covenant of grace was differently administered in the time of the law and in the time of the gospel. In this sense, the law is not at odds with but in accordance with grace, and grace incorporates the law. In this vein, Muller points out that "the system of faith" is not contrary to "a system of obedience."[34] This implies that the use of the law as a rule of life in the covenant of grace indicates how law and grace are not utterly opposed; faith and obedience are not contrary to one another. Grace does not exclude the law but uses and embraces the law. Thus, the covenant of works does not indicate a radical priority of the law over grace, but rather, the classical Reformed understanding of the law in the covenant of works is united with grace through faith.

Given this proper understanding of law and grace, it appears absurd for scholars on the side of neo-orthodoxy to warn that the doctrine of the covenant of works could lead to another works-righteousness. Rather, these scholars are to be criticized for their failure to understand the subtle relationship between law and grace because a repudiation of the law-gospel distinction could destroy the doctrine of the imputation of Christ's righteousness, as well as justification by faith.[35] As Karlberg points out, the distinction between the law and the gospel, "when properly perceived and

33. William Strong, *A Discourse of the Two Covenants: Wherein the nature, differences, and effects of the covenant of works and of grace are ... discussed* (London: J.M, 1678), 3–4.

34. Richard A. Muller, "Covenant and Conscience in English Reformed Theology: Three Variations on a 17th Century Theme," *WTJ* 42, no. 2 (Spring 1980): 308.

35. Karlberg, "Reformed Interpretation of the Mosaic Covenant," 57.

applied, is far from being obscurantist."[36] Thus, the argument of Torrance and Poole that federal theology created a radical dichotomy between law and grace sounds very farfetched.[37]

A historical survey of the doctrine of the covenant of works echoes Edwards's view, in which the covenant of works is never abrogated. If so, the nature of the covenant of works is called into question: What does Edwards mean by no abrogation of the covenant of works? What was Edwards's opinion of the doctrine of the abrogation of the covenant of works? Did he suppose that the covenant of works did not cease to be the covenant of works, so that humanity may obtain salvation by keeping the law of the covenant of works through their own power? Apparently, he had no such notion. This is clear from what has been presented, namely, that he emphasized the inability of humanity to recover their pre-fallen state.

To answer the question of the implications of the abrogation of the covenant of works, one must begin with Edwards's understanding of the state of Adam before and after the fall. Then, as seen above, the relationship between the law and the gospel is significant for Reformed orthodox theologians' understanding of the nature of the covenant of works. The same is true for Edwards; there is an inherent relationship between the law and the gospel in his understanding of the covenant of works. Thus, we will explore Edwards's distinction between the law and the gospel under the Mosaic dispensation. The last section will examine Edwards's view of the Mosaic covenant as a promulgation of the covenant of works. In considering the revelatory character of salvation history, Edwards understands the Mosaic covenant within the covenant of grace. This chapter therefore begins with the recognition of Edwards's commitment to the states of Adam as federal head and of his posterity in the economy of the covenant of works.

---

36. Karlberg, "Reformed Interpretation of the Mosaic Covenant," 57.

37. Torrance, "Covenant or Contract," 67; Poole, The History of the Covenant Concept from the Bible to Johannes Cloppenburg, 183.

ADAM AS THE FEDERAL HEAD OF
THE COVENANT OF WORKS

In his engagement with the doctrine of the covenant of works, Edwards preached distinct but similar sermons on the state of Adam's fall in relation to the covenants of works and grace. Edwards explores the relationship of the first Adam and the second Adam (Christ), original righteousness and original sin, total depravity, the imputation of sin, the imputation of Christ's righteousness, and so forth, in his several sermons on such biblical texts as Genesis 1:27; 3:11; 3:24; 2 Samuel 23:5; Zechariah 4:7; Hebrews 9:13–14, 15–16; and 12:22–24.[38] In particular, it is through his sermons on Genesis 3:11 and 3:24 that Edwards provides a detailed analysis of Adam's state in the covenant of works as a pre-fall covenant.[39] Thus, we will begin by providing a summary of the contents of these two sermons.

First, in his sermon on Genesis 3:11, Edwards aims to describe the nature of the evil acts of Adam in eating the fruit in the middle of Eden, considering the issue of the parallels between the first and second Adams, the federal heads of the covenants of works and grace. With this concern, Edwards begins his sermon by distinguishing between the state of innocence and the state of Adam after depravity. Prior to the fall, Adam enjoyed "a blessed Communion with God" in his innocent state. He could converse with God "in a friendly manner." Adam could answer as "a man speaks with his friend."[40] However, Edwards continues:

---

38. Edwards, "998. Sermon on Gen. 2:17 (August 1751)," (unpublished transcription provided by Ken Minkema of the Jonathan Edwards Center at Yale University); "504. Sermon on Gen. 3:11 (February 1739)," in *Sermons, Series II, 1739*, vol. 54 of *WJE*; "East of Eden" (Gen 3:24)," in *Sermon and Discourses 1730–1733*, WJE 17:329–48; "109. II Sam. 23:5 (Summer-Fall 1729)," in *Sermons, Series II, 1729*, vol. 44 of *WJEO*; "Glorious Grace (Zech 4:7)," in *Sermon and Discourses 1720–1723*, WJE 10:388–99; "495. Sermon on Heb. 9:13–14 (November 1738)," in *Sermons, Series II, 1738*, vol. 53 of *WJEO*; "534. Sermon on Heb. 9:15–16 (Jan. 4, 1740)," (unpublished transcription provided by Ken Minkema of the Jonathan Edwards Center at Yale University); "Sermon on Hebrews 12:22–24 (April 1740)," in *Sermons, Series II, 1740*, vol. 55 of *WJEO*. Edwards preached a series of sermons on Hebrews 12:22–24, each having the same title but internally distinguished by letters from (a) to (g). Information on these materials comes from Douglas Sweeney's survey. See Douglas Sweeney, *Edwards the Exegete: Biblical Interpretation and Anglo-Protestant Culture on the Edge of the Enlightenment* (New York: Oxford University Press, 2016), 296n15. For a brief summary of Edwards's view of the covenant of works, see the "Notes on Scripture" entry no. 398.

39. While Edwards's sermons on 2 Samuel 23:5, Zechariah 4:7, and Hebrews 9:15–16 tend to be related to his understanding of the covenant of grace, his sermon on Hebrews 9:13–14 is involved in his view of the covenant of redemption. Edwards's several sermons in his series on Hebrews 11:22–24 describe how Christians avoid and restrain their sin by coming to the spiritual mount Zion.

40. Edwards, "504. Sermon on Gen. 3:11," L. 1r.

'Tis said in the 8. V. of the Context that our first P[arents]. Heard the voice of the L[ord].——by which it appears that There was something external that Go. Was wont to manifest hims. By of whose approach [-] they could have notic[e] the external sense And Adam Easily distinguish the voice [ ] even [?]—knew the gate or the sound of the feet——they walk what heard at a dist——tis said that our first p[arents]. Hid thems[elves]. When they . H—— They were very guilty & had a sense of their own guilt in their Consciences which made [th]em to fly & hide from G. How different is the Case with [th]em now from what it was before they sin before they were far from flying & hiding when they perceived G. approaching.[41]

The term "first parents" denotes that Adam was a representative of humanity. Edwards notes how the first parents fell into a state of depravity by describing their changed actions toward God. While the first parents not only were fond of hearing "the voice of G[od] walking in the garden & coming to them" but also were eager and "ran to meet him to see & hear their Glor[ious] creator," this was not the case of their state after the fall. Instead, "they lost their love to G[od]," and instead had a "slavish fear" and "hatred."[42]

Edwards continues to deal with the issue of federal headship between the first and second Adams. Edwards stresses the nature of surety in the covenant. The act of Adam was "the act of the surety in whom we fall," so that his sin is imputed to his posterity. At the same time, it rightly relates to "the Righteousness of the second." He asserts, "It is of Infinite Importance that we should know both for the first is our own by which we are undone & the second must be our own if ever we are saved & we must Know the former in order to Know the latter [-] so that is of moment [-] us to be sensible of our sin & guilt by the first Adam as [-] Know our Righ[teousness] & Recovery by the second." Therefore, "our sin and guilt" that comes from the first Adam is twofold: guilt coming from the first sin Adam committed and that arising from the "corruption of nature" as the

---

41. Edwards, "504. Sermon on Gen. 3:11," unpaginated.
42. Edwards, "504. Sermon on Gen. 3:11," unpaginated.

consequence of Adam's first sinful act.[43] However, Edwards distinguishes two kinds of sin, one that is not imputed to Adam's posterity and the other that is applied to his posterity. He writes:

> There was a heinousness in that act of our first F that concerns Adam personally arising from the peculiar station that he stood in. It is not every thing that was in that act that Adam committed [-] where by it was a heinous act in [-] him that is imputed to his Posterity. But there was something peculiar in the act an aggravation that concerned him alone by reason of the peculiar Circumstances that he was in as the F. of mankind that is not imputed.[44]

In analyzing the distinctiveness of the heinousness of Adam's sinful act, Edwards notes a twofold heinousness: (1) the heinousness that Adam committed in a peculiar circumstance that does not relate to his posterity and (2) the sin of Adam, as the head of humanity, that is imputed to his posterity.

Regarding the heinous act of Adam that does not concern his posterity, Edwards argues that the nature of this act is both general and particular. First, "the guilt of that act as it concerned Adam personally depends partly on Innumerable Circumstances that never were revealed to us." There were "all the thoughts & workings of heart Adam had at time which might Greatly aggravate the sin in the sight of G[od] as it concerned him" alone.[45] Edwards continues:

> [We] don't Know Adam did it chiefly to Gratify his wife or out of pity to her ... because he thought the fruit was exceeding pleas[ant] to the taste & so did it to gratify his sensual appetite or whether it was mainly because he thought his eyes should be enlightend or whether it mainly was because he thought he should be like G[od] we don't Know precisely how far he was influenced by the Reprobata[tion] that the Devil made of G[od] as false & deceitfull & saying contrary to what he Knew.[46]

---

43. Edwards, "504. Sermon on Gen. 3:11," L. 3v.
44. Edwards, "504. Sermon on Gen. 3:11," L. 3v.-4r.
45. Edwards, "504. Sermon on Gen. 3:11," L. 5r.
46. Edwards, "504. Sermon on Gen. 3:11," L. 5r.

Therefore, "all the Particular aggravations of that act" that "are not Revealed to us" are not imputed to us, in the sense that "it is impossible for us to Know them."[47] In other words, any sinful considerations in Adam's mind before his eating the forbidden fruit were not imputed to his posterity. Next, these aggravations of Adam's act, which was "an act of murder of all his Posterity," are related to Adam only "as arising from the peculiar Relation he stood in."[48] Edwards argues that if this aggravation is imputed to Adam's posterity, its effect is to "multiply the same guilt to the same persons over & over again without End."[49] Therefore, the consequence of Adam's sin, which was of murdering all humanity, is not imputed to his posterity. In short, the aggravation that arises from the circumstance that he stood as the head of the human race is not imputed to his posterity since this circumstance is "peculiar to him alone and can[']t be reckoned to his posterity."[50]

Edwards then proceeds to discuss the heinousness that is generally imputed to humanity. He attempts to lay out the "Rule" by which aggravations applied only to Adam are distinguished from those that are "Imputed to all his Post[erity]."[51] This rule is that "all aggravations that arise from those things that were in the Cov[enant]" are imputed to all his posterity. After laying down the rule distinguishing between the twofold heinousness, Edwards goes on to speak of the nature of the sin imputed to humanity. A summary of the contents of the nature of the sin is as follows:

1. the sin was "a sin of Heart or thought";

2. our first parents violated God's command "fully & totally";

3. the sin was "not a sin of Ignorance," but rather, Adam and Eve did what they "knew to be directly contrary to God's Command";

---

47. Edwards, "504. Sermon on Gen. 3:11," L. 6r.
48. Edwards, "504. Sermon on Gen. 3:11," L. 6r.
49. Edwards, "504. Sermon on Gen. 3:11," L. 6v.
50. Edwards, "504. Sermon on Gen. 3:11," L. 7v.
51. Edwards, "504. Sermon on Gen. 3:11," L. 9r.

4. their action "was not only Committed against Kn[owledge] but it was a deliberate act of sin";

5. "the Command was Enforced with Threatning Denounced in a most awfull preemptory manner";

6. Adam violated God's commandment against "Exceeding Great Encouragements to obed[ience] for there was not only a threatning to deter from Disobed[ience] but a Glo[rious] Promise even a Promise of Et[ernal] Life if he obeyed";

7. "the heinousness of this act further appears in that he committed it in the perf[ect] exercise of the freedom of his own will";

8. "there were other Commands that Adam was obliged by [-] he was——by every precept of the law of nature";

9. "the Easiness of the [precept] is another aggravation of the violation of it";

10. "This is exceeding aggravated by the Great Goodn[ess] of G[od] to him in the happy state";

11. "this sin was Committed against Great Light" through which Adam knew God; and

12. the sin "was committed with deliberation."[52]

Edwards believes that Adam's first act of sin in eating the forbidden fruit is imputed to his descendants, but other sins that he committed after the fall were not applied to his posterity. According to Edwards, since "the time of Adam's trial as the Covenant of Head of his Posterity was over as soon as that act was Completed," sins following this first sinful act are not imputed to humanity.[53] When Adam "fell the time of his Probation Ceased in his fall," and he "ceased to act as the Publick head of mankind" after the fall.[54] Edwards goes on to repeat in the application portion of the sermon

---

52. Edwards, "504. Sermon on Gen. 3:11," L. 13r–22v.

53. Edwards, "504. Sermon on Gen. 3:11," L. 26r.

54. Edwards, "504. Sermon on Gen. 3:11," L. 27r.

that Adam's sins after the fall are not applied to his posterity. Edwards appears to understand the imputation of sin only in terms of the condition of the covenant.

Last, Edwards comes to the application, in which his emphasis upon the federal headship of Adam, by which the doctrine of the imputation of sin is explained, leads to his focus on the second Adam. His conclusions involve the relationship between the covenant of works and the covenant of grace. Edwards stresses that we are responsible for sins imputed to us by Adam's disobedience to God's command. At the same time, he introduces the nature of the covenant of grace. He writes:

> The Cov[enant] of Grace that was immediately Reveal[ed] after the breach of the first Cov[enant] was made not with a particular Person but with a posterity or Race it was those that were the seed or Posterity of the woman viz X J [that is, Christ Jesus] & his spiritual Posterity Ge. 3. 15 ... & so that Cov[enant] that was Established with Noah was with him & his posterity ... & so the Cov[enant] that was made [-] The Cov[enant] that was made with Phinehas was with him & and his seed ... & so the Cov[enant] that G[od] established with David was with him & and his seed.[55]

Edwards goes on to reveal the consequences of Adam's sin and of the second Adam's suretyship by comparing the two federal heads of the covenants of works and grace, respectively. He lists the differences between them as follows:

1. while "the first Adam in his first Estate was an Excellent Person," "our second Adam" was given "the Glory of the Person";

2. the second Adam "did not fail ... Greater trial by far than the first Adam," though the first Adam had failed and so become "fallible";

---

55. Edwards, "504. Sermon on Gen. 3:11," L. 33v.–34r.

3. "the second surety that was appointed had not only to obey the
    Law that the first had broken but to suffer the Punishm[en]t
    of the breach of those that were guilty";

4. the second Adam satisfied all other sins, as well as the sin
    Adam committed;

5. "the second Adam is given not only Perfectly to Restore the
    Ruining occasioned by the Ruins of the first but to admitt[?]
    him to a much higher pitch of happiness";

6. the appointment of the second Adam brightens "our thought
    of the Grace of G[od]"; and

7. the appointment of the second Adam was not only "Revealed
    but G[od] soon began to save men on the Account of that
    second Adam."[56]

Edwards's emphasis upon the inability of humanity to restore the previous state is clearly spelled out in his sermon on Genesis 3:24, "East of
Eden." In this sermon, Edwards recounts Adam's fall from innocence. He
contrasts Adam and Eve's pre-fall state of innocence with the curse upon
them. In Eden, Adam did not need to work "in order to the providing of
food to sustain his nature," because the trees of the garden of Eden supported his need for food. From this statement, Edwards takes account of
"the irrecoverable loss" of eternal life and blessings that Adam would have
obtained had he kept the law not to eat the fruit of the tree of the knowledge of good and evil.[57]

Much of his sermon exposition occurs in the doctrinal section of the
sermon, in which he fleshes out two doctrines. The first doctrine is, "When
man fell, God drove him away from all his former blessedness." To provide
proof of this, Edwards offers the following three propositions: first, Adam
lost "all his former blessedness"; second, "after man had sinned, there was
a necessity of his parting with all his former blessedness" as implied in
the expression "driven away"; and third, "God in his displeasure separated

56. Edwards, "504. Sermon on Gen. 3:11," L. 44r.–47r.
57. Edwards, "East of Eden (Gen 3:24)," 332.

between man and his former blessedness." In the second doctrine, Edwards says that because of "the displeasure of God" toward human beings, "there was no hope" of humanity obtaining "eternal life a blessedness which otherwise we should have obtained." This doctrine is supported by three propositions: (1) "if we had fulfilled the conditions of the first covenant, we should, by what we did, have obtained eternal life and blessedness"; (2) "there was no hope of our ever obtaining for ourselves this eternal life and blessedness after we had fallen"; and (3) "there was no possibility of it upon this account: that we had by the fall so incurred God's displeasure."[58]

Edwards goes on to contrast the blessedness of Adam in his pre-fall state with his post-fall desperate situation, in which he had no hope to restore the glory that would have been given to him had he kept the law of the covenant of works. If Adam kept the law concerning the tree of the knowledge of good and evil, he would receive two blessings. First, he would be able to have "a living forever." Second, he would be "exalted to a more glorious and blessed life." Then, Edwards relates Adam's situation directly to his posterity. He argues:

> The tree of life was a tree that God planted with the rest of the garden, that man might be the more assured of his reward in case of his obedience, and that this consideration might engage his spirit the more earnestly to seek that he might come to taste of it. 'Tis probable that God told Adam of this tree to encourage his obedience. He might tell him in earnest that man had an opportunity of obtaining the fruit of this tree, and that eternal life and blessedness of which it was a seal, by what he himself did; an obtaining of this blessed reward was in his power. It was in man's own power perfectly to obey the law of God, which is not in our power now since the fall, as it was more in man's power perfectly to obey the law and persevere in it then, than it is for fallen man to perform one act of sincere obedience.[59]

Edwards asserts that based on the knowledge of the tree of life in the garden, Adam would ensure his reward according to his obedience. Moreover, he

---

58. Edwards, "East of Eden (Gen 3:24)," 332–39.
59. Edwards, "East of Eden (Gen 3:24)," 338.

emphasizes Adam's own power to obey the law of God. However, Adam's moral power has two causes: first, he was not under the "power and dominion of" sin; second, there was "a sufficient assistance of God" that enabled Adam to obey the law. Edwards's focus on Adam's moral power in his pre-fall state, which is beyond the capacity of fallen humanity, was intended to describe the plight of his posterity. He clearly articulates that "he had no sin then that he was under the power and dominion of. We can't obey now because we are dead in trespasses." This is true also of Edwards's description of the sufficient assistance God provided Adam. His point is that Adam's posterity lost such an assistance of God.[60]

Given this, it is little surprise that Edwards deals in detail with the nature of God's displeasure in Adam's outlaw acts. As noted above, the third proposition of the second doctrine refers to God's anger, according to which there is "no possibility" to recover the blessedness that Adam lost. He lists four characteristics of God's anger: (1) God "has an infinite abhorrence" of sin; (2) God's anger is "the anger of a just judge"; (3) his anger is "a holy anger," so that he does not allow "a guilty and filthy creature to the possession and enjoyment of eternal life"; and (4) the anger of God toward humanity after the fall is "the resentment of an affronted infinite majesty." Edwards draws the conclusion that "it was the sword of God's dreadful wrath, the sword of divine justice wielded by his infinite power, flaming with holy abhorrence of the filthiness of sin and sharpened by a divine resentment of the affront to his holy majesty."[61] While Edwards describes the nature of God's anger in these four ways, his exposition of God's anger relates to God's attributes of justice, holiness, and omnipotence.

In his application section, Edwards's emphasis upon the state of humanity after the fall goes beyond the inability of a person to restore his or her state. He constantly reiterates the human tendency toward one's own righteousness. "Men are exceeding apt to seek eternal life through their own righteousness though in a fallen state. And the holiness, majesty, justice, wrath, and power of God be engaged to prevent it, and to slay and consume all such that come thus in their own righteousness." Edwards lists four reasons that human nature desires to establish its own righteousness.

---

60. Edwards, "East of Eden (Gen 3:24)," 338.
61. Edwards, "East of Eden (Gen 3:24)," 339–41.

First, humanity is "exceeding loath to perish." Second, "the light of nature" suggests that "the favor of God and his reward must be obtained by righteousness." Third, it is clear that human beings are "ignorant of God's righteousness," given they "keep striving to get a righteousness." Fourth, humanity has a "proud conceit of their own goodness that they are ready to think it sufficient." They have a "high opinion of their own worthiness, excellency, good deeds, prayer, [and] religion, [but are] ignorant what a distance [is] between God and them," claims Edwards.[62] As his Reformed forebears did, Edwards also emphasizes the distorted nature of humanity that has a tendency of seeking its own righteousness.[63]

However, Edwards does not simply reproduce the traditional view of covenant. As noted earlier, while Edwards maintains that Adam's original sin contains two elements, guilt and pollution, his distinction between imputed and non-imputed sins makes a subtle but nonetheless important point. Edwards does not relate Adam's internal aggravation, which happened before and after his eating the fruit of the tree of the knowledge of good and evil, to the condition of Adam's posterity. Edwards contends that Adam's sinful consideration in his heart, which could aggravate sin in the sight of God, is not imputed to his posterity. This point of view, according to Herman Bavinck, differs from classical Reformed theology's view. When it comes to the nature of Adam's original sin, Bavinck insists:

> His [Adam's] trespass, moreover, had not only an exterior but also an interior side .... The very act of eating was itself already a revelation of a sweeping moral change that had occurred in his inner self. Strictly speaking, it was not the first sin, but the first fully matured sin in the sense of James 1:15. Anterior to the sinful deed there were sinful considerations of the mind (doubt, unbelief) and sinful tendencies of the heart (covetousness, pride), which had been prompted by the temptation of the serpent and were fostered by the will of man. Both before, during, and after the act of eating from

---

62. Edwards, "East of Eden (Gen 3:24)," 347–48.

63. This point of view resembles his Reformed forebears' view of the human desire of righteousness. For example, William Strong states, "So far as any man does desire to establish his own righteousness, so far he desires to be under a Covenant of Works for justification and life; but this is the disposition of every man by nature, therefore every man by nature desires to be under the first Covenant still." See Strong, *A Discourse of the Two Covenants*, 25.

the forbidden tree, the relation of humans to God and his law was changed .... Guilt and pollution are two simultaneous consequences of one and the same sin, two aspects of the same occurrence. Finally, the change initiated in Adam .... consisted in that, by his doubt and unbelief, his pride and covetousness, and finally by the sinful deed itself, the person himself progressively detached himself further from God and his law, positioned himself outside the circle of his favor and fellowship and began to use all his gifts and powers above all against God and his commandments ... The same religious and ethical change that occurred in Adam at the time of his fall befalls all his descendants as well.[64]

Guilt and pollution in original sin includes Adam's moral changes before and after eating the fruit from the forbidden tree. Thus, both the religious and ethical changes that happened before and after Adam's eating the fruit are imputed to his posterity. Bavinck believes that this position stands in opposition to Edwards's view of the imputation of sin.[65]

According to Bavinck, another difference between Edwards and his Reformed forebears is Edwards's presentation of the "superior principles" that human beings lost in the fall. In his sermon on Genesis 3:11, Edwards

64. Herman Bavinck, *Reformed Dogmatics*, vol. 3, *Sin and Salvation in Christ*, ed. John Bolt, trans. John Vriend (Grand Rapids: Baker Academic, 2006), 109 (hereafter referred to as *RD*).

65. Bavinck's interpretation of Edwards is wrong, especially when he argues that Edwards denied "immediate imputation in the case of Adam and Christ." Although Bavinck contends that for Edwards "the pollution is actually anterior to guilt," this appears not true at least for the case of the first parents. Rather, Edwards articulated a simultaneous occurrence of both guilt and pollution. Bavinck, *RD*, 3:534, 109. Moreover, Edwards clearly attributes guilt to the first sin Adam committed and regards pollution as the consequence of Adam's first sinful act and humanity's real participation in that act. Nevertheless, there exists a significant difference between Edwards and his Reformed forebears. Sweeney writes that for Edwards, the guilt "did not precede and cause their evil disposition; rather, their disposition led to their indictment." Sweeney, *Jonathan Edwards and the Ministry of the Word: A Model of Faith and Thought* (Downers Grove, IL: IVP Academic, 2009), 159-60. With respect to Edwards's ontological understanding of human nature, Sweeney states, "In his work on original sin, this meant that Edwards thought that Adam was a *real* federal head, the father of the race in whom all people are united, not a distant representative like federal politicians. We were there with him in Eden—not bodily, or course, but ontologically, seminally, like an oak tree is present in an acorn. We were joined in Adam's fall and so are implicated in it." Sweeney, *Jonathan Edwards and the Ministry of the Word*, 158-59. Similarly, E. Brooks Holifield asserts that Edwards's doctrine of imputation of sin "diverged from Reformed orthodoxy" in the sense that his view of the imputation of sin is ontological, while seventeenth-century Calvinist theologians considered imputation of sin to be representative. In the view of Reformed orthodoxy, God imputed Adam's guilt to his posterity due to Adam being "their legal representative." See E. Brooks Holifield, "Edwards as Theologian," in *The Cambridge Companion to Jonathan Edwards*, ed. Stephen J. Stein (Cambridge: Cambridge University Press, 2007), 150.

insists that Adam lost "a sufficient assistance" of God. In the same sermon, Edwards argues that Adam lost "all his inherent good," though he did retain the natural image of God and the inferior principles of self-love and self-preservation with which he was created. As Adam was stripped of "the indwelling [of the Holy Spirit], as a Just Punishment of his Rebellion," his posterity "was deprived of the sp[irit] of G[od]."[66] The same argument is found in *Ethical Writings* and the "Miscellanies". Edwards claims that while "a supernatural principle of divine love" "regulated and directed self-love," since Adam's fall, it has "lost its strength" or "is dead."[67] For Edwards, the "absence of original righteousness" means "the absence of that influence of God's Spirit."[68] In *Original Sin*, Edwards argues that "the inferior principles of self-love and natural appetite, which were given only to serve, being alone, and left to themselves, of course became reigning principles; having no superior principles to regulate or control them, they became absolute masters of the heart."[69] As a result, "the immediate consequence" of this was "a *fatal catastrophe*, a turning of all things upside down, and the succession of estate of the most odious and dreadful confusion."[70] In this vein, Bavinck criticizes Edwards's belief that "the pollution is anterior to guilt," when Edwards "tried to deduce the sinful deed from the sinful inclination that originated earlier," but he "also sought to explain the latter [pollution] in terms of the natural principles inherent in humanity's lower nature."[71]

---

66. Edwards, "504. Sermon on Gen. 3:11," L. 41r.

67. Edwards, *Ethical Writings*, 256; Edwards, *The "Miscellanies": Entry Nos. a-z, aa-zz, 1–500*, 387, 500.

68. Edwards, *The "Miscellanies": Entry Nos. a-z, aa-zz, 1–500*, 387. Note that Edwards considers the Holy Spirit to be "a principle of perfect holiness, to enlighten" Adam. See Edwards, *The "Miscellanies": Entry Nos. 833–1152, WJE* 20:142.

69. Edwards, *Original Sin, WJE* 3:382.

70. Edwards, *Original Sin*, 382.

71. Bavinck, *RD* 3:109. It appears that Edwards regards original righteousness as a superadded or concreated gift. He clearly argues, "All men come into the world without Grace they are destitute of any Gracious Principle of Love to God or Jesus or holiness Grace is what we have not naturally. For nature and Grace in scripture are set as Opposites and the word Grace as it is there used Implies some Gift of God superadded to nature." In this vein, Edwards's distinction between the inferior and superior principles appears to be different from Reformed orthodoxy, which saw that "the service of God, the love for God, and fellowship with God are not superadded gifts but originally and integrally human." Original righteousness for the Reformed orthodox is "called natural," since it is "a natural attribute or quality," rather than "a certain substance or essence." Edwards, "082. Sermon on Matt. 12:30 (ca. 1728–1729; September 1756)," in *Sermons, Series II, 1728–1729, WJEO* 43:L. 3r; Bavinck, *RD*, vol. 2, *God and Creation*, ed. John Bolt, trans. John Vriend (Grand Rapids: Baker Academic, 2004), 552.

A similar kind of difference between Edwards and his Reformed forebears is found in his well-known work *Freedom of the Will*, in which Edwards makes a distinction between natural ability and moral inability.[72] In this book, Edwards contends against Thomas Chubb (1679–1747), Daniel

---

72. In order to explain the distinction between natural ability and moral inability, Edwards employs two parallel terms: moral and natural necessities. First, Edwards argues that the human will is integrally involved in "a motive which is extant in the view or apprehension of the understanding, or perceiving faculty." There are two kinds of motives: "weaker motive" and "strongest motive" according to the extent of the "strength" of the "motive." While the former signifies "a less degree of previous advantage or tendency to move the will," the latter points to "the greatest degree of previous tendency to excite and induce the choice." However, "whatever is perceived or apprehended by an intelligent and voluntary agent, which has the nature and influence of a motive to volition or choice, is considered or viewed *as good*," since "nothing appears inviting and eligible to the mind, or tending to engage its inclination and choice, considered as evil or disagreeable; nor indeed, as indifferent, and neither agreeable nor disagreeable." In other words, the human will is not an independent faculty but "the faculty of perception or apprehension," so that it "is always determined by the strongest motive, or by that view of the mind which has the greatest degree of previous tendency to excite volition." Edwards defines "moral necessity" as a "necessity of connection and consequence, which arises from such *moral causes*, such as the strength of inclinations, or motives, and the connection." Edwards goes on to say that the will is affected by a "previous habitual disposition," or "motive," or "inclination," or "volition of the soul," or "voluntary action." Edwards is emphatic that "moral inability" stems from "the opposition or want of inclination." For example, if a man is not able to "will or choose" something, it is because of "a defect of motives, or prevalence of contrary motives." This implies that as fallen sinners, human beings do not will good because of their disoriented inclination or affection or motives. In this way, the will entails moral necessity. On the other hand, natural ability signifies a fallen man's "being free from hindrance or impediment in the way of doing, or conducting in any respect, as he wills." He argues, "Let the person come by his volition or choice how he will, yet, if he is able, and there is nothing in the way to hinder his pursuing and executing his will, the man is fully and perfectly free, according to the primary and common notion of freedom." In other words, natural ability is nothing more than freedom of will that implies that a person has freedom to do what he will, so that he is responsible for every moral situation. Thus, all human beings commit sin not by natural necessity but by their will, which is affected by the soul's inclination. In this sense, moral necessity is in agreement with natural ability. Edwards, *Freedom of the Will*, WJE 1:142, 143, 148, 156, 158, 159, 163, 164. Scholars have debated Edwards's view of the freedom of the will with respect to whether it deviated from his predecessors. See Richard A. Muller, "Jonathan Edwards and the Absence of Free Choice: A Parting of Ways in the Reformed Tradition," *Jonathan Edwards Studies* 1, no. 1 (2011): 3–22; Paul Helm, "Jonathan Edwards and the Parting of the Ways?" *Jonathan Edwards Studies* 4, no. 1 (2014): 42–60; Richard A. Muller, "Jonathan Edwards and Francis Turretin on Necessity, Contingency, and Freedom of the Will: In Response to Paul Helm," *Jonathan Edwards Studies* 4, no. 3 (2014): 266–85; Paul Helm, "Turretin and Edwards Once More," *Jonathan Edwards Studies* 4, no. 3 (2014): 286–96. Recently, Philip John Fisk, in agreement with Muller, has argued that there is no contingent freedom in Edwards's view of the freedom of will. Philip John Fisk, *Jonathan Edwards's Turn from the Classic-Reformed Tradition of Freedom of the Will* (Göttingen: Vandenhoeck & Ruprecht, 2016), 304–8. For more scholars' works on Edwards's *Freedom of the Will*, see Fisk, *Jonathan Edwards's Turn*, 305n1.

Whitby (1638–1726), and Isaac Watts (1674–1748) that fallen humans do not have moral ability, but they maintain natural ability, thus doing justice to the human will.

However, Edwards's distinction between moral inability and natural ability differs from Calvin's view of a human as the image of God. Calvin argues:

> All parts of the soul were possessed by sin after Adam deserted the fountain of righteousness. For not only did a lower appetite seduce him, but unspeakable impiety occupied the very citadel of his mind, and pride penetrated to the depths of his heart. Thus it is pointless and foolish to restrict the corruption that arises thence only to what are called the impulses of the senses; or to call it the "kindling wood" that attracts, arouses, and drags into sin only that part which they term "sensuality" .... Paul removes all doubt when he teaches that corruption subsists not in one part only, but that none of the soul remains pure or untouched by that mortal disease. For in his discussion of a corrupt nature Paul not only condemns the inordinate impulses of the appetites that are seen, but especially contends that the mind is given over to blindness and the heart to depravity.[73]

For Calvin, the fall of humanity leaves no room for possibility of natural ability. Thus, Bavinck claims that Edwards's distinction between natural ability and moral inability "fostered a lot of misunderstanding and actually aided the cause of Pelagianism."[74] According to Bavinck, the Reformed faith "consistently spoke of natural impotence" rather than moral inability. He asserts:

> But, speaking of natural impotence, one can also have in mind the characteristics of fallen human nature and mean by it that the incapacity for good in this fallen state is "by nature" characteristic for all human beings, congenital and not first introduced in them from without by custom, upbringing, or imitation. In this sense the term "natural impotence" is absolutely correct, and the term "moral

---

73. John Calvin, *Institutes of the Christian Religion* 2 vols., ed. John T. McNeill, trans. Ford Lewis Battles (Philadelphia: Westminster, 1960), 2.1.9.

74. Bavinck, *RD*, 3:122.

impotence" open to misunderstanding. "Morally impossible," after all, is the phrase often used to describe what is considered impossible for a given person on the basis of that person's character, custom, or upbringing. It is morally impossible for a virtuous person all at once to become a thief, for a mother to hate her child, or a murderer to strangle an innocent child. Such a moral "impossibility" nonetheless definitely does occur under certain circumstances. This kind of moral impotence is not what describes the incapacity for good. Though ethical in nature, and an incapacity of the will, natural impotence belongs to humans by nature; it is innate, and a property of the volition itself. And precisely because the will, in its present fallen state, in virtue of its nature cannot do other than to will freely, it cannot do other than what it wills, than that to which it is by nature inclined.[75]

Bavinck hypothesizes that the term "moral inability" lays open the potential for misunderstanding and confusion of the incapacity of the will to do good. His point is that the incapacity for good is attributed not to moral inability but rather to natural inability.

However, in noting Edwards's divergence from the Reformed tradition on these points, one ought not portray Edwards as entirely opposed to the classical Reformed tradition. Rather, Edwards is on the side of Augustine and Calvin in that he contends that human beings do not have a will to do good.[76]

We have discussed Edwards's view of Adam as the federal head and the consequence of his fall that affected his posterity. In considering the impact of Adam's fall upon his posterity, it is vitally important to distinguish between Edwards's understandings of the covenants of works and grace, or the law and the gospel. The following section of this work thus considers Edwards's understanding of the relationship between the law and the gospel, which will shed light on his understanding of the overall structure of the covenant of works in the divine revelation of salvation history.

---

75. Bavinck, *RD*, 3:122.
76. Bavinck, *RD*, 3:122.

THE LAW AND THE GOSPEL

While Edwards's doctrine of the covenant of works is established on the basis of an antithetical relationship between the covenant of works and the covenant of grace, we will see that, for Edwards, the relationship between the two covenants is actually geared toward unity in terms of salvation history. This is clear from Edwards's own view of the relationship between the law and the gospel. Indeed, the covenant of works leads humanity to the law's unity with the gospel. This does not mean that there is a full compatibility between the law and the gospel. Rather, the covenant of works is not compatible with the covenant of grace since the former is based on the condition of perfect obedience by Adam and Eve. Nevertheless, Edwards bases a proper understanding of the relationship between the covenants of works and grace on the theme of the history of redemption.

Along these lines, Edwards, in Miscellany no. 32, asserts, "To say that the covenant of works did admit of a mediator, is something improper. The covenant of works mentioned nothing about it; there is nothing in the covenant of works that opposes."[77] In Miscellany no. 250, he argues that in the Old Testament, "the church, which was then in its infant [state], could not bear a revelation of the covenant of grace in plain terms." Again, Edwards asserts that now, for people under the covenant of grace, the gracious character of the covenant of works glows much brighter than for those when the church was in its "infant [state]."[78] These statements show that in terms of the economy of the New Testament era, the degree of revelation of the covenant of works is much more intense when compared with the Old Testament. As Van der Knijff and Van Vlastuin point out, Edwards considers "the covenant with Israel as a further revelation of the covenant of works."[79]

More importantly, Edwards's focus on the covenant of works is inherently Christological: Edwards places the condition of the covenant of works on an eternally established destiny of the covenant. "For this end," Edwards argues, "came Christ into the world, to fulfill the law, or the covenant of

---

77. Edwards, *Miscellany no. 32*, WJE 13:217.

78. Edwards, *Miscellany no. 250*, WJE 13:362–63.

79. Van der Knijff and Van Vlastuin, "The Development in Jonathan Edwards' Covenant View," 279.

works, for all that receive him."[80] Edwards identifies the covenant of works with the law. As the covenant of grace for Edwards is "synonymous with the gospel,"[81] the covenant of works is identical with the law. In this way, the relationship between the covenants of works and grace implies the law-gospel contrast.

The contrast between the law and the gospel, or between the covenant of works and the covenant of grace, does not imply that there is no harmonious relationship between the two covenants. Rather, there is a unity that results from a contrasting principle between the covenants of works and grace. Why does Edwards contrast the covenant of works with the covenant of grace? To what extent does the former stand in contrast to the latter? Would his view of the covenant of works remain different from his Reformed forebears? As we saw earlier, Reformed orthodox theologians maintained an identical view regarding the abrogation of the covenant of works. Now the question remains: what sort of understanding of the covenant of works is implied by his insisting on non-abrogation of the covenant?

To answer this question, one must focus on Edwards's concept of the revelation of salvation history since the concept of historical revelation plays a crucial role at this point. In other words, Edwards relates the covenant of works or the law to the redemptive works of Christ in terms of salvation history. It is through this viewpoint that Edwards contrasts the covenant of works with the covenant of grace, or the law with the gospel. This again implies that for Edwards, the two covenants stand as a unified whole in terms of the revelation of salvation history.

As mentioned above, the law or the covenant of works for Edwards was fulfilled by Christ. While the covenant of works stands forever as "a rule of judgment," it was already fulfilled by Christ. This perspective plays a significant role in understanding the relationship between the law and the gospel since the law or the covenant of works for Edwards is focused on the anticipation of Christ's redemptive work. In *A History of the Work of Redemption*, Edwards writes:

---

80. Edwards, *The "Miscellanies": Entry Nos. a–z, aa–zz, 1–500*, 217.
81. Van der Knijff and Van Vlastuin, "The Development in Jonathan Edwards' Covenant View," 276.

This law of works indeed includes all laws of God that ever have been given to mankind, both the law of nature and also all political commands that ever were given to man; for 'tis a general rule of the law of works, and indeed of the law of nature, that God is to be obeyed and that he must be submitted to in whatever positive precept he is pleased to give us. 'Tis a rule of the law of works that men should obey their earthly parents, and 'tis certainly as much of a rule of the same law that we should obey our heavenly Father: and so the law of works requires obedience to all positive commands of God. It so required Adam's obedience to that positive command not to eat of the forbidden fruit, and it required the Jews' obedience to all the positive commands given them. When God commanded Jonah to arise and go to Nineveh, the law of works required him to obey. And so it required Christ's obedience to all the positive commands God gave him. But more particularly, the commands of God that Christ obeyed were of three kinds: they were either such as he was subject to merely as man, or such as he was subject to as he was a Jew, or such as he was subject to purely as mediator.[82]

The moral law points to the law of nature, which existed before the Mosaic era. According to Edwards, the law of the covenant of works includes "all laws of God that ever have been given to mankind," and the law of works contains three aspects of Christ's obedience: the moral law, the ceremonial law, and the mediatorial law.[83]

A similar line of thought is found in the Reformed orthodox view. As mentioned in chapter 2, for Mastricht, Witsius, and Turretin, the moral law is applied to human nature, forensic or judicial laws to the Israelites as citizens of the Jewish state, and the ceremonial law as a schoolmaster for the members of the church. This distinction among the laws stands in full agreement with Calvin's view of the Mosaic law. In his *Institutes*, Calvin argues that "the whole law of God published by Moses" is divided into "moral, ceremonial, and judicial laws." First, the moral law "is contained under two heads," that is, "to worship God with pure faith and piety"

82. Edwards, *A History of the Work of Redemption*, WJE 9:309.
83. Edwards, *A History of the Work of Redemption*, 309–10.

and "to embrace men with sincere affection." In this sense, the moral law is "prescribed for men of all nations and times, who wish to conform their lives to God's will." Second, the ceremonial law plays the role of "the tutelage of the Jews, with which it seemed good to the Lord to train this people, as it were, in their childhood, until the fullness of time should come … in order that he might fully manifest his wisdom to the nations, and show the truth of those things which then were foreshadowed in figures." Finally, "the judicial law, given to the Jews for civil government, imparted certain formulas of equity and justice, by which they might live together blamelessly and peaceably."[84] The understanding of the law espoused by both Calvin and Reformed orthodoxy emphasized its application first to the Jewish nation under the Old Testament and by extension to all humanity.

Between Edwards and his forebears, despite some surface resemblance, there is a subtle but significant difference. While both Calvin and Reformed orthodoxy generally regarded the three types of law as public principles of the law that applied either to all humanity or to the Jewish people, Christ's fulfillment of the law lies at the core of Edwards's understanding of the three types of law. Although this does not mean that Edwards's Reformed forebears did not relate the three laws to Christ's redemptive work, it nonetheless appears that Edwards is attempting to focus on Christ's obedience as the federal head of the covenant of grace in achieving the work of redemption rather than on a moral principle of the law.

Edwards's emphasis upon Christ's redemptive work regarding the covenant of works or the law stands out strongly in his application of the three types of law to Christ's obedience. First, Christ obeyed "the commands of the moral law, which was the same with that that was given at Mount Sinai." Second, his obedience is to "all those laws that he was subject to as he was a Jew," that is, the "ceremonial law." This is why Christ "constantly attended the service of the temple and of the synagogues." Last, Christ was subject to "the mediatorial law," which is "related purely to the execution of his mediatorial office."[85] With respect to the mediatorial law, Edwards asserts in Miscellany no. 278 that "the Messiah entered into a covenant of redemption for the recovery of the fallen world, and came under the

---

84. Calvin, *Institutes*, 4.20.14–15.
85. Edwards, *A History of the Work of Redemption*, 309–10.

obligation of the mediatorial law."[86] In short, Christ fulfilled the three laws as a man, as a Jew, and as a mediator.

Although Edwards fashions the division among the three laws after Calvin and his Reformed forebears, their genetic match is sometimes not exact. It is not difficult to see that his forebears' understanding of the judicial law is different from Edwards's own view of the mediatorial law. However, one must carefully explain the sense in which the three types of law are distinguished. Edwards's category of mediatorial law is not one of the formal distinctions maintained by Reformed orthodoxy. However, Edwards does articulate the typical Reformed distinctions of moral, ceremonial, and judicial laws. In *A History of the Work of Redemption*, Edwards writes:

> The next thing that is observable in this period [Mosaic era] was God's giving the typical law in which I suppose [were] included mostly all those precepts that were given by Moses that did not properly belong to the moral law, not only those laws that are commonly called ceremonial in distinction from judicial laws, which are the laws prescribing the ceremonies and circumstances of the Jewish worship and their ecclesiastical state, but also many if not all those divine laws that were political and for regulating the Jewish commonwealth, commonly called judicial laws. These were at last many of them typical.[87]

Therefore, it is clear that Edwards shares the same distinctions of the law with his Reformed forebears. Nonetheless, Edwards's view of the three divisions of the law as moral, ceremonial, and mediatorial is based on his emphasis upon Christ's righteousness and justification. As noted, Edwards applies the moral and ceremonial laws to Christ's redemptive work. Thus, Edwards's understanding of the covenant of works or the law focuses on Christ's righteousness that is obtained by his own obedience.

Having considered the three types of the law Christ fulfilled, Edwards proceeds to reveal the significance of Christ's righteousness by focusing on Christ's mediatorial office. In doing so, Edwards fleshes out the

---

86. Edwards, *Miscellany no. 278, WJE* 13:377.
87. Edwards, *A History of the Work of Redemption*, 181.

relationships among the covenants of redemption, works, and grace. He states:

> To understand this we must consider, that the Messiah entered into a covenant of redemption for the recovery of the fallen world, and came under the obligation of the mediatorial law. The whole matter was wisely agreed and adjusted between the Father and the Son; he was to become incarnate, to reveal the will of God to men, to work miracles, and lay down his life a sacrifice. He *"received a command"* of the father, to *"lay down his life"*; and finished the work which *"he gave him to do."* ... Now his conformity to this rule, or whatsoever he did or suffered by virtue of his consent to the covenant of redemption, and the obligation of the mediatorial law; his whole active and passive obedience, was properly his righteousness. 'Tis true he obeyed the law of nature as he was man and a reasonable creature, and he observed the law of Moses as a Jew and of the seed of Abraham; but that was by virtue of the mediatorial law, and as a part and branch of it: so that all he did in this world, and what he is now doing in heaven, in obedience to his Father's will and for the salvation of men, is properly his righteousness.[88]

When it comes to Christ's fulfillment of the mediatorial law given to him in the covenant of redemption, a similar thought is found in Miscellany no. 794, entitled "Christ's Righteousness. Justification," in which Edwards deals with the threefold division of the law and the righteousness of Christ. Edwards claims that Christ's righteousness "by which he merited heaven for himself and all that believe on him, consists principally in his obedience to the last of these laws."[89] Clearly, Edwards is alert to the difference between the first two laws and the mediatorial law.

Edwards's stress upon the nature of salvation history reveals that Christ's redemptive work is crucial to Edwards's understanding of the relationship between the moral and ceremonial laws. As we have seen, Edwards relates the three types of the law not just to humanity or the Jewish nation but to Christ's redemptive work. Interestingly, while Mastricht and

---

88. Edwards, The "Miscellanies": Entry Nos. a–z, aa–zz, 1–500, 377–78.
89. Edwards, A History of the Work of Redemption, 310.

Turretin deal with a threefold renewal of the covenant of grace regarding the moral, ceremonial, and judicial laws, Edwards's focus lies directly on Christ's obedience as a redemptive work. In this sense, the contrasting principle between the law and the gospel, followed by the divine revelation of redemptive history, means that while the principle of the covenant of works stands in opposition to that of the covenant of grace, its overall structure is nonetheless one of unity in the revelatory sense, revealing the relationship between the condition and fulfillment of the law.[90]

THE MOSAIC COVENANT

Viewed in the close relationship between the law and the gospel, or the covenant of works and the covenant of grace broadly, Edwards's understanding of the covenant of works takes a distinctive perspective on the Mosaic covenant. This perspective concentrates on the progressive revelation of what God initiated in the covenant of redemption. In *A History of the Work of Redemption*, Edwards contends that the Mosaic covenant belongs to the fourth period of the Old Testament, from Moses to David. In doing so, he examines the nature of the Mosaic covenant, revealing how the work of redemption was carried out during this era. Edwards's extensive description of the history of redemption during this stage has three main points in relation to salvation history through Christ. First, "the redemption of the children of Israel out of Egypt" was the "greatest type of Christ's redemption" of his people from Satan, the spiritual Pharaoh. Second, according to God's providence, God separated his own "peculiar people" from all other people, who "were wholly rejected and given over to heathenism," in order to "prepare the way for Christ's coming." Third, one of the greatest works of redemption was "God's giving the moral law in so awful a manner at Mount Sinai." Edwards describes the Mosaic covenant

---

90. This view is not different from the Reformed puritan theologians. Joel Beeke and Mark Jones claim, "To be sure, not all particulars of the doctrine of justification were expressed the same way among Reformed theologians, but they did agree with Lutheran theologians on the basic antithesis between the law and the gospel in this connection. However, as this chapter has shown, the law-gospel distinction cannot simply be reduced to its application to the doctrine of justification by faith. For many Puritans the law and the gospel were redemptive periods correlating to the Old and New Testaments. Therefore the law contained the gospel, and the gospel contained the law." Beeke and Jones, "The Puritans on Law and Gospel," 333. This statement suggests why for Edwards, the covenant of works is identical with the law, and the covenant of grace is regarded as the gospel.

or the Mosaic law either as a "new exhibition of the covenant of works" or as a "rule of life."[91] But what, then, is the nature of the new exhibition of the covenant? Edwards states:

> The covenant of works was here exhibited to be as a schoolmaster to lead to Christ, not only for the use of that nation in the ages of the Old Testament, but for the use of God's church throughout all ages to the end of the world, as an instrument that the great Redeemer makes use of to convince men of their sin and misery and help-lessness and God's awful and tremendous majesty and justice as a lawgiver, and so to make men sensible of the necessity of Christ as a savior. The Work of Redemption in its saving effect in men's souls in all the progress of it, is not carried on without the use of this law that was now delivered at Sinai."[92]

When the moral law in the Mosaic covenant is considered a covenant of works that had functioned as a schoolmaster under the age of the Old Testament, it serves as an instrument by which human beings see the necessity of a mediator. However, if the Mosaic law is considered to be "a rule of life" by "the Redeemer from that time to the end of the world," it "shows them the way in which they must walk, as they would go to heaven." The rule of life as "a way of sincere and universal obedience to" the Mosaic law is "the narrow way that leads to life," giving us no ground of hope, unless in every respect we keep the law.[93]

Regarding the law as both "schoolmaster" and "rule of life," Edwards connects the rule of righteousness and judgment in the covenant of works to Christ's redemptive work. Edwards writes:

> Christ's acts of righteousness may be distributed with respect [to] the legal laws Christ obeyed in that righteousness he performed.

---

91. Edwards, *A History of the Work of Redemption*, 175–80.

92. Edwards, *A History of the Work of Redemption*, 180–81.

93. Edwards, *A History of the Work of Redemption*, 181. This twofold function of the law of Moses is also found in Calvin, Anthony Burgess, William Strong, and Turretin. See John Calvin, *Commentaries on Romans*, trans. John Owen (Edinburgh: Calvin Translation Society, 1849), 385–87; Strong, *A Discourse of the Two Covenants*, 88; Burgess, *Vindiciae Legis*, 229–31; Francis Turretin, *Institutes of Elenctic Theology*, ed. James T. Dennison Jr., trans. George Musgrave Giger, 3 vols. (Phillipsburg, NJ: P&R, 1992–1997), XII.vii. (30). For a brief examination, see Beach, *Christ and the Covenant*, 252.

But here it must be observed in general that all the precepts that Christ obeyed may [be] reduced to one law, and that is that which the Apostle calls "the law of works," *Romans 3:27*. Every command that Christ obeyed may be reduced to that great everlasting law of God that is contained in the covenant of works, that eternal rule of righteousness that God had established between himself and mankind. Christ came into the world to fulfill and answer the covenant of works, that is the covenant that is to stand forever as a rule of judgment, and that is the covenant that we had broken, and that was the covenant that must be fulfilled.[94]

Edwards seems to be critical of the abrogation of the covenant of works. Similarly, in Miscellany no. 30, he explains that the covenant of works is never "abrogated, but is a covenant stands in full force to all eternity without the failing of one tittle."[95] Moreover, he asserts that "we are indeed now under the covenant of works so, that if we are perfectly righteous we can challenge salvation."[96] At first glance, it might seem that Edwards believes people can earn their salvation by fulfilling the conditions of the covenant of works. However, the nuance here is totally different. He argues that the ultimate purpose of the covenant of works in the Mosaic period was to make Israel to find "they could not challenge anything from those promises [on the ground] of obedience, trusted only to the mere undeserved mercy of God and were saved by grace, and expected life only of mere mercy."[97] Moreover, there is a difference between "the children of Israel" and "us" in relation to the covenant of works: one covenant is between God and the children of Israel and the other between God and us. The main purpose of the covenant of works regarding the children of Israel is to help them see "that they could not challenge anything from those promises [on the ground] of obedience, trusted only to the mere undeserved mercy of God … only of mere mercy." With respect to the covenant of works relating to us, Edwards argues that "to us God has plainly declared the impossibility

---

94. Edwards, *A History of the Work of Redemption*, 308.
95. Edwards, *Miscellany no. 30*, WJE 13:217.
96. Edwards, *Miscellany no. 30*, WJE 13:362.
97. Edwards, *Miscellany no. 30*, WJE 13:362.

of obtaining life by that covenant ... and lets us know clearly how we are made partakers of that grace."[98]

Moreover, the covenant of works and its role in judgment are applied not to those who are in Christ but rather to unbelievers.[99] In his "Notes on Scripture," Edwards explains that people are not "judged and condemned by the covenant of grace, but by the law, or covenant of works," which is "the eternal rule of judgment." Since the covenant of grace is "a deliverance from this judgement," those in Christ "are delivered from the law, and escape the condemnation" of the covenant of works. On the contrary, the force of the law is "upon Christ," and "has its full force upon unbelievers."[100] The same thought is found in his sermon on Hebrews 12:22-24, in which Edwards contends that "but after X [Christ] is given and has fulfilled the law G[od] in bestowing the blessings that X[Christ] has purchased still acts as a Strict Judge of the Law," and "he in Justifying & Rewarding believers in X [Christ] does as much do the part of a Strict JUDGE OF THE Law as in Eternally Condemning Sinners."[101] Edwards speaks of the function of the covenant of works or the law: it condemns those who are not in the faith of Jesus, that is, unbelievers. Thus, neither the covenant of works with the children of Israel nor God's covenant with us leaves a loophole through which we can earn our salvation.

Edwards's view of the moral law within the Mosaic law as a republication of the covenant of works matches Calvin's description of the third use of the law in the covenant of grace, which functions first as a mirror

---

98. Edwards, *Miscellany no. 30, WJE* 13:217.

99. Edwards's view clearly bears some resemblance to Reformed orthodoxy. While there are various approaches to the Reformed orthodox view of the renewal of the covenant of works in the Mosaic dispensation, D. Patrick Ramsey's summary is similar to Edwards's own view. Ramsey writes: "The Puritans who believed that the Covenant of Works was renewed or repeated at Mount Sinai understood the condition of obedience to be limited to the Ten Commandments (i.e., the moral law). The promise of life upon obedience was more hypothetical than real since this 'offer' was directed and applied only to the unregenerate in Israel for the purpose of converting them to Christ. For 'when the Law as a Covenant of Works had driven the Israelites to Christ, then it was dissolved to them in that respect and its covenant frame was to be dissolved.' Furthermore, this function or application of the Law of Works will continue today." Ramsey, "In Defense of Moses," 398–99. For more explanation of the relative principle of the covenant of works, see Ferry, "Works in the Mosaic Covenant: Reformed Taxonomy," 93.

100. Edwards, *Notes on Scripture*, 59.

101. Edwards, "547. Sermon on Hebrews 12:22-24 (d) (April 1740)," in *Sermons, Series II, January-June 1740, WJEO* 55:15.

to discover human beings' sinfulness, second as a means of restraining sin, and last as a guide for the Christian life.[102] Given Edwards's understanding of the moral law in the Mosaic dispensation, it is clear that although he does not mention the doctrine of abrogation, the covenant of works for Edwards would be abrogated only as a means through which human beings can obtain the rewards of eternal life and the blessings promised in the covenant. This in turn signifies that the function of the moral law as the covenant of works in the Mosaic dispensation is different from that of the moral law in the pre-fall covenant made between God and Adam. In this sense, it could be said that for Edwards, the covenant of works was abrogated. Thus, Edwards shares a view virtually identical with the Reformed interpretation of the Mosaic covenant, which did not regard the covenant of works as a way for the "sinner to obtain justification by the works of the law."[103] According to Karlberg, traditional Reformed theology maintained that "the works-principle is *subordinate* to that of redemptive grace, and consequently, is never covenantally instituted as a means of justification, not even hypothetically as a punishment for unbelief."[104]

One of the most important aspects of Edwards's distinction between the moral, ceremonial, and judicial laws is that Edwards approaches the three types of law in terms of a progressive revelation by which God reveals his redemptive work during the Mosaic period. As already noted earlier, Edwards's distinction among the three laws matches Calvin's and Reformed orthodoxy's understanding of the laws. However, while Calvin

---

102. Calvin divides the function of the moral law into three aspects. First, the law "warns, informs, convicts, and lastly condemns, every man of his own unrighteousness," by revealing "God's righteousness." Second, the law functions as "a bridle to restrain" people from slackening the reins on the lust of the flesh as to fall clean away from all pursuit of righteousness." Finally, the "third and principal use" of the law "finds its place among believers" in two ways, that is, "teaching" and "exhortation." See Calvin, *Institutes*, 2.7.6 (354), 2.7.11 (359), 2.7.12 (360). Against antinomianism's argument that believers are free from the obligations of the law, Reformed orthodox theologians maintained the third use of the law. For the sixteenth-century context, see Beeke and Jones, "The Puritans on the Third Use of the Law," 555–71. For the Lutheran understanding of the relationship between the law and the gospel, and of the third use of the law, see Steven D. Paulson, "Law and Gospel," in *Dictionary of Luther and the Lutheran Traditions*, ed. Timothy J. Wengert (Grand Rapids: Baker, 2017), 414–18.

103. Karlberg, "Reformed Interpretation of the Mosaic Covenant," 29.

104. Karlberg, "Reformed Interpretation of the Mosaic Covenant," 30. Karlberg maintains that the hypothetical works-principle is not the same as "a hypothetical covenant of works" which undermines the "continuity of the single covenant of grace throughout the period of redemption." See Karlberg, "Reformed Interpretation of the Mosaic Covenant," 30n74; 10n22.

and Reformed orthodoxy dealt with the three laws in a general sense, apply-
ing them to the sinful nature of humanity, the civil laws of the Israelites,
and the rule of the Christian life, Edwards's exposition of the ceremonial
and judicial laws is deeply informed by a progressive history of salvation.
This point of view means Edwards does not raise a novel development that
deviates from his Reformed forebears. Rather, Edwards's biblical exposition providing the covenantal narrative of Exodus appears to be the same
as his Reformed tradition.

Like Edwards's, Calvin's description of the second law, the ceremonial law, reveals a progressive aspect of revelation. Calvin clearly argued
that God "fully manifest[ed] his wisdom to the nations, and show[ed] the
truth of those things which then were foreshadowed in figures."[105] While
Calvin appears to regard the Mosaic covenant as a part of the covenant of
grace, he presents the Mosaic covenant in the progressive unfolding of the
Abrahamic covenant. In this vein, Breno Macedo argues that for Calvin,
"the Mosaic, Davidic, and new covenants are but a progressive revelation
of what God initiated with the patriarchs."[106]

Nonetheless, Calvin's emphasis upon the history of revelation regarding the ceremonial law is not directly related to Christ's redemptive work
but rather belongs to the doctrine of piety. For example, Calvin relates the
three types of law to the doctrine of piety or love. The moral law points to
the love a person has toward both God and neighbors. This is true for his

105. Calvin, *Institutes*, 4.20.15 (1503).

106. Macedo, "Covenant Theology in the Thought of John Calvin: From the Mosaic
Covenant to the New Covenant," *Fides Reformata* 21, no. 1 (2016), 121–48, here 121. Macedo
opposes Karlberg's interpretation of Calvin's view of the law in the Mosaic covenant. Karlberg
asserts that for Calvin, the function of the law in the Mosaic administration is pedagogical.
Against this argument, Macedo claims that the law under the Mosaic covenant should be
understood as "only spiritual." Macedo argues that "the promises of prosperity, land inheritance, and richness, which are indeed present in the covenant, are not conditioned to Israel's
faithfulness to the law." Rather, "obedience to the law should be the fruit of a grateful heart
for both material and spiritual blessings." Karlberg, "Reformed Interpretation of the Mosaic
Covenant," 14; Macedo, "Covenant Theology in the Thought of John Calvin," 129. However,
it seems that Calvin maintained both pedagogical and spiritual blessings in his view of the
Mosaic law. First, Calvin's pedagogical interpretation of the law is clear from his understanding of the threefold usage of the law in the Mosaic dispensation, as Karlberg argues. Moreover,
to reduce the functions of the law in Calvin's view of the Mosaic covenant only to a spiritual
sense is also to oversimplify Calvin's thought on the law. Turretin, Calvin's successor, views
the law in the Mosaic covenant in a pedagogical sense. It is therefore much better for us to
say that pedagogical and spiritual understanding go hand in hand. See Turretin, *Institutes of
Elenctic Theology*, XII.viii.8 (2:235).

view of the ceremonial and judicial laws. He asserts that "as ceremonial laws could be abrogated while piety remained safe and unharmed, so too, when these judicial laws were taken away, the perpetual duties and precepts of love could still remain." Given the title of the chapter of *Institutes*, "Means of Grace: Holy Catholic Church," in which Calvin provides his view of the laws in the Mosaic dispensation, it is understandable that Calvin approaches the meanings of the Mosaic laws in terms of Christian piety.

By contrast, Edwards tends to narrow the meaning of the three types of law in the Mosaic covenant to focus on Christ's redemptive work. As noted earlier, Edwards applies the nature of the moral and ceremonial laws directly to Christ's work, emphasizing that Christ, as a human as well as a Jew, kept the moral and ceremonial laws in the Mosaic covenant. Furthermore, Edwards tends to focus on the meaning of the ceremonial law regarding the redemptive work of Christ. Edwards calls the ceremonial "the typical law" that includes "mostly all those precepts that were given by Moses." Edwards states, "The giving this typical law was another great thing that God did in this period [that] tended [to the] building up this glorious structure of redemption that had been carrying on from the beginning of the world."[107] Interestingly, Edwards no longer provides detailed discussion about the nature of the judicial law in the same work. A question lingers as to why this was so. When one probes Edwards's view of the fourth period from Moses to David presented in *A History of the Work of Redemption*, it certainly seems that Edwards's exposition of the Mosaic covenant is focused not on the theological nature of the laws themselves but rather on the progressive revelation of salvation history. Thus, Edwards provides his exposition of the Mosaic law through the theme of the history of redemption.

Moreover, this revelatory character of redemptive history becomes apparent in Edwards's distinction between the covenants of works and grace. In Miscellany no. 439, Edwards makes a distinction between the covenant of works and the covenant of grace:

If it be inquired, in what sense God gave this covenant to them more than to us, I answer, that although it was as much impossible for

---

107. Edwards, *A History of the Work of Redemption*, 181.

them to be saved by it as it is for us, yet it was really proposed to them as a covenant for them, for their trial (*Exodus 20:20*), that they might this way be brought to despair of obtaining life by this covenant, and might see their necessity of free grace and a Mediator. God chose this way to convince them, by proposing the covenant of works to them, as though he expected they should seek and obtain life in this way, that everyone, when he came to apply it to himself, might see its impracticableness; as being a way of conviction to that ignorable and infantile state of the church. God did with them as Christ did with the young man, when he came and inquired what he should do to inherit eternal life: Christ bid him keep the commandments. There was this difference also: the law, or covenant of works, was more fully and plainly revealed to them than the gospel, or covenant of grace, was.[108]

Edwards's point is that the meaning of the covenant of works could be fully seen in the Mosaic dispensation when it is compared with the covenant of grace under the Old Testament dispensation. This implies that while the meaning of the covenant of grace had been less clearly revealed in the Mosaic period, the covenant of works was fully revealed to the people of the Old Testament. In this sense, the covenant of works in the Mosaic era could be seen in terms of progressive revelation as a developed version of the covenant of works of the pre-fall Adamic administration.

Edwards goes on to note different conditions between the covenant with the children of Israel, that is, the covenant of works, and the covenant of grace. Having set out the sense in which the condition of the Mosaic covenant is distinguished from that of the covenant of grace, Edwards examines faith and obedience, which are applied differently in both dispensations. Although the principle of faith and obedience is at work in both covenants, "the particular matter of that faith [and] obedience was in considerable part different," when one compares the Mosaic dispensation with the Christian dispensation. First, the "explicit acts of faith with respect to the Mediator and the gospel doctrines" were not necessary to the people of the Mosaic period. Second, the same principle is true for obedience.

---

108. Edwards, *Miscellany no. 439*, WJE 13:487-88..

Although the moral laws of the covenant of works were required to be kept by the children of Israel under the covenant of works, Israelites could be saved "in great neglect of them." However, this is not the case of the believers in the New Testament era. There are "some moral duties" to which believers in the gospel under the covenant of grace are subject for their "salvation." While these moral duties were not applied to the children of Israel for their salvation, they are necessary for the salvation of the people of the covenant of grace due to the "reason of much clearer revelations of" the laws. Emphasizing the virtue of its "different state of the church and of revelation" under the covenant of grace, Edwards concludes that although the people in the Mosaic dispensation of the covenant of works "could not be saved without the same principle and spirit, of old, yet they might be saved without such exercise and explicit acts thereof." In this sense, the covenant of grace is called "a new covenant, because the conditions of it are in some respect new."[109] Edwards understands the republication of the covenant of works in the Mosaic dispensation in terms of the continuous nature of revelation throughout salvation history.

CONCLUSION

After considering Edwards's Trinitarian doctrines, this chapter turned to his views of the covenant of works as exemplified in two sermons, on Genesis 3:11 and 3:24, respectively. It was found that his doctrine reflects a thoroughly Reformed understanding of the relationship between the law and the gospel. He understands the Mosaic law as a developed version of the pre-fall covenant of works and sees the gospel as an outworking of the covenant of grace. Edwards also, in keeping with the Reformed tradition, separates the Mosaic laws into three categories: moral, ceremonial, and judicial.

While Edwards shares the same distinction of the Mosaic laws with his Reformed forebears, his understanding of the laws in the Mosaic covenant is focused much more on historical reality in the sense that it was revealed to Adam's posterity at a particular moment in history. As noted earlier, Edwards distinguishes the conditions of the Mosaic covenant from those of the covenant of grace in terms of the continuous nature of revelation

---

109. Edwards, *Miscellany no. 439, WJE* 13:488.

regarding salvation history. He focuses primarily on how Christ's work fulfilled the Mosaic laws. He believes that the Mosaic law was given not so that people could earn redemption but rather so that the law would lead Old Testament Israel to Christ. Thus, as with his Trinitarian doctrines, Edwards's theology of the covenant of works demonstrates an unwavering focus on redemptive history.

5
—

THE DOCTRINE OF THE COVENANT OF GRACE AND THE HISTORY OF REDEMPTION

INTRODUCTION

For Edwards's federal theology, the covenant of grace takes ultimate priority. Bogue even calls it the "theological locus *par excellence*" with respect to Edwards's view of "the soteriological relation of God and man in Christ."[1] For Edwards, the covenant of grace concerns both the covenant of redemption and the covenant of works. He believes that the covenant of grace is the implementation of the covenant of redemption and that the latter without the former would be "a charlatanic doctrine."[2] At the same time, the covenant of works provides the nature of the benefits of the covenant of grace since the two covenants also work together in providing continuity from the Old Testament to the New Testament. Thus, for Edwards, the close relationships among the covenants of redemption, works, and grace seem to suggest that the entire covenant schema is constructed with great intricacy.

Despite its importance in his theology, Edwards did not write a monograph or treatise on the covenant of grace.[3] However, the topic of this chapter, the history of redemption, invariably leads to an examination of Edwards's view of the covenant of grace in terms of historical stages. There are several discussions of the covenant of grace throughout Edwards's

---

1. Carl W. Bogue, *Jonathan Edwards and the Covenant of Grace* (Cherry Hill, NJ: Mack, 1975), 7.
2. Bogue, *Jonathan Edwards and the Covenant of Grace*, 116.
3. Bogue, *Jonathan Edwards and the Covenant of Grace*, 14.

massive literary corpus. In particular, Edwards employs the redemption theme in the "Letter to the Trustees," the three notebooks, the 1739 sermon series known as the "Redemption Discourse," and the whole of "Miscellanies."[4]

However, of these, the 1739 sermon discourses play the most pivotal role in our understanding of Edwards's view of the covenant of grace in terms of the history of redemption. Here, in thirty sermons, Edwards draws out the history of redemption theme throughout the covenant schema, especially the covenant of grace. The sermon series follows the historical order of the work of redemption as Edwards understood it. For example, there are distinct periods that reveal what he sees as three stages in which God's work of redemption takes place in the world.[5] Edwards defines the work of redemption as "a work that God carries on from the fall of man to the end of the world." Therefore, the Redemption Discourse is the primary example of Edwards's thoughts on the historical aspect of the covenant of grace. Indeed, that the covenant of grace has "historical stages" is "the basic theme of the extensive work on *The History of Redemption*."[6]

This chapter is limited to a descriptive account of Edwards's sermons entitled "A History of the Work of Redemption," which form a prototype of the *history* project .[7] In this exploration, it is apparent that Edwards draws on the heritage of Reformed orthodoxy in his redemptive-historical approach. However, he does not merely regurgitate this tradition. As will be seen, his use of the theme is creative, especially when compared with Calvin, Cocceius, and Witsius. Edwards lays out the biblical story in such

---

4. According to John Wilson, a large number of the "Miscellanies" concentrate on the topic of redemption. Moreover, "'the Miscellanies' dramatically confirm that this was *a*, if not *the*, central focal point of his theological reflection." See John F. Wilson, "Jonathan Edwards' Notebooks for *A History of the Work of Redemption* " in *Reformation, Conformity and Dissent: Essays in Honour of Geoffrey Nuttall*, ed. R. Buick Knox (London: Epworth, 1977). With respect to the descriptive nature of the history of redemption in the letter to the trustees and the notebooks, Wilson points out, "The 'Letter to the Trustees' includes a fuller and more precise 'outline' of the projected *Work of Redemption* than the notebooks." See John F. Wilson, "Jonathan Edwards as Historian," *CH* 46, no. 1 (1977): 14n34.

5. The three great stages are as follows: (1) the fall of man to Christ's incarnation, (2) Christ's humiliation from the incarnation of Christ to his resurrection, and (3) Christ's resurrection to the end of the world.

6. John H. Gerstner, *Steps to Salvation: The Evangelistic Message of Jonathan Edwards* (Philadelphia: Westminster, 1960): 183–84.

7. Stephen M. Clark, "Jonathan Edwards: The History of the Work of Redemption," *WTJ* 56, no. 1 (1994): 46; Adriaan C. Neele, *Petrus van Mastricht (1630-1706): Reformed Orthodoxy: Method and Piety* (Leiden: Brill, 2009), 320.

a way that it builds toward the consummation of redemptive history. In its examination, this chapter begins with a summary of the contents of the sermon series of 1739, which is followed by a detailed analysis of Edwards's theology in that series.[8]

OVERVIEW OF THE CONTENTS OF
THE REDEMPTION DISCOURSE

In the first sermon in which Edwards formulates a doctrine from the biblical text, he gives a brief definition of the work of redemption. He argues that redemption has two distinct meanings: that which is with respect to its "effect" and that which is with respect to "the grand design (purpose)." The "effect" here indicates "the application of redemption," which includes the "converting, justifying, sanctifying and glorifying" of believers. "By these things," Edwards contends, "the souls of particular persons are actually redeemed—do receive the benefit of the Work of Redemption as carried on in all ages from the fall of man to the end of the world."[9] He maintains that the effect of the work of redemption is applied to believers' souls repeatedly throughout all ages. Thus, with respect to the effect, the work of redemption relates to the individual experience of salvation.

Yet Edwards does not stop there. For him, the grand design or purpose of redemption holds a weightier role than the individual experience. He writes:

> The Work of Redemption with respect to the grand design in general as it relates to the universal subject and end of it, is carried on from the fall of man to the end of the world in a different manner, not merely by the repeating and renewing the same effect on the different subjects of it, but by many successive works and dispensations of God, all tending to one great end and effect, all united as the several parts of a scheme, and altogether making up one great work.[10]

For Edwards, although the order of salvation occupies its place in the work of redemption, there is also "one great work," a final purpose, that will be

---

8. Since Wilson analyzes the sermon series of 1739, I will briefly deal with an analysis of the sermons. Cf. John F. Wilson, "Editor's Introduction," in *A History of the Work of Redemption*, *WJE* 9:1–109.

9. Edwards, *A History of the Work of Redemption*, *WJE* 9:120–21.

10. Edwards, *A History of the Work of Redemption*, 121.

accomplished at the end of the world. Edwards then goes on to describe "successive works" using the metaphor of building a house.[11] He maintains that the elements of the work of redemption happen in a historical process, progressing from lesser to greater importance, which will in turn accomplish "one great work" at the end. He argues that the final purpose is the glory of the Trinity "in an exceeding degree."[12]

Edwards's emphasis on the historical nature of redemption is also reflected in the sermon series' structure and content. The sermons are divided into three stages, each of which Edwards finds in redemptive history. First, sermons two through thirteen deal with the dispensations from "the fall of man to Christ's incarnation." This period is subdivided into "six lesser periods": (1) the fall to the flood, (2) the calling of Abraham, (3) the calling of Moses, (4) the anointing of David, (5) the captivity into Babylon, and (6) the incarnation of Christ.[13] In these sermons, Edwards stresses that all of the events in the Old Testament occurred to prepare for Christ's coming. In sermons fourteen to seventeen, Edwards examines the period of "Christ's humiliation from the incarnation of Christ to his resurrection."[14] Here, Edwards furnishes "a rational theological analysis" of Christ's humiliation.[15] Last, in sermons eighteen to twenty-nine, Edwards addresses the work of redemption in the third and final period: Christ's resurrection to the end of the world, including "the day of judgment."[16]

As already mentioned, Edwards's distinction between redemption as effect and grand design, together with the structure of these sermons themselves, suggests that he stresses the redemptive-historical aspect rather than the individual salvific experience. This implies that while Edwards falls in the same camp as Witsius, who also applied the history of redemption to the order of salvation, Edwards's emphasis on the historical theme

---

11. Edwards says that "like a house or temple that is building, first the workmen are sent forth, then the materials are gathered, then the ground fitted, then the foundation is laid, then the superstructure erected one part after another, till at length the topstone is laid. And all is finished." Edwards, *A History of the Work of Redemption*, 121.

12. Edwards, *A History of the Work of Redemption*, 125.

13. Edwards, *A History of the Work of Redemption*, 127.

14. Edwards, *A History of the Work of Redemption*, 294.

15. Wilson, "Editor's Introduction," in *A History of the Work of Redemption*, 36.

16. Edwards, *A History of the Work of Redemption*, 344, 502.

differentiates him from Witsius, who stressed the order of salvation for the individual believer.

REDEMPTIVE-HISTORICAL THOUGHT
IN THE REDEMPTION DISCOURSE

The emphasis upon salvation history is also evident in Edwards's method: he draws the federal schema from the text of Scripture, which is studied through a redemptive-historical lens. For Edwards, redemption and history are relationally indivisible. Yet here, the obvious question arises: How did Edwards define the relationship between salvation history and the Bible? In order to understand what factors play into this relationship, it is first necessary to answer these two questions: (1) What is the relationship between the doctrine of the covenant of grace and the history of redemption? And (2) how does the covenant schema stem from the text of the Bible? Thankfully, answers to both of these questions can be found in Edwards's sermon series of 1739.

THE COVENANT OF GRACE AND SALVATION HISTORY

Edwards begins his series with the purpose of the first sermon. He writes:

> The drift of this chapter is to comfort the church under her sufferings and the persecutions of her enemies. And the argument of consolation insisted upon is the constancy and perpetuity of God's mercy and faithfulness towards her, which shall be manifest in the continuance of the fruits of that mercy and faithfulness in continuing to work salvation for her, protecting her against all assaults of her enemies, and carrying her safely through all the changes of the world and finally crowning her with victory and deliverance.[17]

Here, Edwards gives a broad hint that he is about to describe God's faithful acts on behalf of his people throughout history. Given this focus on the continuous gracious acts of God, it is not surprising that Edwards contrasts "the happiness of the church of God" with "the contrary fate of his enemies." He argues that the church's enemies, those who hate and persecute

---

17. Edwards, *A History of the Work of Redemption*, 113.

God's people, are like "a garment" and "wool," which will be eaten by the moth and worm.[18]

In contrast, the happiness of God's church will continue "from generation to generation (Isaiah 51:8)."[19] Edwards considers two aspects of the

---

18. Edwards, *A History of the Work of Redemption*, 114.

19. Edwards, *A History of the Work of Redemption*, 113. The phrase "happiness of the church" is related to God himself. The close relationship between the happiness of the church and God is also found in Edwards's *End of Creation*. According to Nichols, in *End of Creation*, the first part of "Two Dissertations," *Concerning the End for which God Created the World* in *Ethical Writings*, (*WJE* 8:405-536), Edwards rejects both eighteenth-century moral philosophers who regarded "man's happiness as the central concern of God's governance of the world" and deists who "painted God as distant from and disinterested in the daily affairs of his creation." Against these two wrong concepts, Edwards argues that God is intimately related to his creatures, "directing all of history to just one end: not man's happiness as an end in itself, but his own divine glory." Stephen R. C. Nichols, *Jonathan Edwards's Bible: The Relationship of the Old and New Testaments in the Theology of Jonathan Edwards* (Eugene, OR: Pickwick, 2013), 109. In response to Holmes, who sees Edwards's view of "God's chief end" in the believers' knowledge of redemption, Oliver Crisp and Nichols claim that Edwards's chief end must be distinguished from the ultimate end. Their argument is based on these words of Edwards: "In the creature's knowing, esteeming, loving, rejoicing in, and praising God, the glory is both exhibited and acknowledged," *End of Creation*, 531. From this statement, Crisp and Nichols agree that there is a crucial distinction between Edwards's chief and ultimate ends. While the ultimate end is related to the believer's conversion, i.e., the creature's knowing, esteeming, loving, rejoicing and praising, Edwards's chief end points to God's glory, which is exhibited in the creature's conversion. See Stephen R. Holmes, *God of Grace and God of Glory: An Account of the Theology of Jonathan Edwards* (Grand Rapids: Eerdmans, 2001), 44-59; Oliver D. Crisp, *Jonathan Edwards and Metaphysics of Sin* (Burlington, VT: Ashgate, 2005), 5-24; Nichols, *Jonathan Edwards's Bible*, 109n2. Crisp and Nichole are correct when one considers Edwards's own distinction between the ultimate and chief ends. Edwards classifies three kinds of ends which an agent has: subordinate, ultimate, and chief. A subordinate end means that "an agent seeks and aims at in what he does; but yet don't seek it, or regard it at all upon its own account." An ultimate end indicates that "the agent seeks in what he does for its own sake." And a chief end is "an end that is most valued; and therefore most sought after by the agent in what he does." Edwards, *End of Creation*, 405-7. While the last two ends (the ultimate end and the chief end) could be regarded as "both ultimate ends," they are not "chief ends." Edwards uses an example to clarify. "A man may go a journey partly to obtain the possession and enjoyment of a bride that is very dear to him, and partly to gratify his curiosity in looking in a telescope, or some new-invented and extraordinary optic glass: both may be ends he seeks in his journey, and the one not properly subordinate or in order to another. One may not depend on another; and therefore both may be ultimate ends: but yet the obtaining his beloved bride may be his chief end, and the benefit of the optic glass, his inferior end. The former may be what he sets his heart vastly most upon, and so be properly the chief end of his journey." Edwards, *End of Creation*, 408. For the debate on Edwards's concept of the divine disposition, see Sang Hyun Lee, ed., *The Princeton Companion to Jonathan Edwards* (Princeton, NJ: Princeton University Press, 2005); Nichols, *Jonathan Edwards's Bible*, 142-95. On the debate over Edwards's doctrine of justification, see J. V. Fesko, *The Covenant of Redemption: Origins, Development, and Reception* (Göttingen: Vandenhoeck & Ruprecht, 2016), 127n94; Douglas A. Sweeney, *Edwards the Exegete: Biblical Interpretation and Anglo-Protestant Culture on the Edge of the Enlightenment* (New York: Oxford University Press, 2016), 202-18.

happiness of the church: (1) "God's righteousness" and "salvation" and (2) "its continuance." For the first aspect, the happiness of the church consists of two things: righteousness and salvation. Both are related through the covenant of grace. On the one hand, God's righteousness refers to "faithfulness," that the promises of the covenant of grace have been achieved for the church. That is, God has been faithful in conferring "the benefits of the covenant of grace." These benefits are "bestowed of free and sovereign grace" and given "in the exercise of God's righteousness or justice." Edwards maintains that because of the "promise of the covenant of grace," God was pleased "to bind himself to bestow" these promises on his people. Thus, the righteousness that God performs is the same as "covenant mercy."[20]

On the other hand, Edwards relates God's righteousness to the concept of salvation. While the former is "the cause," the latter is "the effect." Edwards defines salvation here as "the sum of all those works of God by which the benefits that by the covenant of grace are procured and bestowed."[21]

Second, the happiness of God's church consists of its "continuance." Here, the relationship between redemption and history appears. For Edwards, the praises of "forever" and "from generation to generation" in Isaiah 51:8 point ultimately to "the end of the world" or "the end of the generations of men." Thus, with respect to the connection between salvation and the covenant of grace, salvation implies the redemptive works of God, which allow the benefits of the covenant of grace to be "procured and bestowed."[22] Edwards is emphatic here that "the work of redemption itself towards the church shall continue to be wrought till then, till the end of the world."[23] This implies that the benefits of the covenant of grace are fulfilled through the divine historical work of redemption.

Edwards then turns to a formulation of doctrine: "The Work of Redemption is a work that God carries on from the fall of man to the end of the world." Here, Edwards attempts to explain this doctrine using

---

20. Edwards, *A History of the Work of Redemption*, 114.
21. Edwards, *A History of the Work of Redemption*, 115.
22. Edwards, *A History of the Work of Redemption*, 115.
23. Edwards, *A History of the Work of Redemption*, 116.

phrases such as "the grand design" and "Work of Redemption." He argues
that the work of salvation and the work of redemption are synonymous
since Scripture teaches that "God's saving his people is called 'his redeem-
ing them.' " It is for this reason that Jesus is called "both the Savior and the
Redeemer of his people."[24]

Edwards then explains in more detail the definition of the work of
redemption and how the grand design is carried out. With respect to the
phrase "the Work of Redemption," Edwards contends that in a restrictive
sense, it ought to be regarded as "the purchase of salvation" by Christ. In
this case, the work of redemption signifies something "not so long a-doing"
but something which "was begun and finished with Christ's humiliation,"
"incarnation," and "resurrection." In this view, the work of redemption was
finished on "the day of Christ's resurrection," while it was not "actually"
but "virtually done."[25]

However, Edwards's interest is in the whole application of the benefits
of the covenant of grace throughout history rather than the fulfillment of
salvation itself by Christ, which is applied to an individual. In other words,
the work of redemption should be understood in a broad sense. He writes:

> But then sometimes the Work of Redemption is taken more largely,
> including all that God works or accomplishes tending to this end,
> not only the purchasing of redemption but also all God's works that
> were properly preparatory to the purchase, or as applying the pur-
> chase and accomplishing the success of it. So that the whole dis-
> pensation as it includes the preparation and the imputation and
> application and success of Christ's redemption is here called the
> Work of Redemption.[26]

For Edwards, the whole process of the work of redemption is for the enact-
ing of "the eternal covenant of redemption." Thus, to clarify the meaning
of the work of redemption, Edwards points out three things that need to
be considered. First, "the persons of the Trinity" entered into a covenant of
redemption as follows: the Father appointed the Son (as a mediator) from

---

24. Edwards, *A History of the Work of Redemption*, 116–17.
25. Edwards, *A History of the Work of Redemption*, 117.
26. Edwards, *A History of the Work of Redemption*, 117.

all eternity, the Son undertook the office, and "all things" were agreed to in the covenant of redemption between the Father and the Son. Second, while the work of redemption has "an end," its fruits (the glory and blessedness) are eternal. Third, the work of redemption has a final purpose, which will be accomplished at the end of the world.[27]

Having considered both the term of the work of redemption and the manner in which it is applied,[28] Edwards proceeds to explain what the great design is and how the work of redemption is carried on from the fall of man in two respects.[29] In this explanation, the work of the redemption is closely related to the benefits of the covenant of grace. Also, Edwards's definition of the work of redemption is focused on the historical aspect of salvation rather than on individual faith. While Edwards maintains the typical Reformed understanding of salvation history with regard to these two concepts of redemption, his theological method for the interpretation of Scripture rests particularly on the historical aspect of salvation.

Given his interest in the historical character of salvation, it is no surprise that in his second sermon, Edwards turns to an account of how the work of redemption is accomplished in history. He maintains that redemptive history is the progressive history of salvation, in which the fulfillment of the promise of the covenant of grace is increasingly revealed to believers.

To deal with the nature of the salvation-historical aspect of the covenant of grace in detail, Edwards divides the entire historical period from the beginning to the end of the world into three eras: the fall of man to Christ's incarnation, Christ's incarnation to his resurrection, and Christ's resurrection to the end of the world.[30] He then begins to analyze the history

---

27. Edwards, *A History of the Work of Redemption*, 118–19.

28. As he explains in the beginning of the sermon, Edwards repeats that redemption is applied to both the spiritual effect on an individual and the grand design, the series of successive works of redemption through history.

29. As mentioned in chapter 1, Edwards's concept of the work of redemption focuses on the final purpose, which was made in the covenant of redemption among the persons of Trinity. Edwards presents the purpose as follows: (1) to put God's enemies under his feet, (2) to restore all the ruins of the fall, (3) to bring all elect creatures to a union in one body, (4) to complete the glory of all the elect by Christ, and (5) to accomplish the glory of the Trinity to an exceeding degree. These purposes are accomplished by the work of redemption as "the principal mean." In this way, the work of redemption reveals God's eternal purposes. In other words, parts of the grand purpose can be seen through the process of their becoming perfect through history, even though they will be complete not in this world but rather in heaven.

30. Edwards, *A History of the Work of Redemption*, 127.

of the work of redemption during the first era. His main argument here is that the works of redemption during this period were "forerunners and earnests" and "working out redemption and work preparatory" to Christ's coming. "The great works of God in the world during this whole space of time," Edwards writes, "were all preparatories to this." In short, the first great period refers to preparation for Christ's coming.[31]

While Edwards believes the number of people who obtained salvation during this period was "very small to what it was afterwards," such salvation was given as "way of anticipation."[32] He argues:

> All this salvation was as it were by way of anticipation, all the souls that were saved before Christ came were only as it [were] the earnests of the future harvest. God wrought many lesser salvations and deliverances for this church and people before Christ came. These salvations were all but so many images and forerunners of the great salvation Christ was to work out when he came. God revealed himself of old from time to time from the fall of man to the coming of Christ.[33]

The preparatory character of the first era shows that Edwards's view of redemption is oriented toward Christ's work. In fact, Edwards describes each era according to the degree to which that era aligns with the revelation of the gospel. Thus, while Edwards argues that the church in that period enjoyed "the light of the gospel," those revelations "were only so many forerunners and earnests of the great light." While the church at that time "had the light of the sun," it was "but as reflected from the moon and stars."[34]

Edwards subdivides the first era into six lesser periods: (1) history "from the fall to the flood," (2) "to the calling of Abraham," (3) "to Moses," (4) "to David," (5) "to the captivity into Babylon," and (6) "to the incarnation of Christ."[35] He then elaborates on the period from the fall to the flood.

---

31. Edwards, A History of the Work of Redemption, 128.
32. Edwards, A History of the Work of Redemption, 128.
33. Edwards, A History of the Work of Redemption, 128–29.
34. Edwards, A History of the Work of Redemption, 129.
35. Edwards, A History of the Work of Redemption, 129.

Edwards stresses that God's work of redemption "was began to be carried on" as soon as Adam fell.

Salvation history is Christocentric for Edwards. He believes that Christ began his threefold office as prophet, priest, and king as early as the fall of man. Genesis 3:15 ("And I will put enmity between thee and the woman, and between thy seed and her seed; it shall bruise thy head, and thou shalt bruise his heel"), which Edwards believes refers to "God's design of subduing his enemies under the feet of his Son," figures prominently in this portrait.[36] Edwards believes God's design is declared through Christ's threefold office. Given that one of the great works of redemption was to prepare for Christ's coming, "the first thing Christ did in the Work of Redemption" was to carry on "his prophetical office."[37] In other words, Christ's first work of redemption as a prophet was to reveal God's grand design.

For Edwards, Christ's priestly office is interrelated with his prophetic work since the former is based on the latter. He argues that Christ's priesthood is foreshadowed in "the custom of sacrificing," which was implemented to help us understand the "type of the sacrifice of Christ." Thus, sacrifice was "by divine appointment" rather than merely "natural worship." Edwards holds that sacrifice itself was given by "some positive command or institution for man, for God has declared his abhorrence of such worship as is taught by the precept of men without his institution."[38] But Edwards does not stop there. He turns to Genesis 3:15, which he considers to be prophecy and through which the "covenant and promise was the foundation" of the "custom of sacrificing."[39] Edwards insists, "That promise [of the covenant of grace] was the first stone that was laid towards this glorious building the Work of Redemption which will be finished <at the end of the world>. And the next stone which was laid upon this was the institution of sacrifices to be a type of the great sacrifice."[40] For Edwards, Christ's priesthood follows his role as prophet.

---

36. Edwards, *A History of the Work of Redemption*, 134.
37. Edwards, *A History of the Work of Redemption*, 134.
38. Edwards, *A History of the Work of Redemption*, 134–35.
39. Edwards, *A History of the Work of Redemption*, 135.
40. Edwards, *A History of the Work of Redemption*, 135.

Furthermore, the priestly and prophetic offices undergird Christ's king-ship. Edwards finds Christ's kingly office in the practical redemption of man. He writes:

> God did soon after the fall begin actually to save the souls of men through Christ's redemption. In this Christ who had newly taken upon [himself] the work of mediator between God and man did first then begin that work wherein he appeared in the exercise of his kingly office, as in the sacrifices he was represented in his priestly office, and in the first prediction of redemption by Christ he had appeared in the exercise of his prophetical office. In that prediction the light of Christ's redemption first began to dawn in the prophe-cies of it; in the institution of sacrifice it first began to dawn in the types of it; in this, viz. his beginning actually to save men, it first began to dawn in the fruit of it.[41]

Given Edwards's use of Genesis 3:15, it appears that this biblical text is crit-ical in revealing his understanding of Christ's threefold office as prophet, priest, and king. Noteworthy is Edwards's understanding that Christ began to discharge the office of mediator (through his threefold office) even during the earliest moments after the fall. In using this theme, he iden-tifies covenantal aspects of the Old Testament. Instead of rushing to the New Testament, he attempts to show how much more fully the covenant of grace has been revealed through the periods recorded in the Old Testament.

Having discussed the threefold office of Christ in the first period of the Old Testament, Edwards moves on to his third sermon, which addresses the period from the fall to the flood. Notably, he places an emphasis on the pouring out of the Holy Spirit. He writes, "The next remarkable thing that God did in further carrying on this great affair of redemption was the first remarkable pouring out of the Spirit through Christ that ever was, which there was in the days of Enos."[42]

Why does he emphasize this pneumatological event? Although his summary is brief, the relationship between Christ's threefold office and the Holy Spirit's being poured out should not be overlooked. For Edwards,

---

41. Edwards, *A History of the Work of Redemption*, 137–38.
42. Edwards, *A History of the Work of Redemption*, 141.

the pouring out of the Holy Spirit is the application of Christ's redemptive works that began when Christ entered into the threefold office. This
is apparent from his statement, "the first remarkable pouring out of the
Spirit through Christ," as cited above. Here, one scholar's view of Edwards's
intention in preaching this sermon series is relevant. "The Redemption
Discourse," argues Wilson, "had controlling theological premises and was
intended to eventuate in religious practice or conversion."[43] This is echoed
by Lucas's comment on the Redemption Discourse: "The engine of redemptive history was revival."[44]

This interpretation is supported by Edwards's focus on the practical
life of believers. Edwards insists that as a result of the pouring out of the
Holy Spirit, there appeared "something new in the visible church of God
with respect to the duty of prayer, or calling on the name of the [Lord]."
The "uncommon influences of God's Spirit" came to bring about "a great
increase of the performance of the duty of prayer."[45] Although "there had
[been] a saving work of God in the hearts of some" people of the previous
time, "God was pleased to grant a more large effusion of his Spirit for the
bringing in an harvest of souls to Christ."[46] This exposition of the pouring
out of the Holy Spirit as one of greatest works of redemption is a creative
application of Trinitarian thought to the doctrine of the covenant of grace.
At the same time, it reveals that the benefit of the covenant of grace is not
unrelated to the practical response of believers in positive obedience.

Edwards then gives an example of this work of redemption in Enoch,
who lived in the days of Enosh. According to Edwards, Enoch's "soul as it
was built on Christ was built up in holiness to a greater height than there
had been any instance of before."[47] Moreover, Enoch's translation into
heaven without death resulted from the fact that the work of redemption
"was carried on further than ever it had been before." Edwards stresses
that the light of gospel during this period increased with great intensity.[48]

---

43. Wilson, "Editor's Introduction," in *A History of the Work of Redemption*, 37.

44. Sean Michael Lucas, "*A History of the Work of Redemption*," *A Reader's Guide to the Major Writings of Jonathan Edwards* (Wheaton, IL: Crossway, 2017), 181.

45. Edwards, *A History of the Work of Redemption*, 142.

46. Edwards, *A History of the Work of Redemption*, 143.

47. Edwards, *A History of the Work of Redemption*, 143–44.

48. Edwards, *A History of the Work of Redemption*, 146.

Here, Edwards's thoughts bear some similarities to those of Cocceius. For example, Van Asselt observes that for Cocceius, each stage in salvation history from the beginning to the end "gives the experience of salvation its peculiar form." In other words, "each period in salvation history coincides with a corresponding state or condition in the believer."[49] This also holds true for Edwards's view of the relationship between salvation history and individual faith. Edwards writes:

> And here by the way I would observe that the increase of gospel light and the carrying on the Work of Redemption as it respects the elect church in general, from the first erecting of the church to the end of the world, is very much after the same manner as the carrying on of the same work and the same light in a particular soul from the time of its conversion till it is perfected and crowned in glory. The work in a particular soul has its ups and downs. Sometimes the light shines brighter, and sometimes 'tis a dark time. Sometimes grace seems to prevail; at other times it seems to languish for a great whole together and corruption prevails and then grace revives again. But in the general grace is growing from its first infusion till it is perfected in glory; the kingdom of Christ is building up in the soul. So it is with respect to the great affair in general as it relates to the universal subject of it, as 'tis carried on from the first beginning of it after the fall till it is perfected at the end of the world, as will more fully appear by a particular view of this affair from beginning to end in the prosecution of this subject, if God gives opportunity to carry it through as I propose.[50]

For Edwards, an individual believer's spiritual growth through the light of the gospel matches the progression of salvation history.

However, the thoughts of Edwards and Cocceius fail to overlap completely. For Edwards, the relationship between the historical stages of the covenant of grace and its spiritual effect on believers is nothing other than progression. In other words, he avoids a meticulous structuring of the

---

49. Willem J. Van Asselt, *The Federal Theology of Johannes Cocceius, 1603–1669*, trans. Raymond A. Blacketer (Leiden: Brill, 2001), 281.

50. Edwards, *A History of the Work of Redemption*, 144–45.

doctrine of the covenant of grace. This sets him apart from Cocceius, who matched the stages of the abrogation of the covenant of works to the progressive effect on an individual soul.

Edwards then moves on to a discussion of the second period of the Old Testament, from the Noahic deluge to the calling of Abraham. He regards the flood as a redemptive work of God in that the flood itself played a significant role in promoting God's work of redemption.[51] Such a universal catastrophe was the "fulfilment of the covenant of grace" predicted in Genesis 3:15.[52] When the seed of the woman was "in utmost peril" by the seed of the serpent, it was saved by God's destruction of nations through the flood.[53] While God could have used "other methods" for delivering his church, he destroyed the world in a way in which the church would see God's glory, similar to when the Egyptians were drowned in the Red Sea. He argues that all of these events took place agreeable to the "promise of the covenant of grace."[54]

Edwards then argues that in this period, God "*renews* with Noah and his sons" the covenant of grace. When Noah offered a sacrifice, it represented "the true sacrifice of Christ." Edwards also maintains that God promised his church "the new grant of the earth" in accordance with the covenant of grace, which is established upon Christ's sacrifice.[55] Edwards even sees God's disappointment of "the design of building the city and tower of Babel" as a part of "the great Work of Redemption."[56] In this regard, Edwards repeatedly mentions Christ's blood as the foundation of the tower. "Therefore," he asserts, "God saw it tended to frustrate the design of that great building that was founded not on the haughtiness of men but Christ's blood."[57] In fact, in his exposition of God's work of redemption in the time of Enosh, Edwards argues that Christ's blood had

---

51. Edwards, *A History of the Work of Redemption*, 149.

52. Edwards, *A History of the Work of Redemption*, 150.

53. Edwards, *A History of the Work of Redemption*, 150.

54. Edwards, *A History of the Work of Redemption*, 151.

55. Edwards, *A History of the Work of Redemption*, 152.

56. Edwards observes seven stages during the second period of the Old Testament: (1) flood, (2) family of Christ preserved, (3) new covenant, (4) renewing covenant, (5) Babel, (6) dispersion of humanity, and (7) preservation of the church.

57. Edwards, *A History of the Work of Redemption*, 153–54.

a "great efficacy so long before it was shed."[58] This shows that God's work of redemption in the Old Testament is not unrelated to Christ's blood shed during the New Testament era. Rather, the opposite is true. For Edwards, every event in the Old Testament is understood and interpreted in terms of the fulfilled redemption enacted through Christ's blood.

The historical venture is, for Edwards, ultimately and wholly about God's work of redemption through Christ's sacrifice, and so he consistently relies on the salvation-historical theme to reveal the nature of redemption. Clearly, he has already committed himself to showing how God's work of redemption has been carried on from beginning to end. When he analyzes the historical events that occurred in the Bible and the secular world, he consistently draws attention to God's continuously redemptive works in revealing the light of the gospel, protecting the church, and fulfilling (to various degrees) the covenant of grace. It is therefore enough to provide, as briefly as possible, a survey of the historical events described in *A History of the Work of Redemption*.

Compared with the prior periods, Edwards finds that the covenant of grace during the time of Abraham's call includes "a more particular and full revelation and confirmation of the covenant of grace."[59] Along with "a further revelation of the covenant of grace," there was a further confirmation of revelation.[60] Moreover, he believes that the covenant of grace during this period was more frequently renewed than it had been before.[61]

In the fourth period, from Moses to David, Edwards contends that God renewed the covenant of grace with his people under Moses and the guidance of Joshua, so that the work of redemption was advanced.[62] Later on, God made the covenant of grace with David, promising the Messiah as his seed.[63] In describing the progressive characteristic of the light in the cov-

---

58. Edwards, *A History of the Work of Redemption*, 148.

59. Edwards, *A History of the Work of Redemption*, 160

60. Edwards lists the confirmations as follows: (1) "circumcision," (2) the blessings of Melchizedek, (3) "the vision that he had in the deep sleep that fell upon him of the smoking furnace and burning lamp that passed between the parts of his sacrifice," (4) the promise of giving Abraham a son, and (5) the event of delivering Isaac upon the wood of the sacrifice to be slain. See Edwards, *A History of the Work of Redemption*, 161–64.

61. Edwards, *A History of the Work of Redemption*, 170.

62. Edwards, *A History of the Work of Redemption*, 192, 215.

63. Edwards, *A History of the Work of Redemption*, 214.

enant of grace in the Old Testament, Edwards writes, "Thus you see how the light of the gospel, which first began to dawn and glimmer immediately after the fall, gradually increases the nearer we come to Christ's time."[64]

Thus, Edwards identifies aspects of the covenant of grace in a series of periods in which God promises, renews, confirms, preserves, and more fully reveals the covenant of grace in increasing measure. However, he does not go beyond a general description of the renewal of the covenant. As Wilson points out, while Edwards employs the covenant scheme, he eschews "the minutiae" of covenant theology.[65] Moreover, he does not directly deal with the terms and contents of the covenant in his further discussion of the work of redemption during the second and third great periods.[66] This does not mean that Edwards jettisons the covenantal aspects. Rather, the covenantal description of the history of redemption persists throughout the sermon series. Nevertheless, the redemptive-historical lens, and not the covenantal system, is the driving force behind Edwards's reading of the Bible.

Furthermore, while Edwards's distinction of six periods in the Old Testament is similar to Witsius's view, the two approaches are nonetheless different. While Witsius describes progressive redemption in the Old Testament, his emphasis lies on the degree of benefit derived from the covenant of grace during the Old Testament as compared with the New Testament. This is also true for Edwards, who "deemed the Old Covenant inferior to the New" covenant.[67] On the surface, Edwards's way of thinking does not seem to differ substantially from his Reformed predecessors. Yet Edwards's focus is not an attempt to present the benefit of the covenant of grace in the Old Testament as inferior to the benefit obtained in the New Testament. Rather, his interest in the covenant of grace is the progress of revelation that undergirds the whole Bible. He attempts to draw out how God's salvific act was progressively revealed throughout history.

---

64. Edwards, *A History of the Work of Redemption*, 189.

65. Wilson, "Editor's Introduction," in A History of the World, 54.

66. Edwards, *A History of the Work of Redemption*, 172, 185, 189, and 315. Edwards frequently uses the phrase the "light of the gospel" throughout the sermon series.

67. Douglas A. Sweeney, *Edwards the Exegete: Biblical Interpretation and Anglo-Protestant Culture on the Edge of the Enlightenment* (New York: Oxford University Press, 2016), 61.

THE REDEMPTIVE-HISTORICAL THEME AND THE BIBLICAL TEXT

After this discussion of the first great period and the work of redemption, Edwards begins to focus on how a redemptive-historical approach aids our understanding of biblical texts. In dealing with the last period of the first great period (the Babylonian captivity to the coming of Christ), he employs the redemptive-historical theme. Here it appears that Edwards regards the Bible as an account of the events by which the work of redemption was carried out.

Edwards argues that Scripture communicates about the work of redemption in two ways: through history and through prophecy. As for the first, although Scripture does involve history, it does not include all history. As for the second, Edwards believes prophecy is substituted for history in some places. He writes that where "Scripture history fails, there prophecy takes place." In this way, Edwards believes that the whole chain of events revealing the work of redemption continues until the "consummation of all things."[68] This is how he finds doctrinal harmony in the Bible.

Edwards goes on to note that there are two reasons Scripture does not provide an account of the history of the sixth period, from the Babylonian captivity to the coming of Christ. First, "the spirit of prophecy" ceased, which, albeit with God's intention, resulted in the absence of prophets to write the history of that period. Second, God allowed non-biblical history to preserve the "authentic and full accounts of the events of this period." Non-biblical history, which Edwards calls "profane history," does not give an accurate account of the five preceding periods (from the fall of man to the Babylonian captivity). However, in this age, Edwards maintains that God allowed that "profane history related things with some certainty" and that, as a result, prophecy became sufficient for delivering historical accounts of the work of redemption.[69]

Edwards also applies these three sources (biblical history and prophecy as well as secular history) to understand the historical events of the third great period (from the end of Christ's humiliation to the end of the world). For example, in dealing with the success of Christ's redemption during the period of "the destruction of Jerusalem," Edwards interprets

---

68. Edwards, *A History of the Work of Redemption*, 242.

69. Edwards, *A History of the Work of Redemption*, 243–44.

biblical texts using "Scripture history," "Scripture prophecy," and "God's providence as related in human histories."[70] After examining the success of the gospel in light of the historical events described in Scripture, Edwards examines the fate of those who opposed the gospel during this period. He argues that they experienced the last judgment, which was "the terrible destruction of their city and country by the Romans" and included the destruction of Jerusalem.[71]

Moreover, he describes the third major segment of the work of redemption, including the destruction of Jerusalem, as a period in which God accomplishes "the success and end of Christ's purchase."[72] Noting the events that happened during this period, Edwards attempts to show that "the kingdom of Christ is gradually prevailing and increasing" in several great stages as Christ's resurrection is increasingly fulfilled as history moves closer to the end of the world. Finally, at the end of sermon eighteen, Edwards presents the reason why the work of redemption appears progressively: "the glory of God's wisdom in the manner of doing this is more visible to the creatures' observation," and "Satan is the more gloriously triumphed over."[73] At this point, Edwards's focus is on the manner in which the benefits of the covenant of grace are revealed and bestowed: in a manner that is beheld by believers.

As seen in chapter 2, Witsius regards the destruction of Jerusalem as the final abrogation of the ceremonial law. Likewise, for Edwards, the collapse of Jerusalem represents "a final end to the Old Testament world."[74] However, there is a distinct difference in their views. Witsius understands the fall of Jerusalem in terms of the progressive characteristics of the benefits of the covenant of grace. However, Edwards treats the same event as evidence of "how the success of Christ's purchase of redemption

---

70. Edwards, *A History of the Work of Redemption*, 383.

71. Edwards, *A History of the Work of Redemption*, 383–85.

72. Edwards, *A History of the Work of Redemption*, 371. This period is also divided into "four successive great events" describing Christ's coming in his kingdom as "the success of Christ's purchase": (1) the destruction of Jerusalem, (2) Constantine's era in the destruction of the heathen Roman empire, (3) the destruction of Antichrist, and (4) Christ's coming to the last judgment.

73. Edwards, *A History of the Work of Redemption*, 356.

74. Edwards, *A History of the Work of Redemption*, 385.

was carried on."[75] Edwards thus approaches the Old and New Testaments in terms of how the work of redemption takes place throughout history without ceasing (through the lens of both biblical prophecy and recorded history). He relates the events of the Old Testament to those of the New Testament in terms of a progressive view of redemptive history. That is, Edwards regards redemptive history as a continuous activity of God, in Christ and through the Holy Spirit.

CONCLUSION

The previous chapters demonstrated how Edwards uses the history of redemption as a framework for understanding the doctrines of the immanent Trinity, the economic Trinity, and the covenant of works. In this chapter, we turned our attention to the covenant of grace. Of all the doctrines examined thus far, it is here where we see Edwards's emphasis on redemptive history come most clearly to the forefront. For Edwards, redemptive history is none other than the story of how the covenant of grace is fulfilled and revealed to believers. Thus, Edward builds the Redemption Discourse around three historical stages: the fall of man to Christ's incarnation, to Christ's resurrection, and to the end of the world. For Edwards, every event that occurs in history moves the process of salvation history forward, intensifying the light of the gospel toward the final state of the church. Thus, Edwards's historical perspective of salvation is not static but rather eschatological.

The perspective of progressive revelation encapsulates the events of the Old Testament. Edward repeatedly maintains that Christ's blood is the conduit of the power and efficacy of salvation activity, even long before Christ's crucifixion. In fact, he contends that Christ carried out his redemption in the moments immediately after the fall. This reflects Edwards's assumption that there is a Christocentric relationship between the Old and New Testaments.

Finally, Edwards does not attempt to explain the relationship between the Old and New Testaments in terms of the benefits of the covenant of grace. Rather, he interprets all the events in the Bible in terms of how God prepares for redemption, accomplishes that redemption, and then

---

75. Edwards, *A History of the Work of Redemption*, 374.

applies it to his church. He uses salvation history as an interpretive grid for understanding events in the Bible and secular history. He thus employs three sources (biblical history, biblical prophecy, and secular history) in analyzing the work of redemption.

To this point, our approach has been rigorously focused on salvation history in the thought of Edwards and his Reformed predecessors. We have sought to explore how redemptive history is present in his theology to better understand if and how Calvin and his successors influenced Edwards. We have also sought to understand the differences between Edwards and several Reformed forebears to better understand Edwards's uniqueness. In the following section, our approach will focus solely on his biblical exegesis and the doctrinal harmony that emerged from his Christocentric approach to the Bible.

Part 3

—

THE DOCTRINAL HARMONY
of SCRIPTURE

6

—

THE EXEGETICAL BASIS OF THE DOCTRINE OF THE COVENANT OF REDEMPTION

INTRODUCTION

OVERVIEW OF THE DOCTRINAL HARMONY OF SCRIPTURE

In the previous part (chapters 3, 4, and 5), it was shown that Edwards lays the foundation for his understanding of federal theology in the redemptive-historical aspect of divine revelation. Indeed, the central event of divine revelation, that is, the salvation history of Christ, leads directly to Scripture, since biblical history is read as the divine revelation of salvation. However, this perspective poses a question: Is the history of salvation a key to understanding how Edwards interprets Scripture? The analysis in the previous chapter regarding salvation history in the federal schema shows that this is precisely the case. For Edwards, the redemptive-historical theme is pivotal to his interpretation of the Bible, as it was for his Reformed forebears, especially Cocceius.[1]

However, Edwards does not view redemptive history as the single interpretive framework that drives his biblical exegesis. Rather, Edwards employs various hermeneutical methods while considering the unity of the Bible. This leads to a secondary question: How does Edwards's engagement with the Bible help us understand his view of history? It has already been noted that Edwards attempts to understand the nature of redemptive

---

1. Willem J. Van Asselt, *The Federal Theology of Johannes Cocceius, 1603-1669*, trans. Raymond A. Blacketer (Leiden: Brill, 2001), 233.

history in terms of the harmony of the Bible. However, what doctrinal harmony does Edwards find in the Bible? Or perhaps a better question might be, what leads Edwards to see that successive stages in redemptive history are consistent throughout the Bible?[2]

Regarding the first question, Edwards does not provide the key concepts that typify his exegetical methods, although it is clear he used various methods.[3] Unfortunately, this makes it difficult for the reader to understand the nature of the doctrinal harmony in Edwards's thought. However, it is clear that he regards salvation history in two respects: the order of salvation (as regards an individual) and redemptive history (as regards the universe). This leads Nichols to argue that the work of redemption

> encompasses both the grand scheme of history directed to God's glory, and the application of salvation to individuals common throughout history. The relationship of these two aspects of the work of redemption is the key to understanding the doctrinal harmony of the Testaments in Edwards's theology. Here another image helps, an image Edwards employs in numerous places, and one that links for Edwards the two senses of redemption that he outlines in his 1739 sermons: that of a wheel.[4]

Nichols describes Edwards's metaphor of a wheel as follows:

---

2. According to Van Asselt, salvation history is to be called "covenantal history," especially when it refers to "federal theology." See Van Asselt, *The Federal Theology of Johannes Cocceius*, 291. These questions echo the scholarly debates on Cocceius's view of salvation history. According to Van Asselt, some scholars argue that Cocceius's aim was "to introduce into theology an immanent and evolutionary concept of history: history as an autonomous and immanent process of development." In contrast to this critical approach to Cocceius's federal theology, Busch claims that Cocceius's covenant system "accentuates the historical aspect of that which revelation makes known in the various dispensations of salvation history." On the other hand, C. S. McCoy and H. Faulenbach deny "any idea of historical development." Classifying these diverse interpretations of Cocceius's federal system into two major groups (the evolutionary model and the synthetic model), Van Asselt suggests a Pneumatological model that provides "a more satisfactory solution to the question that we encountered in our analysis of the evolutionary and synthetic models, namely, that of the relationship of salvation history (the linear or horizontal dimension) to the predestinarian, salvation-order, or experiential aspect (the vertical dimension)." Van Asselt, *The Federal Theology of Johannes Cocceius*, 3, 12, 14, 303.

3. Douglas A. Sweeney, *Edwards the Exegete: Biblical Interpretation and Anglo-Protestant Culture on the Edge of the Enlightenment* (New York: Oxford University Press, 2016), x.

4. Stephen R. C. Nichols, *Jonathan Edwards's Bible: The Relationship of the Old and New Testaments in the Theology of Jonathan Edwards* (Eugene, OR: Pickwick, 2013), 116.

One great wheel represents "'the entire series of events in the course of things through the age of the visible universe." It performs one great revolution. Inside this great wheel is a lesser wheel that performs two revolutions to its one. Inside these are further wheels, each smaller than the previous. Within them all and smallest of all, man's life is depicted as a wheel that rises from the nakedness of his mother's womb and returns to the dust of the earth. The grand scheme of redemption and the individual human life are connected in this depiction of God's providence.[5]

For Nichols, the doctrinal harmony of the Bible can be seen in Edwards's twofold concept of redemptive history. Similarly, McClymond and McDermott present the concept of the history of redemption as the governing theological theme that dominated Edwards's reflection during his final years.[6] Barshinger, agreeing with McClymond and McDermott, argues that for Edwards, "God's work of redemption was the all-encompassing theological concept around which all others were oriented."[7]

However, these scholars, especially Nichols and Barshinger, tend to focus on the role of the concept of individual redemption. Nichols devotes little time to Edwards's fundamental theme of the grand design, despite his engagement with Edwards's sermon series of 1739.[8] Rather, he focuses on the concept of individual redemption as a parallel to the grand design of redemption.[9] This is also true for Barshinger, who emphasizes the concept of the history of redemption as applied to individual faith through the gospel and the influence of the Holy Spirit.[10] This point of view, however, appears to misunderstand Edwards's original intention in his sermon series of 1739. Although Edwards maintains the close relationship between

---

5. Nichols, *Jonathan Edwards's Bible*, 117.

6. Michael J. McClymond and Gerald R. McDermott, *The Theology of Jonathan Edwards* (New York: Oxford University Press, 2012), 181.

7. David P. Barshinger, *Jonathan Edwards and the Psalms: A Redemptive-Historical Vision of Scripture* (New York: Oxford University Press, 2014), 270–72.

8. He seeks in Edwards's sermon series of 1739 not so much the theme of grand design but just four images (a building work, a river's course, an imperial army, and a tree) that Edwards employs to describe God's grand scheme of redemption.

9. See Nichols, *Jonathan Edwards's Bible*, 111–18.

10. Barshinger, *Jonathan Edwards and the Psalms*, 259, 270–72.

the history of salvation as it relates to the individual soul and to all of creation,[11] the latter, rather than the former, lies at the core of Edwards's view of history.

This understanding echoes Wilson's rejection of Scheick's interpretation of Edwards's twofold nature of salvation. Scheick argues that "as the soul grows in grace and as history approaches eternity, both by means of *a posteriori* phases, the more luminous they become."[12] In response, Wilson argues:

> Edwards was well aware of the distinction between the subjective side of redemption and the objective side. He took a great interest in how redemption affected the individual saint and sinner. Indeed, his experience with and observation of the awakenings in Northampton, and his subsequent analysis of them, underlay his own major contribution to the Puritan literature on the morphology of the religious life. But the Redemption Discourse was not concerned with the effect of redemption upon the soul of the saint—that he plumbed in *Religious Affections*. The objective side was the focus, that is, the divine Work of Redemption. For him, if there was an analogy, it was from that greater redemption of creation to its pale shadow in the soul, not vice versa.[13]

Wilson argues that while Edwards refers to the two senses of redemption repeatedly throughout his corpus, the greater historical aspect of divine revelation is more pivotal to his theology than salvation realized in a

---

11. As Sweeney points out, one of the fundamental elements of the doctrinal harmony of the Bible in Edwards could be a spiritual harmony that "tends to bring the texts themselves to mind, on proper occasions; as the particular state of the stomach and palate, tends to bring such particular meats and drinks to mind, as are agreeable to that state." Sweeney, *Edwards the Exegete*, 75.

12. William J. Scheick, "The Grand Design: Jonathan Edwards' History of Redemption," *Eighteenth-Century Studies* 8, no. 3 (Spring 1975): 313. Scheick's interpretation of Edwards's view of salvation history resembles Cocceius's view of the historical stages of the covenant of works: "The covenant of works with Adam is no theological construct, but rather, like the Fall into sin, it is an historical fact. On the other hand, the stages in this historical series give the experience of salvation its peculiar form. Each period in salvation history coincides with a corresponding state or condition in the believer." See Van Asselt, *The Federal Theology of Johannes Cocceius*, 281.

13. John F. Wilson, "Editor's Introduction," in *A History of the Work of Redemption*, WJE 9:100.

believer's life. Thus, it does not seem to be Edwards's intention to reveal "a direct parallel between the stages of salvation in the soul and creation."[14]

Wilson's appreciation of Edwards's intention in his sermon series resonates with Edwards's own view of the Bible as a unified whole. He expresses this thought in the 1757 "Letter to the Trustees," in which he discusses his goals for the *history* project. He writes that he aims to consider

> all parts of the grand scheme in their historical order. The order of their existence, or their being brought forth to view, in the course of divine dispensations, or the wonderful series of successive acts and events; beginning from eternity and descending from thence to the great work and successive dispensations of the infinitely wise God in time, considering the chief events coming to pass in the church of God, and revolutions in the world of mankind, affecting the state of the church and the affair of redemption, which we have an account of in history or prophecy; till at last we come to the general resurrection, last judgment, and consummation of all things; when it shall be said, "it is done. I am Alpha and Omega, the Beginning and the End" [Rev. 22:13]. Concluding my work, with the consideration of that perfect state of things, which shall be finally settled, to last for eternity. This history will be carried on with regard to all three worlds, heaven, earth, and hell: considering the connected, successive events and alterations, in each so far as the Scriptures give any light; introducing all parts of divinity in that order which is most scriptural and most natural: which is a method which appears to me the most beautiful and entertaining, wherein every divine doctrine, will appear to greatest advantage in the brightest light, in the most striking manner, showing the admirable contexture and harmony of the whole.[15]

In summary, Edwards refers to a harmony that was something successive encompassing all historical events that have occurred in creation and those that have been recorded in the Bible. This viewpoint is supported by

---

14. Wilson, "Editor's Introduction," in *A History of the Work of Redemption*, 100.

15. Edwards, "Letter to the Trustees of the College of New Jersey, Oct. 19, 1757," in *Letters and Personal Writings*, WJE 16:728.

Edwards's mention of "another great work" that he planned to write. In the same letter, he writes:

> I have also for my own profit and entertainment, done much towards another great work, which I call *The Harmony of the Old and New Testament*. The first considering the prophecies of the Messiah, his redemption and kingdom; the evidences of their references to the Messiah, etc. comparing them all one with another, demonstrating their agreement and true scope and sense; also considering all the various particulars wherein these prophecies have their exact fulfilment; showing the universal, precise, and admirable correspondence between predictions and events. The second part: considering the types of the Old Testament, showing the evidence of their being intended as representations of the great things of the gospel of Christ: and the agreement of the type with the antitype. The third and great part, considering the harmony of the Old and New Testament, as to doctrine and precept.[16]

Edwards's intended work, "The Harmony of the Old and New Testament," was to include various harmony schema, that is, three areas of testamental harmony (prophecy and fulfillment, types, and doctrine and precept). This signifies that Edwards's view of the harmony of the Bible is not limited to doctrinal harmony through the framework of salvation history.[17]

Nevertheless, it should be noted that these three elements are easily integrated into the salvation-historical aspect, grounded in fundamental themes of Edwardsian theology. That is, prophecy, typology, and doctrine and precept all are involved in redemptive history. According to Wallace E. Anderson, Edwards assembled his notebooks, entitled "The Harmony of the Genius, Spirit, Doctrines and Rules of the Old and New Testaments," "Defense of the Authenticity of the Pentateuch as a Work of Moses and the Historicity of the Old Testament Narratives," and "Scripture Prophecies of the Old Testament," in order to defend the historicity of the biblical narrative of the Old Testament and to demonstrate the historical reliability

---

16. Edwards, "Letter to the Trustees of the College of New Jersey, Oct. 19, 1757," 728.

17. For a brief analysis of the nature of harmony, see Nichols, *Jonathan Edwards's Bible*, 11–14.

of prophecies. Anderson argues that these notebooks, when related to the larger work, "The Harmony of the Old and New Testament," reveal "how in his opinion prophecy and typology, though different modes of discourse, could not be arbitrarily separated."[18]

This is also suggested in Cocceius's view of typology and prophecy. "Prophecy and world history," asserts Van Asselt, "are closely linked in" Cocceius's prophetic theology.[19] Prophecy gives an account for "history in a manner that is very tangible and demonstrable, but never definitive." In fact, it is through Cocceius's prophetic theology that he "is able to introduce the concept of salvation history and the notion of the progressive understanding of revelation."[20] The same principle of history can be applied to Cocceius's use of typology. Van Asselt goes on to say that Cocceius's use of typology can be classified into "a progressive, forward-looking typology (from the past to the present), and a regressive, backward-looking typology (from the present to the past)." Van Asselt thus concludes that "prophecy, analogy, typology, and the history of salvation together form a coordinated system in the hermeneutics of Cocceius."[21]

Thus, these three areas (prophecy, type, and doctrine) do not depart from each other but rather are tightly interwoven. In this light, it could be argued that one encompassing principle of the harmony between the Old and New Testaments has to do with the exact fulfillment of the word of God in all of the historical events of the world.[22] This implies that Edwards's emphasis on history of redemption comes as a necessary outpouring of his view of the harmony of the Bible.

Further, the key to understanding Edwards's view of the harmony of the Bible lies in his own biblical exegesis. In his exegesis, Edwards employs a variety of hermeneutical methods. These exegetical methods include literal, linguistic, allegorical, tropological, anagogical, typological, prophetical, Christological, historical, contextual, theological, and pedagogical. In

---

18. Wallace E. Anderson, "Editor's Introduction to 'Images of Divine Things' and 'Types,'" in *Typological Writings, WJE* 11:12–13.

19. Willem J. Van Asselt, "Covenant, Kingdom, and Friendship: Johannes Cocceius's Federal Framework for Theology," in Johannes Cocceius, *The Doctrine of the Covenant and Testament of God*, trans. Casey Carmichael (Grand Rapids: Reformation Heritage, 2016), xxv.

20. Van Asselt, *The Federal Theology of Johannes Cocceius*, 128.

21. Van Asselt, *The Federal Theology of Johannes Cocceius*, 129.

22. See Edwards, *Letters and Personal Writings*, 728.

other words, he develops the covenant schema from biblical exegesis, in which various exegetical methods are employed to interpret the history of redemption. His biblical exegesis forms the basis of the covenant schema, which in turn provides an overarching interpretive framework for understanding the history of redemption—a doctrinal harmony of the Bible. This echoes Sweeney's argument that Edwards "refused to settle tensions in the Bible one-sidedly."[23] In the following analysis of Edwards's biblical exegesis of the covenant schema, it will be shown that the redemptive-historical theme is grounded in Edwards's interpretation of Scripture. This demonstrates that Edwards's view of the history of redemption in his covenant schema is more appreciative of biblical exegesis than the systematic approach of his Reformed forebears.

STATE OF THE PROBLEM

The foregoing analysis of Edwards's doctrine of the Trinity and the covenant of redemption argued that the history of redemption functions as an interpretive framework. Moreover, as noted, Edwards does not simply follow a traditional Reformed view but rather has a developed pneumatology in his understanding of the covenant of redemption. This gives rise to the question of what Edwards sees as the covenant's basis. That is, how does Edwards use the Bible to formulate the doctrine of the covenant of redemption? As seen in chapter 3, Edwards uses reason as well as Scripture in his consideration of the Trinity. In defense of his use of reason, Edwards comments, "If they call this what is not said in the Scripture, I am not afraid to say twenty things about the Trinity which Scripture never said."[24] In this vein, Sang Hyun Lee argues that although Edwards "was serious about Scripture as the norm and source of theology," he is bold to "engage in philosophical and theological reflection."[25]

While Edwards's view of the covenant of redemption is distinct from Puritan Reformed orthodoxy, it was not devised based on Edwards's metaphysical musings or concern for the Christian life. Moreover, although Edwards uses rationality to explore his understanding of the Trinity, his

23. Sweeney, *Edwards the Exegete*, 217.

24. Edwards, *Miscellany no. 94*, WJE 13:257.

25. Sang Hyun Lee, "Editor's Introduction," in *Writings on the Trinity, Grace, and Faith*, WJE 21:9–10.

conception nonetheless rests on his exegesis of Scripture. Edwards's doctrine of the covenant of redemption derives not from his idealism but from his exegetical considerations focused on the history of redemption. In fact, a study of Edwards's biblical basis for the covenant of redemption reveals that this doctrine aligns with his interpretive framework, the doctrinal harmony of Scripture.

Thus far, no scholarly work has attempted to uncover the relationship between Edwards's biblical exegesis and his doctrine of the covenant of redemption. This chapter will demonstrate that Edwards's exegetical consideration of the doctrine of the covenant of redemption, which focuses on the history of redemption, reveals his desire to perceive the history of redemption within a governing principle of the doctrinal harmony of Scripture. The first section examines Edwards's use of biblical texts to find evidence for the doctrine of the Trinity. The second section explores Edwards's biblical approach to the covenant of redemption. The final section presents the exegetical methods Edwards employs to shape his view of the covenant of redemption. The chapter will demonstrate that Edwards's understanding of the covenant of redemption rests on his biblical, linguistic, spiritual, typological, and historical considerations of the history of redemption. The chapter begins by reexamining the Trinitarian writings of Edwards, including his exegetical works on the covenant of redemption.

BIBLICAL BASIS OF THE THREE
PERSONS OF THE TRINITY

In *Discourse on the Trinity*, Edwards begins his portrayal of the Trinity with an interpretation of 1 John 4:8, 16, "God is love."[26] In these verses, Edwards finds evidence for the persons of the Trinity. He argues that love is "essential and necessary to the Deity." The reasoning continues that love itself assumes a subject and an object since "all love respects another."[27] Thus, for Edwards, the word "love" implies a plurality of persons. In his words, "By love here the Apostle certainly means something beside that which is commonly called self-love, that is very improperly called love, and is a thing

---

26. Edwards, "Discourse on the Trinity," in *Writings on the Trinity, Grace, and Faith*, WJE 21:114.

27. Edwards, "Discourse on the Trinity," 114.

of an exceeding diverse nature from that affection or virtue of love the Apostle is speaking of."[28] Edwards seeks to consider authorial intention as well as context. In other words, he does not attempt to invent the concept of persons through the use of these verses but rather seeks to affirm what he believes the Apostle intended to reveal through the word *love*.

After considering authorial intention, Edwards moves on to context. "In the context of which place," Edwards writes, "I think it is plainly intimated to us that the Holy Spirit is that love, as in the twelfth and thirteenth verses." Edwards contends that verses 12–13 describe the Holy Spirit as love "dwelling" in believers. That "God lives in us" (v. 12) signifies the giving of the Holy Spirit to believers. This interpretation, according to Edwards, is in accordance with "the last verses of the foregoing chapter."[29] In *Treatise on Grace*, Edwards states, "I have before observed that the Scripture abundantly reveals that the way in which Christ dwells in the saints is by his Spirit's dwelling in them."[30] Thus, the Holy Spirit's indwelling is the manner Christ dwells in believers. After considering the authorial intent and the context of the verses, Edwards interprets the Holy Spirit as God dwelling in us in terms of the benefit of the covenant of redemption.

In light of this interest in the Holy Spirit, he then describes the Son as the second person of the Trinity. To do so, he uses words such as idea, "love," "representation," "brightness," "delight," "form," "wisdom," and "logos". These words, he argues, are rooted in Scripture. "Nothing can more agree with the account the Scripture gives of the Son of God, his being in the form of God and his express and perfect image and representation."[31] In support of this, Edwards references 2 Corinthians 4:4 ("Lest the light of the glorious gospel of Christ, who is the image of God"); Colossians 1:15 ("Who is the image of the invisible God"); Philippians 2:6 ("Who being in the form of God"); and Hebrews 1:3 ("Who being the brightness of his glory, and the express image of his person").[32]

All of these verses not only include the term "image" or an analogous word but also belong to texts that refer to Christ's redemptive work in

---

28. Edwards, "Discourse on the Trinity," 114.
29. Edwards, "Discourse on the Trinity," 121.
30. Edwards, "Treatise on Grace," in *Writings on the Trinity, Grace, and Faith*, 185.
31. Edwards, "Discourse on the Trinity," 117.
32. Edwards, "Discourse on the Trinity," 117.

relation to the Trinity. First, in 2 Corinthians 4:4, the word "image" parallels "the light." In Philippians 2:6, the writer refers to the "form," a concept similar to "image." Likewise, in Hebrews 1:3, the writer refers to "brightness," another term akin to "image."[33] Second, these biblical texts appear to reflect a Trinitarian narrative in which Christ's work of redemption and the redemptive economy of the Trinity are clearly expressed. In other words, not only are the terms Edwards employs drawn from scriptural exposition that describes Christ as the image of God, but Edwards's view of the Trinity is bound up with his view that the history of redemption began and was realized through the covenant of redemption.

Further scriptural evidences that Edwards uses to support his view of the Son as the idea involving the image, representation, love, delight, wisdom, and logos of God are John 12:45–46; 14:7–9; 15:22–24; 3:35; 5:20; 8:12; Exodus 33:14; Isaiah 63:9; 1 Corinthians 1:24; Luke 11:49; Matthew 11:27; 23:34; Proverbs 8:30; and 1 John 4:8.[34] A close examination of these verses suggests that Edwards tends to rely on the New Testament, especially Johannine literature, which portrays Christ as redeemer.

Why does Edwards rely so heavily on Johannine literature in his exposition of the persons of the Trinity?[35] A possible answer is that Edwards's interpretation of Johannine literature focuses on Christ's role as the revelation of God in the history of redemption. This would explain Edwards's use of words that parallel the idea of the image of God in his description of Christ. In his *Discourse*, Edwards portrays five aspects of the Son: the "representation of the Godhead," "delight," "face," "brightness," and "God's own eternal and perfect idea."[36]

While these five phrases attempt to depict Christ as the image of God, all of them are also associated with the concept of revelation. For example, in his discussion of an epistemological understanding of the Philip episode,[37]

---

33. Edwards, "Discourse on the Trinity," 117.

34. Edwards, "Discourse on the Trinity," 118–21.

35. According to McClymond, one of most important Johannine motifs in Edwards appears to be a "motive for salvation-history, and for salvation itself." Michael J. McClymond, "Of His Fullness Have All We Received," in *Jonathan Edwards and Scripture*, ed. David P. Barshinger and Douglas A. Sweeney (New York: Oxford University Press, 2018), 166.

36. Edwards, "Discourse on the Trinity," 117–19.

37. Edwards cites John 14:7–9, "If ye had known me, ye should have known my Father also: and from henceforth ye know him, and have seen him. Philip saith unto him, Lord, show us

Edwards mentions that to see something is to have an idea of it in terms of its "intents and purposes." In other words, to see an image is nothing other than having the idea of it. Edwards applies this interpretation to John 15:22–24 (v. 23, "whoever hates me hates my Father"). This indicates that Edwards understands Christ as the image of God in terms of Christ revealing God. This is clear from Edwards's own words: "But that the Son of God is God's own eternal and perfect idea is a thing that we have yet much more revealed in God's Word."[38]

With respect to Edwards's notion of Christ as the perfect idea of God, two considerations are of particular importance. The first is that Edwards emphasizes Christ as the wisdom and logos of God. For Edwards, "things" in God's Word refers to three aspects of the Son. First, Christ is "the wisdom of God."[39] That is, the Son as wisdom is "the same with God's perfect and eternal idea." For evidence of this, Edwards cites Proverbs 8:22–31, which depicts Wisdom calling out. According to Edwards, these verses demonstrate that the Son, as "the personal wisdom of God," was present before the creation of the world.[40] Second, Christ is the "logos of God," which means "the inward word" of God. Thus, "the outward word," such as "the Scripture," originates from the inward word. In this sense, the Bible has "its own interpreter," that is, Christ. Finally, the Son as the idea of God refers to the "Amen," which implies "truth." Edwards argues that there is no other "original and universal truth" except for Christ, who is the "eternal or infinite knowledge or idea."[41] Hence, Edwards's description of wisdom is associated with revelation.

The second consideration is that for Edwards, the realization of wisdom is geared toward Christ's redemptive works. That is, wisdom is associated with the saving presence of God. This is proved by Edwards's preference for the word "perfect." He uses this word to describe the Son as the idea of God and indicate nothing less than God's communicable attributes. Although

---

the Father, and it sufficeth us. Jesus saith unto him, Have I been so long time with [you, and] yet hast thou not seen me. Philip? He that hath seen me hath seen the Father; and how sayest thou, show us the Father." See Edwards, "Discourse on the Trinity," 118.

38. Edwards, "Discourse on the Trinity," 119.
39. Edwards, "Discourse on the Trinity," 119.
40. Edwards, "Discourse on the Trinity," 119–20.
41. Edwards, "Discourse on the Trinity," 120.

Edwards does not refer to the communicable attributes of God, Edwards's idea of perfection reflects these attributes. As Bavinck argues,

> All the attributes of God discussed above are summed up in his perfection. Accordingly, in speaking of God's perfection here, we are not referring exclusively to his moral perfection (i.e., his goodness or holiness), but mean that God is the sum total of all his perfections, the One than whom no greater, higher, or better can exist either in thought or reality. In other words, God fully answers to the idea of God. A creature is perfect, that is, perfect in its kind and in its creaturely finite way, when the idea that is its norm is fully realized in it. Similarly, God is perfect inasmuch as the idea of God fully corresponds to his being and nature.[42]

The Son as the perfect idea of God is considered the same as the Father since God "fully answers to the idea" of himself. Given this, there is a high degree of consistency between the perfect idea and its realization. Wisdom, in a practical sense, is concerned with ultimate reality involving the history of redemption.

Edwards's focus on the realization of revelation can be clearly seen in his description of the Son as the perfect idea of God. He argues:

> And how well doth this agree with his office of being the great prophet and teacher of mankind, the light of the world, and the revealer of God to creatures .... John 8:12, "I am the light of the world." Matt 11:27, "No man knoweth the Father, save the Son, and he to whomsoever the Son will reveal him." John 1:18, "No man hath seen God at any time; the only begotten Son, which is in the bosom of the Father, he hath declared him." Who can be so properly appointed to be [the] revealer of God to the world, as that person who is God's own perfect idea or understanding of himself? Who can be so properly appointed to be the light by which God's glory shall appear to creatures, as he is that effulgence of his glory by which he appears to himself? And this is intimated to us in the Scripture to be the reason why Christ is the light of the world and the revealer

of God to men, because he is the image of God ... 2 Cor 4:4, "Lest the light of the glorious gospel of Christ, who is the image of God, should shine unto them." John 12:45-46, "And he that seeth me seeth him that sent me. I am come a light into the world, that whosoever believeth on me should not abide in darkness."[43]

The biblical texts to which Edwards refers point to Christ as the revealer of God and redeemer of sinners. For Edwards, the office of Christ correctly corresponds to his nature. This means that Edwards's exegetical consideration of the Son is interwoven with his interest in the office of the Son as mediator.

Having discussed the relationship between the Son and his office of redemption, Edwards moves on to the nature of the Holy Spirit. According to Edwards, the Holy Spirit is the personification of the divine will. He argues for this as follows. First, the "Godhead or the divine nature and essence" has its subsistence in "love." Second, the name of the Holy Spirit indicates "the disposition, inclination, or temper of mind." Third, "the office of the Holy Spirit" relates to creatures in three ways: (1) to quicken, enliven, and beautify creatures; (2) "to sanctify intelligent creatures"; and (3) "to comfort and delight them." Fourth, a "dove" as "the symbol" of the Holy Spirit implies "the emblem of love." Fifth, the Holy Spirit, as the act of the divine will, is confirmed by the "types of the Holy Ghost," such as "oil," which signifies a "soft, smooth-flowing and diffusive nature." Sixth, there are "metaphors" of the Holy Spirit, such as "water, fire, breath, wind, oil, wine, a spring, a river, a being poured out and shed forth, a being breathed forth." Seventh, believers' "communion with God" is contained in "their partaking of the Holy Ghost." Finally, the Holy Spirit is the "blessing" itself from "the Father and the Son."[44]

The scriptural proofs that Edwards uses to support these attributes of the Holy Spirit include Proverbs 8:30; 1 John 1:3; 4:8, 12–13; Numbers 14:24; Psalm 36:7–9; 51:10; 68:13; 133:2; Luke 9:55; 1 Thessalonians 1:6; 5:23; 1 Peter 3:4; Ephesians 1:3, 14; 4:23; 2 Peter 1:4; John 3:6; 4:10–15; 7:38–39; 10:14; 14:16–18, 21, 23; 17:13, 22–23, 26; Genesis 1:2; Romans 5:5; 8:9–10; 11:36; 14:17;

---

43. Edwards, "Discourse on the Trinity," 120–21.
44. Edwards, "Discourse on the Trinity," 121–27.

15:30; 2 Corinthians 1:22; 5:5; 6:6; Colossians 1:8; Galatians 3:2, 13–14; 5:13; Acts 9:31; 13:52; Song of Songs 1:15; 5:2; 2:14; 6:9; Matthew 3:17; 7:11; Leviticus 1:14; Ezekiel 1:28; 47; Revelation 4:3; 10:1; 21; 22:1; Titus 3:5–6; Hebrews 12:10; Daniel 2:22; 1 Corinthians 2:10; 8:6; Isaiah 54:11–12; 1 Chronicles 29:2.[45] The list could go on, given his exposition of the Holy Spirit as saving grace in *Treatise on Grace*.[46]

Compared with the scriptural proofs Edwards provides for the nature of the Father and the Son, these references for the nature of the Holy Spirit are considerable. As Ralph Cunnington points out, Edwards devotes about "two-thirds of his discourse on the Trinity to the Holy Spirit."[47] This shows that Edwards is preoccupied with the nature of the Holy Spirit.

Moreover, Edwards's exegetical concern with the Holy Spirit rests not on the doctrine of the covenant of redemption itself but on the theme of the history of redemption. For instance, while Edwards attempts to reveal the attributes of the Holy Spirit by using many biblical texts, two foci come to the forefront. First, he emphasizes the Holy Spirit's significant role in the work of redemption in terms of the equality of the Holy Spirit to the other persons of the Trinity. This is evident in Edwards's approach to the Bible. Before he even discusses the Holy Spirit, Edwards describes the Deity, which is an important key to understanding the divine attributes of the Holy Spirit. When discussing the biblical texts he uses to argue for the divine attributes of the Holy Spirit, Edwards repeatedly emphasizes that the Holy Spirit is the mutual love of the Trinity. Thus, the Holy Spirit, as the Trinity's mutual love, is the manner of the Godhead's existence and action. This explains what Edwards intends by the phrase "The Deity becomes all act."[48] Thus, all the biblical texts Edwards uses as evidence of love being the way of existence and action of the Godhead testify to the equality of persons in the Trinity.

---

45. Edwards, "Discourse on the Trinity," 121–38.

46. In "Treatise on Grace," Edwards devotes much space to the description of the Holy Spirit as grace, emphasizing the importance of the Holy Spirit as saving grace in salvation and the Christian life in response to the Holy Spirit's dwelling in believers. In doing this, Edwards employs a large number of scriptural proofs. See Edwards, "Treatise on Grace," 153–97.

47. Ralph Cunnington, "A Critical Examination of Jonathan Edwards' Doctrine of the Trinity," *Themelios (Online)* 39, no. 2 (July 2014): 222n6, http://themelios.thegospelcoalition.org/article/a-critical-examination-of-jonathan-edwardss-doctrine-of-the-trinity.

48. Edwards, "Discourse on the Trinity," 121.

Second, Edwards's view of the Holy Spirit as the mutual love of the Trinity is closely related to the Holy Spirit's work in the history of redemption. Edwards writes, "It is a confirmation that the Holy Ghost is God's love and delight, because the saints' communion with God consists in their partaking of the Holy Ghost." According to Edwards, communion with God is "twofold": communion with God and communion among believers. This is supported by 1 John 1:3, "That ye also may have fellowship with us: and truly our fellowship is with the Father, and with his Son Jesus Christ." Further, 2 Peter 1:4 describes believers as "partakers of the divine nature," an idea also found in Hebrews 12:10, John 17:13, 22–23, and 2 Corinthians 13:14.[49] Additionally, Edwards asserts that Romans 5:5, "The love of God is shed abroad in our hearts by the Holy Ghost which is given unto us," signifies "the manner of communicating the Spirit of God himself."[50] In this way, the love among the Godhead is at work in the minds of believers.

Edwards's interest in the role of the Holy Spirit in the history of redemption is distinct from Puritan Reformed orthodoxy. In fact, Edwards believes Reformed orthodoxy has overlooked the role of the Holy Spirit. He asserts:

> If we suppose no more than used to be supposed about the Holy Ghost, the concern of the Holy Ghost in the work of redemption is not equal with the Father's and the Son's, nor is there an equal part of the glory of this work belonging to him: merely to apply to us or immediately to give or hand to us the blessing purchased after it was purchased (as subservient to the other two persons), is but a little thing to the purchasing of it by the paying an infinite price by Christ's offering up himself in sacrifice to procure it.[51]

Thus, Edwards believes that the doctrine of the covenant of redemption in Reformed orthodoxy focuses too much on the relationship between the Father and the Son. Accordingly, Edwards is uncomfortable with saying that the Holy Spirit's role is merely to apply the benefits of the covenant of redemption. Considering the equality of the three persons of the Trinity,

---

49. Edwards, "Discourse on the Trinity," 129–30.
50. Edwards, "Discourse on the Trinity," 141.
51. Edwards, "Discourse on the Trinity," 137.

Edwards assumes that the emphasis of Reformed orthodoxy on the Father and the Son tends to weaken the role of the Holy Spirit.

Given Edwards's view on the Holy Spirit, Cocceius deserves a mention in this context. With respect to Cocceius's view of the role of the Holy Spirit in the covenant of redemption, Willem Van Asselt argues:

> With regards to the role of the Holy Spirit within the *pactum salutis*, therefore, we must conclude that the Holy Spirit is certainly involved in the immanent Trinitarian pact, but not as a legal partner. He is not a negotiating subject, but an implementing subject in his role as the *potential Deitatis*. It is not surprising, however, that the Holy Spirit is not a legal partner in the pact. His work, of course, does not involve any humiliation or submission, as does that of the Son. The Holy Spirit does not submit himself to the law (of works) in the way that the Son submits himself to the Father in the *pactum salutis*.[52]

According to Van Asselt, Cocceius asserts that the Holy Spirit is not subservient to the Son and the Father in the covenant of redemption since the Holy Spirit is not a legal partner of the covenant. The same argument is found in Edwards, who contends that the Holy Spirit's subjection to the Son as God-man does not involve "abasement" since his subjection results from "the economy of the Trinity." In other words, the subjection the Holy Spirit gives to the Son arises not from the establishment of the covenant of redemption but from the economy of the Father. Thus, the Holy Spirit is subject to the Son not in terms of "abasement" but in terms of "the gift by the Father" as his "economical character."[53]

However, there are subtle differences between Cocceius and Edwards with regard to their denial of the subjection of the Holy Spirit in the covenant of redemption. First, as seen in the previous section, while Edwards emphasizes the equality of the three persons of the Godhead, Cocceius does not regard the concept of humiliation in terms of the equality of the Trinity. In other words, Cocceius's portrayal of the Holy Spirit's subjection to the Son is in the context of the Father and the Son as the legal parties

---

52. Van Asselt, *The Federal Theology of Johannes Cocceius*, 235.

53. Edwards, *Miscellany no. 1062, WJE* 20:441.

of the covenant of redemption. Edwards, in contrast, focuses on the Holy Spirit himself.

Second, although both Cocceius and Edwards involve the role of the Holy Spirit in the economy of the persons of the Trinity, Edwards's emphasis on the Holy Spirit's role within the Trinity comes more to the forefront compared with Cocceius. For instance, offering a brief summary of the roles of the Trinity in the covenant, Cocceius attributes the roles of "legislator" and "ruler" to the Father and that of "testator" to the Son. However, the Holy Spirit is described as the one who "exercises the power of the Godhead by regenerating us, and its charity by uniting us to God and by sealing our inheritance."[54] While the Father and the Son are considered the legal parties of the eternal pact, the role of the Holy Spirit is related merely to the application and realization of the covenant of redemption. Van Asselt provides a summary of Cocceius's view:

> Cocceius distinguishes three aspects of the Spirit's functioning within the counsel of peace: 1) the power of God (*potentia Dei*); 2) love (*charitas*); and 3) sealing (*Obsignatio*). These, however, are externally, directed movements of the Spirit, in which *power* highlights the realization of the testament in those who are reborn, *love* emphasizes the element of fellowship with God, and *sealing* accentuates the assurance, as well as the eschatological element. There is no mention, however, of the internal functions of the Spirit within the counsel of peace; Cocceius is silent on this point.[55]

As Van Asselt rightly notes, for Cocceius, the Holy Spirit is involved in "the immanent Trinitarian pact." However, Cocceius does not mention "the internal functions of the Spirit within the counsel of peace."[56]

As noted in the first section, Edwards identifies the Holy Spirit as the mutual love of the Father and the Son. As Studebaker rightly points out, the Holy Spirit for Edwards is "not the third with whom the Father and the Son share their mutual love, but the subsistence of the Father and the

---

54. Johannes Cocceius, *The Doctrine of the Covenant and Testament of God*, trans. Casey Carmichael, (Grand Rapids: Reformation Heritage, 2016), 88–89.

55. Van Asselt, *The Federal Theology of Johannes Cocceius*, 234.

56. Van Asselt, *The Federal Theology of Johannes Cocceius*, 234.

Son's mutual love."[57] The Holy Spirit is "not a loving and beloved member of the Trinitarian society, but the divine love itself."[58] This relationship implies that although Edwards does not refer to the Holy Spirit as one of the contracting parties, the work of the Holy Spirit is ontologically involved in the eternal pact between the Father and the Son.

A brief comparison between Cocceius and Edwards hints at the underlying difference in Edwards's exegetical consideration of the Trinity, which focuses on the work of redemption.[59] Not only does Edwards's discussion of the Holy Spirit throughout the *Discourse* emphasize the role and equality of the Holy Spirit within the Trinity, but Edwards also pays attention to the ontological attendance of the Holy Spirit in the covenant of redemption.

Edwards's use of the biblical texts must be seen in this context. In other words, all of the verses attributed to the exposition of the Holy Spirit refer not only to the equality of the Holy Spirit but also to the abundant and profound role of the Spirit in the history of redemption. In this way, Edwards attempts to do justice to the doctrine of the Trinity: "Under the Old Testament, the church of God was not told near so much about the Trinity as they are now; .... And so also it has come to pass in the church, being told more about the incarnation and the satisfaction of Christ and other glorious gospel doctrines."[60] This suggests that Edwards employs, reads, understands, and interprets the biblical texts in the light of the New Testament and doctrinal history, in the hope that his portrayal of the Trinity, particularly of Holy Spirit, will be consistent with the biblical witness.

---

57. Steven M. Studebaker and Robert W. Caldwell III, *The Trinitarian Theology of Jonathan Edwards: Text, Context, and Application* (Burlington, VT: Ashgate, 2012), 121.

58. Amy Plantinga Pauw, *The Supreme Harmony of All: The Trinitarian Theology of Jonathan Edwards* (Grand Rapids: Eerdmans, 2002), 44.

59. This is not to suggest that the theme of the history of redemption for Puritan Reformed theologians was unimportant. Rather, as seen in Cocceius, the history of redemption plays a critical role in their approach to biblical exegesis. According to Van Asselt, Cocceius draws his attention not to "the work of the Spirit within the pact" but to "the Spirit's work outside of the counsel of peace, that is, to the Spirit's work in the history of redemption." See Van Asselt, *The Federal Theology of Johannes Cocceius*, 235.

60. Edwards, "Discourse on the Trinity," 139–40.

EXEGETICAL THEOLOGY FOR THE
COVENANT OF REDEMPTION

What has so far been said is only intended to briefly indicate Edwards's interest within his exegetical consideration of the Trinity and offer a first approximation of his understanding of its nature. As noted, Edwards uses various biblical texts in describing the persons of the Godhead, maintaining their equality and distinction. The next section will show that Edwards's use of biblical texts regarding the covenant of redemption is closely related to his concern for God's supreme sovereignty and divine excellency through God's works of redemption.

GOD'S SOVEREIGNTY

For Edwards, God's sovereignty in offering redemption to believers is a theological fountainhead for all other doctrines. He believes the basis of the covenant of redemption is in the persons of the Trinity themselves. Thus, it is not difficult to see that the agreement and stipulation among the persons of the Godhead implies God's unchangeable love and promise to his people. In the "Blank Bible," Edwards cites Genesis 1:26 as evidence for "a consultation of the persons of the Trinity" in the creation of man. According to Edwards, Genesis 1:26, "Let us make man," shows that "the Father employed the Son and the Holy Ghost" in creating man. Edwards elaborates, "The Son endued man with understanding and reason. The Holy Ghost endued him with a holy will and inclination, with original righteousness."[61] As Stephen Stein comments, it is not obvious why "Edwards assigned the endowments of the 'understanding and reason' and of the 'will and inclination' " to the Son and the Holy Spirit, respectively.[62] However, it is apparent that Edwards assigns distinct roles to the three persons as the operators of the covenant of redemption.

For Edwards, the divine consultation among the divine persons assumes the Father and Son as the contracting parties. In his sermon on John 15:10, Edwards portrays the nature of the Father's command and the Son's obedience in the covenant of redemption. The Son obeyed the command of the Father to come "into the world," take "upon him the human nature," and

---

61. Edwards, The "Blank Bible," WJE 24:126.
62. Stephen J. Stein, "Editor's Introduction," in The "Blank Bible," 26.

dwell "among" people. Christ "became Mediatour by virtue of the covenant of redemption" or the "eternal Agreement between the father and the son, wherein the son Agreed to be the mediatour between G[od] and man." Edwards finds in Psalm 40:6 that it is in obedience that the Father delights. Christ speaks "nothing but what the Father Appointed him Joh 8. 26."[63] Finally, Edwards describes the nature of the commandments the Father gave the Son in the covenant of redemption.

A description of the Father and the Son as contracting parties of the covenant of redemption is also found in Luke 22:29, "καγω διατιθεμαι υμιν καθος διεθετο μοι ο πατηρ μου βασιλειαν, I do by covenant dispose unto you a kingdom, as my father by covenant disposed unto me." The term διατιθεμαι implies to "make a contract or testament" or to "appoint or dispose by covenant or testament." This word usage is also found in Acts 3:25, "Ye are the children of the prophets and of the covenant which God made (διαθησομαι) with our fathers." It is again seen in Hebrews 8:10, "This is the covenant I will make (διαθησομαι) with the house of Israel." This leads Edwards to conclude that the word διαθηκη indicates covenant.[64]

Moreover, Edwards emphasizes the free will of the Son in his appointment as mediator. Edwards describes the nature of the Son's appointment in 1 Peter 1:20. He uses this text to formulate his doctrine that "the love wherewith God has loved his saints, is an everlasting love." In fact, he attributes one of the grounds of God's everlasting love to the covenant of redemption, in which God showed his love to believers before creation. In his words, God created "the whole world—sun, moon, and stars, heaven and earth—out of love to them." God's love for his people stems from "what was one from eternity, particularly in the covenant of redemption that made between the Father and the Son." Jesus Christ was appointed as "security" for God's people. This is supported by 1 Peter 1:20: "Who verily was ordained before the foundation of the world, but was manifest in these last times for you." For Edwards, this verse implies that "Christ became engaged to the Father to become incarnate" as well as to "go through such

---

63. Edwards, "190. John 15:10 (Mar. 1736)," in *Sermons and Discourses, 1731-1732*, WJEO 46:L. 5v.

64. Edwards, *Miscellany no. 1064*, WJE 20:445.

great labors and extreme sufferings."[65] Therefore, the certainty of salvation for believers is closely bound to the eternal pact between the Father and the Son.

Edwards's emphasis on the mutuality of the covenant is also found in Cocceius, who stresses God's unilateral and bilateral actions in the covenant. In *The Doctrine of the Covenant and Testament of God*, Cocceius argues:

> One may be sure that the pact (between God and the Father and the Son) is not with fallen man but with the Mediator. To be sure, the will of the Father giving the Son to be head and λυτρωτην, Redeemer, of a foreknown people, and the will of the Son presenting Himself to attend to this salvation, contain the account of the agreement.[66]

Cocceius maintains that the validity of the covenant rests on a pact between the Father and the Son.[67] This emphasis on God's sovereignty in salvation appears in other Reformed scholastics, such as Anthony Burgess. Burgess contends that a covenant assumes "agreement" and "stipulations" between two parties, which in turn make the covenant valid. The agreement and stipulations involve "a promise" that both parties should keep.[68] Although Burgess's statement regards the covenant of works, the meaning of *covenant* can also be applied to the covenant of redemption. In this case, Edwards's description of the pact between the Father and the Son shares the emphasis on God's sovereignty as found in his Reformed predecessors.

THE EXCELLENCY OF GOD

As noted earlier, based on Psalm 40:6, Edwards thinks that the Son's obedience is solely what the Father delights in. Edwards thus relates the Son's obedience to the excellency of his reward. "It shows," Edwards argues, "the infinite dignity and excellency of the Father, that the Son so delighted and prized his honor and glory, that he stooped infinitely low rather than man's

---

65. Edwards, "The Everlasting Love of God (Jer 31:3)," in *Sermons and Discourses, 1734–1738*, WJE 19:479–80.

66. Cocceius, *The Doctrine of the Covenant and Testament of God*, 85.

67. Cocceius, *The Doctrine of the Covenant and Testament of God*, 85.

68. Anthony Burgess, *Vindiciae Legis, Or, A Vindication of the Morall Law and the Covenants, from the Errours of Papists, Arminians, Socinians, and More Especially Antinomians*, 121.

salvation should be to the injury of that honor and glory."[69] This relationship between Christ's obedience and reward raises the question of how
Edwards understands the excellency of the Son.

Given this context, it is not surprising that Edwards further explores
the nature of the Son's obedience. He argues in various places that the
Son's obedience is not compulsory but voluntarily, thus making clear his
belief that the Son is appointed as a mediator by his free agreement. In
his sermon on Psalm 40:6-8, "The Sacrifice of Christ Acceptable," Edwards
addresses this issue. Christ's sacrifice originated from his "own power."
No obligation was given to Christ until "he became mediator." Thus, the
sacrifice of Christ is based on his voluntary act "freely consented to in the
covenant of redemption."[70] For more evidence of Christ's voluntary obedience, Edwards quotes Zechariah 13:7, "Awake, O sword, against the man
that is my fellow." He believes the word "fellow" signifies the equality of
the Father and the Son, thus proving that what Christ offers is "his own."[71]

For Edwards, the Son's willingness to obey is essential to understanding the excellency of God. But what is also essential to this understanding
is the glorious state of Christ in his reward. With respect to that reward,
Edwards argues that Isaiah 53:10-12 signifies as follows:

> The success of Christ in his work of redemption, in bringing home
> souls to himself, applying his saving benefits by his spirit, and the
> advancement of the kingdom of grace in the world, is the reward
> especially promised to him by his Father in the covenant of redemp-
> tion, for the hard and difficult service he performed while in the
> form of a servant.[72]

In these verses, Edwards finds clear evidence for Christ's success being his
reward. In "Notes on Scripture" regarding this same text, Edwards argues
that Isaiah 53:12 describes the reward as "Christ's portion," which is "the
most perfect and glorious kingdom of the earth." He then cites Isaiah 60:13

---

69. Edwards, "Discourse on the Trinity," 136.

70. Edwards, "The Sacrifice of Christ Acceptable" (Ps 40:6-8), in *Sermon and Discourses 1723-1729*, WJE 14:451.

71. Edwards, "The Sacrifice of Christ Acceptable," 451.

72. Edwards, "True Saints, When Absent from the Body, Are Present with the Lord (Oct. 1747)," in *Sermons and Discourses, 1743-1758*, WJE 25:238.

and Psalm 72:10 as descriptions of the great glory of Christ's rewards.[73] Edwards's interpretation of Isaiah 60:13 and Psalm 72:10 reflects his belief that Christ's reward has been fulfilled in the history of redemption.[74]

In "Notes on Scripture," no. 351, Edwards takes various verses as proof of Christ's reward. He argues that these verses have been fulfilled and will be fulfilled in the future. He writes, "See Is. 60:5–6, 9–10, 13, 16–17; and 61:6, which was fulfilled in the days of Constantine the Great, and will be more gloriously fulfilled at the fall of Antichrist. Thus the wealth of the sinner is laid up for the just, and Christ shall have a portion divided to him with the great, and shall divide the spoil with the strong [Is. 53:12]."[75] Edwards understands that it is this portion, including all the nations that Christ obtains throughout the history of redemption, that is the reward of Christ.

Similarly, Edwards uses 1 Corinthians 15:24–28 as the evidence for the economic order of the Trinity, which as time goes on will become visible much more than the state of the economy established before creation was apparent. In Miscellany no. 1062, Edwards asserts:

> But then the economical order of the persons of [the] Trinity shall yet remain, whereby the Father acts as head of the society and supreme Lord of all, and the Son and the Spirit subject unto him. Yea, this economical order shall not only remain, but shall then, and on that occasion, become more visible and conspicuous; and the establishment of things by the covenant of redemption shall then as it were give place to this economy as prior. For thus the Apostle represents the matter, I Cor. 15:24–28.[76]

For Edwards, then, the economic order of the persons of the Trinity will appear more clearly when the Son completes his work of redemption at the end of the world.

Concerning the promise in the covenant of redemption, a similar assertion is found in Edwards's interpretation of the same biblical text in "Notes on Scripture," no. 158. "But with respect to government," he argues, "God

---

73. Edwards, *Notes on Scripture*, WJE 15:52.
74. Edwards, *Notes on Scripture*, 52.
75. Edwards, *Notes on Scripture*, 337.
76. Edwards, *Miscellany no. 1062*, WJE 20:434.

will be respected as Supreme Orderer, and Christ with his church united to him and dependent on him, shall together be received of the benefit of his government." Edwards's entries on 1 Corinthians 15:24 in "Miscellanies" nos. 86, 609, and 736 portray Christ's eternal reign over his kingdom as the result of his obtaining the reward.[77] That Christ's rule over his kingdom is eternal is proved by Bible texts such as Luke 1:33, Romans 11:29, Isaiah 9:7, Micah 4:7, and Hebrews 1:8.[78]

Given his view of the nature of the rewards Christ acquires throughout the whole history of redemption, it is not difficult to see that Edwards's exegetical consideration proceeds from his concern of the harmony of the Bible, in which the redemptive-historical theme is explained. From Matthew 25:34,[79] Edwards argues that all things happened for the work of redemption. The persons of the Trinity "were confederated in a design and a covenant of redemption, in which covenant the Father appointed the Son and the Son had undertaken their work, and all things to be accomplished in their work were stipulated and agreed." The work of creation refers to the "work before man fell." Thus, Edward argues that "the creating heaven was in order to the Work of Redemption."[80]

For Edwards, all of God's works are focused on the work of redemption, which incorporates all the works of God. Edwards distinguishes among the decrees of God, especially the work of creation, the "work of providence," and "the work of redemption." Edwards believes God's providence is "the end of God's works of creation," and thus is considered as the "building of an house" or the "forming an engine or machine."[81] He believes God's work of providence "is greater than the work of creation." However, the work of providence is lesser than the work of redemption since the latter is "the sum of God's works of providence." As a result, the work of redemption is "the greatest of all the works of God," while all of the other works are considered "part of it [the work of redemption]" or "appendages" to it. In

---

77. Edwards, *Miscellany no. 86, WJE* 13:250–51; *Miscellany no. 609, WJE* 18:144; *Miscellany no. 736, WJE* 18:359–61.

78. Edwards, *Miscellany no. 736, WJE* 359.

79. Edwards does not quote but inserts the citation Matthew 25:34, "Come, ye blessed of my Father, inherit the kingdom prepared for you from the foundation of the world." See Edwards, *A History of the Work of Redemption, WJE* 9:118n3.

80. Edwards, *A History of the Work of Redemption*, 118.

81. Edwards, *A History of the Work of Redemption*, 118.

this regard, Edwards asserts that "all the decrees of God" are reducible to the "eternal covenant of redemption."[82] This means that all the works of God are established and administered in accordance with the covenant of redemption. Here, Edwards makes no distinction between the covenant of redemption and the work of redemption. However, for Edwards, the covenant of redemption is included within the work of redemption. Thus, Edwards concludes that "the work of redemption is the great subject of the whole Bible."[83] As David Barshinger finds, the redemptive-historical approach "gave structure to Edwards' theology" and was "a framework" for interpreting Scripture.[84]

As noted above, Edwards's interpretation of 1 Corinthians 15:24 is closely related to the theme of the history of redemption. Paul Ramsey, citing Edwards in *A History of the Work of Redemption*, points out that Edwards makes two references to the covenantal frame: "Retrospective reference to the covenant protologically" and "the eschatological completion of *that* covenant."[85] In the twenty-ninth sermon of his thirty-sermon series on the history of redemption, Edwards writes, "Now shall all the promises made to Christ by God the Father before the foundation of the world, the promises of the covenant of redemption, be fully accomplished."[86] He believes the fulfillment of the promises of the covenant of redemption is linked to the eschatological completion of that covenant. Edwards writes:

> And as Christ when he first entered upon the Work of Redemption, after the fall of man, had the kingdom committed to him of the Father, and took on himself the administration of the affairs of the universe, to manage all so as to subserve to the purposes of this affair; so now that work being finished, he will deliver up the kingdom to the Father, I Cor. 15:24, "Then cometh when he shall have delivered up the kingdom to God, even the Father; when he shall have put down all rule and all authority and power."[87]

---

82. Edwards, *A History of the Work of Redemption*, 118.
83. Edwards, *A History of the Work of Redemption*, 118.
84. Barshinger, *Jonathan Edwards and the Psalms*, 5.
85. Paul Ramsey, "Appendix III: Heaven Is a Progressive State," in *Ethical Writings*, WJE 8:737.
86. Edwards, *A History of the Work of Redemption*, 509.
87. Edwards, *A History of the Work of Redemption*, 510.

As Ramsey rightly notes, the commission of Christ as the Father's delegate "was to subserve" God's grand design of the history of redemption, so that Christ's redemptive works cease when his kingdom is fully delivered to the Father.[88]

Regarding Christ's rewards, Edwards's interpretation of John 17:24, part of the high priestly prayer, is notable:

> By the glory that God had given Christ, he [John] meant the glory that God was about to exalt him to at his ascension into heaven, and sitting at God's right hand, wherein he should be invested with kingly glory; as appears by the beginning of his prayer, where he prays for that glory and exaltation and dominion over all flesh that … was to be given him in reward for his going through the work of our redemption, as may be evident by comparing John 17:1, John 17:2, John 17:4…. And therefore, Christ's crown and kingdom, that he has in reward for his doing the work of redemption, shall not cease at the day of judgment, for not till then will he have perfected all that belongs to this work.[89]

John 17:24 for Edwards makes it clear that Christ's rewards will be fully acquired at the end of the world. In other words, Edwards understands Christ's rewards in the covenant of redemption in terms of the excellency of the glory of God. Therefore, Edwards's biblical exegesis of the covenant of redemption focuses on God's sovereignty before creation and excellency after the covenant's fulfillment. The underlying implication of Edwards's interest in the sovereignty and excellency of God signifies that Edwards understands the Bible, and specifically the covenant of redemption, in terms of the administration and fulfillment of the work of redemption.

LINGUISTIC, CULTURAL, AND SPIRITUAL EXEGESIS

Edwards approaches the covenant of redemption with various exegetical considerations, all of which focus on the realization of the history of redemption. This echoes Reformed orthodoxy's view of covenant: "The

---

88. Ramsey, "Appendix III: Heaven Is a Progressive State," 738.
89. Edwards, *Miscellany no. 736, WJE* 361.

Reformed orthodox understanding of covenant rested on a complex of exegetical, etymological, theological, and legal considerations," asserts Muller.[90] The same is true for Edwards's exegetical methods. When examining the covenant of redemption, he considers the linguistic and cultural context in Greek and Hebrew and the spiritual and practical application. To consider how much Edwards's thought follows Reformed exegetical tradition goes beyond the scope of this chapter. Rather, this last section addresses Edwards's linguistic, cultural, and spiritual interpretation of the covenant of redemption, with an emphasis on the theme of the history of redemption.

Edwards's understanding of the Trinity and the covenant of redemption emerges from careful linguistic and contextual considerations. The Son as the image of God is found in 2 Corinthians 4:4, "Christ, who is the image of [God], should shine unto them." Similarly, Edwards believes Philippians 2:6, Colossians 1:15, and Hebrews 1:3 reveal the Son of God as the divine idea. Hebrews 1:3 clearly articulates "the express image of his person." Edwards confirms Christ as the representation of the Trinity after considering the original language of the phrase "the express image of his person." The original language, χαρακτὴρ τῆς ὑποστάσεως αὐτοῦ,[91] denotes "one person as like another, as the impression on the wax is to the engraving on the seal." From this, he argues that "Christ is this most immediate representation of the Godhead."[92]

This linguistic consideration is also found in Edwards's etymological approach to the name *Elohim* in Genesis 1:1 and the image of God in Genesis 1:26. In Genesis 1:1, which begins "In the beginning God created," the root of the word *Elohim* comes from אלה, which means *adjurare*, that is, to enter an agreement. For Edwards, this word implies that as for "the grand scheme and design of the creation," there is confederation among "the three persons of the Trinity" in the "eternal covenant of redemption." *Elohim* implies "the plural number of *El*." Moreover, *Elohim* has its root

---

90. Richard A. Muller, "The Covenant of Works and the Stability of Divine Law in Seventeenth-Century Reformed Orthodoxy: A Study in the Theology of Herman Witsius and Wilhelmus à Brakel," *Calvin Theological Journal* 29, no. 1 (April 1994): 80.

91. Edwards's use of this term does not include the vowels in the original Greek. The term fully spelled out with both consonants and vowels is χαρακτὴρ τῆς ὑποστάσεως αὐτοῦ.

92. Edwards, "Discourse on the Trinity," 137.

from both אֵל (deus; "God") and אַיִל (fortitudo; "strength"), and thus Elohim involves the "power of the Creator."[93]

Edwards's view on the cultural context of the covenant of redemption can be found in "Notes on Scripture," nos. 62 and 171, in which he describes the nature of Christ's obedience. He refers to Psalm 40:6, "Mine ear hast thou opened." According to Edwards, "open" here is understood as "bored." He believes this refers to a slave whose ear is required to be bored, and he argues that the verse suggests a type of Christ. Edwards continues the argument by writing that just as a slave whose ear is bored to the door must serve "his master forever [vv.5-6]," "Christ has his ear bored" to "the door of God's house" for his people.[94] This means that in accordance with his own will, Christ became the slave of God for the redemption of his people. Similarly, in "Notes on Scripture," no. 171, Edwards connects Psalm 40:6–8 to Christ's willing obedience. The ancient Jewish custom of piercing the ear of a slave indicates a slave's love and willing service to his master. Thus, as a slave's love to his master is the cause of his obedience, the Son's love of the Father and his voluntary will are essential factors that validate the covenant of redemption.

Moreover, Edwards employs typology as an exegetical method to interpret the Bible text in terms of the covenant of redemption. In "Notes on Scripture," Edwards's exegesis of Deuteronomy 9:5 describes Abraham, Isaac, and Jacob as "types of Christ," in terms that Christ is "our spiritual father" who was given a promise from God in the covenant of redemption.[95] For Edwards, that the promises God made to these forefathers are applied to their posterity is closely related to the benefits of the covenant of redemption. In this sense, Edwards boldly sees types of Christ in Abraham, Isaac, and Jacob. Edwards's strict typology, according to Wilson, is used in his Redemption Discourse in A History of the Work of Redemption.[96] As Stein points out, Edwards sees "the type through the antitype; that is, his view of the 'eternal covenant of redemption,' clarified by New Testament documents, provided a window back into the origins of the world."[97]

---

93. Edwards, The "Blank Bible," 123.
94. Edwards, Notes on Scripture, 67.
95. Edwards, Notes on Scripture, 291.
96. Wilson, "Editor's Introduction," in A History of the Work of Redemption, 59.
97. Stephen J. Stein, "Editor's Introduction," in The "Blank Bible," 25.

Nonetheless, Edwards's use of typology does not seem to be little more than a strict application of the covenant frame to the biblical texts. That is, Edwards's typological understanding is interwoven with a careful linguistic consideration and the spiritual application of the benefits of the covenant of redemption. In his engagement with Psalm 72:15, Edwards uses typology with a linguistic concern. The verse reads, "Prayer also shall be made through him continually, and daily shall he be blessed." Edwards argues:

> The word translated "for" is sometimes used for "through," as *Joshua* 2:15, "Then she let them down by a cord *through the window*." If we hold translation "for him," then it must be understood of the saints' praying for the Father's accomplishment of the promises made to the Son in the covenant of redemption, that his kingdom may come, his name glorified, and that he may see his seed, and that the full reward may be given him for his sufferings, and so that he may receive "the joy that was set before him" [Hebrews 12:2].[98]

Edwards identifies Christ in the psalm after considering the usage of the word "for him" (בַּעֲדוֹ). As for the syntax of בַּעֲדוֹ, the interpretation of it is appositional, so there is little difficulty in taking it as referring to the Father's accomplishment of the promises. For Edwards, to understand בְּעַד as "for," that is, for the fulfillment of the promises, is quite reasonable. Thus, Edwards concludes that "the saints' prayer" is for "the Father's accomplishment of the promises made to the Son."[99]

The same principle of typology, which takes into consideration linguistics and the spiritual application of the covenant of redemption, is found in Edwards's interpretation of 1 Kings 7:15–22. Edwards believes that the two bronze pillars, "Jachin and Boaz," signify that "the entrance of God's elect and covenant people into heaven is secured by God's immutable establishment and almighty power." He supports this interpretation with Revelation 3:12, "Him that overcometh will I make a pillar in the temple of my God." According to Edwards, *Jachin* (יָכִין, "he shall establish") indicates

---

98. Edwards, The "Blank Bible," 509.

99. Edwards, The "Blank Bible," 509.

"both God's decree and promise," since the decree and promise become "the same" through the covenant of redemption.[100]

In another example, Edwards argues that lilies and flowers symbolize "a presentation of honor, glory, and beauty in Scripture." For instance, in Isaiah 28:1, "beauty" is described as "flowers." This is the same as the meaning of "lily" in Canticles 2:1-2. Moreover, the "pomegranate" means "sweet fruit." Edwards writes, "These spiritual fruits are often compared to pomegranates in Solomon's Song, and more frequently than to any other sort of fruit, as Cant. 4:3, 13, and 6:7, 11, and 7:12, and 8:2." At the end of "Notes on Scripture," no. 274, Edwards asserts that these spiritual fruits reveal "how the graces of God's Spirit and the spiritual fruits of holiness and happiness are interwoven one with another."[101]

Edwards's view of the Holy Spirit as a spiritual fruit also appears in his argument that the Holy Spirit is "the thing purchased" itself.[102] He uses Galatians 3:13-14 as evidence that "the sum of all that Christ purchased for man was the Holy Ghost" because the biblical text promises the "Spirit through faith." He refers to Psalm 133:2, in which the Holy Spirit is described as the "oil," a word that indicates the communicative characteristics of the Holy Spirit to church members.[103] Edwards argues that the "oil" running down to "the members of his body and to the skirts of his garment (Ps 133:2)" implies that believers enjoy God's love, which is "the Holy Spirit."[104] Similarly, John 4:10-15 and 7:38-39 describe the Holy Spirit as water and a river, which Edwards believes signify "the sum of all spiritual good." He goes on to cite biblical texts that evidence the Holy Spirit as the purchased inheritance or promise of God. Among these are Ephesians 1:14, 2 Corinthians 1:22 and 5:5, and Galatians 3:2. This is the same as his "Blank Bible," where he argues that the Holy Spirit "was poured forth upon Christ," connecting Psalm 133:2 to John 1:16 ("grace for grace").[105]

Edwards ascribes the attributes of water or river, which imply the communication of God to the believer, to the Holy Spirit. As Ramsey points

---

100. Edwards, *Notes on Scripture*, 229.
101. Edwards, *Notes on Scripture*, 230.
102. Edwards, "Discourse on the Trinity," 136.
103. Edwards, "Discourse on the Trinity," 136.
104. Edwards, "Discourse on the Trinity," 136.
105. Edwards, *The "Blank Bible,"* 536.

out well, for Edwards, "the great fruit of the Spirit is now looked on as everlastingly 'communicated' to the church."[106] Therefore, Edwards's use of typology in describing the Holy Spirit is carried over in terms of the benefit of the covenant of redemption. This point of view differs from that of Cocceius, who denies that "the Scriptures have multiple senses and assigned typology to the *sensus literalis*."[107] As seen so far, Edwards's use of typology considers a linguistic, contextual, and spiritual interpretation within the framework of the covenant of redemption in that he emphasizes the Holy Spirit as the benefit of the covenant of redemption for believers.

CONCLUSION

The present chapter focused on Edwards's exegesis as it relates to his doctrines of the Trinity and the covenant of redemption. It showed that he uses many passages in the Bible and considers both authorial intention and cultural context. He consistently maintains that his doctrines arise from the biblical witness.

For Edwards, the persons of the Godhead are equal. In addition to being an equal person of the Trinity, the Holy Spirit is also mutual love itself. In this way, Edward argues, the Holy Spirit plays a distinct role in the covenant of redemption. As for the Son, Edwards relies on texts that describe Christ as the revelation of God and the Word of God. Edwards argues the Son's willingness to obey leads to a perfect and glorious kingdom on earth.

In these views, Edwards clearly follows the Reformed tradition. In addition, his interpretation is clearly Christocentric and based on the belief that both Testaments speak about the Son's work of redemption. The uniqueness of Edwards's exegesis should be understood as follows. First, it seeks to develop the equality of the persons of the Trinity, making up for what was lacking in the Reformed tradition's view of the Holy Spirit's role. Second, it strives to emphasize God's sovereignty in offering salvation to believers as a way of resisting the "twin threats of Arminianism and Arianism."[108] Third, it endeavors to show how the history of redemption integrates the entire

---

106. Paul Ramsey, "Editor's Introduction," in *Ethical Writings,* 93.

107. Van Asselt, "Covenant, Kingdom, and Friendship," xxiii.

108. Pauw, *The Supreme Harmony of All,* 93.

Bible and the whole history of earth. In short, Edwards sees Scripture as unified truth and redemptive history as the guide for its interpretation.

7

—

THE EXEGETICAL BASIS OF THE DOCTRINE OF THE COVENANT OF WORKS

INTRODUCTION

As the previous chapter observed, Edwards's exegesis utilizes a salvation-historical theme for the covenant of redemption. In other words, the doctrine of the covenant of redemption in Edwards's theology rests upon his biblical exegesis, in which he focuses on the theme of salvation history and employs a variety of interpretive methods drawing upon the unity of the Bible. The same is true for Edwards's biblical exposition of the doctrine of the covenant of works. As will be demonstrated, Edwards attempts to demonstrate the unity of the Bible when explaining the central themes of the covenant of works, such as federal headship and the law-gospel distinction, by using a variety of interpretive methods.

Moreover, although Edwards's biblical interpretation of the dispensations of covenants appears similar to that of his Reformed forebears, Edwards sought to listen to the Bible itself. This does not mean that Reformed orthodoxy's biblical exposition of the covenant of works is different from Edwards's or that their view of the covenant is less biblical than Edwards. When it comes to the biblical characteristics of the doctrine of the covenant of works in Reformed orthodoxy, the *Westminster Confession* (1647) provides the rule of the interpretation of Scripture as follows: "The whole counsel of God, concerning all things necessary for his own glory, man's salvation, faith, and life, is either expressly set down in Scripture, or by good and necessary consequence may be deduced from Scripture: unto which nothing at any time is to be added, whether by new revelations of the Spirit, or traditions of men."[1]

Resting on this statement, Richard Muller identifies the doctrine of the covenant of works as an example of a consequent doctrine derived from Scripture.[2] The ensuing discussion in the *Westminster Confession* makes it clear that there was widespread acceptance of the doctrine of the covenant of works' dependence upon Scripture. Scholars like C. J. William, Ryan M. McGraw, and Mark Jones agree with Muller that the formulation of the doctrine of the covenant of works is "necessary as a consequence deduced from Scripture."[3] Van Asselt finds that for Cocceius, biblical exegesis and doctrine "form a unity, in that the Scripture itself supplies the *corpus doctrinae* and the means of its own interpretation." "True doctrine," asserts Van Asselt, "rests upon the comparison and analogy of biblical pericopes: it attempts to discover coherence in biblical statements."[4] Given the correlation between Scripture and doctrine, it is clear that seventeenth-century Reformed theologians were aware of the problem with the terminology

---

1. *Westminster Confession*, I.6, in Philip Schaff, *Creeds of Christendom*, 3 vols. (1931; reprint Grand Rapids: Baker, 1983), 3:603.

2. Richard Muller, "The Covenant of Works and the Stability of Divine Law in Seventeenth-Century Reformed Orthodoxy: A Study in the Theology of Herman Witsius and Wilhelmus à Brakel," *Calvin Theological Journal* 29, no. 1 (1994): 75; Muller, "'Either Expressly Set Down ... or by Good and Necessary Consequence': Exegesis and Formulation in the Annotations and the Confession," *Scripture and Worship: Biblical Interpretation and the Directory for Public Worship*, ed. Richard A. Muller and Rowland S. Ward (Phillipsburg, NJ: P&R, 2007), 59–82.

3. C. J. William, "Good and Necessary Consequences in the Westminster Confession" in *The Faith Once Delivered: Essays in Honor of Dr. Wayne Spear*, ed. Anthony T. Selvaggio (Phillipsburg, NJ: P&R, 2007), 171–90; Ryan M. McGraw, *By Good and Necessary Consequence* (Grand Rapids: Reformation Heritage, 2012); Joel R. Beeke and Mark Jones, "The Puritans on the Covenant of Works," in *A Puritan Theology: Doctrine for Life* (Grand Rapids: Reformation Heritage, 2012), 219. William defines "good" and "necessary" as follows: "'Good' and 'necessary' may also be seen as the terminological equivalents of the two standard criteria for sound, logical deductions. For any argument to be sound, it must meet two specific criteria, namely, (1) the premises must be true and (2) the conclusion must follow necessarily from the premises ('deductive validity'). True premises make an argument 'good,' while deductive validity makes its conclusion 'necessary.' Therefore, a 'good and necessary consequence' requires verifiably true premises and deductive validity." See William, "Good and Necessary Consequences in the Westminster Confession," 179. For various criticisms of the doctrine of the covenant of works, see Cornelis P. Venema, "Recent Criticisms of the Covenant of Works in the Westminster Confession of Faith," *Mid-America Journal of Theology* 9 (Fall 1993): 165–98.

4. Willem J. Van Asselt, *The Federal Theology of Johannes Cocceius, 1603–1669*, trans. Raymond A. Blacketer (Leiden: Brill, 2001), 124.

of the covenant of works in relation to the biblical texts employed as the exegetical basis for the doctrine.[5]

This increasing recognition of the deductive character of federal theology echoes Edwards's biblical exposition of the doctrine of the covenant of works. Again, Edwards attempts to introduce the historical progress of salvation from the Bible by using various interpretive methods. In order to examine the relationship of the doctrine of the covenant of works to his biblical exegesis, this chapter will first look at the collations of some central texts pertaining to the covenant of works and then look at interpretive approaches of Christ's redemptive works as a ground of the unified whole of the Bible. It will begin by returning to Edwards's exegetical works that were discussed in chapter 4, analyzing his biblical exegesis of the covenant of works.

THE COLLATIONS OF THE CENTRAL TEXTS

Like his Reformed forebears,[6] Edwards perceives a collation of Genesis 2:17 and Romans 5. Genesis 2:17 plays an important role in Edwards's understanding of the covenant of works, especially with respect to his view of the relationship between Adam and his posterity. Edwards considers Genesis 2:17 as indicating the inclusion of Adam's posterity in his sin. In his sermon on Genesis 3:11, Edwards relies on Genesis 2:17 when he argues, "I say tis manifest these words had not Respect to Adam alone but to mankind in

---

5. See Ernest F. Kevan, *The Grace of Law: A Study in Puritan Theology* (1964; reprint Grand Rapids: Baker, 1976), 110–13; Muller, "The Covenant of Works and the Stability of Divine Law," 75–76; Muller, "'Either Expressly Set Down ... or by Good and Necessary Consequence,'" 59–82; William, "Good and Necessary Consequences in the Westminster Confession," 172; Beeke and Jones, "The Puritans on the Covenant of Works," 218. In his essay, Muller examines the relationship of the confessional standards to the exegesis of the sixteenth and seventeenth centuries with respect to three doctrines: the divine decrees, providence, and the covenant of works.

6. Edwards's biblical basis for the doctrine of the covenant of works has much in common with Reformed orthodox theologians' use of the biblical texts. Muller points out, "The early orthodox Reformed theologians had developed their understanding of the prelapsarian covenant on the basis of Genesis 2:17 and various Pauline texts," especially Romans 5. According to Muller, these biblical texts indicate "the inclusion of Adam's posterity in his sin and their being made subject to the same punishment." In this way, Genesis 2:17, for Reformed orthodox theologians, is collated to the Pauline antitheses of Adam and Christ. Muller, "'Either Expressly Set Down ... or by Good and Necessary Consequence,'" 81, 77, 80. For more discussion of this, see Richard Muller, *Post-Reformation Reformed Dogmatics: The Rise and Development of Reformed Orthodoxy, ca. 1520 to ca. 1725*, Vol 4: *The Triunity of God* (Grand Rapids: Baker, 2003), 4, 7.

General. G[od] spoke to Adam as the head of the human Race."[7] In the same sermon, Edwards cites Romans 5:15, which parallels Adam and his posterity: "It was only that one offence that is imputed to Adam's posterity Rom 5.15.16. ... There it is said by the offence of one & not the offences of one that many are said to be dead."[8] In the "Blank Bible" note on Genesis 2:17, Edwards writes, "These words [in Gen 2:17] signify that perfect obedience was the condition of God's covenant that was made with Adam, as they signify that for one act of disobedience he should die."[9] Again, Edwards's view of the federal heads, the first and second Adams, is clearly explained in his exegesis of Romans 5:15-16, in which Edwards extrapolates the nature of the gift from the promissory aspects that point to Christ's fulfillment of the covenant. In his "Blank Bible" note on Romans 5:16, Edwards states, "We receive much more benefit by the grace of God in Christ than we did mischief by the sin of Adam, in this respect, that that brought the guilt but of one sin upon us, but Christ's satisfaction and the grace of God through that, removes the guilt of many sins from us."[10] Thus, Edwards's use of Genesis 2:17 and Romans 5 shows that he cited these two texts in order to indicate a confederation between Adam and his posterity and an antithesis between Adam and Christ.[11] Of course, Edwards's biblical basis for the doctrine of the covenant of works is not limited to the collation of Genesis 2:17 and Pauline texts. For example, Edwards's interpretation of Genesis 2:17 is correlated to Revelation 20:14, 1 Kings 2:42, 2 Peter 2:1, Deuteronomy 32:35, Ephesians 2:1, Colossians 2:13, Matthew 8:22, and John 5:25. This is also true for the Reformed orthodox theologians who considered various assemblies of texts in formulating their view of the covenant of works.[12]

However, a careful examination of Edwards's biblical exegesis of Genesis 2:17 reveals that Edwards is inclined to listen to the witness of the Bible itself as an interpretive method of harmonizing biblical texts.

---

7. Edwards, "504. Sermon on Gen. 3:11 (February 1739)," in *Sermons, Series II, 1739, WJEO* 54:L. 31r.

8. Edwards, "504. Sermon on Gen. 3:11," L. 25v–L. 26r.

9. Edwards, The *"Blank Bible," WJE* 24:134.

10. Edwards, The *"Blank Bible,"* 1000.

11. See Muller, "'Either Expressly Set Down ... or by Good and Necessary Consequence,'" 74.

12. See Muller, "'Either Expressly Set Down ... or by Good and Necessary Consequence,'" 69–82.

Edwards's interpretation is focused on the biblical exposition of the text, particularly the Hebrew idiomatic expression. For example, in his "Notes on Scripture" entry on Genesis 2:17, Edwards emphasizes that the expression "dying thou shalt die" indicates not only the certainty of death but also the extremity of it because the text mentions "dying twice over."[13] The text points to two kinds of death. While the certainty of death implies a temporal death of the body, the extremity of death points to eternal death. Edwards repeats a similar exposition of the nature of death in his sermon on Genesis 3:15 and "Notes on Scripture," nos. 320 and 325.[14] In so doing, Edwards relates Genesis 2:17 to Revelation 20:14. Edwards contends, "And that 'tis to these words the apostle John refers, in the 20th [chapter] of Revelation and 14th [verse], when he says, 'This is the second death.' ... There he explains who the serpent was that beguiled Eve: 'the dragon, that old serpent, who is the devil and Satan.' So here he explains what the second of these deaths that was threatened to Adam was."[15] In his "Blank Bible" note on Revelation 20:14, Edwards argues that the phrase "this is the second death" is nothing other than the repetition of "the threatening to our first parents" in Genesis 2:17.[16] His consideration of what might be the author's intention of this Hebrew idiom led Edwards to distinguish between the first and the second deaths.

Edwards finds the same linguistic approach employed in Solomon's threat to Shimei in 1 Kings 2:42 and 37, "For it shall be, that on the day thou goest out, and passest over the brook Kidron, thou shalt know for certain that thou shalt surely die." Edwards considers the phrase "dying thou shalt die" as an expression belonging to "the idiom of the Hebrew tongue." Edwards claims that "a repetition or doubling of a word" points to "speaking" with "a very extraordinary emphasis."[17] This kind of Hebrew idiom, according to him, appears elsewhere in 2 Peter 2:1 and Deuteronomy 32:35,

13. Edwards, *Notes on Scripture*, WJE 15:72.

14. Edwards, "504. Sermon on Gen. 3:11," L. 16r.–L. 18r. See "Notes on Scripture," no. 320, which deals with the nature of death with respect to spiritual and physical aspects. Edwards, *Notes on Scripture*, 302.

15. Edwards, *Notes on Scripture*, 72.

16. Edwards, *The "Blank Bible,"* 1242.

17. Edwards, *Notes on Scripture*, 310.

which indicate swift destruction, and in Ephesians 2:1, 5; Colossians 2:13; Matthew 8:22; and John 5:25; which denote the twofold death.[18]

Similarly, in *Original Sin*, Edwards identifies the death of Adam as eternal death, which resulted from sin, following his examination of the language found in a large number of texts.[19] This leads to the question of why Edwards devotes so much attention in *Original Sin* to his argument for the nature of the death of Adam, especially his second death. Although, as Bavinck points out, Edwards argued that moral pollution arises from the sinful inclination of humanity,[20] Edwards emphasizes the miserable state of human beings.[21] This is clear from the context, in which Edwards opposes Taylor's argument that the death with which God threatened Adam and Eve (Gen 2:17) pointed to a physical death to which Adam and his posterity were destined. According to Edwards, although the Hebrew word "death" implies "external and visible," it should be understood as "figurative." Edwards writes:

> There are many words in our language, such as "heart," "sense," "view," "discovery," "conception," "light," and many others, which are applied to signify external things, as that muscular part of the body called "heart"; external feeling called "sense"; the sight of the bodily eye called "view"; the finding of a thing by its being uncovered, called "discovery"; the first beginning of the foetus in the womb, called "conception"; and the rays of the sun, called "light": yet these words do as truly and properly signify other things of a more spiritual internal nature, as those: such as the disposition, affection, perception and thought of the mind, and manifestation

---

18. See Edwards, "504. Sermon Gen. 3:11," L. 16r; L. 17v; Edwards, *Notes on Scripture*, 302.

19. Among those texts are Rom 6:23; 7:5; 8:13; 2 Cor 3:7; 1 Cor 15:56; Rev 20:6, 14; 21:8; 2:11; 1 John 3:14; John 5:24; 6:50; 8:51; 11:26; Matt 10:29; Luke 10:28; Ezek 3:18; Jer 31:30; Isa 11:14; Prov 12:28; Eccl 2:14; 7:15; Ps 34:21; 139:19; 69:28; Deut 27; 28; 30:15; Rom 10:5; Gal 3:12; etc. See Edwards, *Original Sin*, WJE 3:237–44.

20. Herman Bavinck, *Reformed Dogmatics*, vol. 3, *Sin and Salvation in Christ*, ed. John Bolt, trans. John Vriend (Grand Rapids: Baker Academic, 2006), 109.

21. For a more comprehensive summary of *Original Sin*, see Clyde A. Holbrook, "Editor's Introduction," in *Original Sin*, 1–101; Stephen R. Yarbrough, "The Beginning of Time: Jonathan Edwards' *Original Sin*," in *Early American Literature and Culture: Essays Honoring Harrison T. Meserole*, ed. Kathryn Zabelle Derounian-Stodola (Newark: University of Delaware Press, 1992), 149–64; Robert W. Caldwell III, "*Original Sin*," in *A Reader's Guide to the Major Writings of Jonathan Edwards*, ed. Nathan A. Finn and Jeremy M. Kimble (Wheaton, IL: Crossway, 2017): 153–74.

and evidence to the soul. Common use, which governs the propriety of language, makes the latter things to be as much signified by those words, in their proper meaning, as the former.[22]

This passage presents Edwards's consideration of the text as more analogical, with a series of rather less defensible physical interpretations of the text. He argues, for example, that various terms in Hebrew and other Oriental languages "no less properly and usually signify something more spiritual." Edwards goes on to say:

So the Hebrew words used for "breath," have such a double signification; *neshama*

> signifies both "breath" and the "soul"; and the latter as commonly as the former: is used for "breath" or "wind," but yet more commonly signifies "spirit." "Nephesh" is used for "breath," but yet more commonly signifies "soul." So the word *lébh*, "heart," no less properly signifies the "soul," especially with regard to the will and affections, than that part of the body so called. The word "shalom," which we render "peace," no less properly signifies prosperity and happiness, than mutual agreement. The word translated "life" signifies the natural life of the body, and also the perfect and happy state of sensible active being; and the latter as properly as the former. So the word "death" signifies "destruction," as to outward sensibility, activity and enjoyment: but it has most evidently another signification, which, in the Hebrew tongue, is no less proper, viz. "perfect, sensible, hopeless ruin and misery."[23]

The real intention in Edwards's doctrine of original sin is the interest of the "perfect, sensible, hopeless ruin and misery" of the human race.

Edwards's interpretation of Genesis 2:17 focuses on the meaning of and the distinction between the first and second deaths. Why does Edwards focus on the twofold meaning of the term "death"? The collations between Genesis 2:17 and Romans 5, and Genesis 2:17 and various other biblical texts, evidence that a Hebrew idiom like "dying thou shalt die" plays a pivotal role

---

22. Edwards, "Observations on Holy Scripture," in *Original Sin*, 242.
23. Edwards, "Observations on Holy Scripture," 242–43.

in deciding the meaning of the biblical texts. This means that Edwards's doctrine of the covenant of works proceeds from the doctrine of original sin and that his understanding of the sin of Adam rests on a complex of exegetical and theological considerations that examine etymological, linguistic, cultural, analogical, figurative, and idiomatic expressions. Thus, Edwards's understanding of original sin, which differs from the typical Reformed tradition, stems from his own interpretation of the Bible, based upon various exegetical considerations.

What is the biblical text used as the ground of the doctrine of the covenant of works? This question has to do with the key biblical source of the covenant of works in Edwards's theology. As observed in chapter 4, it is through his sermons on Genesis 3:11 and 3:24 that Edwards explores in depth the bond between Adam's guilt and his posterity's sinful state. This means that Genesis 3, rather than Genesis 2, is a primary biblical *locus* from which Edwards developed his doctrine of the covenant of works.[24] Closely related is the question of why Edwards chose Genesis 3 to be a central text of the covenant of works. This question leads us to see Edwards's intent in the sermons on 3:11 and 3:24.

Edwards reads Genesis 3 theologically, emphasizing that the first parents lost their willful obedience by which they could have obtained eternal life and blessedness. One of the important aims in the two sermons is to reveal the nature of the heinous acts of Adam as the federal head of humanity in his eating the forbidden fruit and then to describe the miserable condition of Adam and his posterity. Given this purpose, it is not difficult to note the reason Edwards would choose Genesis 3 as the central text for establishing the doctrine of the covenant of works. In other words, Genesis 3:11 and 3:24 would be the most significant place from which to begin describing the miserable state of Adam and his posterity as well as the anger of God based upon his divine attributes.

---

24. Reformed orthodox theologians also considered Genesis 3 the ground of the doctrine of the covenant of works. However, the Reformed formulators of the concept of a covenant of works, such as Fenner, Polanus, Perkins, and Rollock, tended to focus their attention on Genesis 2:17 rather than Genesis 3. See Muller, "'Either Expressly Set Down ... or by Good and Necessary Consequence,'" 70–71.

THE INTERPRETIVE METHODS

Given Edwards's central texts for examining the covenant of works, which are similar but not identical to those his Reformed forebears used, one can assume that Edwards's theological interpretation of the covenant of works is based on his own exposition of the texts that underpin the doctrine of the federal headship. For example, Edwards carefully examines the psychological state of Adam provided by the biblical texts. This is apparent in his comparison of Adam's physical and spiritual states before and after the fall. In his sermon on Genesis 3:11, Edwards compares Adam's state described in Genesis 3:11 with that of Genesis 3:8, which reads, "And they heard the voice of the LORD God walking in the garden in the cool of the day: and Adam and his wife hid themselves from the presence of the LORD God amongst the trees of the garden." Edwards considers not only the biblical narrative in which Adam could hear God's voice and recognize the climatological feeling physically but also the anthropomorphic description of God's stroll. For Edwards, the text emphasizes "a friendly manner" that existed between Adam and God.[25]

Edwards's emphasis on the undisturbed fundamental relationship between Adam and God is again found in his description of God's interrogation of the first parents in Genesis 3:9–10. Edwards focuses on the anthropomorphic elements of this text. He asserts that there are "three things" in the manner in which the interrogation is expressed: (1) "a Calling him to an account as his Judge," (2) "a Charge of the act of Eating the forbidden fruit," and (3) "a [sense] reproof of this act."[26] God is described as one who calls, charges, and reminds Adam of how the heinousness of Adam's sin brings about a breach of relationship between God and Adam. In other words, the anthropomorphic expression becomes a significant tool in revealing the degree of Adam's sin and the misery derived from the disturbed relationship between Adam and God.

In this trial, the human race was ultimately held responsible since they are subject to the curse upon Adam. Edwards utilizes the narrative of Genesis 3:15–19 to elucidate that there are federal relationships between the serpent and the Devil, the woman and her female posterity, and Adam

---

25. See Edwards, "504. Sermon on Gen. 3:11," L. 1r.
26. Edwards, "504. Sermon on Gen. 3:11," L. 3r.

and his posterity. "What is said after the fall," Edwards claims, " … was plainly not meant only of those Individuals but of the Kind or race to which they appertained. Part of the curse that is denounced on the serpent is to be understood not only of the Devil that actuated the serp[ent] but of the serp[ent]" that "is denounced on the serpent." The curse falls not only upon the "Individual serp[ent]" but also upon "the whole serpentine race or progeny as it was to continue through all future ages." The curse upon the woman is applied not only to Eve but also to "her female Posterity or woman kind in all ages." Last, the curses upon the man (vv. 17, 18, 19) are applied to both the first parents and their posterity.[27]

Edwards sees the serpent, the woman, and Adam not only as individuals but also as representing the human race. When Edwards takes the interrogative declaration of 3:15 to be speaking of ordinary reptiles and the real first parents, his interpretive method is a literal anagoge: the author intended us to apply the text to the future event. Edwards goes on to emphasize the author's intention in the text that the meaning of death declared in Genesis 2:17 is applied to both Adam and his posterity. Edwards asserts:

> All that is said of our first Parents in these Chapters is so plainly
> to be extended to their posterity it would be very unreasonable to
> exempt those words only in 2. Chap. 17 v … & to say that they refer
> only to Adam & Eve & not to their posterity yet more unreason-
> able to interpret those words for there is more in these Chapters to
> shew that them G[od] had Respect to mankind in General than in
> any other. For all that is said in what God says when he Comes to
> Judge man & pronounce sentence on him for this evince does shew
> plainly that all his Posterity were liable to the Penalty.[28]

This interpretation exceeds the plain meaning of the text on the basis of a crucial interpretive approach. The curse of the serpent is applied even to unbelievers as well as to Satan. At the same time, Edwards believes that the author intended the meaning of the curse in Genesis 3:15 as collective. That is, Edwards understands the curse declared to the serpent as something referring to both a sentence against ordinary reptiles and to

---

27. Edwards, "504. Sermon on Gen. 3:11," L. 32r.–32v.

28. Edwards, "504. Sermon on Gen. 3:11," L. 32v.–33r.

the eventual defeat of Satan. Edwards's use of literal anagoge is similar to Calvin's interpretation of Genesis 3:15. "We must now make a transition from the serpent to the author of this mischief himself; and that not only in the way of comparison, for there truly is a literal *anagogy*," asserts Calvin.[29] Indeed, "God has not so vented this anger upon the outward instrument as to spare the devil, with whom lay all the blame. That this may the more certainly appear to us, it is worth the while first to observe that the Lord spoke not for the sake of the serpent but of the man."[30]

This literal anagoge is correlated with Edwards's use of a fourfold sense of the text, one that was largely rejected by the Reformers: the literal, anagogical, tropological, and allegorical senses.[31] His note on Genesis 3:7-8 in the "Blank Bible" considers that the tree of the garden, according to the literal sense, means a real tree created by God. Tropologically speaking, "the trees of the garden" are "the ordinances and duties of religion." Allegorically, the garden is "a type of the church." Anagogically, the trees of the garden reveal "the manner of sinner's flying from one refuge to another."[32]

However, Edwards's use of literal anagoge should not be read as disregarding a grammatical approach to the texts. In his "Blank Bible" note on Genesis 3:15, Edwards argues that the word "woman" signifies not only the woman literally but also the church referred to in Revelation 12. He goes on to argue that the meaning of the "seed" of woman is twofold: either Christ or believers. Edwards reads the Genesis narrative in light of Revelation, which deals with the meaning of the Genesis text. In so doing, he explains the grammatical meanings of the words (the pronoun "he," the verb "bruise," and the affix "his") involved in the text. Further, Edwards emphasizes that since these words are used in "the singular number," the

29. John Calvin, *Commentary on Genesis*, trans. John King (Edinburgh: Calvin Translation Society, 1847), 168. According to the editor of Calvin's commentary on Genesis, this means that "there was an intentional transition from the serpent to the spiritual being who made use of it." See Calvin, *Commentary on Genesis*, 168n5.

30. Calvin, *Commentary on Genesis*, 168-69.

31. See David C. Steinmetz, "Divided by a Common Past: The Reshaping of the Christian Exegetical Tradition in the Sixteenth Century," *Journal of Medieval and Early Modern Studies* 27, no. 2 (Spring 1997): 249. For the medieval use of fourfold sense of Scripture, see Steinmetz, "Divided," 248.

32. Edwards, *The "Blank Bible,"* 137.

word "seed" points to "a particular person and not her posterity in general." This is "agreeable to" Paul's interpretation of the word (Gal 3:16, "He saith not, To seeds, as of many, but as of one, And to thy seed, which is Christ.").[33]

Notably, Edwards's interpretation of the seed in Genesis 3:15 is similar to Calvin's and some Reformed orthodox theologians' understanding of the text. Understanding the word "seed" as "a *collective* noun," Calvin argues that while the seed in Genesis 3:15 refers to "the posterity of the woman generally," the second seed in Genesis 3:15d indicates Christ as the head of the human race and "the whole Church of God."[34] The same, according to Beeke and Jones, is true for Thomas Goodwin and Francis Roberts, who considered "the seed" in Genesis 3:15d to "be understood collectively."[35] For Calvin and the Reformed orthodox theologians mentioned above, the first use of "seed" in Genesis 3:15 refers to the whole human race, and the second use, in 15d, points to Christ and his church.

Edwards's "Blank Bible" entry on Genesis 4:25 shows his grammatical approach to the text. "Eve [doesn't] say," he emphasizes, "'God hath appointed us another seed,' but 'hath appointed ME [another seed].' " Edwards focuses on the biblical author's intention that Eve was aware of the meaning of her giving birth to Seth as the promised son. Edwards writes, "She speaks of Abel and Seth, the righteous children of Adam and Eve, as 'her seed'; and so the church or generation of the righteous, which was to proceed from Seth, she calls, 'her seed,' doubtless with respect to the promise."[36] This grammatical approach is applied to the "seed of Abraham, who should 'possess the gate of his enemies, and in whom all the families of the earth should be blessed.' "[37] Edwards's point is that the seed of Abraham is nothing other than the type of Christ. Edwards's exegesis of Genesis 3:15 rests on the collation of other texts, especially Revelation 12 and Galatians 3:16, with consideration of the intentions of the authors of those texts as they discuss Genesis 3:15.

Given that Edwards deals with Genesis 3:11 under the theme of God's interrogation, it is not difficult to see that typology plays a significant role

---

33. Edwards, The "Blank Bible," 138.
34. Calvin, Commentary on Genesis, 171.
35. Beeke and Jones, "The Puritans on the Covenant of Works," 262–63.
36. Edwards, The "Blank Bible," 143.
37. Edwards, The "Blank Bible," 138.

in uniting Edwards's literal, theological, and Christocentric approaches to the Bible. Edwards reads the text typologically, not merely historically. In doing so, his concern lies with the anger of the Lord against Adam's sin and with Christ's suffering that satisfied the justice and wrath of God. Edwards does not deal with a juridical investigation of Adam's sin in detail.[38] Rather, he turns to a more detailed exposition of the nature of Adam's sin, noting Christ as the ultimate antitype of Adam. Edwards writes:

> It concerns us all to Consi[der] & be sensible of the nature of that act of our First F[ather]. ... for we are all to look upon as our act it was the act of the surety in whom we fall & that act by which we fall in our surety it nearly Concerns us to be well sensible of two things viz. our sin by the first Adam & the Righteousness of the second [Adam] it is of Infinite Importance that we should know both for the first is our own by which we are undone & the second must be our own if ever we are saved & we must Know the former in order to Know the latter [-] so that is of moment [-] us to be sensible of our sin & guilt by the first Adam as [-] Know our Righ[teousness] & Recovery by the second [Adam].[39]

Christ is juxtaposed with Adam. Edwards structured his sermon on Genesis 3:11 based on this parallel between the two federal heads, providing a biblical exposition of the antithesis between Adam's failure to keep the covenant of works and Christ's fulfillment of the covenant of works.

The typological reading of the covenant of works freed him to read the Bible Christologically in order to make a unity of these biblical texts. As we saw in chapter 4, Edwards repeatedly distinguishes between imputed and non-imputed sins. This principle is applied to the second Adam, whose obedience is imputed to believers. Edwards claims that "all the Obedience of the man X [Christ] Jesus" is not always imputed to believers. While the obedience Christ performed "during the time of his trial" on earth is imputed to us, the perfect obedience Jesus now performs in heaven is "not

---

38. It is not until his analysis of the second Adam, Christ, as the Mediator between God and humanity that Edwards engages in a juridical investigation of the serpent, the woman, and the man, in his application section of the sermon. See Edwards, "504. Sermon on Gen. 3:11," L. 31v.–32v.

39. Edwards, "504. Sermon on Gen. 3:11," L. 3r.–4v.

Imputed to believers."[40] For evidence, Edwards cites 1 Corinthians 15:28: "And when all things shall be subdued unto him, then shall the Son also himself be subject unto him that put all things under him, that God may be all in all." This text for Edwards provides an important clue for the distinction between imputed and non-imputed sins. Christ's obedience being performed in heaven is not imputed to believers, since "the time of X' [Christ's] trial as a Publik Head & surety" was completed at his resurrection.[41] This shows that Edwards's typological reading of the federal heads of the covenant of works interlocks smoothly with his efforts to demonstrate the unity of the Bible under the theme of the work of redemption, which has a Christocentric focus.

Similarly, Edwards in his sermon on Genesis 3:24 offers a biblical exposition of the inability of humanity to restore their previous state, emphasizing God's displeasure with Adam's disobedience. In doing this, Edwards uses a literal-historical interpretation of the Bible. This is clear from his reading of Genesis 3:24, "So he drove out the man; and he placed at the east of the garden of Eden cherubims, and a flaming sword which turned every way, to keep the way of the tree of life." Edwards uses this image of the flaming sword to emphasize God's anger against Adam's sin. "It was," asserts Edwards, "the sword of God's dreadful wrath, the sword of divine justice wielded by his infinite power, flaming with holy abhorrence of the filthiness of sin and sharpened by a divine resentment of the affront to his holy majesty."[42] Because of this sword of wrath, man is forever banished and never again allowed to enter Eden.

Edwards's literal-historical reading of the text is again found in his understanding of the Edenic imagery, which plays a significant role in his theological reflections on the nature of the human fall and on the blessings Christ acquired though his sufferings. This is apparent from the nickname Edwards gives to Genesis 3, his consistent reflection on the divine attributes, and his application of the flaming sword to Christ. First, Edwards begins this sermon by calling Genesis 3 "the most sorrowful and

---

40. Edwards, "504. Sermon on Gen. 3:11," L. 28.r–28v.

41. Edwards, "504. Sermon on Gen. 3:11," L. 28v.

42. Edwards, "East of Eden (Gen 3:24)," in *Sermons and Discourses 1730–1733*, in *Sermons and Discourses 1730–1733*, 342.

melancholy chapter that we have in the whole Bible."[43] Second, his comprehensive description of Genesis 3 is not unrelated to his concern for the divine attributes, such as God's anger toward his enemies and his justice, holiness, and majesty.[44] Edwards's sermon on Genesis 3:24 repeatedly contrasts Adam and Eve's pre-fall state of innocence with their condemnation, after which they can never restore their pre-fall state by their own power. It is by considering their damnation in terms of God's attributes that Edwards provides his theological reflection on Adam's fall.

Third, in the application part of this sermon, Edwards considers the flaming sword of God to be fulfilled by Christ. He states:

> Christ undertook to lead us to the tree of life, and he went before us. Christ himself was slain by that flaming [sword]; and this sword, having slain the Son of God appearing in our name, who was a person of infinite worthiness, that sword did full execution in that. And when it had shed the blood of Christ, it had done all its work, and so after that was removed. And Christ arising from the dead, being a divine person himself, went before us; and now the sword is removed, having done its execution, already having nothing more to do there, having slain Christ. There is no sword now, and the way is open and clear to eternal life for those that are in Christ.[45]

Considering this metaphorical image, Mark Valeri provides a summary: "Edwards offers one of the more striking images in the sermon: God ultimately wielded the flaming sword to slay his own Son. Through Christ's death, believers experience the joy of holiness and obedience in a measure even fuller than that enjoyed by Adam in paradise."[46] Here, although Edwards does not refer to Christ as the antitype of the Old Testament sacrificial lamb slain by God's wrath, such a theme is involved in his description of the blood of Christ. Moreover, he claims that Christ is the second Adam, referencing 1 Corinthians 15:45, "And so it is written, The first man Adam was made a living soul; the last Adam was made a quickening spirit."

---

43. Edwards, "East of Eden (Gen 3:24)," 331. See Edwards, *A History of the Work of Redemption*, 360.
44. Edwards, "East of Eden (Gen 3:24)," 340–41.
45. Edwards, "East of Eden (Gen 3:24)," 346.
46. Mark Valeri, "Editor's Introduction to 'East of Eden' (Gen 3:24)," *WJE* 17:330.

As Adam was the federal head of his posterity, Christ "became our representative and surety."[47] According to this typological approach, Genesis 3:24 is certainly a major text from which the concept of federal heads is drawn. As noted above, his typological exegesis, as found in this sermon, underpins Edwards's Christological reading of the covenant of works in the antithesis between the first and second Adams.

Other texts Edwards considers to refer to the curses, the garden of Eden, or the second Adam include Genesis 3:22, 23, 19, 7; Ephesians 2:1; 2 Corinthians 3:18; Revelation 2:7; 1 Corinthians 15:45; and Romans 10:3.[48] For Edwards, the first citations (Gen 3:22, 23, 19, 7; Eph 2:1; 2 Cor 3:18) and the last (Rom 10:3) point to the consequence of the curse upon Adam as confirming the doctrine of original sin.[49] With the exception of those from Genesis and Revelation, all these citations are drawn from the Pauline epistles.

Edwards employs literal-theological exegesis. This does not mean that his method falls into a wooden literalism that does not consider the usage of the literal meaning of the biblical texts, contexts, and other interpretive methods. Quoting Edwards's comments on Revelation 2,[50] Glenn R. Kreider argues that, "assuming that 'real' is a synonym for 'literal,' " Edwards rejects literal hermeneutics, "at least as applied to this text."[51] Kreider is partly correct in the sense that Edwards sought a spiritual meaning of the Bible. However, he is incorrect if he is suggesting that in Edwards there are no literal approaches to biblical texts, especially Revelation 2.

Edwards, very much like his Reformed predecessors, took great pains to focus on the typological sense of the text, which enunciates the literal-spiritual (or prophetic) meaning understood in Christocentric terms.[52]

---

47. Edwards, "East of Eden (Gen 3:24)," 346.

48. Edwards, "East of Eden (Gen 3:24)," 331, 334, 338, 342, 344, 346, 347.

49. Edwards, "East of Eden (Gen 3:24)," 331, 334, 338, 342.

50. The citation is as follows: "The angels of the churches do no more represent real, particular persons, than the riders upon the horses in the 6th chapter signified particular, real persons, or [the] four angels that were bound in the river Euphrates in the 9th chapter, or the angel that preached the everlasting gospel to the whole world, represented any one real person." Edwards, "Apocalypse Series," in *Apocalyptic Writings*, WJE 5:143.

51. Glenn R. Kreider, *Jonathan Edwards's Interpretation of Revelation 4:1–8:1* (Lanham, MD: University Press of America, 2004), 6–7.

52. Indeed, on this point one finds Edwards closely aligned with Reformed exegetical methods. Steinmetz claims that "by Luther's time, the literal sense was understood to include

For example, Edwards maintained both literal and spiritual meanings of the Bible, even in Revelation 2. The trees of the garden of Eden are a dwelling place in which Adam lived. They become an image of pristine beauty, when Adam and Eve lose "their former blessedness" by God's casting them out of paradise.[53] Physical access to the garden of Eden and to the tree of life is closed to humanity.[54] At the same time, the tree of life in the middle of the garden of Eden is meant to be Christ. According to this literal-typological reading, Edwards legitimizes that Genesis tells how Adam, as the federal head of the human race, could be the type of Christ. Employing Revelation 2:7, Edwards maintains, "Christ himself now stands instead of that tree of life that grew in the midst of the garden of Eden."[55] Thus, for Edwards, one image of God's salvation through Christ is that of a return to Eden. While Christ is interpreted in a spiritual sense, it is clear that Edwards's description of the garden of Eden points to the real place in which the tree of life stood.

The literal-theological approach to the Bible is apparent from his further reading of Genesis in light of Revelation 22 and Ezekiel 47:12, which, according to Edwards, focus on Christ's fulfillment of the covenant of works. In "Notes on Scripture," no. 397, "Genesis 2:9 and 3:22–24," Edwards

---

both the unfolding historical narrative (the literal-historical sense) and whatever typological meanings were foreshadowed in the story (the literal-prophetic sense)." Steinmetz, "Divided by a Common Past," 248. In his study of Calvin's exegesis of Old Testament prophecies, Muller argues that Calvin considered the literal sense of the texts [the Davidic Psalm 72 and 78:70] "the historical succession of the promise as it moves toward its highest fulfillment." Richard A. Muller, "The Hermeneutic of Promise and Fulfillment in Calvin's Exegesis of the Old Testament Prophecies of the Kingdom," in *The Bible in the Sixteenth Century*, ed. David C. Steinmetz (Durham, NC: Duke University Press, 1990), 77. Understanding Edwards in the time of mainstream Protestants who maintained "the supremacy of Scriptural literal sense," Sweeney emphasizes, "Like many early Protestants, then, Edwards practiced literal and spiritual exegesis. He majored in the literal sense. Scholars sometimes overwork his spiritualizing tendencies. He labored as a preacher, though, a minister of the Word. So he took advantage of all the tools that helped him make its contents come alive for those in his care." Douglas A. Sweeney, *Edwards the Exegete: Biblical Interpretation and Anglo-Protestant Culture on the Edge of the Enlightenment* (New York: Oxford University Press, 2016), 48. Thus, Kreider is incorrect when he argues that "the claim that Edwards followed the practice of literal hermeneutics is unfounded." Kreider, *Jonathan Edwards's Interpretation of Revelation*, 7.

53. Edwards, "East of Eden (Gen 3:24)," 331–32.

54. Edwards, "East of Eden (Gen 3:24)," 332.

55. Edwards, "East of Eden (Gen 3:24)," 344. A similar argument is found in Edwards's sermon "God Glorified in Man's Dependence." See Edwards, "God Glorified in Man's Dependence (1 Cor 1:29–31)," in *Sermons and Discourses 1730–1733*, 208.

indicates that the fruit of the tree of life "was intended as a seal of Adam's confirmation in life" and was "reserved by God to be bestowed as a reward of his obedience and overcoming all temptations, when his time of probation was ended."[56] Edwards cites Revelation 22:14, 2:7, 22:2, and Ezekiel 47:12 in connection with the interpretation of the Genesis texts. Edwards uses these texts as evidence that confirms eternal life as the reward of Adam's obedience. Further, Edwards speaks of the garden of Eden and the tree of life as being real, presupposing the possibility that the tree of life would yield its fruit every month of the year. "Some trees were hung with ripe fruits, and others in the blossom in each month in the year. St. John's vision, Rev. 22, may be so understood, that each single tree bore 'twelve manner of fruit' [v. 2] on different branches (and yet perhaps there is no necessity of so understanding it), and so one sort bore ripe fruit in one month, and another in another," Edwards asserts.[57] Edwards's use of cross-references here shows that his Christological reading of Genesis is closely interconnected with Revelation and Ezekiel through his literal-theological reading of the Bible.

We find a similar theological exposition of Adam as the federal head of the covenant of works in Edwards's brief treatment of Genesis 1:27–30, which he addresses in "Notes on Scripture," no. 398, "Covenant with Adam"; in a "Blank Bible" entry; and in a sermon on Genesis 1:27. In "Notes on Scripture," no. 398, Edwards addresses the blessings resulting from the covenant with Adam. According to Edwards, the blessings God gave Adam as his own image-bearer in creation entail two significant considerations. Edwards claims, "In order to man's being happy in the blessings, two things were needful: first, that the enjoyments granted should be good; and second, that the subject should be good, or in a good capacity to receive and enjoy them." Edwards believes that the blessings of the covenant, stemming from humanity's creation as the image-bearers of God, presuppose both Adam's willful obedience and the excellency of the reward. The blessings, at the same time, indicate the threat deriving from "his disobedience." Thus, that threat and the "implicit promise of life" provide evidence for Edwards

---

56. Edwards, *Notes on Scripture*, 393.

57. Edwards, *Notes on Scripture*, 393–94, 561–62.

that "the covenant must be made with Adam, not only for himself, but all his posterity."[58]

Edwards's theological reflection on the blessings given to Adam is based on this inference and upon Edwards's textual, cultural, linguistic, and cross-referential considerations of the biblical term *image*. In his "Blank Bible" entry on Genesis 1:27, the biblical references Edwards employs are Ephesians 4:24 and Colossians 3:10. He writes:

> Plato in his *Critias* affirms that in the days of old, there flourished in the first men Θεοῦ μοῖρα, a particle of God, also Θεῖα φύσις, a divine nature, which rendered them blessed, and more particularly in his *Theætetus*, discoursing of this likeness of man to God, makes it to consist in this, that man be holy with wisdom and righteousness, agreeable to Eph. 4:24 and Col. 3:10. Man's creation after the image of God is set forth by Ovid in his *Metamorphoses*.[59]

Edwards relates Plato's use of the term Θεοῦ μοῖρα (part or portion of God) and Θεῖα φύσις (divine nature) to flesh out the biblical teaching on the image of God. These terms are rendered by Edwards to indicate holiness with "wisdom and righteousness," which are grounded upon biblical statements such as those found in in Ephesians 4:24 and Colossians 3:10.

In so doing, Edwards not only notes the similarity between the creation story of the Bible and the pagan fables of Saturn, but he also pursues an etymology of the term *covenant*, drawing a conclusion that such fables were influenced by the story of Adam.

Interestingly, Edwards considers ancient Near Eastern literature to be an aid in interpreting the biblical narrative in order to account for the response of the Phoenicians to Abraham. In particular, Edwards appeals to a phrase in Ugaritic, a language and literature closely akin to the background of Melchizedek. By referencing the ancient Near Eastern background literature, especially through Gale's *Court of the Gentiles*, Edwards provides an argument for biblical influence on Greek myth. Edwards asserts, "For the Greeks, having no words terminating in 'm' for 'Adam' they pronounced 'Adan.' Adam is called the 'son of God'; so Saturn is called the

---

58. Edwards, *Notes on Scripture*, 395–96.
59. Edwards, *The "Blank Bible,"* 126.

'son of heaven.' Adam was formed out of the dust of the earth; so Saturn's mother was called Tellus."[60] Examining the similarities between the creation narrative of Genesis and the ancient world's fables, Edwards finds an implicit meaning of the term *covenant*. He states:

> No wonder that when the Phoenicians heard the Israelites speaking of Abraham their father, they should understand them of the same παγγεννέτωρ, or grand progenitor, for his name Abram signifies "high father" or "great father"; and his name Abraham signifies that he is "the father of a multitude," and the great promise to him was that he should be the "father of many nations" [*Genesis 17:5*]. They were all of them, according to the Hebrew idiom, sons of the covenant, or sons of *Berith*, which might lead the Phoenicians to suppose Berith to be God's wife. God did particularly in a remarkable manner establish his covenant with each of these: Adam, Noah, and Abraham. And they possibly might look back upon Abraham as the son of heaven and earth, as they asserted of Saturn, or Adam. *Genesis 14:19*, "Blessed be Abraham of the most high God, the generator of heaven and earth," as Bochart renders it. And the Phoenicians, hearing the Israelites speaking of Abraham as their great father, and also Israel, might easily confound them.[61]

Edwards argues that the biblical narrative shows that the Phoenicians understood Abraham's name as the father of the human race according to their understanding of Saturn in their own fables. As Saturn was the son of heaven and earth, so it was with Abraham. The evidence Edwards adduces for the meaning of the name of Abraham is the usage of Genesis 14:19. As mentioned in the citation above, that Abraham was considered to be the son of heaven and earth in the ancient Near East context is supported by Melchizedek's calling Abraham's God "the most high God, the generator of heaven and earth."[62] Edwards goes on to speak about the similarities

---

60. Edwards, *The "Blank Bible,"* 127.

61. Edwards, *The "Blank Bible,"* 129–30.

62. Edwards argues that Melchizedek, who was a Phoenician, considered "the covenant" or *"Berith"* in the Hebrew idiom to be God's wife, and thus he used the phrase "the generator of heaven and earth" (Gen 14:19), which was originally set for Saturn, when he blessed Abraham. As Sweeney points out, Edwards considers Melchizedek to be a Canaanite king who would "have been familiar to the Jews, at least in many times and places, whose acquaintance with the

between the biblical narrative of Genesis and the creation stories of the ancient Near East, considering the linguistic resemblances.[63] In this way, the creation stories from elsewhere in the ancient Near East play a role in Edwards's textual, linguistic, and cultural accounts of the Bible. This means that Edwards's linguistic exegesis is based not on a wooden, literalistic understanding of the text but rather on thoughtful consideration of the larger cultural context as the background for the biblical text.

Again, Edwards provides a theological reflection on the image of God in an unpublished 1751 sermon on Genesis 1:27, saying that the image of God indicates both "Reason & underst[anding]" and "Holiness."[64] First, Edwards considers the narrative of the text, which speaks about the distinction between the humans and all other creatures. With all other creatures ("Birds," "Beasts," and "fishes"), the emphasis falls on the fact that none of them has "understanding." With the created man and woman, their likeness to their creator is emphasized instead: humans are "able to know what is right & what is wrong & capable of Knowing what the will of G[od] & his duty is." Thus, all other creatures were "made for man," as if they were "the furniture & provision of the House." Second, the image of God goes beyond human reason and understanding. Adam and Eve were made holy because God "is an infinitely Holy Being." He asserts, "If men have Reason without Holiness they [be not] the better for it. If he had great understanding & is wicked he is so much the worse." Thus, while both reason and holiness pertain to the image of God, the latter is "the most Excellent."[65]

Pentateuch is seen throughout the Bible and is evidence that Moses (or a similarly venerable authority) had compiled it." See Sweeney, *Edwards the Exegete*, 80. Note that Edwards's rest upon Bochart's interpretation of the word "generator" is similar to the modern interpretation of the usage of the Phoenician language. J. C. L. Gibson argues, "The participle קנה points to 'creator' or 'owner' of the earth." In this view, the Ugaritic language of the Hebrew verb קנה ("to get, own") could mean "to create." However, John Collins argues that "the attested Ugaritic ideology lacks the notion of 'to create' in the sense that the biblical authors use it, namely, 'to originate the being of,' and 'to possess' makes better sense of the context of both the Ugaritic and the Genesis texts." Collins's point is that both the Ugaritic text and the Hebrew text that contain the verb קנה signify "to possess" rather than "to create." See J. C. L. Gibson, *Canaanite Myths and Legends* (Edinburgh: T&T Clark, 1977), 63; C. John Collins, *Genesis 1-4: A Linguistic, Literary, and Theological Commentary* (Phillipsburg, NJ: P & R, 2006), 195–96.

63. See Edwards, The *"Blank Bible,"* 130ff.

64. Edwards, "998. Sermon on Gen. 1:27 (August 1751)," (unpublished transcription provided by Ken Minkema of the Jonathan Edwards Center at Yale University), 2, 25.

65. Edwards, "998. Sermon on Gen. 1:27 (August 1751)," 2–10.

For Edwards, wisdom and holiness are the fundamental elements that comprise the image of God.

A seventeenth-century example of a similar expository conclusion is found in Cocceius's interpretation of the image of God. Cocceius argues that the image of God (Gen 1:26) is meant to be "wisdom (Col 3:10)" and "the sanctity of truth (Eph 4:24), 'ὁσιότητης τῆς ἀληθείας,' " indicating at the point of "a will loving the truth learned by the mind and keeping it for a rule of actions to reign in the members." Cocceius understands the image of God in terms of the law as "the book of the law" engraved in the image of Adam. In this vein, Adam possessed "Righteousness," which "pertains to the image of God."[66] Edwards's use of the biblical texts and his understanding of the terms are identical with Cocceius's interpretation of the image of God.

As with the relationship between the federal heads in the covenant of works, Edwards's exegetical approach to the relationship between the law and the gospel is largely Christological. However, Edwards's Christological reading of the Bible should not be understood as if it is always describing the spiritual effects of redemption. Rather, Edwards's exegesis focuses on a historical-prophetic sense of the text geared toward a redemptive-tele-ological dimension.

Edwards explains the nature of the moral law as being identical with the covenant of works, focusing on the promise of the covenant fulfilled by Christ. In so doing, Edwards focuses on authorial intention in the biblical texts.[67] For Edwards, the biblical authors were fully aware of the principle contrasting the law and the gospel, and they were aware that the human race is sinful. This means that Edwards's understanding of redemptive history involves a literary approach to the Bible. Indeed, Edwards believes that the biblical writers wanted their intentions to be clear to the reader.[68]

---

66. Johannes Cocceius, *The Doctrine of the Covenant and Testament of God*, trans. Casey Carmichael (Grand Rapids: Reformation Heritage, 2016), 28.

67. Edwards's focus on the authorial intention of the interpretation of the Bible is in line with both premodern and modern biblical exegesis, which sought or recognized the author's intended meaning of the texts. For premodern and modern biblical exegesis, see Kevin J. Vanhoozer, *Is there a Meaning in this Text? The Bible, the Reader, and the Morality of Literary Knowledge* (Grand Rapids: Zondervan, 1998), 47–48.

68. Collins defines a literary approach as follows: "A literary approach starts from rec-ognizing that authors use aesthetic devices to a greater or lesser extent, both to make their

Among these biblical texts are Romans 3:12, 27; 8:3–4; Galatians 3:12; Hebrews 10:1; and Colossians 2:7, which all mention the antithesis between the law and the gospel. In his "Blank Bible" entry on Romans 3:13ff., Edwards argues that the author of Romans quotes Romans 3:10–18 out of the first five verses of Psalm 36. The Apostle's aim in Romans 3:12 is to prove that "mankind are universally sinful; that everyone is corrupt."[69] Similarly, in his Redemption Discourse, Edwards appeals to Romans 3:27, which refers to the law-gospel juxtaposition, arguing that "Every command that Christ obeyed may be reduced to that great and everlasting law of God that is contained in the covenant of works." The reason Christ came into the world is nothing other than to fulfill the law of the covenant of works.[70] The same can be said for the "Notes on Scripture" entry on Galatians 5:18, in which Edwards sets justification under the law over against justification through faith. "Christ," asserts Edwards, "was to answer the law, and satisfy that; he in his death endured the curse of the law (Gal 3:10–13, and Rom 8:3–4)."[71] Romans 3, 5, and 8 and Galatians 3:12 are certainly major covenant-of-works texts for Edwards's exegesis.

In "Notes on Scripture," no. 288, Edwards comments on the law-gospel contrast in his exegesis of Hebrews 10:1 using anagogical and historical interpretive methods. The word "shadow" is "distinguished from images or pictures, as being a more imperfect representation of the things. ... The shadow was accompanied with darkness and obscurity; gospel things were then hid under a veil."[72] Edwards relates this text to Hebrews 8:5 and Colossians 2:17. In his "Blank Bible" entry on Hebrews 8:5, Edwards argues that the author of Hebrews means that Mount Sinai "represented heaven."[73] Anagogically speaking, Mount Sinai is the heavenly place. Edwards interprets Colossians 2:17 similarly at this point, indicating that a shadow is a type of historical event that adumbrates another event to come. "The

---

works interesting and to help the audience focus attention on the main communicative concerns." Collins, *Genesis 1–4*, 9.

69. Edwards, *The "Blank Bible,"* 991. Cf. Edwards, "Observations on Romans 3:9–24," in *Original Sin*, 290–91.

70. Edwards, *A History of the Work of Redemption*, WJE 9:308–9.

71. Edwards, *Notes on Scripture*, 129.

72. Edwards, *Notes on Scripture*, 247–48.

73. Edwards, *The "Blank Bible,"* 1147.

types of the Old Testament were given, not without an aim at their instruction to whom they were given, but yet they were given much more for our instruction under the New Testament; for they understood but little, but we are under vastly greater advantage to understand them than they."[74]

It is clear that Edwards sought not only a spiritual sense but also a literal-historical sense of the texts. Since Edwards's Christological reading of the doctrine of the covenant of works employs a promise-fulfillment structure, this structure makes indispensable the relationships between the federal heads (Adam and Christ), the law and the gospel, and the Old and New Testaments. It is according to this promise-fulfillment structure that God carries on his redemptive work through Christ in a manner that displays the divine wisdom in both design and execution—a notion that Edwards expresses using the phrase "the history of redemption." This structure presupposes a similarly indispensable interpretive method, that is, typology. "Throughout *A History of the Work of Redemption*," Lucas points out, "Edwards relied heavily on typology as a means for linking together the Old and New Testaments and showing how it all points to Christ and his redemptive work."[75]

---

74. Edwards, "Types," in *Typological Writings*, WJE 11:148.

75. Sean Michael Lucas, "*A History of the Work of Redemption*," *A Reader's Guide to the Major Writings of Jonathan Edwards* (Wheaton, IL: Crossway, 2017), 181. While Edwards's typology is grounded in the Bible, it is not limited to biblical descriptions. Mason I. Lowance Jr. and David H. Watters argue that Edwards's typology is "an expanded and broadened typology which would permit allegorizing of the world of nature in a Platonic fashion." Mason I. Lowance Jr. and David H. Watters, "Editor's Introduction to 'Types of the Messiah,' " in Edwards, *Typological Writings*, 173. In the same vein, Barbara Kiefer Lewalski insists that Edwards "attempted to systematize and defend types from the natural world as an extension of biblical typology." Barbara Kiefer Lewalski, *Protestant Poetics and the Seventeenth-Century Religious Lyric* (Princeton, NJ: Princeton University Press, 1979), 139. Indeed, in "Images" in *Typological Writings*, Edwards argues, "Why should we not suppose that He makes the inferior in imitation of the superior, the material of the spiritual, on purpose to have a resemblance and shadow of them? We see that even in the material world, God makes one part of it strangely to agree with another, and why is it not reasonable to suppose that He makes the whole as a shadow of the spiritual world?" Edwards, "Images of Divine Things," in *Typological Writings*, 53. He also claims, "This may be observed concerning types in general, that not only the things of the Old Testament are typical; for this is but one part of the typical world. The system of created beings may be divided into two parts, the typical world and the antitypical world. The inferior and carnal, i.e., the more external and transitory part of the universe, that part of it which is inchoative, imperfect and subservient, is typical of the superior, more spiritual, perfect and durable part of it, which is the end and as it were the substance and consummation of the other. Thus the material and natural world is typical of the moral, spiritual and intelligent world, or the City of God. And many things in the world of mankind, as to their external and worldly parts, are typical of things pertaining to the City and kingdom of God, as many things

Although there are many sorts of interpretive methods, it is through typology that Edwards approaches the promise-fulfillment structure of the covenant of works. This again implies that the interpretive method of typology plays a significant role in Edwards's vision of the unity of the Bible. Edwards defines "Types" as follows: "Texts of Scripture that seem to justify our supposing the Old Testament state of things was a typical state of things, and that not only the ceremonies of the Law were typical, but that their history and constitution of the nation and their state and circumstances were typical. It was, as it were, a typical world."[76] As Mason I. Lowance Jr., and David H. Watters point out, Edwards's typology represents an attempt at revealing "God's progressive dispensation through history and human time while providing continuities between the Old and New Testaments and contemporary events."[77] For Edwards, typology neither disregards the literal sense nor opposes historical reality. Rather, typology is a means not only to affirm "both the literal meaning and historical reliability of the biblical narratives"[78] but also to do justice to allegorical, mystical, spiritual, and metaphorical interpretations of the Bible.

---

in the state of the ancient Greeks and Romans, etc. And those things belonging to the City of God, which belong to its more imperfect, carnal, inchoative, transient and preparatory state, are typical of those things which belong to its more spiritual, perfect and durable state, as things belonging to the state of the church under the Old Testament were typical of things belonging to the church and kingdom of God under the New Testament. The external works of Christ were typical of his spiritual works. The ordinances of the external worship of the Christian church are typical of things belonging to its heavenly state." Edwards, "Types of the Messiah," in *Typological Writings*, 191–92. For more information, see John F. Wilson, "Editor's Introduction," in Edwards, *A History of the Work of Redemption*, 47–48; Barshinger, *Jonathan Edwards and the Psalms: A Redemptive-Historical Vision of Scripture* (New York: Oxford University Press, 2014), 174; Kreider, *Jonathan Edwards's Interpretation of Revelation*, 99–100; Janice Knight, "Learning the Language of God: Jonathan Edwards and the Typology of Nature," *WMQ* 48 (1991): 531–51; Diana Butler, "God's Visible Glory: The Beauty of Nature in the Thought of John Calvin and Jonathan Edwards," *WTJ* 52 (1990): 13–26.

76. Edwards, "Types," 146.

77. Lowance and Watters, "Editor's introduction to 'Types of the Messiah,'" in *Typological Writings*, 157.

78. Wallace E. Anderson, "Editor's Introduction to 'Images of Divine Things' and 'Types,'" in *Typological Writings*, 12. According to Anderson, Edwards, in response to Enlightenment rationalism and deism, whose interpretive principle was based on reason, adopting a skeptical method of scriptural interpretation, maintained the literal and historical interpretations of the biblical text. On the other hand, against the Catholic and Anglican exegetes who sought the allegorical sense of the text at the expense of historicity, Edwards places an emphasis on the significance of the progress of redemptive history. For more context of the eighteenth century and Edwards's objections to rationalists and deists, to Catholic and Anglican exegetes, to the Cabalists, and to English dissenters, see Anderson, "Editor's Introduction to 'Images of Divine Things' and 'Types,'" 3–33.

Edwards's use of typology follows a double-literal exegesis, which is found in medieval exegetes such as Nicholas of Lyra. Steinmetz describes Lyra's double-literal sense as

> a literal-historical sense, corresponding to the story line of the text in its original setting, and a literal-prophetic sense, incorporating at least some of what had been regarded as the spiritual sense of the text. The same text might have two referents, one in the present and one in the more distant future. Isaiah 53, which speaks of Israel as a suffering servant according to the literal-historical sense, may also have reference to Christ according to the literal-prophetic sense, whose innocent suffering expiated the sins of the world. The letter, in other words, is not barren surface, but is pregnant with deeper meanings that are recoverable without recourse to the spiritual senses of Scripture. Promise and fulfillment, type and antitype, are embedded in the letter, which is not mere history but prophecy as well.[79]

According to Steinmetz, it is in this sense that the Protestants rejected allegory as a tool for interpretation and advocated the literal sense.[80] This implies that they maintained "a letter pregnant with spiritual significance, a letter big-bellied with meanings formerly relegated by the quadriga to allegory or tropology." The same was true for Calvin, who identified the ladder in Jacob's dream with Christ.[81] Puritan historian Barbara K. Lewalski argues, "Typology occupied a more central and more precisely defined place in Calvin's exegesis than in Luther's," and his "hermeneutical recommendations and practice" offered "a model for later exegetes."[82] According to Wilson, William Perkins, who was one of the most influential Elizabethan Puritans, "made room for" the tradition of "double literal sense."[83] Likewise, Edwards maintains double-literal senses of the text by

79. Steinmetz, "Divided by a Common Past," 249.

80. Similarly, Stephen J. Stein notes that Protestant exegetes in the post-Reformation era focused upon "the literal sense of the text, rejecting a multiple scheme of interpretation." Stephen J. Stein, "Jonathan Edwards and the Rainbow: Biblical Exegesis and Poetic Imagination," *New England Quarterly*, 47, no. 3 (September 1974): 453.

81. Steinmetz, "Divided by a Common Past," 249.

82. Lewalski, *Protestant Poetics and the Seventeenth-Century Religious Lyric*, 118.

83. Wilson, "Editor's Introduction," in *A History of the Work of Redemption*, 46.

emphasizing that prophecies had a "twofold accomplishment."[84] In this way, Edwards sought the harmony of prophecies concerning Christ and their salvation-historical fulfillment.

CONCLUSION

In this chapter, we examined Edwards's discussion of the doctrine of the covenant of works and how he uses biblical texts to support this doctrine. There is no question that in Edwards's mind, the covenant of works is derived from Scripture.[85]

As with his Reformed forebears, Edwards employs a literal method to interpret biblical narratives. However, his literal approach does not downplay spiritual and historical aspects of the text. Instead, he uses typology in both a literal-historical sense and a literal-prophetic sense. Edwards reads the biblical narrative not only as something that happened in the past but also as a mirror that reflects the future event of Christ's redemption, which is a literal-prophetic sense or, better, a literal-historical-prefiguring-Christological sense.

The analysis presented in this chapter strongly suggests that for Edwards's understanding of the covenant of works, the fundamental ground is redemptive history through Christ. A central theme of the covenant of works consists of parallels between Adam and Christ and between the law and the gospel. These parallels focus on Christ's obedience to his Father and his subsequent glorification by the Father.

Given the exegetical and theological sophistication that lies behind how Edwards develops his doctrine of the covenant of works, it is apparent that although the links between the biblical texts Edwards uses for his exegesis of this doctrine are intricate, immense, and far-reaching, his exegetical perspective requires, and even helps to establish, the unity of the Old and New Testaments. In the following chapter, we will move on to consider Edwards's exegesis of the doctrine of the covenant of grace.

---

84. Edwards, Miscellany, no. 1172, in The "Miscellanies": Entry Nos. 1153–1360, WJE 23:88.

85. Beeke and Jones, "The Puritans on the Covenant of Works," 219.

8

—

THE EXEGETICAL BASIS OF THE DOCTRINE OF THE COVENANT OF GRACE

INTRODUCTION

This chapter advances Edwards's main concern about the doctrinal harmony of Scripture through examining the biblical basis for his doctrine of the covenant of grace. As Glenn R. Kreider points out, Edwards reads the book of Revelation Christocentrically.[1] According to him, while Edwards used "literal, allegorical, typological, and metaphorical" methods of interpretation, "none of them by itself adequately describes his prevailing approach to the Scripture."[2] Rather, Edwards's prevailing approach to the Bible is Christological typology.[3] The question Kreider fails to ask is how these interpretive methods relate to each other in the interpretation of the whole Bible. David P. Barshinger claims that although there are various interpretive methods, such as literal, typological, Christological, and other methods, Edwards "used them as tools that were guided by his broad redemptive-historical understanding of the Psalms."[4] It is also true that Edwards's redemptive-historical exegesis plays a significant role in his use of exegetical methods to understand the Bible.

---

1. Glenn R. Kreider, *Jonathan Edwards's Interpretation of Revelation 4:1–8:1* (Lanham, MD: University Press of America, 2004), 18.

2. Kreider, *Jonathan Edwards's Interpretation of Revelation*, 8.

3. Kreider, *Jonathan Edwards's Interpretation of Revelation*, 18, 287, 289.

4. David P. Barshinger, *Jonathan Edwards and the Psalms: A Redemptive-Historical Vision of Scripture* (New York: Oxford University Press, 2014), 26.

THE FEDERAL THEOLOGY OF JONATHAN EDWARDS

However, when we note Edwards's various exegetical approaches to the Bible in relation to the doctrine of the covenant of grace, we need to relocate them within the wider scheme of his interest in the harmony of the Bible, in which the structure of promise and fulfillment lies. As chapters 6 and 7 showed, the promise-fulfillment structure in Edwards is understood in terms of the twofold purpose of redemption: the salvation of man and the grand design of salvation.[5] Indeed, the work of redemption is a means of achieving a "design of glorifying himself [God] from eternity." In Miscellany no. 982, "The Work of Redemption The Sum of All God's Works," Edwards cites Colossians 2:2-3 as attesting to God's glory; these texts are read as follows: "to the acknowledgment of the mystery of God, even of the Father and of Christ, in whom or in which are hid all the treasures of wisdom and knowledge." According to Edwards, these words imply that "the gospel ... unfolds the grand mystery of all God's counsels and works, and opens to view the treasures and divine wisdom and knowledge in God's proceedings, which before were, from the beginning of the world, hidden treasures."[6] As E. Brooks Holifield puts it, Edwards "sought

---

5. See chapter 6: 3-4; chapter 7: 27.

6. Edwards, *A History of the Work of Redemption*, WJE 9:125; *The "Miscellanies": Entry Nos. 833–1152*, WJE 20:301-2. This theological theme matches the final goal of theology in Reformed orthodoxy. "The end or goal of theology, in most of the orthodoxy systems, is defined as twofold: theology has an ultimate or primary end (*finis ultimus*) in the glory of God (*Gloria Dei*), and an intermediate or secondary end (*finis intermedius*) in the salvation of man," asserts Muller. As Beeke and Jones point out, the goal of both the covenants of works and grace in Puritan theology is "the glory of God." Notably, Beeke and Jones distinguish the goal of the former from that of the latter: "The end of the covenant of works was God's glory as Creator, but in the covenant of grace, the goal is God's glory as Redeemer. Thus, God's attributes are manifested more abundantly in the covenant of grace because His grace and mercy shine forth in the salvation of men. In Jesus Christ the attributes of God are glorified with a 'new and glorious luster. ... They are much more glorified than they were or could have been by the Covenant of Works (John 12:28, 17:4).' " Similarly, Edwards defined his exposition of the Old and New Testaments' dispensations of the covenant of grace in terms of their revelatory character of the glory of God. For example, in "Notes on Scripture," Edwards's discussion of the parallels between Mt. Sinai and Mt. Zion focuses on revelation in that God's manner of giving the law at Mt. Sinai reveals God's glory. As we already saw in chapter 5, the benefits of the covenant of grace are revealed "in the exercise of God's righteousness or justice." From this, one can expect that Edwards's biblical exegesis of the covenant of grace would focus on the progressive revelation of the attributes of God as righteous Redeemer. In "Notes on Scripture," no. 389, "Ezekiel 1," Edwards draws his attention to the meaning of "wheel" in Ezekiel's inaugural vision. Edwards writes, "The entire series of events in the course of things through the age of the visible universe may fitly be represented by one great wheel, exceeding high and terrible, performing one great revolution. In the beginning of this revolution, all things come from God, and are formed out of a chaos; and in the end, all things shall return

the 'grand design' hidden within the scriptural accounts of history," find-ing Christ as "a figure of awe because of the way he brought opposites into harmonious unity."[7] This signifies that such a structure of promise and fulfillment in Edwards is oriented to his doctrinal harmony of the Bible as an interpretive framework.

This chapter will explore the biblical basis for the covenant of grace, particularly considering Edwards's distinction of six covenantal adminis-trations in the Old Testament from the fall of Adam to Christ's incarnation: Adam to Noah, to Abraham, to Moses, to David, the Babylon captivity, and to Christ's incarnation.[8] In doing so, the chapter will show how Edwards's use of these exegetical methods is oriented to accomplish the harmony of the Bible. While chapter 4 limited its survey of the redemptive-histor-ical theme within the covenant of grace found in Edwards's Redemption Discourse of 1739, this chapter will examine Edwards's exegesis of this topic in exegetical materials such as the Redemption Discourse, "Notes on Scripture," the "Blank Bible," and the "Miscellanies," as well as other places where he considers this topic, such as *Religious Affections, Ecclesiastical*

---

into a chaos again, and shall return to God, so that he that is the Alpha will be the Omega. This great wheel contains a lesser wheel, that performs two revolutions while that performs one. The first begins at the beginning of the world, and ends at the coming of Christ, and at the ending of the Old Testament dispensation, which is often represented as the end of the world in Scripture. The first revolution began with the creation of the world; so the second revolution began with the creation of new heavens and a new earth." Edwards believes that God reveals himself by performing one great wheel which is classified into two revolutions: the first creation through God and the second creation through Christ. With respect to the former, the purpose of this series of events is "to bring things about to Christ again, and to prepare the way for his coming, and to introduce him as the Redeemer of man." Richard A. Muller, *Post-Reformation Reformed Dogmatics: The Rise and Development of Reformed Orthodoxy, ca. 1520 to ca. 1725*, vol 1, *Prolegomena to Theology* (Grand Rapids: Baker Academic, 2003), 5,3 (D), 245; Joel R. Beeke and Mark Jones, "Puritan Hermeneutics and Exegesis," in *A Puritan Theology: Doctrine for Life* (Grand Rapids: Reformation Heritage, 2012), 28, 30; Edwards, *Notes on Scripture*, WJE 15:135–40; *A History of the Work of Redemption*, 114; *Notes on Scripture*, 375.

7. E. Brooks Holifield, "Edwards as Theologian," in *The Cambridge Companion to Jonathan Edwards*, ed. Stephen J. Stein (Cambridge: Cambridge University Press, 2007), 159. For a brief exposition of debates between Edwards's followers and opponents, see Holifield, "Edwards as Theologian," 157–58.

8. Edwards's classification of the six periods of the Old Testament is similar to classical Reformed orthodoxy's understanding of the dispensations of the covenant of grace. See Beeke and Jones, "The Puritans on the Covenant of Grace," in *A Puritan Theology*, 259–78. For an example of this classification in Reformed orthodoxy, see Won Taek Lim, "The Covenant Theology of Francis Roberts" (PhD diss., Calvin Theological Seminary, 2000), 135–205.

Writings, Typological Writings, Apocalyptic Writings, Letters and Personal Writings, and several sermons.

THE BIBLICAL BASIS AND
INTERPRETIVE METHODS

THE COVENANT OF COMMENCEMENT: ADAM TO NOAH

When it comes to the covenant of grace, the initial biblical text Edwards focuses on is Genesis 3:15, in which he finds the revelation of the promise of the covenant of grace. "Presently upon this the gospel was first revealed on earth in these words, Gen. 3:15," states Edwards.[9] Edwards claims that Genesis 3:15 was given as the revelatory foundation of "covenant and promise" on which "the custom of sacrificing was built."[10] Notably, Edwards distinguishes promise from types. "This light of the sun of righteousness to come," Edwards writes, "they [the church] had chiefly two ways. One was by predictions of Christ to come whereby his coming was foretold and promised, and another was by types and shadows of Christ whereby his coming and redemption was prefigured." Thus, while the promise in Genesis 3:15 was "the dawn of gospel," it was through "the institution of sacrifice" that we see the first type of the sacrifice of Christ.[11]

Then, Edwards moves on to Genesis 3:21, where God made for Adam and Eve garments of skins and clothed them. This event was "the second stone" that was laid in the work of redemption.[12] Edwards details that the leather garments required an animal to be slain as the first sacrifice, relying on a traditional interpretation and textual witnesses that prove that the sacrifice was an animal. In doing so, he emphasizes a spiritual effect of the event upon Adam and Eve. "'Tis said that God made them coats, as the righteousness our naked bodies are clothed with is not our own righteousness but the righteousness which is of God, 'tis he only clothed the

---

9. Edwards, *A History of the Work of Redemption,* 132. Genesis 3:15 was also a major covenant verse in sixteenth- and seventeenth-century Reformed orthodoxy. See Beeke and Jones, "The Puritans on the Covenant of Grace," 262.

10. Edwards, *A History of the Work of Redemption,* 135.

11. Edwards, *A History of the Work of Redemption,* 136–37.

12. Edwards, *A History of the Work of Redemption,* 135.

naked soul."[13] According to Edwards, not only was "the institution of sacrifice" in the Old Testament the most important type of "Christ and his
redemption," but it was also intended to "establish in the minds of God's
visible church the necessity of a propitiatory sacrifice in order to the deity's being atoned for sin."[14]

Edwards's description of the work of redemption is closely connected
with ecclesiological visibility. In *Religious Affections*, Edwards writes:

> And the nature of the covenant of grace, and God's declared ends
> in the appointment and constitution of things in that covenant, do
> plainly show it to be God's design to make ample provision for the
> saints having an assured hope of eternal life, while living here upon
> earth. For so are all things ordered and contrived in that covenant,
> that everything might be made sure on God's part. The covenant is
> "ordered in all things, and sure" [II Samuel 23:5]: the promises are
> most full, and very often repeated, and various ways exhibited; and
> there are many witnesses, and many seals; and God has confirmed
> his promises with an oath. And God's declared design in all this is,
> that the heirs of the promises might have an undoubting hope, and
> full joy, in an assurance of their future glory.[15]

As noted, the promises of the covenant of grace are historically exhibited
as seals that assure the believers' hope of eternal life. This understanding
stems from his interpretation of Hebrews 6:17–18, which reads, "Wherein
God, willing more abundantly to show to the heirs of promise the immutability of his counsel, confirmed it by an oath; that by two immutable
things, in which it was impossible for God to lie, we might have a strong
consolation, who have fled for refuge to lay hold on the hope set before
us."[16] God's will appears and is confirmed in the form of seals and an oath,
providing consolation and hope to the true believer.

The visible church is a considerable focus in the early sermons, especially the third sermon of the Redemption Discourse, which emphasizes

---

13. Edwards, *A History of the Work of Redemption*, 136.
14. Edwards, *A History of the Work of Redemption*, 137.
15. Edwards, *Religious Affections*, WJE 2:169.
16. Edwards, *Religious Affections*, 169.

the event of the pouring out of the Holy Spirit as one of Christ's redemptive works. Edwards tends to relate Christ's redemptive work to the visible church. For the pneumatological event of the pouring of the Holy Spirit, Edwards provides an exegesis of Genesis 4:26, which reads, "Then began men to call upon the name of the Lord," with a linguistic sense of the text. Edwards argues:

> The meaning of these words have been considerably controverted among divines. ... Some divines think that the meaning is that then men first began to perform public worship. ... Whether it be to be [so] understood or no, yet so much must necessarily be understood in it, viz. that there was something new in the visible church of God with respect to the duty of prayer, or calling on the name of the [Lord], that there was a great addition to the performance of this duty, and that in some respect or other it was carried far beyond whatever it had been before, which must be the consequence of a remarkable pouring out of the Spirit of God.[17]

Edwards highlights the meaning of the word *beginning* in the text. "And when it is said then *began* men to call upon the name of the Lord, no more can be understood by it than that this was the first remarkable season of this nature that ever was; it was the beginning or the first of such a kind of work of God," asserts Edwards.[18] According to him, this expression is "commonly used in Scripture." Among the biblical texts Edwards uses in connection with Genesis 4:26 are Zephaniah 3:9, 1 Samuel 14:35, and Hebrews 2:3, to which Edwards applies the same interpretive approach, emphasizing the remarkable event of the pouring out of the Holy Spirit. In this way, Edwards interprets Saul's attempt to build an altar (1 Sam 14:35) as to *begin* building the altar.[19] As Wilson points out, Edwards's reference to Hebrews 2:3 in connection with 1 Samuel 14:35 reveals that "outpourings of the Spirit (salvation) are frequently indicated in Scripture by the word *began*."[20]

---

17. Edwards, *A History of the Work of Redemption*, 141–42.

18. Edwards, *A History of the Work of Redemption*, 142.

19. Edwards, *A History of the Work of Redemption*, 142–43.

20. See Edwards, *A History of the Work of Redemption*, 143n3. A similar line of thought is found in Calvin and Turretin. In his comment on Genesis 4:26, Calvin argues, "The face of the Church began distinctly to appear." Similarly, Turretin in his *Institutes* understands

When he does give careful attention to the linguistic aspect of the biblical words, he also considers issues of biblical translation. In the "Blank Bible" note on Genesis 4:26, Edwards claims that "the right translation probably is, 'Then began men to call by the name of the Lord, or 'in' the name of the Lord'; i.e. then they began to call themselves and their children 'by' or 'in' his name." Edwards notes that a similar usage of the preposition *in* is found in Numbers 27:4; Deuteronomy 9:14; 25:7; 1 Samuel 24:21; 2 Samuel 14:7; 18:18; Ruth 4:5; Job 18:17; Isaiah 14:22; and Genesis 48:16. Edwards's point is that there was "a visibly distinct society" in the church of God. From this analysis, he derives the concept of headship of the covenant of grace, in which the children of God are called into "the place of public worship."[21]

Edwards again emphasizes the visible church in his description of the Noahic flood. Here Edwards distinguishes the seed of promise from the seed of Satan. In doing so, he shows how the church had been preserved "in the posterity of Seth."[22] Edwards asserts, "God restored it in the midst of all this flood of wickedness and violence. He kept it up in that line of which Christ was to proceed."[23] Although the flood "overthrew the world," it "did not overthrow" the "building of God, the Work of Redemption." Rather, the flood was "a work of God" that promoted redemption.[24] In *The Christ of the Covenants*, O. Palmer Robertson states, "The covenant with Noah appears in the context of the unfolding of these two lines, and manifests God's attitude toward both. Total and absolute destruction shall be heaped on the seed of Satan, while free and unmerited grace shall be lavished on the seed of the

---

Genesis 4:26 as meaning "divine worship with greater frequency." However, neither Calvin nor Turretin seem concerned about the meaning of the word *began* itself, nor convey their use of the texts including Zephaniah 3:9 and Hebrews 2:3 the idea that through the result of the pouring out of the Holy Spirit, there exists on earth a visible church. See John Calvin, *Commentary on Genesis*, trans. John King (Edinburgh: Calvin Translation Society, 1847), 224; Turretin, *Institutes of Elenctic Theology*, 3 vols., ed. James T. Dennison Jr., trans. George Musgrave Giger (Phillipsburg, NJ: P&R, 1997), 3:45. Cf. John Calvin, *Commentary on Zephaniah*, trans. John Owen (Edinburgh: The Calvin Translation Society, 1848), 282–5; Calvin, *Commentary on Hebrews*, trans. John Owen (Edinburgh: Calvin Translation Society, 1853), 53–54; Turretin, *Institutes of Elenctic Theology*, 3:636; 1:101.

21. Edwards, *The "Blank Bible," WJE* 24:143.

22. Edwards, *A History of the Work of Redemption*, 147.

23. Edwards, *A History of the Work of Redemption*, 148.

24. Edwards, *A History of the Work of Redemption*, 149.

woman."[25] This echoes Edwards's use of Genesis 3:15 and his view of God's destruction of the "enemies of the church" as the work of redemption.[26]

Moreover, Edwards views the redemptive work of Christ as directly related to the idea of the visible church ontologically, as he understands salvation history as both real and mystical (allegorical). For example, Edwards considers the flood to be the seal of Christ's redemption. He describes the saving work of Noah and his family in two respects. First, Noah's family "was the church" in which the "Redeemer was to proceed." Second, Noah's family was the "church" that God saved; it was "the mystical body of Christ" that God redeemed. Not only does Edwards consider the Noahic flood to refer to a real historical salvation of the church, but he also seems to consider that there was a mystical presence of Christ in the event. In a September 1749 sermon on Genesis 6:22, Edwards claims that Noah's warning to people meant Christ's warning. "Every knock of the workmen was a knock of Jesus Christ at the door of their hearts," asserts Edwards.[27] This interpretation is from his consideration of 1 Peter 3:19-20, "By which also he went and preached unto the spirits in prison; which sometime were disobedient, when once the longsuffering of God waited in the days of Noah, while the ark was a preparing, wherein few, that is, eight souls were saved by water."[28]

In the "Blank Bible" note on 1 Peter 4:6, Edwards references Romans 8:13 and Ephesians 4:22 and 24, which speak about the life according to the Spirit, to support his argument about the spiritual presence of Christ. Edwards claims that the apostle Peter referred to the story of the Noahic flood "because the state of the Jews at this day a little before the destruction of Jerusalem was very parallel with that of the old world at the time when the longsuffering of God waited, and his Spirit was striving or preaching, while the ark was preparing." Here again, Edwards argues that Christ's Spirit is preaching through Noah, who was preparing the ark.[29] Edwards

25. O. Palmer Robertson, *The Christ of the Covenants* (Grand Rapids: Baker, 1980), 109.

26. Edwards, *A History of the Work of Redemption*, 149–50.

27. Edwards, "566. Sermon on Gen. 6:22 (September 1740)," (unpublished transcription provided by Ken Minkema of the Jonathan Edwards Center at Yale University), 21.

28. Edwards, "Sermon on Gen. 6:22 (Sep 1740)," 21.

29. Edwards, *The "Blank Bible,"* 1180–81.

interprets the story of the Noahic flood not just spiritually but, rather, considers Christ to be ontologically (spiritually) present in Noah.

Edwards's typological, or allegorical-spiritual, or, better, mystical interpretations, are not unrelated to an anagogical sense with hope. In the Redemption Discourse, Edwards goes on to say that God's act of saving Noah and his family "was a wonderful work of God and a remarkable type of the redemption of Christ, of that redemption that is sealed by the baptism of water." This interpretation is based on 1 Peter 3:20–21, which describes the Noahic flood as "baptism."[30] Following Peter's interpretation of the flood, Edwards argues that "the water" that delivered Noah and his sons is a "type of the blood of Christ that takes away the sin of the world."[31] Indeed, Edwards believes that Peter "seems to signify that the destruction of God's visible church of old by the flood … is a type of the death and resurrection of Christ, as our baptism is."[32] In "Types of the Messiah," Edwards finds a similar typological understanding of the text. He argues, "The things that we have an account of in Moses' history of the Deluge have a great resemblance of many of the Old Testament representations of things that shall be brought to pass in the times of the Messiah's kingdom."[33] God's preservation of Noah and his family typifies Christ's redemption of his people. To describe the Noahic covenant as an event typifying the Messiah, Edwards employs the Isaiah texts and the Psalms. Among them are Isaiah 32:2; 4:6; 25:4; 43:2; Psalms 46:1–3; 32:6; and 91:7, in which Edwards describes Christ as a hiding place from the storm—anagogical exegesis.[34] As we have demonstrated, Edwards's interpretation of the covenant of commencement with Adam shows that his use of typology is ontological, allegorical, and anagogical. Here, we see that Edwards's distinctions among typology, allegory, and anagogy are blurred.

---

30. Edwards, *A History of the Work of Redemption*, 151.
31. Edwards, *A History of the Work of Redemption*, 151.
32. Edwards, *The "Blank Bible,"* 1179.
33. Edwards, "Types of the Messiah," in *Typological Writings, WJE* 11:221.
34. Edwards, "Types of the Messiah," 222.

THE NOAHIC COVENANT AS PRESERVATION: NOAH TO ABRAHAM

Edwards deals with seven themes under the Noahic covenant: (1) the flood, (2) the preserved family of Christ, (3) the new covenant with Noah, (4) the renewal of Noah and his sons, (5) Babel, (6) dispersion, and (7) preserving. The texts that serve as a source for Edwards's view of the Noahic covenant in his exposition of the covenant of grace are primarily Genesis 8:20–22 and 9:1–3, 7, and 10. For Edwards, God's promise to Noah is based proleptically on the sacrifice of Christ. Edwards writes:

> The next thing I would observe was the new grant of the earth God made to Noah and his family immediately after the flood, as founded on the covenant of grace, when Noah moved out of the ark. The sacrifice of Christ was represented by Noah's building an altar to the Lord and offering a sacrifice of every clean beast and every clean fowl. ... And thereupon [God] blessed Noah and established his covenant with him and with his seed, promising no more in like manner to destroy the earth, signifying how, here too by the sacrifice of Christ, God's favor is obtained and his people are in safety from God's destroying judgment and do obtain the blessing of the Lord.[35]

God does not destroy the earth but rather has mercy on Noah and his family according to the promise that is "founded on" the covenant of grace.[36] Since Christ was "the surety" of the covenant, such a promise is given not to Adam but to Noah, nor could it be broken. The phrase "my covenant" in Genesis 9:10 signifies the very covenant of grace that already existed before Noah, so that "Noah would understand what covenant it was by that denomination."[37] In "Notes on Scripture," no. 166, "Genesis 8:21," Edwards

---

35. Edwards, *A History of the Work of Redemption*, 152.
36. Edwards, *A History of the Work of Redemption*, 153.
37. Edwards, *A History of the Work of Redemption*, 153. Note that Edwards asserts that God preserved Noah and his family from the flood before his making a new covenant with Noah. With respect to the relationship between the pre-flood and post-flood covenant with Noah, Robertson argues, "The pre-diluvian and post-diluvian covenantal commitments of God to Noah fit the frequent pattern of covenantal administration in Scripture. It is not necessary to posit two covenants with Noah, one preceding the flood and one following the flood. Preliminary dealings precede formal inauguration procedures. God's commitment to 'preserve' Noah and his family prior to the flood relates integrally to the 'preservation' principle, which forms the heart of God's covenantal commitment after the flood." See Robertson, *The Christ of the Covenants*, 110n2. For more information on the correlation of the covenantal commitments within its administration, see D. J. McCarthy, "*Běrît* and Covenant

explains that it was not through "the acceptableness" of Noah's burnt offerings but through "the acceptableness of the sacrifice of Christ represented by it" that God decided not to "curse the ground."[38] This shows that typology helps Edwards understand the nature of the covenant of grace in terms of a Christocentric focus.

Edwards goes on to emphasize that the covenant with Noah reveals that Noah received a new right to maintain the earth, affirming God's preservation of the earth. Indeed, the covenant with Noah repeatedly is renewed not only with Noah but also with "his sons."[39] In these renewals, God preserved the true religion. In this vein, Edwards interprets the event of the tower of Babel as a demonic attack on God's "great Work <of Redemption>." The building of the tower of Babel "tended to frustrate" the grand design of redemption, which "was founded not on the haughtiness of men but Christ's blood."[40] Edwards bases this interpretation on Isaiah 2, in which "the prophet is foretelling of God's setting up the kingdom of Christ in the world." God's purpose in the destruction of the tower of Babel was to "bring down the haughtiness of men, and how the 'day of the Lord shall be on every high tower and [every fenced wall].' " Indeed, "Christ's kingdom is established by bringing down every high thing to make way for it, II Cor. 10:4–5." Thus, it is necessary to destroy Babel in order for "soul to make way for the setting up Christ's kingdom."[41]

For Edwards, Isaiah 2 and 2 Corinthians 10:4–5 deal with God's power to make all things obedient to Christ. The former text is read as a prophecy, and the latter is considered a fulfillment. Once again, for Edwards, the visible church was a necessary aspect of God's redemptive work in both the individual soul and his grand design. Moreover, Edwards's interpretation of the Old Testament prophets has a Christocentric focus. We will study his ecclesiology at length in chapter 9. Here, we will be satisfied with offering exegetical warrant for Edwards's understanding of the covenant of grace.

---

in the Deuteronomistic History," in *Studies in the Religion of Ancient Israel*, G. W. Anderson, et al., eds., VTSup 23 (Leiden: Brill, 1972), 81, 81n6. According to Robertson, McCarthy finds "several instances in Scripture in which a covenantal bond seals a relationship already existing." Robertson, *The Christ of the Covenant*, 110n2.

38. Edwards, *Notes on Scripture*, 98.
39. Edwards, *A History of the Work of Redemption*, 153.
40. Edwards, *A History of the Work of Redemption*, 154.
41. Edwards, *A History of the Work of Redemption*, 154.

Although Edwards's Christological reading through his typology some-times goes beyond the classical Reformed theologians, who also read Scripture Christologically through typology, his exegesis approaches the biblical texts from the whole Bible—the analogy of Scripture.[42] Edwards labored to understand the historical and regional contexts of biblical passages, interpreting the texts according to the way in which he found God's grand design of salvation in the biblical narrative. As Sweeney argues, Edwards falls within the "twin interpretive pillars" of traditional Protestant readings of the Bible. That is, Edwards upholds (1) "the 'anal-ogy of Scripture' (*analogia Scripturae*)," which means that "*individual* texts were read in light of other texts in other parts of holy Scripture," and (2) "the 'analogy of faith' (*analogia fidei*)," which implies that "*diffi-cult* texts were read in view of the kerygmatic core and doctrinal drift of the Bible."[43] Thus, it is not difficult to see that Edwards understands the meanings of the texts to be found in other biblical texts. For example, Edwards believes that the city of Babylon was set over against "the city of God." Indeed, "Palestine and Jerusalem and Zion is opposed often in both Old Testament and New." The city of Babylon was intended to prosecute "the great design of redemption." In order to make "the building of Babel to cease," God dispersed "the nations" and divided "the earth among its inhabitants." Edwards claims that God's scattering the nations is achieved for the purpose of the "great design" because God saw "the future propa-gation of the gospel among the nations." Understandably, this plan caused them to be "placed, the ends of their habitation so limited round about the land of Canaan, the place laid out for the habitation of God's people, as most suited the design of propagating the gospel among them." The loca-tion of the land of Canaan is supported by Deuteronomy 32:8–9 and Acts 17:26–27, which indicate that "the inhabited world was chiefly in the Roman

---

42. Edwards's use of typology and allegory should not be understood as deviating from Protestant typology. Noting a dangerous trend by some who see Edwards's hermeneutical method as something entirely new, Sweeney claims that although Edwards "often went beyond what other Protestants had said about the Christological meanings of his Old Testament texts, he refused to go beyond what the rule of faith allowed." Douglas A. Sweeney, *Edwards the Exegete: Biblical Interpretation and Anglo-Protestant Culture on the Edge of the Enlightenment* (New York: Oxford University Press, 2016), 102, 100–101.

43. Sweeney, *Edwards the Exegete*, 55–56. Sweeney cites Richard Muller's definition of the terms. For this, see Richard A. Muller, *Dictionary of Latin and Greek Theological Terms: Drawn Principally from Protestant Scholastic Theology*, 2nd ed. (Grand Rapids: Baker Academic, 2017), 25.

empire in the times immediately after Christ, which was in the countries round about Jerusalem."[44] Without specifically referring to the relationship between these two texts, Edwards believes that the land of Canaan is a type of Jerusalem in the New Testament, and the habitations of the nations is a type of the inhabited world in the Roman empire.

A similar reflection on the boundaries of the nations' habitations is found in "Notes on Scripture," no. 387, on Acts 17:26–27, in which Edwards argues that because of their location, "the Gentile world might always be under a capacity of receiving light from the Jews." Edwards goes on to assert, "The world had great advantage to obtain the knowledge of the true God by their being all 'made of one blood'; by this means the knowledge of true religion was for some time kept up in the world by tradition." God allowed the nations "a clue in their search after truth" through a way of "tradition and memory" till Moses' era.[45] In sum,

> God appointed the particular place of the habitation of the Jews to be as it were in the midst of the earth, between Asia, Africa, and Europe; and in the great contests there were between the great empires of the world, they were always in the way. And before the days of the gospel, the bounds of the world of mankind seem not to have been near so extensive as since; and particularly, 'tis probable that America has been wholly peopled since. See *Isaiah 45:19*; *Ezekiel 5:5*.[46]

With respect to other nations that were not placed in that area, Edwards claims, "The devil afterwards led many nations unto remote parts of the world to that end to get 'em out of the way of the gospel, led 'em unto America. Others were led unto northern cold regions that are almost inaccessible."[47] For Edwards, the boundaries of the nations' habitations were set for the purpose of the gospel. Thus, the human race, after the destruction of the tower of Babel, was placed to inhabit the earth, especially around the midst of the earth, that is, Israel. This implies that Edwards reads

---

44. Edwards, *A History of the Work of Redemption*, 155.
45. Edwards, *Notes on Scripture*, 370.
46. Edwards, *Notes on Scripture*, 372.
47. Edwards, *A History of the Work of Redemption*, 155.

the textual description of the biblical cities, regions, or countries with an eye toward seeing history as a vehicle that announces the gospel. Notably, this interpretation is in line with the Pauline view of the boundaries of the nations, as seen in Acts 17:27, "That they should seek the Lord, if haply they might feel after him, and find him, though he be not far from every one of us."[48]

In his "Blank Bible" note on Deuteronomy 32:8, Edwards gives a more detailed exposition of the places of the inhabitants. Sharing a typological explanation of the land of Canaan with Matthew Henry, Edwards identifies Noah's imprecatory statements regarding the descendants of Canaan as prophecies that were fulfilled in time. He asserts that God "ordered that the posterity of Canaan ... should be planted there in the meantime, to keep possession as it were till Israel was ready for it, because those families were under the curse of Noah, by which they were condemned to servitude and ruin (Gen. 9:25), and therefore would be the more justly, honorably, easily, and effectually rooted out, when the fullness of time was come that Israel should take possession."[49] Edwards believes that Noah's curse upon Canaan was fulfilled according to the grand design of salvation.

Edwards's dependence upon biblical history, however, does not mean that he restricts his own reflections to a literal-historical exposition of the Bible or that he believes there is no biblical genre except history. Rather, Edwards's exegetical methods used in his exposition of the covenant of grace include a massively poetic tendency. In Miscellany no. 1033, "Imprecations of the Old Testament," Edwards claims, "It was an ancient way of prophecy to prophesy of future blessings and calamities in the language of prayer or petition." As examples, Edwards presents "Isaac prophesies of the future lot of Jacob" (Gen 27:28–29), Moses' blessings of the tribes (Deut 33:6–8, 24), Jotham's curse upon Abimelech, the men of

---

48. Eckhard J. Schnabel states, "Paul asserts that the human race was created by God so that people are in fellowship with him. Beyond the (physical and) historical existence of the human race, God created human beings so that they would 'seek' (ζητεῖν) him, i.e., that they would try to find him. The use of this verb here implies that human beings do not know God and do not know how or where to find God, but it also implies that they desire to find him and have a relationship with him." Eckhard J. Schnabel, *Acts*, Zondervan Exegetical Commentary on the New Testament (Grand Rapids: Zondervan, 2012), 735.

49. Edwards, *The "Blank Bible,"* 306.

Shechem, and the house of Millo (Judg 9:20).[50] While Edwards does not refer to Noah's curse upon Canaan in Genesis 9:25 as a prophecy, for him the curse in Genesis 9:25 belongs to a literary device that indicates future calamities, which will be fulfilled according to the words of God.

A similar line of poetic understanding is found in Edwards's exegesis of the story of Noah and the rainbow. In "Notes on Scripture," no. 348, "Genesis 9:12–17," Edwards attends to the rhetorical figures in the biblical text. He places a great emphasis upon the tropes and schemes that made biblical language poetic. For example, Edwards believes that the rainbow is "the token of the covenant" as a "special promise."[51] This image of tokens also appears in Isaiah 54:8–10 and 7:14, which mention the same promise.[52] Edwards goes on to interpret the light of the rainbow as "the symbol of God's favor and blessed communications to those that are the objects of his favor" and "a symbol of hope, comfort and joy, excellency and glory."[53] Edwards's interpretation is not only allegorical, as applied to a spiritual communion of the church with Christ, but also anagogical, indicating hope.

Further, light represents "grace and love that is manifested in the covenant of grace." The light "in all the variety of its beautiful colors" signifies "the beauties and sweetness of the divine Spirit of love, and those amiable sweet graces and happy influences that are from the Spirit." The light is the symbol of "the divine presence, and especially of God manifest in the flesh, or in the human nature of Christ, and therefore fitly represents the pleasant grace and sweet love of God as appearing in Christ, God-man." Edwards goes on to use figurative imagery, such as "the cloud," "the multitude of drops," "the bow," the shape of "the rainbow," "the sun," "a drop of rain," "the drops of rain," considering biblical language to be radically poetic.[54] For example, the cloud indicates "the human nature of Christ's

---

50. Edwards, Miscellany no. 1033, in The "Miscellanies": Entry Nos. 833–1152, 370.

51. Edwards, Notes on Scripture, 329.

52. Edwards, Notes on Scripture, 329.In his "Blank Bible" note on Isaiah 7:14, Edwards argues that "those things" which are "'mentioned in Scripture'" are "signs of things predicted ['did not take place'] till after the thing signified has been accomplished." See Edwards, The "Blank Bible," 636.

53. Edwards, Notes on Scripture, 329.

54. Edwards, Notes on Scripture, 329–35. For an excellent analysis of this entry, see Stephen J. Stein, "Jonathan Edwards and the Rainbow: Biblical Exegesis and Poetic Imagination," New England Quarterly 47, no. 3 (September 1974): 440–56.

person." The multitude of drops, which make "the light of the sun … so beautifully reflected," typifies "the saints" as the children of Christ. "The whole rainbow" is the type of a diverse but united church as an organic whole.[55] For the rest of description of the rainbow, Edwards uses a comprehensive exegetical method, including typological, allegorical, tropological, anagogical, ethical, and eschatological dimensions.[56]

Again, the covenant with Noah was the covenant of preservation, which is renewed according to the covenant of grace. This concept is not created by Edwards himself but results from his consideration of the textual witnesses that provide a narrative of the preservation of the church. Edwards believes that the narrator of the Bible, especially Moses, described the biblical events within a literary framework for readers of the Bible to understand the work of redemption in the grand design of God. "Another thing … ," contends Edwards, "was God's preserving the true religion in the line of which Christ was to proceed when the world in general apostatized to idolatry." Edwards claims that although "even God's people themselves … became corrupted in the measure with idolatry," they were not "wholly drawn off to idolatry to forsake the true God."[57] For this argument, Edwards focuses on biblical events in which God's people remain faithful despite of their corruption. For example, Edwards cites Genesis 31:53, "The God of Nahor judge betwixt us," in which Jacob describes God as "the Lord of Nahor." He also mentions Solomon, who was to a certain extent "infected with idolatrous corruption" (1 Kgs 11:1–10). Similarly, "the children of Israel" served "other gods in Egypt" (Josh 24:14). Jacob's family kept "images for a considerable time," and he took his wife, who is from "Padan Aram" (Gen 28:6; 31:17–19). Nonetheless, "the true religion was kept up in <the line of whom Christ was to come>, which is another instance of God's remarkably preserving his church in a time of a general deluge of wickedness."[58] Edwards's descriptions of the flood, the Noahic covenant, its renewals, and the destruction of the tower of Babel are followed by the witnesses of the biblical texts. It is in this exegetical way that the Noahic covenant

---

55. Edwards, *Notes on Scripture*, 330–31.
56. See Edwards, *Notes on Scripture*, 331–35.
57. Edwards, *A History of the Work of Redemption*, 156.
58. Edwards, *A History of the Work of Redemption*, 156.

provides for Edwards the historical framework in which God carries on his grand design of salvation.

THE ABRAHAMIC COVENANT AS THE CONFIRMATION OF PROMISE: ABRAHAM TO MOSES

If the Noahic covenant was for Edwards the way of preservation through destruction, the covenants with Abraham, Moses, and David are considered the way of redemption through separation. Again, this point of view represents Edwards's understanding of Moses' intention. In "Notes on Scripture," no. 416, "Whether the PENTATEUCH was written by Moses," Edwards attempts to demonstrate that the Pentateuch was indeed written by Moses. In doing so, he argues that Moses was aware of the history through which God intended to separate the seed of Abraham from other nations. He writes:

> That great affair that Moses most evidently wrote the history of, and which takes up all the historical part of the Pentateuch, from Gen. 10:26 to the end of Deuteronomy, is God's separating the seed of Abraham and Israel from all nations, and bringing [them] near to himself to be his peculiar people; but to the well understanding of this, it was requisite to be informed of the origin of nations, the peopling of the world, and the Most High, his dividing the nations their inheritance. And therefore the 9th, 10th, and 11th chapters of Genesis are but a proper introduction to the history of this great affair. And in that song of Moses, of which there is mention made in the law, and which Moses in the law was required to write, and the people in the law were required to keep, and learn, and often rehearse, there is an express reference to the separating the sons of Adam, and God's dividing the earth among its inhabitants, which is unintelligible without the 10th and 11th chapters of Genesis. And in this place also is plainly supposed a connection between this affair and that great affair of separating the children of Israel from all nations to be his peculiar people, about which most of the history of the Pentateuch is taken up.[59]

---

59. Edwards, *Notes on Scripture*, 439.

Edwards's view of Moses' intention in writing the Pentateuch shows that even for Moses, the Abrahamic covenant was the covenant of promise, in which Christ and his redemptive works are revealed much more strongly than previously through the narrative of separating the church from the world. In his exposition of the Abrahamic covenant, Edwards tends to relate the biblical events more directly to Christ. As already noted, Edwards's Christocentric view of history in his description of the two lesser periods of the Old Testament is focused on typology foreshadowing Christ's blood as the ultimate sacrifice. Even in his treatment of the Noahic covenant, Edwards also deals with Christological themes such as Christ's human nature, his state of humiliation, his suffering and death, and his resurrection.[60] Nevertheless, Edwards's exegesis of the Abrahamic covenant finds numerous types of Christ in the texts, illuminating in more detail the redemptive work of Christ, such as Christ's incarnation, humiliation, and ascension, as well as the salvation of the Gentiles.

Edwards highlights that God's revelation is more fully made known in the time of Abraham than in the previous periods. During this period, God called Abraham and made him and his family "remain a people separate from all the rest of the world" in order to uphold "the true religion."[61] Since "the land of the Chaldees" in which Abraham had lived "was the country" near Babel, these two places "were the original and chief seat of the worship of idols." In response, God moved Abraham to a new place, which was "separate from" these evil areas. Edwards sees this event as "a new thing" that had never happened before. This work of redemption happens because this period was coming closer to "the coming of Christ." Edwards notes, "By this calling of Abraham, the ancestor of Christ, foundation was laid for the upholding the church of Christ in the world till Christ should come, for the world having become idolatrous there was a necessity that the seed of the woman should thus be separated from the idolatrous world in order to that." The call of Abraham happened not just for the preservation of the true religion but specifically in preparation for the coming of Christ. "It was needful," claims Edwards, "that there should be a particular nation separated from the rest of the world to receive these

---

60. See Edwards, *Notes on Scripture*, 329–35.
61. Edwards, *A History of the Work of Redemption*, 158.

types and prophecies that were needful to [be] given of Christ to prepare the way for this coming."[62] Thus, God's calling of Abraham is considered "a kind of new foundation laid for a visible church of God in a more distinct and regular state, to be upheld ... till Christ should actually come, and then through him to be propagated to all nations."[63]

Again, Edwards's Christocentric focus in the history of the Abrahamic covenant stems from his exegetical-theological approach to the biblical narrative and depends on the witnesses of the New Testament's interpretations of these Genesis texts. For example, Edwards focuses on the meaning of the biblical expression "the father" of all believers: "Abraham is represented in Scripture as though he were the father of all the church." The Bible describes him as "a root whence the visible church thence forward through Christ, rose as a tree distinct from all other plants, of which tree Christ was the branch of righteousness and from which tree, after Christ came, the natural branches were broken off and the Gentiles were grafted onto the same tree."[64] This interpretation, as Wilson points out, "echoes a characteristically Pauline interpretation of the Old Testament" found in passages such as Galatians 3:8–9, 29 and Romans 4:16 and 11:13–20.[65]

Edwards goes on to highlight Christocentric revelation by asserting that "the great condition of the covenant of grace" was made known in this period (cf. Gen 15:5–6), and this fact is supported by the New Testament, especially Romans 4:16, in which Paul refers to believers who have the faith of Abraham. The formal introduction of the covenant of grace begins with circumcision. "There was a further confirmation of it by seals and pledges than ever it had been before, as particularly, God did now institute a certain sacrament to be a steady seal of this covenant in the visible church till Christ should come, viz. circumcision," claims Edwards.[66] Citing Romans 4:11 ("the sign of circumcision as a seal of the righteousness of faith") Edwards emphasizes that "God saw the principal wall

---

62. Edwards, *A History of the Work of Redemption*, 158–59.
63. Edwards, *A History of the Work of Redemption*, 160.
64. Edwards, *A History of the Work of Redemption*, 160.
65. Edwards, *A History of the Work of Redemption*, 160n2.
66. Edwards, *A History of the Work of Redemption*, 161.

of separation."[67] As did his Reformed forebears,[68] Edwards believes that Romans 4:11 is the text that evidences circumcision as sealing the righteousness of Abraham. In this way, Edwards believes that his exposition of the Abrahamic covenant follows the Pauline interpretation.

Edwards proceeds to examine the biblical texts that narrate the Abrahamic covenant and its renewal through Abraham's descendants. In the Redemption Discourse, the biblical texts Edwards directly employs for the Abrahamic covenant are Genesis 10:10–12; 14:4–7, 19–20; 15, particularly verse 16; 19:1–9, 24–28; 22:15; 24:3; 26:3–4, 34–35; 27:29; 27:46–28:2; 28:10–22; 31:24; 32:1–33:5; 34:30; 35:5; 37–50, particularly 49:8–12 and 50:20; Isaiah 41; Hebrews 2:11; 3:6–10; 7:1–17; 11:11–12; John 8:56; 1 Peter 2:7, 8; Psalm 105:12–15; Galatians 3:24; Exodus 19:16; Jude 1:7; Mark 12:10; Acts 4:11; Philippians 2:5–11; and Revelation 5:5.[69] Through his exegesis of these verses, Edwards describes the nature of the history of separation between Abraham's seed and the world and analyzes how the contents of the covenant of grace were revealed and confirmed in the time of Abraham.

Importantly, while Edwards treats the contents of the covenant, such as circumcision as the covenantal seal, and the external blessings of the covenant promises (i.e., "his victory [over] Chedorlaomer and the kings" and the blessing of Melchizedek the priest of the most high God as the confirmation of the promise of the covenant of grace),[70] he puts most emphasis on the revelatory character of Christ and on his redemptive work in the covenant of grace. One of the great examples of this is found in Wilson's appreciation of Edwards's view of Romans 4:18–21. "This passage and the one above," Wilson argues, "extol Abraham and Sarah's faith; they trusted that God would grant them a son. In arguing that Isaac's birth was a further confirmation of the covenant, JE [Jonathan Edwards] puts the emphasis on the revelation of the covenant rather than on their faith, although he connects this covenant with faith by emphasizing that it was a covenant of grace."[71] Indeed, Edwards believes that Genesis 14:14–16 signifies "the

---

67. Edwards, *A History of the Work of Redemption*, 162.

68. Beeke and Jones, "The Puritans on the Covenant of Grace," 267.

69. These texts are from Edwards's own citation and references observed by Wilson. See Edwards, *A History of the Work of Redemption*, 162–72, and Wilson's footnotes on the same pages.

70. Edwards, *A History of the Work of Redemption*, 161–63.

71. Edwards, *A History of the Work of Redemption*, 164n5.

victory that Christ his seed should obtain over all nations of the earth whereby he should possess the gate of his enemies," alluding to Isaiah 41, which prophesies "the future glorious victory the church shall obtain over the nations of the world." Melchizedek was the "great type of Christ," and his bread and wine signify "the sacrament of the Lord's Supper." Further, Edwards believes that "the smoking furnace and burning lamp" described in Genesis 15 was a sign of "the sacrifice of Christ." While "the smoking furnace" was the type of "the sufferings of Christ," the burning lamp indicates "the glory" after "Christ's sufferings." Furthermore, for Edwards, Hebrews 11:11–12 and Romans 4:18 allude to Genesis to confirm the "promise God gave Abraham of the covenant of grace." Isaac's deliverance referred to in Hebrews 11:17–19 typifies "the resurrection of Christ from the dead."[72] Edwards even believes that Abraham literally saw Christ's "'day and saw it and was glad' [John 8:56]." As a result, Abraham had a "clear understanding and sight of Christ."[73]

Edwards elaborates on the significance of this point, employing the stories of God's redemptive work through Abraham, Isaac, and Jacob, from whom "Christ was to proceed."[74] In Edwards's view, this redemptive history is supported by Psalm 105:12–15, which addresses God's protection of Israel over against other nations. Interestingly, Edwards believes that Jacob "wrestled with Christ" (Gen 32:1–33:5).[75] When the covenant of grace was "renewed and confirmed to Jacob," the ladder Jacob saw in his dream "was a symbol of the way of salvation by Christ" (Gen 28:10–22).[76] In his "Blank Bible" note on Genesis 28:11–12ff, Edwards's typological and allegorical treatment of Christ comes to the fore. Edwards argues that "the angels of God ascending and descending" (v. 12) in Genesis 28:12 signifies Christ, which is alluded to by John 1:51, "You shall see heaven open, and the angels of God ascending and descending on the Son of man." Jacob's

---

72. Edwards, *A History of the Work of Redemption*, 162–64. According to Edwards, Hebrews 11:19 is an example of types in the Old Testament that is given with an "aim at their instruction to whom they were given, but yet they were given much more for our instruction under the New Testament; for they understood but little, but we are under vastly greater advantage to understand them than they." See Edwards, *Typological Writings*, 148–49.

73. Edwards, *A History of the Work of Redemption*, 162–65.

74. Edwards, *A History of the Work of Redemption*, 165.

75. Edwards, *A History of the Work of Redemption*, 166.

76. Edwards, *A History of the Work of Redemption*, 170.

sleep is a type of "the death of Christ," representing that "there should be a way to heaven from the earth" through Christ's death. He goes on to say that Jacob is rendered as "a type of Christ." At the same time, Jacob also "represents a believer, or rather all believers collective, or the church, or spiritual Israel."[77]

Further, that the rock Jacob used for his pillow is Christ is confirmed by the fact that Jacob "anointed it (v. 18)." The emphasis on the stone as a type of Christ is affirmed by Genesis 28:22, which reads, "And this stone, that I have set up for a pillar, shall be God's house," since the idea of Christ as God's house is alluded to by New Testament texts such as Colossians 2:9 ("all the fullness of the Godhead bodily"), John 2:19 ("Destroy this temple, and in three days I will build it up"), and Revelation 21:22, which describes the Lamb as "the temple of the New Jerusalem."[78] Edwards goes on to assert that Jacob represents Christ. "Jacob's sleeping or resting on" the stone means "God's people's believing in or resting on Christ" (Matt 11:28, which sets out Christ's invitation and promise to the weary). Even Jacob's sleeping is a type of Christ's "death," as well as his "rest." Edwards writes:

> If we look on Jacob here as a type of Christ, his sleep is a type of death. If as a type of the church or of the Israel of God, then it represents spiritual rest. But let us take the type which way we will, we may observe that the great privilege and blessing is obtained of having heaven's gate opened, and a way to heaven from the earth; and the ministration is enjoyed in Bethel, in the house of God, i.e. in God's church, and in the improvement of the ordinances of his house.[79]

77. Edwards, The "Blank Bible," 172–73.

78. Edwards, The "Blank Bible," 173–74. In his "Blank Bible" note on Daniel 9:25, Edwards provides the meanings of anointing in four respects: (1) Christ in his divine nature is "the object of the infinite love and delight of the Father," who "eternally pours forth the Spirit of love"; (2) Christ in human nature is given the Holy Spirit "from the first moment of his existence in that degree and measure as to be a bond of union with the eternal Logos so as to be the same person"; (3) "The Father poured forth the Holy Spirit abundantly on him to consecrate him to and qualify him for this work at his conception and birth, and more publicly and visibly at his baptism"; and (4) Christ "is anointed by the church, or by every believing soul, by the exercise of the grace of the Holy Spirit towards him, and as it were pouring out his soul in divine love in him." See Edwards, The "Blank Bible," 767–68.

79. Edwards, The "Blank Bible," 175.

Here again, Edwards's view that Jacob is a type of both Christ and the spiritual rest of the church obscures the line between typology and allegory.

An examination of Edwards's interpretation of Jacob shows that the more he observes the texts canonically, the more he desires to find Christological meaning in the texts. Kreider rightly notes:

> Beginning with the Fathers, exegetes were interpreting the text of the Old Testament Christologically. If all of Scripture finds its fulfillment and significance in Christ, then perhaps the exegete should be able to find Christological significance in each text. This seems to be the practice of many of the interpreters surveyed. In this case, although the historical context and the original setting of the text are not unimportant, there is the desire to find the fuller or deeper meaning in the text in light of the coming of Christ.[80]

As with Jacob's story, Edwards argues that Joseph's story shows how God has preserved his people. In so doing, Edwards attempts to interpret Joseph allegorically and typologically. "This salvation of the house of Israel by Joseph was upon many accounts very much a semblance of the salvation of Christ," he insists.[81]

Notably, for Edwards, the literal and typological senses go hand in hand in revealing Christ's redemptive works. For example, Edwards explains Christ's humiliation and exaltation through Joseph's story.[82] As "Joseph was first in a state of humiliation," Christ came to the world "in the form of a servant." Joseph's being cast into a dungeon signifies Christ's descending "into the grave." However, as Joseph "rose out of the dungeon," became exalted unto "the king's right hand," and "[provided] food to preserve life," Christ in his exaltation "dispensed food to his brethren and so gives them life." Furthermore, the prophecy in Jacob's blessing to Judah (Gen 49:8–10)

---

80. Kreider, *Jonathan Edwards's Interpretation of Revelation*, 52–53.

81. Edwards, *A History of the Work of Redemption*, 171.

82. Note that Witsius finds the meanings of Christ's humiliation and exaltation in Abel and Enoch as the historical types of the Old Testament, respectively. Witsius classifies the types of the Old Testament into three categories: the natural, historical, and legal types of Christ. See Herman Witsius, *The Economy of the Covenants Between God and Man: Comprehending a Complete Body of Divinity*, trans. William Crookshank, 2 vols. (Edinburgh: John Turnbull, 1803), 2:192–231. For a brief summary of Witsius's work, see D. Patrick Ramsey and Joel R. Beeke, *Analysis of Herman Witsius's The Economy of the Covenants* (Grand Rapids: Reformation Heritage, 2003).

specifies "Christ's pedigree" as Judah's posterity.[83] In this way, Edwards does not disregard a literal sense of the texts, but rather he uses the literal sense to help his understanding of salvation history.[84] In this case, the literal sense of the text is considered to be historical and prophetical, and its fulfillment can be understood by typology. As we saw above, Edwards highlights the advances and confirmations of the promise of the covenant of grace, unfolding and prefiguring Christ's work of redemption.

THE MOSAIC COVENANT AS PEDAGOGY: MOSES TO DAVID

Typology plays a significant role in Edwards's understanding of the spiritual and progressive character of salvation, which is apparent in his understanding of the Mosaic covenant.[85] According to Wallace E. Anderson, Edwards's formulation of "his view of typology" is to "conform to his perception of how God manifested himself and his work of redemption in the

---

83. Edwards, *A History of the Work of Redemption*, 171–72.

84. This hermeneutic in Edwards is not to be regarded as interpretive innovation. According to Lewalski, one of the important Protestant revisions of medieval theory was Protestants' "understanding of the types as an integral part of the literal text whose meanings are progressively clarified in history." For "the usual medieval conception," "Old Testament personages and typical things are merely literal signs, shadows, or corporal figures, important only as they point to the substance, the body, the true spiritual reality found solely in Christ and the New Testament." On the contrary, the Protestants placed an emphasis on "the continuities between the two covenants in regard to the spiritual condition of the faithful." Although the Protestant exegetes maintained that the "Old Testament ceremonies and practices have been abrogated," they "saw the spiritual situation of Christians to be notably advantaged by the New Covenant but not different in essence from that of the Old Testament people, since both alike depend on signs which will be fulfilled in Christ at the end of the time." For the Protestants, "the ultimate antitype for all the types" is not "the incarnate Christ of the Gospel," but "the Christ of the *eschaton*." See Barbara Kiefer Lewalski, *Protestant Poetics and the Seventeenth-Century Religious Lyric* (Princeton: Princeton University Press, 1979), 125–26. Note that with respect to the interpretation of the types of the Old Testament, Witsius maintains that there are two senses to most things the Old Testament: the literal sense and the mystical sense. According to him, even the literal sense of the texts could "represent other things, which they were appointed to prefigure long before they happened." Both Christ and Paul "have informed us of this, when they apply most of the things which happened under the old dispensation to the Messiah, and to the oeconomy of a better testament." The "mystical" meaning "points to Christ, in his *person, states, offices, and works*, and in his *spiritual body*, the church." See Witsius, *The Economy of the Covenants*, 2:188–89. Emphasis original.

85. Note that Reformed orthodox theologians, such as John Ball and Francis Roberts, locate the Davidic covenant and the covenant with Israel in the Babylonian captivity within the administration of the Sinai covenant. See Lim, "The Covenant Theology of Francis Roberts," 205.

corporeal realm."[86] Importantly, Edwards maintains both the literal-historical sense and the literal-prophetic sense. Edwards believes that the redemption of the children of Israel out of Egypt was "the greatest pledge and forerunner of the future redemption of Christ." Edwards goes on to say that "the bush" on Mount Sinai indicates "a dry place, as the human nature of Christ," who was described as "a root out of a dry ground." The bush burning with fire implies "the sufferings of Christ." That the bush was not consumed signifies that Christ "suffered extremely yet perished not, but overcame at last and rose from his suffering."[87]

According to Edwards, the angel of the Lord in Exodus 3:2–3, by whom Moses was sent to redeem Israel, was Christ.[88] This point of view is striking since Edwards believes that Christ was literally and historically present in the time of the Mosaic era. That Christ "redeemed with a strong hand and outstretched arm and great and terrible judgments" on Israel's enemies implies that "Christ with mighty power triumphs over principalities [and powers] and executes complete judgment on his church's enemies, bruising the serpent's head." It was Christ himself who redeemed Israel from "the devils, the gods of Egypt" as well as from the Egyptians. According to Wilson, these interpretations in Edwards clearly allude to Isaiah 11:1 and 53:2, which Edwards reads as prophecies of Christ's coming, as well as to Colossians 2:15 and Genesis 3:15.[89] Edwards goes on to say:

> And Christ, the seed of the woman, did now in a very remarkable manner fulfill the curse on the serpent in bruising his head, Exodus 12:12, "For I will pass through the land of Egypt this night, and will smite all the first born in the land of Egypt, both man and beast; and against all the gods of Egypt will I execute judgment." Hell was as much and much more engaged in this affair as Egypt was; the pride and cruelty of Satan, that old serpent, was more concerned in it than Pharaoh's. He did his utmost against the people, and to his utmost opposed their redemption. But 'tis said that when God

---

86. Wallace E. Anderson, "Editor's Introduction to 'Images of Divine Things' and 'Types,'" in Edwards, *Typological Writings*, 9.

87. Edwards, *A History of the Work of Redemption*, 175–76.

88. Edwards, *A History of the Work of Redemption*, 175.

89. See Edwards, *A History of the Work of Redemption*, 175n7, 8, 4; 176n6.

redeemed his people out of Egypt, then he broke the heads of the dragons in the waters. He broke the heads of leviathan in pieces and gave him to be meat, Psalms 74:12–14. God forced their enemies to let 'em go that they might serve him, as Zacharias, Luke 1:74–75.[90]

Edwards's point is that Christ made Israel free from their servitude to Satan, as well as from the Egyptians, in order to fulfill the curse on the serpent written in the Bible.

Edwards's reading of Psalm 106:34 follows a similar pattern. Edwards believes that the deliverers alluded to in the psalm typify Christ. Among them, there are Barak, Jephthah, Gideon, and Samson. In particular, when Christ "appeared to manage the affairs of his church in this period he often appeared also in the form of that nature that he took upon him in his incarnation." The person Moses beheld as "the 'similitude of the Lord' " in Numbers 12:8 was Christ. Moses saw not Christ's face but "the back parts of a glorious human form in which Christ appeared to him." Likewise, Christ appeared to "the seventy elders" (Exod 24:9–11). It was also Christ whom Joshua met by Jericho (Josh 5:13–15). The same is true for Judges 6:11, in which the angel was meant to be Christ, and 13:17–20, in which God appeared to Manoah. Edwards emphasizes that this latter passage signifies that Christ "appeared to Manoah in a representation both of his incarnation and death: of his incarnation in that he appeared in an human form, and of his death and sufferings represented by the sacrifice of his kid."[91]

Edwards's exegesis of the story of Exodus is striking. For example, the redemption event of the exodus is understood as a fulfillment of the consequences of the covenant of works, and at the same time, Edwards sees it as reflecting the future event of salvation for the church of God. Similarly, Edwards's notes on Exodus 2 in "Notes on Scripture" and the "Blank Bible" reveal his understanding in terms of the literal-prophetic sense. In "Notes on Scripture," no. 95b, Edwards notes that Moses was "a type of the church of the Jews in their oppressed condition in Egypt," but he was also "a type of every elect soul who is naturally overwhelmed in sin, in misery and danger, and is redeemed and delivered, in terms that Moses was taken out of the

---

90. Edwards, *A History of the Work of Redemption*, 176.
91. Edwards, *A History of the Work of Redemption*, 196–98.

water."[92] In his note on Exodus 2:10 in the "Blank Bible," Edwards argues that Moses' being preserved in the midst of the waters was "a figure of Christ's coming forth out of his state of humiliation and suffering, wherein he was as it were in the midst of great waters."[93] One notes four dimensions of the character of Moses. Moses could be understood as a real figure, a type of the church under the Mosaic era, a type of the soul of the elect, and a type of Christ being humiliated in the era of New Testament.[94]

As for Edwards's understanding of the Mosaic covenant as the republication of the covenant of works, it is important to note that the Mosaic covenant is under the first great period, during which God's work of redemption is to prepare for Christ's coming. This echoes Sweeney's observation of Edwards's pedagogical exegesis, which "gave him rules for faith and life."[95] Edwards loves to unpack the text in practical pedagogy. Edwards's interpretation of 1 Corinthians 1:21 is a prime example of how he practices pedagogy. He argues that God gave the Mosaic covenant in an awful manner.[96]

---

92. Edwards, *Notes on Scripture*, 77–78.

93. Edwards, *The "Blank Bible,"* 207.

94. A similar line of thought is found in James Durham's definition of typology. According to Durham (1622–1658), typology is distinguished from allegory in terms of five aspects: historical, factual, prefiguring, antitypical, and Christological senses. See James Durham, *Clavis Cantici, or An Exposition of the Song of Solomon* (Edinburgh: G. Swintoun and J. Glen, 1668), 5–6. In analyzing typology, the ancient mode of Christian symbolism, Lewalski maintains a similar exposition of the distinction between typology and allegory. See Lewalski, *Protestant Poetics and the Seventeenth-Century Religious Lyric*, 111, 122. From these two sources, Doug Landrum argues that, despite his distinction between two different modes, Durham provided "the opportunity for a more inclusive measurement of Edwards's exegesis." Doug Landrum, *Jonathan Edwards's Exegesis of Genesis: A Puritan Hermeneutic?* (Mustang, OK: Tate, 2015), 83. For more information on the distinction between the two different modes, see Peter Cotterell and Max Turner, *Linguistics and Biblical Interpretation* (Downers Grove, IL: InterVarsity, 1989), 294; Kreider, *Jonathan Edwards's Interpretation of Revelation*, 12. For Edwards, the distinction between two different modes could be marginal. See Stephen J. Stein, "The Quest for the Spiritual Sense: The Biblical Hermeneutics of Jonathan Edwards," *Harvard Theological Review* 70, no. 1 (1977): 112–13; Mason I. Lowance Jr., "'Images or Shadows of Divine Things' in the Thought of Jonathan Edwards," in *Typology and Early American Literature*, ed. Sacvan Bercovitch (Amherst: University of Massachusetts, 1972), 228; Mason I. Lowance Jr. and David H. Watters, "Editor's Introduction to 'Types of the Messiah,'" in Edwards, *Typological Writings*, 179. However, Edwards was cautious with his use of typology, emphasizing that such use of typology should be linked explicitly with biblical references. In this vein, some scholars reject Stein's depictions of Edwards as if he had no warranted rule of interpretation. See Stephen R. C. Nichols, *Jonathan Edwards's Bible: The Relationship of the Old and New Testaments in the Theology of Jonathan Edwards* (Eugene, OR: Pickwick, 2013), 95; Landrum, *Jonathan Edwards's Exegesis of Genesis*, 146; Sweeney, *Edwards the Exegete*, 72.

95. Sweeney, *Edwards the Exegete*, x.

96. Edwards, *A History of the Work of Redemption*, 180–81.

Edwards cites 1 Corinthians 1:21, which reads, "For after that in the wisdom of God the world by wisdom knew not God, it pleased God by the foolishness of preaching to save them that believe."[97] For Edwards, this verse offers evidence that God let the Gentiles know about the insufficiency of human ability to deliver themselves from darkness and misery. God carried on his redemptive works in the Old Testament by making the heathen face their ignorance of salvation. A similar interpretation of 1 Corinthians 1:21 is found in Edwards's *Apocalyptic Writings*, the "Miscellanies," and the sermon, "The Pure in Heart Blessed."[98] While Edwards's understanding of 1 Corinthians 1:21 is not limited to such a pedagogical sense,[99] he is emphatic that the text reveals God's pedagogical design for salvation history. In "An Humble Attempt," in *Apocalyptic Writings*, Edwards argues that 1 Corinthians 1:21-22 observe that "the insufficiency of human abilities ... does now remarkably appear."[100] The same is true for his sermon "The Pure in Heart Blessed," in which Edwards argues that although God "delivered his Law" from Mount Sinai, "the principal discoveries of God's mind and will to mankind were reserved to be given by Jesus Christ."[101]

Thus, for Edwards, the Mosaic covenant is given as pedagogy for the children of Israel. As mentioned earlier, the law in the Mosaic covenant serves as a schoolmaster, leading people to Christ. The reason for the revelation of the covenant of works in the Mosaic dispensation was that God intended to convince his people of their inability to obtain salvation on their own. Edwards emphasizes this pedagogical sense in his sermon on

---

97. Edwards, *A History of the Work of Redemption*, 180.

98. See Edwards, *An Humble Attempt to Promote Explicit Agreement and Visible Union of God's People in Extraordinary Prayer for the Revival of Religion and the Advancement of Christ's Kingdom on Earth, Pursuant to Scripture-Promises and Prophecies Concerning the Last Time*, in *Apocalyptic Writings*, WJE 5:441.

99. Edwards applies 1 Corinthians 1:21 to the historical aspect of salvific revelation under the theme of conviction of an individual in the order of salvation. This implies that Edwards draws a pedagogical principle of God from 1 Corinthians 1:21 that deals with salvation history and applies it to conviction. This is why Edwards connects this verse with other texts, such as Matthew 15:22-28, 18:24, John 16:21, Revelation 12:2, 1 Samuel 22:2, Ezekiel 20:33-37, Judges 6:8-10, Psalm 126:5, and Luke 8:43, in which he finds God's pedagogical method in service of the need of conviction before conversion. See Edwards, *The "Miscellanies": Entry Nos. a-z, aa-zz, 1-500*, WJE 13:439-41.

100. Edwards, "An Humble Attempt," 359.

101. Edwards, "The Pure in Heart Blessed (Matt. 5:8)," in *Sermons and Discourses 1730-1733*, WJE 17:59.

Hebrews 12:22–24a. In this sermon, Edwards preaches that Christians must avoid the way of sin. In doing so, he describes Mt. Sinai as a metaphor serving as a means to lead those who "are far" away from Mt. Zion, that is, the heavenly Jerusalem, to Christ.[102] Throughout the sermon, he compares God's presence on Mt. Sinai with that on Mt. Zion. "There was a Great deal to Restrain from sin that their Fathers saw and heard when they came to m[oun]t Sinai," asserts Edwards. God manifested his "terrible majesty" in "the m[oun]t burnt with fire with blackness & darkness & tempest and the sound of the trumpet and the voice of words giving forth the ten Commands." Thus, the people of Israel became "sensible how terrible his wrath would be against the breakers of the commands."[103] However, while the children of Israel "heard the voice of G[od] as a Strict Lawgiver" at Mt. Sinai, "Xtians are brought to hear the voice of X as a Savior" at Mt. Zion.[104] Edwards repeats the same theme in his sermon on Hebrews 12:22–24d.[105]

While Edwards contrasts the voice of God heard at Mt. Sinai with the voice of God as heard in the gospel, he uses the former as a means to lead people to God's church, or the spiritual Jerusalem. In the application part of the sermon, Edwards exhorts his people to "consider how miserable a condition you are in in this your distance from this Holy mountain you are wandering in a wilderness in a naked defenseless condition you have no foundation better than the sand for a dependence for your Et[ernal] welfare and happiness ... & instead of being of the Household of G[od] you are the children of the Devil." Then, he argues that "the silver trumpet" from Mt. Zion invites God's people to come to Mt. Zion. In other words, for Edwards, the ten commandments in the Mosaic dispensation of the covenant of works express "the dreadful wrath threatened at Mt Sinai" in order for believers not to neglect the avoidance of sin.[106] In this vein,

---

102. Edwards, "544. Sermon on Hebrews 12:22–24 (a) (April 1740)," in *Sermons, Series II, 1740, WJEO* 55, unpaginated.

103. Edwards, "544. Sermon on Hebrews 12:22–24 (a) (April 1740)," 1.

104. Edwards, "544. Sermon on Hebrews 12:22–24 (a) (April 1740)," 10.

105. Edwards, "547. Sermon on Hebrews 12:22–24 (d) (April 1740)," in *Sermons, Series II, 1740*, vol. 55 of *WJEO*, unpaginated.

106. Edwards, "544. Sermon on Hebrews 12:22–24 (a) (April 1740)," 18. Edwards's discussion of the parallels between Mt. Sinai and Mt. Zion is repeated in "Notes on Scripture." However, his focus is not on pedagogy but rather on revelation in that God's manner of giving the law at Mt. Sinai reveals God's glory. In other words, while Edwards's sermon on Hebrews 12:22–24a emphasizes the dreadful manner in which the ten commandments were given at

Sweeney sees the function of the schoolmaster in the Mosaic law as the "method of divine propaedeutics."[107] Similarly, Michael Horton points out, one of the distinct characteristics of the Mosaic covenant was its role as "a pedagogue unto Christ [showing] the Savior who alone could fulfil the terms of the law."[108]

Given this, it is not surprising that Edwards's view of the pedagogical exegesis of the text in relation to the Mosaic covenant appears to be the same as that of his forebears, who saw the covenant of works or the Mosaic law as a bridle restraining sin and as a schoolmaster to bring the Jewish people in the Old Testament to Christ. Specifically, Edwards's pedagogical exegesis resembles Calvin's view of the law in the Mosaic dispensation. For example, Calvin's exegeses of 1 Corinthians 1:21 and Romans 5 have a pedagogical focus. In his commentary on Romans 5, Calvin argues that Paul sought to harmonize the law with faith. Calvin contends:

> In order to instruct the people in the doctrine of repentance, it was necessary for him to teach what manner of life was acceptable to God. ... It was now the duty of the people to consider in how many ways they drew curses on themselves, and how far they were from deserving anything at God's hands by their works, that being led to despair as to their own righteousness, they might flee to the haven of divine goodness, and so to Christ himself. This was the end or design of the Mosaic dispensation.[109]

Calvin believes that the law given in the Mosaic administration functions as a means to lead Israel to Christ. The very same is true for his commentary on 1 Corinthians 1:21, in which Calvin interprets the phrase "for since the world knew not" as follows:

Mt. Sinai, warning about sin, his interpretation of God's descent on Mt. Sinai in "Notes on Scripture" is intended to reveal the greatness of the glory of God. See Edwards, *Notes on Scripture*, 135–40.

107. Sweeney, *Edwards the Exegete*, 60. According to Sweeney, a propaedeutic is a preliminary instruction, or something that prepares the way for our understanding of something else.

108. Michael S. Horton, "Obedience Is Better Than Sacrifice," in *The Law is Not of Faith: Essays on Works and Grace in the Mosaic Covenant*, ed. Bryan D. Estelle, J. V. Fesko, and David Van Drunen (Phillipsburg, NJ: P&R, 2009), 315.

109. John Calvin, *Commentary on the Epistle of Paul the Apostle to the Romans*, trans. John Owen (Edinburgh: Calvin Translation Society, 1849), 386.

The right order of things was assuredly this, that man, contemplating the wisdom of God in his works, by the light of the understanding furnished him by nature, might arrive at an acquaintance with him. As, however, this order of things has been reversed through man's depravity, God designs in the first place to make us see ourselves to be fools, before *he makes us wise unto salvation* (2 Timothy iii.15).[110]

When we consider the pedagogical function of the Mosaic covenant and Edwards's use of the texts, it is clear that Edwards explains the Mosaic covenant in terms of God's redemptive purpose found in the biblical texts mentioned above.

Finally, Edwards employs canonical exegesis when he connects the Mosaic covenant to Christ and redemptive history. As we have seen from Edwards's own exposition of the biblical narratives of the four covenants with Adam, Noah, Abraham, and Moses, Edwards deems the Bible to be the most significant source for redemptive history. It is through his canonical reading that Edwards sees succession in the events portrayed in Scripture. For example, the final period of the Mosaic covenant, to which Edwards pays attention, is "the beginning of a succession of prophets and erecting a school of the prophets in Samuel's time." While "the spirit of prophecy" had existed during the previous periods,[111] such a prophecy was not constant before Samuel. Edwards writes:

> But there was no such order of men upheld in Israel for any constancy before Samuel. The want of it is taken notice of in 1 Sam. 3:1, "And the word of the Lord was precious in those days; there was no open vision." But in Samuel there was begun a succession of prophets that was maintained continually from that time, at least with very little interruption, till the spirit of prophecy ceased about Malachi's time. And therefore Samuel is spoken of in the New Testament as the beginning of this succession of prophets, Acts 3:24, "And all the prophets from Samuel and those that follow after, as

---

110. John Calvin, *Commentary on the First Epistle of Paul the Corinthians*, trans. John Pringle (Edinburgh: Calvin Translation Society, 1848), 84.

111. Edwards, *A History of the Work of Redemption*, 199.

many as have spoken, have foretold of these days." After Samuel was Nathan, and Gad, and Iddo, and Heman, and Asaph, and others. And afterwards at the latter end of Solomon's reign we read of Ahijah, and in Jeroboam and Rehoboam's time we read of prophets, and so continually, one prophet succeeded another till the captivity. We read in the writings of those prophets that are inserted into the canon of the Scriptures, of prophets as being a constant order of men upheld in the land in those days. And in the time of the captivity there were prophets still, as Ezekiel and Daniel, and after the captivity then more prophets, as Zechariah, Haggai, and Malachi.[112]

For Edwards, 1 Samuel 3:1 offers an important clue that during the period from Adam to Moses, there were no successive prophecies provided by a series of prophets. In the "Blank Bible" note on 1 Samuel 3:1, Edwards cites Matthew Henry's exegesis of the text: "Now and then a man of God was employed as a messenger upon an extraordinary occasion, but there were no settled prophets to whom the people might have recourse for counsel, or from whom they might expect the discoveries of the divine will. What was, it seems, was private; none were publicly known to have visons." On the contrary, "there was open vision during the time of Samuel, and this claim is supported by 1 Sam. 3:20 and 4:1 which evidence that all Israel knew that 'Samuel was established to be a prophet of the Lord.' "[113]

Moreover, Acts 3:24, which reads, "Yea and all the prophets from Samuel and them that follow after, as many as have spoken, have likewise foretold of these days," is significant for Edwards's conclusion that "God intended a constant succession of prophets" from Samuel's era. For more evidence, Edwards cites Acts 10:43, "To him give all the prophets witness," and Acts 3:18, "But those things, which God before had shewed by the mouth of all his prophets, that Christ should suffer, he hath so fulfilled." Edwards finds similar support from 1 Peter 1:10-11, "of which salvation the prophets have inquired and searched diligently, who prophesied of the grace that should come unto you; searching what, or what manner of time the Spirit of Christ which was in them did signify, when it testified beforehand the

---

112. Edwards, *A History of the Work of Redemption*, 199–200.
113. Edwards, *The "Blank Bible,"* 346–47.

sufferings of Christ, and the glory that should follow." Further, Ephesians 2:20's phrase "built on the foundation of the prophets and apostles" offers the same exposition of the redemptive work through a constant succession of prophets.[114] Edwards's interest in Israel's history from Samuel to Jeremiah lies not in various historical events but rather in constancy of prophecy. More importantly, this concern is not from his own interpretation of the Bible but from his affirmation of the biblical evidence. It is through his canonical reading that he approaches the historical books and the prophetic books, emphasizing God's redemptive work in the preparation of the coming of Christ.

As we have seen, Hebrews 12:22–24 and 1 Corinthians 1:21 provide Edwards with a proper place to engage in theological interpretation of the Mosaic covenant, and the Exodus 2 and 3 narratives, which describe God's calling of Moses, his deliverance from Egypt, and his administration of the Sinaitic or Mosaic covenant, show how God kept his promise alluded to in Genesis 3:15. Edwards believes that the biblical writers of the New Testament drew their theological conclusions regarding the Mosaic covenant from the careful examination of their Old Testament narratives and the intention of the biblical authors, especially Moses. This implies that for Edwards, the New Testament's authors share the Old Testament's historical and theological framework and therefore the Old Testament authors' understanding of the nature and function of the Mosaic covenant. Edwards's use of interpretive methods including the literal, prophetical, and pedagogical senses of the texts for his understanding of the Mosaic covenant is based on an essential framework, that is, a doctrinal harmony of the Old and New Testaments, showing the close relation of the historically interpreted texts in accordance with a promise-fulfillment structure.

THE DAVIDIC COVENANT: DAVID TO
THE BABYLONIAN CAPTIVITY

Edwards considers David "the greatest personal type of Christ of all under the Old Testament."[115] As noted earlier, Witsius classifies the types of Christ in the Old Testament into three categories: the natural types (the creation

---

114. Edwards, *A History of the Work of Redemption*, 202.
115. Edwards, *A History of the Work of Redemption*, 204.

of the world, and man and woman), the historical types (during the first age of the world, i.e., Abel, Enoch, Noah, Isaac, and Moses), and the legal types (the ark of the covenant and the day of expiation or atonement).[116] By comparison, Edwards divides the types of Christ in the Old Testament into three different categories: institutional types, providential types, and personal types. Representative examples of the institutional types and the providential types are "the ordinance of sacrificing" and "the redemption out of Egypt". Further, David is "the greatest of the personal types." This classification reveals that Edwards's description of the elements of the covenant of grace undergoes a positive development, progressing from lesser to greater in relation to a Christocentric focus. However, such divisions result from his observations of the historical narrative of Scripture. "The dispensations of providence that have been taken notice of through the last period from Moses to this time, respect the people whence Christ was to proceed. But now the Scripture history leads us to consider God's providence towards that particular person whence Christ was to proceed," asserts Edwards.[117]

Edwards stresses the abundant revelations that took place under the Davidic covenant. Edwards lists these revelations under nineteen headings: (1) anointing David as "the ancestor of Christ to be king over his people," (2) "preserving David's life," (3) additions to "the canon of the Scripture," (4) "inspiring David to show forth Christ and his redemption in divine songs," (5) "exalting David to the throne of Israel," (6) choosing "a particular city" to place God's name, (7) the promise of the Messiah, (8) giving David "the whole of the promised land," (9) perfecting "all institutions of the Jewish worship," (10) the addition to the canon of the Scripture by the prophets Nathan and Gad, (11) "continuing the kingdom of his visible people in the line of Christ's legal ancestors," (12) "the building of the temple," (13) the Jewish church "risen to its highest external glory," (14) a gradual declension of "the glory of the Jewish church," (15) the additions to the canon of the Scripture in and after Solomon's reign, (16) "upholding his church and the true religion" during this period, (17) the preservation of "the Book of the Law," (18) the preservation of "the tribe of which Christ was to proceed

---

116. See Ramsey and Beeke, *Analysis of Herman Witsius's The Economy of the Covenants*, 49–50.

117. Edwards, *A History of the Work of Redemption*, 203.

from," and (19) God's raising up of "a set of eminent prophets" to write prophecies and leaving such prophecies "for the use of his church."[118]

Although these nineteen elements of revelation include various contents with respect to Christ and his redemptive work, most of them relate to the development of the canon. In other words, Edwards's main concern is God's progressive revelation, through which Christ is revealed as the scope of all Scripture. Edwards offers this summary of the periods from Adam to David:

> And if we consider the abundant prophecies of this and the other prophets, what a great increase is here of the light of the gospel which had been growing from the fall of man to this day; how plentiful are the revelations and prophecies of Christ now to what they were in the first Old Testament period from Adam to Noah. Or in the second from Noah to Abraham, or to what they were before Moses, or in the time of Moses, Joshua, and the judges. This dispensation that we are now speaking of was also a glorious advance of the Work of Redemption by the great additions that were hereby made to the canon of the Scripture. Great part of the Old Testament was written now from the days of Uzziah to the captivity into Babylon. And how excellent are those portions of it. What a precious treasure have those prophets committed to the church of God tending greatly to confirm the gospel of Christ, and which has been of great comfort and benefit to God's church in all ages since, and doubtless will be to the end of the world.[119]

Edwards thus examines the Davidic covenant in terms of the additions to the canon of the Scripture.

Again, Edwards's interest in canonicity leads him to approach the biblical texts Christologically. Here Edwards's use of typology is fundamental in the proleptic revelation of Christ and his redemptive work. God's anointing of David typifies Christ "being solemnly anointed by God to be king."[120] With respect to the anointing of Christ, Edwards cites collateral texts that link

---

118. Edwards, *A History of the Work of Redemption*, 203, 206, 208, 209, 211, 212, 214, 215–16, 218, 220, 221, 224, 226, 228, 232, 233, 234, 237.

119. Edwards, *A History of the Work of Redemption*, 204.

120. Edwards, *A History of the Work of Redemption*, 204.

the kingdom of David to that of Christ, such as Psalm 89:20, "I have found David my servant; with mine holy oil"; Luke 1:32, "Give him the throne of his father David"; Isaiah 11:1, "a branch shall grow out of his roots"; Jeremiah 23:5, "I will cause the branch of righteousness to grow up unto David"; and Revelation 22:16, "the root and offspring of David."[121] Edwards offers a Christological reading of several OT passages. That God took away the crown from Saul and gave it to David foreshadows "how Christ who appeared despicable, without form [or comeliness], and was despised and rejected [of men], should take the kingdom from the great ones of the earth."[122] David as the youngest of Jesse's sons shows the accomplishment of Christ's teaching, "The last shall be first and [the first last.]" The last, Edwards believes, points to Christ.[123] As we can expect from Edwards's consideration of David as a personal type of Christ, Edwards relates every personal experience of David to the Christological event. For Edwards, the whole process of providential history in preserving David's life represents the life of Christ, who was preserved from Satan and who conquered him and saved his people.[124]

Noting the significance of David's songs, Edwards asserts:

> Hereby the canon of the Scripture was further added, and an excellent portion of divine writ was it that was added. This was a great advance that God made in this building, as the light of the gospel which had been gradually growing from the fall was exceedingly increased by it. For whereas before there was but here and there a prophecy given of Christ in a great many ages, now here Christ is spoken of by his ancestor David abundantly in multitudes of songs, speaking of his incarnation, life, death, resurrection, ascension into heaven, his satisfaction, intercession, his prophetical, kingly, and priestly office, his glorious benefits in this life and that which is to come, his union with the church, and the blessedness of the church in him, the calling of the Gentiles, the future glory of the church near the end of the world, and Christ's coming to the final

---

121. Edwards, *A History of the Work of Redemption*, 205.
122. Edwards, *A History of the Work of Redemption*, 205.
123. Edwards, *A History of the Work of Redemption*, 205–6.
124. See Edwards, *A History of the Work of Redemption*, 206–8.

judgment. All these things and many more concerning Christ and his redemption are abundantly spoken of in the book of Psalms.[125]

David's life anticipates the Christological fulfillment of those types.[126]

Edwards's biblical exposition of Christ and his redemptive work tends to focus on the glory of God as the redeemer. In other words, Edwards subsumes Christology under the glory of God. "This was," Edwards insists, "also a glorious advancement of the affair of redemption as God hereby gave his church a book of divine songs for their use in that part of their public worship, viz. singing his praises throughout all ages to the end of the world."[127] The reason God gave the book of Psalms is related to his glorious revelation of redemption. God is not just one who reveals his redemptive work without indicating his greater purpose. Rather, God reveals his glory through the redemptive work of Christ. In other words, the whole process of redemptive history is oriented to reveal his glory as redeemer. The reason why God chooses a particular city, that is, Jerusalem, is to "place his name there."[128] Indeed, Christ deserves "so much more glory" "than Moses, Joshua, David, and Solomon, and all the great prophets, priests and princes, judges and saviors of the Old Testament put together."[129] The abolishment of the tabernacle by Moses was caused by God for his purpose to "set up the spiritual gospel temple which was to be far more glorious and of greater extent, and to stand forever."[130] Even "the declining of the glory" of the legal dispensation through corruptions such as superstition and self-righteousness "made way for the introducing the more glorious dispensation of the gospel."[131] God intended this gradual decline of "the glory of the Jewish dispensation" to "make the glory of God's power in the great effects of Christ's redemption the more conspicuous."[132]

---

125. Edwards, *A History of the Work of Redemption*, 210–11.

126. Reformed orthodoxy similarly referred to these revelations in its explanation of the Davidic covenant. Beeke and Jones, "The Puritans on the Covenant of Grace," 269.

127. Edwards, *A History of the Work of Redemption*, 211.

128. Edwards, *A History of the Work of Redemption*, 212.

129. Edwards, *A History of the Work of Redemption*, 218.

130. Edwards, *A History of the Work of Redemption*, 220.

131. Edwards, *A History of the Work of Redemption*, 230.

132. Edwards, *A History of the Work of Redemption*, 231.

The glory of God as the ultimate purpose of the history of redemption, which is promised, revealed, and known to Israel through God's self-disclosure, is known at a deeper level through the history of the Bible. In particular, Edwards relates the biblical narrative of the Babylonian captivity to Christian history during the era of the Roman empire, employing the analogy of faith. Edwards writes:

> This prepared the way for Christ's coming as it made the salvation of the Jews by Christ, those of them that were saved, the more sensible, visible. Though the bigger part of the nation of the Jews was rejected, and the Gentiles called in their room, yet there were a great many thousands of the Jews that were saved by Christ after his resurrection. Act. 21:20. They being taken from so low a state under temporal calamity in their bondage to the Romans, and from a state of great superstition and wickedness that the Jewish nation was then fallen into it, made their redemption the more sensibly and visibly glorious.[133]

Edwards believes that as a great number of the Jews were saved by Christ according to God's preparation, in which the Jews first were persecuted during the reign of the Romans, the same was true during the times of Gideon, Solomon, and the Babylonian captivity, when God diminished his people.[134] According to the analogy of faith, Edwards considers the biblical history of these eras to point to the divine preparation of redemption as an instrument of revealing his glory more abundantly.

THE LAST PERIOD OF THE COVENANT OF GRACE AS A PREPARATORY COVENANT: THE BABYLONIAN CAPTIVITY TO CHRIST'S INCARNATION

As chapter 5 showed, Edwards deals with redemptive history from the Babylonian captivity to Christ's incarnation through three lenses: Scripture history, prophecy, and secular history. In doing so, Edwards contends that secular history can be a means to discern the work of redemption in that it depicts events alluded to in the prophecies found in Scripture. Given

---

133. Edwards, *A History of the Work of Redemption*, 232.
134. See Edwards, *A History of the Work of Redemption*, 231.

this, it is not surprising that Edwards's distinction between history and prophecy leads to selective use of Scriptures having pedagogical significance for redemption. For instance, while the history of Scripture gives no account of the last period of the Old Testament, prophecies found in the books of Daniel, Isaiah, Jeremiah, and Ezekiel allude to redemptive events that occurred during this period.[135] For Edwards, the prophets mention all the redemptive-historical events that occurred during this period of the Old Testament.

Specifically, Edwards understands the texts of the prophets in terms of the great "revolutions," "overturnings," or "shakings" that made way for Christ's coming. He applies these descriptions to historical events recorded in secular history.[136] For example, the Babylonian Empire's occupation of all lands was predicted by biblical prophecies, and secular history tells us that the Babylonian Empire was in fact overthrown by Cyrus, the Persian empire by Alexander, and the Grecian empire by the Romans. These secular histories correspond exactly to what is found in passages of the biblical prophets (Isa 24:1; Jer 25:15–27; and Dan 2, 7, and 11).[137] Edwards considers "these great overturnings" to be a preparatory stage of Christ's coming. Indeed, "these great overturnings were because the time of the great messiah drew nigh."[138]

As further biblical evidence, Edwards cites Ezekiel 21:27, Revelation 8:13, and Haggai 2:6–7. With respect to the two former texts, Edwards gives his careful attention to the biblical expression, especially three repetitions of the word woe. Noting the third repetition, Edwards gives an account of the meaning of the word:

> It must be noted that the prophet Ezekiel prophesied in the time of the Babylonish captivity, and therefore there were three great and general overturnings of the world to come after this prophecy before Christ came: the first by the Persians, [the] second by [the] Grecians, [the] third by [the] Romans, and then after that Christ whose right it was to rule and reign. Here these three great

---

135. Edwards, *A History of the Work of Redemption*, 243–44.
136. Edwards, *A History of the Work of Redemption*, 244–47.
137. Edwards, *A History of the Work of Redemption*, 244–45.
138. Edwards, *A History of the Work of Redemption*, 246.

overturnings are evidently spoken as preparatory to the coming and kingdom of Christ.[139]

That Edwards employs a pedagogical exegetical method does not mean that he disregards the grammatical expressions of the text, nor does he fail to consider canonical exegesis. Rather, the opposite is true.

First, Edwards focuses on the meaning of the word grammatically in order to emphasize the Christological aspect of redemption. With respect to the word *woe*, which appears in both Ezekiel 21:27 and Revelation 8:13, Edwards asserts:

> But to understand the words aright we must note the particular expression, "I will overturn, overturn, overturn, it," i.e. the diadem, crown of Israel, or the supreme temporal dominion over God's visible people. Thus God said, "be no more," that is, the crown should be taken off and the diadem removed, as it is said in the foregoing verse. The supreme power over Israel should be no more in the royal line of David to which it properly belonged, but should be removed away and given to others, and overturned from one to another. First the supreme power over Israel should be in the hands of the Persians, and then it should be overturned again, and again then [it should be in the hands of the] Grecians, and then [it should be] overturned and be in the hands of the Romans, and should be no more in the line of David till that very person come that was the son of David, whose proper right it was. And then God would give it him.[140]

Considering the biblical expression, "the diadem," Edwards interprets the history from the Babylonian captivity to Christ's incarnation in terms of a process of a succession of earthly kingdoms until the incarnation of Christ. These overturning events, according to Edwards, are also described in Haggai 2:6–7, which reads, "For thus saith the Lord of hosts; Yet once, it is a little while, and I will shake the heavens, and the earth, and the sea,

---

139. Edwards, *A History of the Work of Redemption*, 246.
140. Edwards, *A History of the Work of Redemption*, 246–47.

and the dry land; And I will shake all nations, and the desire of all nations shall come: and I will fill this house with glory, saith the Lord of hosts."[141]

Second, Edwards's interpretation of the great overturnings is canonical. Edwards considers these great turnings to be the event of "the church's being in travail to bring forth Christ" in his exposition of Revelation 12:2.[142] In "Exposition on the Apocalypse," Edwards argues that Revelation 12:2 points to "the dreadful pains" the church "endured in her travail with Christianity."[143] Similarly, Romans 8:19–22 shows "the whole creation groaning and travailing in pain together till now, to bring forth the liberty and manifestation of the children of God." God indeed "suffered the devil to do his utmost and to establish his interest by setting up the greatest, strongest, and most glorious kingdoms in the world that he could, before the despised Jesus overthrew him and his empire." As prophesied in Isaiah 2:12, "The day of the Lord of the hosts shall be upon every one that is proud and lofty," so that "Christ might appear so much the more glorious in being above them." Edwards links the texts mentioned above with the New Testament witnesses on the basis of his historical understanding of redemption. He writes:

> I now proceed to show how the Work of Redemption was carried on through the remaining times that were before Christ, in which we have not that thread of Scripture history to guide us that [we] have had hitherto, but have these three things to guide us, viz. the prophecies of the Old Testament, and human histories of those times, and some occasional mention made and evidence given of some things that happened in those times in the New Testament.[144]

Edwards believes that the New Testament witnesses all events in the Old Testament as being set for preparation of Christ's coming. Again, in his sermon "God Glorified in the Work of Redemption," which he preached in a public lecture in Boston in 1731, Edwards even understands the relationship

---

141. Edwards, *A History of the Work of Redemption*, 247.
142. Edwards, *A History of the Work of Redemption*, 247.
143. Edwards, "Exposition on the Apocalypse," in *Apocalyptic Writings*, 108.
144. Edwards, *A History of the Work of Redemption*, 270.

between secular history and biblical history in terms of pedagogy, resting on 1 Corinthians 1:29-30. He claims:

> The Apostle therefore observes to them how that God by the gospel destroyed, and brought to naught, their human wisdom. The learned Grecians, and their great philosophers, by all their wisdom did not know God, they were not able to find out the truth in divine things. But after they had done their utmost to no effect, it pleased God at length, to reveal himself by the gospel which they accounted foolishness.[145]

Thus, Edwards interprets secular history through his canonical reading of the Bible. According to Sweeney, Edwards sought to interpret the biblical text "in a canonically balanced way."[146] Edwards harmonizes the Old and New Testaments through his canonical reading of the text. Edwards's canonical reading of the Bible again leads him to use redemptive-historical exegesis in interpreting those parts of history not described in the Bible. In this regard, secular history during the intertestamental period serves as a means to understand the work of redemption.

CONCLUSION

This chapter examined Edwards's exegetical methods as they pertain to the doctrine of the covenant of grace. It showed how his use of Scripture is deeply shaped by his view of the harmonious character of the Bible.[147]

---

145. Edwards, "God Glorified in the Work of Redemption, by the Greatness of Man's Dependence upon Him, in the Whole of It (1731)," in *The Sermons of Jonathan Edwards: A Reader*, ed. Wilson H. Kimnach, Kenneth P. Minkema, and Douglas A. Sweeney (New Haven: Yale University Press, 1999), 66.

146. Sweeney, *Edwards the Exegete*, 217.

147. This exegetical principle is similar to Calvin's approach to the Bible. "The Christological interpretation in Calvin's Old Testament commentaries looks to the future for the fulfillment of promises and prophesies, and his New Testament commentaries have as the determinative factor for exegesis a movement toward Christ, a movement that is always based on the conviction that the clarity of sacred Scripture is grounded in Christ alone," Kraus asserts. For Calvin, Christ and his redemptive work as fulfillment of Old Testament prophecy are the key to the unity of the whole Bible. Hans Joachim Kraus, "Calvin's Exegetical Principles," trans. Keith Crim, *Interpretation* 31, no. 1 (1977): 17-18. For a brief analysis by Muller of Kraus's understanding of Calvin's exegesis of the Old Testament, see Richard A. Muller, "The Hermeneutic of Promise and Fulfillment in Calvin's Exegesis of the Old Testament Prophecies of the Kingdom," in *The Bible in the Sixteenth Century*, ed. David C. Steinmetz (Durham, NC: Duke University Press, 1990), 76.

A study of his exegesis of this doctrine gives rise to several principles of macro-interpretation. First, Edwards understands the text in the context of what he believes is the biblical authors' intended meaning. Second, he interprets in terms of canonicity. That is, he does not move far from the New Testament's interpretation of the Old Testament. Rather, Edwards adheres to the biblical witnesses, especially following what he perceives to be the New Testament interpretation of the covenant of grace. In other words, his canonical reading of the Bible serves as an outstanding tool for his exposition of the covenant of grace. Third, Edwards believes that Scripture interprets itself and that the meanings of texts should be determined in accordance with the rest of the Bible. Each of these principles highlights Edwards's strong conviction of the harmonious nature of Scripture.

When it comes to micro-exegetical methods, typology plays a major role in Edwards's understanding. His Christocentric focus leads him to interpret the historical events of the Old Testament as types of Christ, in which he finds prophetic descriptions of Christ's humanity, humiliation, suffering, death, and resurrection. However, Edwards's typology is not limited to Christology but is widely applied because of his literal-historical and literal-prophetic senses. Indeed, Edwards believes that the literal texts, while recording historical facts, may not only be fulfilled in Christ but may also reflect future aspects of salvation for the church. Again, Edwards is deeply convinced of the harmony of Scripture.

Last, Edwards finds the methods of pedagogical and redemptive-historical exegesis important. In terms of the promise-fulfillment structure, the Old Testament is the preparatory stage of the fulfillment of the covenant of grace until Christ comes. Through this pedagogical method, Edwards also finds continuities between the old and new covenants. This reflects the views of some of Edwards's Reformed forebears, such as Calvin.

Regarding how Scripture relates to secular history, Edwards maintains that salvation history helps us understand the teachings of the Bible. One significant example is his view of the destruction of Jerusalem during the New Testament era. For Edwards, this represents not merely the end of the Old Testament world but also an accomplishment of the work of redemption.

Edwards is clearly confident that his doctrine of the covenant of grace follows the biblical witness. He seeks to listen to the biblical witness about redemptive history and thereby develop a theology of the covenant of grace. To do so, he selects texts and exegetical methods that result from his belief that Scripture is harmonious. His exegetical methods are clearly bound by the inner unity of the Bible. It is through this exegetical perspective that Edwards developed his federal theology by seeking the doctrinal harmony of the Bible, within which the divine revelation of salvation history could be understood as consistent.

Part 4

—

FEDERAL THEOLOGY *and* ECCLESIOLOGY

9

—

EDWARDS'S FEDERAL THEOLOGY IN ECCLESIASTICAL PERSPECTIVE

INTRODUCTION

Edwards was convinced that the church had two natures: visible and invisible. Further, he was convinced that Scripture testified to these two natures. While the visible church included the converted as well as people who still needed conversion, the invisible, or true, church included only those who had, by conversion, entered into the covenant of grace, that is, those who possessed both visible and invisible faith. Since he believed that there were members of visible churches who had never entered into the covenant of grace with God in Christ by the Holy Spirit, he placed a strong emphasis on true Christianity, true religion, entered into by conversion and the covenant of grace, which made one a part of the true/invisible church.[1]

---

1. Indeed, in his sermon on Colossians 1:24, Edwards writes, "The church of Christ is that company of men that is effectually called out from this fallen undone & gathered together in one in Christ Jesus through him to worship G[od] & have the peculiar enjoyment of him." There are "true saints and those only" who "are effectually called" and "have a true & saving faith born again." In "An Humble Inquiry," Edwards asserts, "Visibility is a relative thing, and has relation to an eye that views or beholds. Visibility is the same as to appear to be a real saint in the eye that beholds; not the eye of God, but the eye of man. Real saints or converts are those that are so in the eye of God; visible saints or converts are those who are so in the eye of man." Edwards, "738. Sermon on Col. 1:24" (unpublished transcription provided by Ken Minkema of the Jonathan Edwards Center at Yale University), L. 3r; L. 4r; Edwards, "An Humble Inquiry into the Rules of the Word of God, Concerning the Qualifications Requisite to a Complete Standing and Full Communion in the Visible Christian Church," in *Ecclesiastical Writings*, WJE 12:185. This shows that, for Edwards, the true church is the invisible church, which is effectually called, rather than the visible church, which is externally called. With respect to union with Christ, Edwards sees "a two-fold union between Christ and the church": "Real and Relative." The former signifies a "real tie or bond between them whereby they are united and really become one," as between "branches and stock [the trunk or woody stem of a living tree]," that is a "natural bond." The latter implies "mutual" relationship. For example, "The apostle Paul was united to the City of Rome," or "a person that is naturally a stranger

Perhaps the foremost example of this is Edwards's doctrine of the Lord's Supper, which emerged as a result of polemic with the Northampton church over the question of true faith. Edwards complained, "I had have difficulties in my mind for many years, with regard to admission of members into the church who made no pretense to real godliness."[2] Edwards "had harbored reservations about his church's sacramental policy"[3] since the church had followed Solomon Stoddard, who believed that the Lord's Supper is a converting ordinance. Stoddard adopted the half-way covenant in order to permit those who professed their belief in Christ without "making a public profession of the Christian faith" to participate in communion.[4] The Northampton church's participation in the half-way covenant convinced Edwards of the need for further reformation in the congregation. Stoddard and the Northampton church even allowed "excommunicated persons" to be "members" of the church. Against this policy, Edwards argued that "no orthodox divines would hold these to be properly and regularly qualified for the Lord's Supper."[5]

Specifically, in December 1748, Edwards refused a young man's request for church membership since he "declined coming into the church" in the way Edwards believed proper, that is, by professing his godliness publicly. In February 1749, Edwards expressed his thoughts on this matter to "the committee of the church, and proposed it to them whether they were willing" for Edwards to deliver his idea of a new policy "from the

---

may be united to a prince by espousals though she never saw him face to face." Edwards, "738. Sermon on Col. 1:24," L. 6r; L. 6v. For a brief summary of the *real* and *relative* unions in the thought of Edwards, see Douglas A. Sweeney, "The Church," in *The Princeton Companion to Jonathan Edwards*, ed. Sang Hyun Lee (Princeton: Princeton University Press, 2005), 170–71.

2. Edwards, "An Humble Inquiry," 507.

3. Douglas A. Sweeney, *Jonathan Edwards and the Ministry of the Word* (Downers Grove, IL: InterVarsity, 2009), 140.

4. Edwards, "An Humble Inquiry," 174. For a detailed exposition of the sacramental controversy, see Edwards, "Narrative of Communion Controversy," in *Ecclesiastical Writings*, 507–619. For Stoddard's own position of the sacrament, see Solomon Stoddard, *The Doctrine of Instituted Churches Explained and Proved from the Word of God* (London: Ralph Smith, 1700); Stoddard, *The Inexcusableness of Neglecting the Worship of God, under a Pretence of Being in an Unconverted Condition…* (Boston: B. Green, 1708); Stoddard, *An Appeal to the Learned: Being a Vindication of the Right of Visible Saints to the Lords Supper, Though They Be Destitute of a Saving Work of God's Spirit on Their Hearts…* (Boston: B. Green, 1709). I am indebted to Sweeney for this material. See Sweeney, *Jonathan Edwards and the Ministry of the Word*, 140n70.

5. Edwards, "An Humble Inquiry," 175.

pulpit."[6] However, because of his rejection of Stoddard's admission policies, Edwards encountered opposition, and his plan to change their policy on membership and sacraments resulted in his dismissal from the church. In opposing the admission of unregenerate persons to the Lord's Supper, Edwards emphasized that true believers are those who maintain the condition of the covenant of grace. This is why Edwards, in "An Humble Inquiry," claims that "to own this covenant [the covenant of grace] is to profess the consent of our *hearts* to it."[7] This story shows that Edwards attempted to relate the outward profession, that is, visible faith, to true religious affection, that is, invisible faith. It is in this way that, for Edwards, visible faith is closely related to true piety.

Edwards sees his federal theology as being characterized by both faith and piety. The basis for unity between faith and piety is located in Edwards's understanding of the doctrinal harmony of the Bible. With respect to the ecclesiastical and practical significance of his federal theology, while faith is distinguished from piety, the former is never separate from the latter. This is clear from his doctrine of justification, in which he seeks unity between faith and piety. In his sermon on "Justification by Faith Alone" as "one of the sparks for the revival of 1734,"[8] he writes, "God don't give those that believe, an union *with*, or an interest *in* the Savior, in reward for faith, but only because faith is the soul's active uniting with Christ, or is itself the very act of unition, on their part."[9] Edwards believes that faith is something more than the means to receive the righteousness of Christ. In Edwards's thought, there is no dividing faith from the pious life, but rather, both are considered one organic whole.

Edwards's emphasis on practical life in his doctrines of union with Christ and justification has produced intense debate among the secondary literature on Edwards.[10] There are many factors in this debate. For

---

6. Edwards, "Narrative of Communion Controversy," 508.

7. Edwards, "An Humble Inquiry," 205. Emphasis in original.

8. E. Brooks Holifield, "Edwards as Theologian," in *The Cambridge Companion to Jonathan Edwards*, ed. Stephen J. Stein (Cambridge: Cambridge University Press, 2007), 152.

9. Edwards, "Justification by Faith Alone," in *Sermons and Discourses 1734–1738, WJE* 19:158.

10. A series of scholars have insisted that Edwards's understanding of faith is dispositional. This insistence finds its support in the following scholars: Thomas A. Schafer, Conrad Cherry, Anri Morimoto, George Hunsinger, Gerald R. McDermott, Gerald McClymond, Sang Hyun Lee, Steven M. Studebaker, Lawrence R. Rast Jr. and J. V. Fesko. Notably, Fesko argues

example, Edwards did not discuss the role of faith in justification in

that Edwards opposes "the idea that faith is the instrument of justification, a tenet that was virtually universally confessed since the earliest days of the Reformation." Further, he argues that for Edwards, "a person is not completely justified until faith issues forth in works, that is, a person's justification hinges upon faith producing works." Thomas A. Schafer, "Jonathan Edwards and Justification by Faith," *CH* 20 (1951): 55–67; Conrad Cherry, "Justification by Faith," in *The Theology of Jonathan Edwards: A Reappraisal* (New York: Doubleday, 1966), 90–106; Anri Morimoto, *Jonathan Edwards and the Catholic Vision of Salvation* (University Park: Pennsylvania State University Press, 1995), 162; Gerald R. McDermott, *Jonathan Edwards Confronts the Gods: Christian Theology, Enlightenment Religion, and Non-Christian Faiths* (New York: Oxford University Press, 2000), 110–29, 339; McDermott, "Salvation as Divinization: Jonathan Edwards, Gregory Palamas and the Theological Uses of Neoplatonism," in *Jonathan Edwards: Philosophical Theologian*, ed. Paul Helm and Oliver D. Crisp (Aldershot, VT: Ashgate, 2003), 127–38; McDermott, "Jonathan Edwards on Justification by Faith—More Protestant or Catholic?" *Pro Ecclesia* 17, no. 1 (2008): 92–111; George Hunsinger, "Dispositional Soteriology: Jonathan Edwards on Justification by Faith Alone," *WTJ* 66, no. 1 (2004): 107–20; Sang Hyun Lee, "God's Relation to the World," in *The Princeton Companion to Jonathan Edwards*, ed. Sang Hyun Lee (Princeton: Princeton University Press, 2005), 59; Lee, "Does History Matter to God?: Jonathan Edwards's Dynamic Re-conception of God's Relation to the World," in *Jonathan Edwards at 300: Essays on the Tercentenary of His Birth*, ed. Harry S. Stout, Kenneth P. Minkema, and Caleb J. D. Maskell (Lanham, MD: University Press of America, 2005); Steven M. Studebaker, "Jonathan Edwards' Pneumatological Concept of Grace and Dispositional Soteriology: Resources for an Evangelical Inclusivism," *Pro Ecclesia* 14, no. 3 (2005), 339; Lawrence R. Rast Jr., "Jonathan Edwards on Justification by Faith," *CTQ* 72 (2008): 347–62; Michael J. McClymond and Gerald R. McDermott, *The Theology of Jonathan Edwards* (2012), 267–68, 361–62; J. V. Fesko, *The Covenant of Redemption: Origins, Development, and Reception* (Göttingen: Vandenhoeck & Ruprecht, 2016), 122–43. This claim, however, is challenged by those who agree that Edwards's doctrine of justification remained faithful to Reformed orthodoxy's view of faith. These scholars include Carl Bogue, Samuel T. Logan Jr., Stephen R. Holmes, Jeffrey C. Waddington, E. Brooks Holifield, Oliver D. Crisp, Michael McClenahan, Josh Moody, Hyun-Jin Cho, Stephen R. C. Nichols, Reita Yazawa, and Douglas Sweeney. Carl W. Bogue, *Jonathan Edwards and the Covenant of Grace* (Cherry Hill, NJ: Mack, 1975), 227–51; Samuel T. Logan Jr., "The Doctrine of Justification in the Theology of Jonathan Edwards," *WTJ* 46 (1984): 26–52; Stephen R. Holmes, "Does Jonathan Edwards Use a Dispositional Ontology? A Response to Sang Hyun Lee," in *Jonathan Edwards: Philosophical Theologian*, 99–114; Jeffrey C. Waddington, "Jonathan Edwards's 'Ambiguous and Somewhat Precarious' Doctrine of Justification?" *WTJ* 66 (2004): 357–72; E. Brooks Holifield, "Edwards as Theologian," 152; Oliver D. Crisp, "Jonathan Edwards on the Divine Nature," *Journal of Reformed Theology* 3 (2009): 175–201; Michael McClenahan, *Jonathan Edwards and Justification by Faith* (Aldershot, VT: Ashgate, 2012); Josh Moody, "Edwards and Justification Today," in *Jonathan Edwards and Justification*, ed. Josh Moody (Wheaton, IL: Crossway, 2012), 17–43; Hyun-Jin Cho, *Jonathan Edwards on Justification: Reformed Development of the Doctrine in Eighteenth-Century New England* (Lanham, MD: University Press of America, 2012); Stephen R. C. Nichols, *Jonathan Edwards's Bible: The Relationship of the Old and New Testaments in the Theology of Jonathan Edwards* (Eugene, OR: Pickwick, 2013), 11, 14, 142–44, 172–73; Reita Yazawa, "Covenant of Redemption in the Theology of Jonathan Edwards: The Nexus between the Immanent and the Economic Trinity" (PhD dissertation, Calvin Theological Seminary, 2013); Douglas A. Sweeney, "Justification by Faith Alone? A Fuller Picture of Edwards's Doctrine," in *Jonathan Edwards and Justification*, 129–54; Sweeney, *Edwards the Exegete: Biblical Interpretation and Anglo-Protestant Culture on the Edge of the Enlightenment* (New York: Oxford University Press, 2016), 202–18. For more on the scholarly literature on Edwards's view of dispositional ontology, see Yazawa, "Covenant of Redemption," 118–36.

primarily Aristotelian/Reformed scholastic terms. As Ava Chamberlain puts it, "the primary focus" of Edwards's doctrine of justification is not "the forensic transaction that occurs by means of justification but the ontological transformation that occurs by means of union with Christ."[11] Further, he "spoke in great detail about the importance of good works, sometimes saying things that sound remarkably Catholic."[12] Related to these factors is that Edwards spoke more about "conditions" of justification than about "causes" of justification. Understandably, Edwards's view of the conditions of the covenants of redemption, works, and grace has led some scholars to investigate developments in Edwards's federal theology.[13]

Considering the number of issues raised by the scholarship and the limited space of this chapter, it would be impossible to address a comprehensive understanding of the relationship between federal theology and ecclesiology in Edwards's thought. Rather, this chapter's goal is to address the question of the doctrine of justification, Edwards's concept of conditions of covenants, and the meaning of redemption that is particularly involved in the doctrine of the Lord's Supper as a sign of covenant, all of which will shed light on the ecclesiological and practical significance of Edwards's federal theology.

In this chapter, I will demonstrate that Edwards seeks the essential unity between faith and piety through his ecclesiological perspective on federal theology within his perception of the doctrinal harmony of the

---

11. Ava Chamberlain, "Editor's Introduction," in The "Miscellanies": Entry Nos. 501–832, WJE 18·39.

12. Sweeney, Edwards the Exegete, 212. For more on Edwards's Catholic language, see Sweeney, Edwards the Exegete, 209–16.

13. As introduced in chapter 1, McClymond and McDermott argue that Edwards developed his federal theology through three phases, especially in 1723, 1733, and 1739, changing his view of the conditions of the covenants. According to them, the first stage of development occurred when Edwards argued that the covenant of redemption is the same as the covenant of grace. The second period can be seen in 1733, during which Edwards called faith a condition of entering into the covenant of grace as "a marriage covenant between Christ and his church." Last, in 1739, Edwards distinguished between the covenants of redemption and grace in response to Thomas Boston's argument that the covenant of redemption is not different from the covenant of grace. Correcting McClymond's and McDermott's interpretation of the developments over the course of these three phases in Edwards's career, Cornelis van der Knijff and Willem van Vlastuin claim that while the first transition between 1723 and 1733 is correct, the second phase, between 1733 and 1739, appears improper. McClymond and McDermott, The Theology of Jonathan Edwards, 325–26; Cornelis van der Knijff and Willem van Vlastuin, "The Development in Jonathan Edwards' Covenant View," Jonathan Edwards Studies 3, no. 2 (2013): 281.

Bible. The first section supports this claim by examining Edwards's doctrine of justification found in his conception of harmony between God's sovereignty and the freedom of human agency in establishing union with Christ. Then, the next section will examine Edwards's distinctions among the conditions of the covenants of redemption, works, and grace. Specifically, I will show that the doctrinal harmony of the Bible in Edwards's thought, true to his doctrine of justification, is the central interpretive framework within which human agency actively participates in the history of redemption through keeping the conditions of covenants. Last, the chapter will explore Edwards's view of redemption by examining his works related to the controversy over qualifications for communion, including *Religious Affections*; "An Humble Inquiry"; *Narrative of Communion Controversy*; "Misrepresentations Corrected"; *Lectures on the Qualifications for Full Communion in the Church of Christ* (1750); *True Grace, Distinguished From the Experience of Devils*; *The Faithful Narrative*; and a series of "Miscellanies" and sermons. In doing so, the chapter will demonstrate the practical-spiritual significance of Edwards's federal theology from an ecclesiological perspective, in consideration of Edwards's practice-focused exegesis of key biblical texts. This brief foray into the rich substance of Edwards's federal theology will serve to demonstrate the doctrinal harmony of the Bible as a central principle through which Edwards understands the church.

THE DOCTRINE OF JUSTIFICATION

To make sense of Edwards's doctrine of justification, which is deeply related to his federal theology, one must first take seriously his concern regarding the relationships among government, church, and Christian piety, which he inherited from the seventeenth-century Puritans and from his New England forebears. Before Edwards, a close relationship between federal theology and its moral principles was evident in Reformed orthodoxy and in New England, where Edwards lived.[14] For example, William

---

14. Perry Miller argues that Edwards abandoned the covenant schema of his predecessors (the first generation of New Englanders), which had deviated from Calvin's theology. As mentioned in chapter 1, Peter De Jong, Joseph Haroutunian, Sydney Mead, Sydney Ahlstrom, and William McLoughlin maintain a similar position to Miller. Particularly, according to McLoughlin, the New Divinity's concept of the covenant finds its origins in "the Mayflower Compact of the Pilgrims in 1620, the first code of laws adopted in Virginia in 1610, the famous

Perkins (1558–1602), according to David D. Hall, "characterized" equity "as 'so excellent as the careful practice thereof is the marrow and strength of a commonweal.' "[15] For Perkins, equity "pointed beyond conscience to the fundamental nature of covenant." Hall emphasizes that Perkins considered the moral law to be "an instrument of justice," as "binding on Christians as it had been on the people of Israel because of its perpetual 'equity.' "[16] Ministers in New Haven kept a record of their colony from its beginning in 1639, which is called *Records of the Colony and Plantation of New Heaven*. It declares, "The Scriptures do holde forth a perfect rule for the direction and government of all men in all dueties which they are to performe to God and men as well in the government of families and commonwealths as in matters of the church."[17] This record, Hall argues, was an attempt for ministers and laymen in New Haven to seek "godly rule."[18] Theodore Dwight Bozeman claims that "all essential elements of the National Covenant" in

---

sermon of John Winthrop on board the *Arabella* in 1630, and the Cambridge Platform of Massachusetts of 1648." In the sermon, Governor Winthrop spoke of his entire group as being in covenant with God. From this, McLoughlin contended that Puritans emphasized obedience to authority for social order as well as individual freedom. From this, he argued that the covenant for the Puritans bound each individual to obey God first and foremost and at the same time bound him to submit himself to the will of the group for the common good. The Edwardsians regard God as "a guardian spirit, capable of helping those who seek it," because of the covenant with his chosen people. If individuals adhere to God's rules, then God allows them "a glorious new day of peace." In this vein, the Edwardsians' concept of the covenant places an emphasis on the duty of individuals to social order, and thus, there exists a tension between authority and freedom. McLoughlin's argument is in accordance with Miller and Morgan's view that there was "a conflict between the demands of authority and the permissiveness of freedom." Like McLoughlin, Ahlstrom also gives an example of the covenant in John Winthrop's sermon. On the federal idea in the relationship between the church and society, Ahlstrom says, "What all this meant in a practical sense was that the Puritans thought about economic, political, and social problems in extraordinarily corporate terms. The Church consequently directed its attention not only to the problems of the individual before God but to the state before God. The Church assumed a responsibility for society because Puritans thought in terms of a social or national covenant." See William G. McLoughlin, *Revivals, Awakenings, and Reform: An Essay on Religion and Social Change in America, 1607–1977* (Chicago: University of Chicago Press, 1978), 35–38; Sydney E. Ahlstrom, "Theology in America: A Historical Survey," in *The Shaping of American Religion*, ed. James Ward Smith and A. Leland Jamison (Princeton: Princeton University Press, 1961), 241–42.

15. David D. Hall, *A Reforming People: Puritanism and the Transformation of Public Life in New England* (New York: Knopf, 2011), 144.

16. Hall, *A Reforming People*, 144.

17. Cited in David D. Hall, *A Reforming People*, 100. For the original document, see Charles J. Hoadly, ed., *Records of the Colony and Plantation of New Haven*, Hoadly, 2 vols. (Hartford: Case, Tiffany, 1857), 1:12.

18. Hall, *A Reforming People*, 100.

England or New England "were derived primarily from the Pentateuch and from the books of Kings and Chronicles."[19] As Sweeney rightly points out, "Scripture gave structure to New England's 'Bible commonwealths,' whose laws and other mores were derived from the Word of God."[20]

Sweeney also argues that between 1620 and 1630, the earnest British colonists, who "were dissatisfied with the progress of the Reformation in England," proclaimed purification of "their national church by means of biblical teaching, bold liturgical reforms, as well as an emphasis on genuine conversion."[21] Further, Joel Beeke describes Herman Witsius (1636–1708) as one who argued, "Only when purity of doctrine was accompanied by purity of life could the state and church expect God's blessing."[22] Thus, Sweeney asserts that in the same ecclesiological soil as his Reformed forebears, Edwards attempted to define the church as "the mystical body of Jesus Christ" in a realistic sense.[23] Edwards was loyal to the practical meaning of the teaching of the Bible, seeking to live such an obedient life to the commands of God for receiving salvation and teaching his people to maintain the pietistic life that flows from love for God.

Given this coherent unity between faith and piety, it is not surprising that the doctrinal harmony of the Bible sheds light on some

19. Theodore Dwight Bozeman, *To Live Ancient Lives: The Primitivist Dimension in Puritanism* (Chapel Hill: University of North Carolina Press, 1988), 32.

20. Sweeney, *Edwards the Exegete*, 20.

21. Sweeney, *Jonathan Edwards and the Ministry of the Word*, 23. Indeed, Edwards refers to God's Moral Government and Spiritual Worship (see Edwards, *The "Miscellanies": Entry nos. 833–1152*, WJE 20:246–48). For more on Edwards's view of moral government, see Oliver D. Crisp, "The Moral Government of God: Jonathan Edwards and Joseph Bellamy on the Atonement," in *After Jonathan Edwards: The Courses of the New England Theology*, ed. Oliver D. Crisp and Douglas A. Sweeney (New York: Oxford University Press, 2012), 78–90.

22. Joel R. Beeke, *Puritan Reformed Spirituality: A Practical and Biblical Study from Reformed and Puritan Heritage* (Grand Rapids: Reformation Heritage, 2004), 339.

23. Sweeney describes Edwards's realism when it came to conceiving of the church as follows: "Edwards' descriptions of the church shared in common a basic commitment to the metaphysical notion that the church *really* is the mystical body of Jesus Christ. As such, it includes within its (true) membership only those who are born again, who have died to sin and risen with Christ, who share a new life together in him and a common mission to embody the presence of Christ in the secular world. Or as Edwards once insisted to the people of Northampton, ''Tis the relation and concern that the members of the church have with Christ that is the thing wherein above all things the essence of the church consists' (Col. 1:24, F. 791, L. 5r)." Sweeney, "The Church," 169. For more on Edwards's realism in his understanding of the church, see Thomas A. Schafer, "Jonathan Edwards' Conception of the Church," *CH* 24 (1955): 62.

misunderstandings of Edwards's doctrine of justification. One of the misunderstandings among those who maintain a dispositional-ontological view of faith is that they tend to overlook the harmonious relationship between God's sovereignty through the Holy Spirit's role in salvation and the active role of human faith in forming union with Christ. Indeed, Edwards was emphatic that while "God makes use of means," such as church ordinances, a divine and supernatural light is "produced by God immediately." Even "the Word of God is not proper cause" of the effect of such a divine light. Although "the notion that there is a Christ, and that Christ is holy and gracious, is conveyed to the mind by the Word of God," it is through the immediate "work of the Holy Spirit" that believers can possess "the sense of the excellency of Christ."[24] In a similar way, Edwards in his sermon of 1730, "God Glorified in Man's Dependence," formulates a doctrine that "God is glorified in the wisdom of redemption in this, that there appears in it so absolute and universal a dependence of the redeemed on him."[25] In this work, Edwards writes, "Though means are made use of in conferring grace on men's souls, yet 'tis of God that we have these means of grace, and 'tis God that makes them effectual ... and their [the means of grace] efficacy depends on the immediate influence of the Spirit of God."[26] Thus, Edwards attributes the effectual cause of faith to the work of Holy Spirit.

With respect to the work of the Holy Spirit in justification, human agency is distinguished from the work of the Holy Spirit with human nature. Yazawa writes:

> When Edwards talks about participation in God's fullness, it does not mean that human nature is somehow transformed into the divine or that human nature is identical with the divine nature. The language of participation in Edwards means that, through the indwelling of the Holy Spirit, the elect become a part of the flow

---

24. Edwards, "A Divine and Supernatural Light" in *Sermons and Discourses 1730-1733*, *WJE* 17:417.

25. Edwards, "God Glorified in Man's Dependence (1 Cor 1:29-11)," in *Sermons and Discourses 1730-1733*, 202.

26. Edwards, "God Glorified in Man's Dependence," 203.

of divine self-communication without losing the human nature. Simply put, the elect come under the influences of the Holy Spirit.[27]

This echoes how the pneumatological aspect of salvation plays a significant role in Edwards's doctrine of justification by faith alone. This is why Edwards in his sermon "Justification by Faith Alone" goes on to say that believers' obedience to the requirements of God in relation to union with Christ could not be a source of the reward promised by God. At the end of the sermon, Edwards draws this conclusion: "How far a wonderful and mysterious agency of God's Spirit, may so influence some men's hearts, that their practice in this regard may be contrary to their own principles, so that they shall not trust in their own righteousness, though they profess that men are justified by their own righteousness."[28] As Kyle Strobel rightly points out, Edwards was "concerned to delineate redemption by Word and Spirit, which necessarily entails forensic justification."[29]

Edwards's understanding of union with Christ through the Holy Spirit resembles Calvin's doctrine of union with Christ. Scott M. Manetsch points out, "Calvin is clear that faith is the instrument by which sinners receive the benefits of Christ. Moreover, the Holy Spirit is the divine agent who unites the believer to Christ: 'To sum up,' Calvin notes, 'the Holy Spirit is the bond by which Christ effectually unites us to himself.' "[30] Like Calvin, Edwards "grounded the imputation of Christ's righteousness to sinners on their real, mystical union with the resurrected Lord," asserts Sweeney.[31] Thus, Edwards's emphasis on union with Christ and the role of the Holy Spirit in salvation indicates that Edwards would agree that faith is *an*

---

27. Yazawa, "Covenant of Redemption," 121.

28. Edwards, "Justification by Faith Alone," 242.

29. Kyle Strobel, "By Word and Spirit: Jonathan Edwards on Redemption, Justification, and Regeneration," in *Jonathan Edwards and Justification*, ed. Josh Moody (Wheaton, IL: Crossway, 2012), 68.

30. Scott M. Manetsch, "John Calvin's Doctrine of the Christian Life," *JETS* 61, no. 2 (2018): 265. For more on Calvin's understanding of the doctrine of union with Christ, see Cornelis P. Venema, "Union with Christ and the 'Twofold Grace of God,' " in *Accepted and Renewed in Christ: The "Twofold Grace of God" and the Interpretation of Calvin's Theology*, Reformed Historical Theology Series (Göttingen: Vandenhoeck & Ruprecht, 2007), 83–94; J. Todd Billings, *Calvin, Participation, and the Gift: The Activity of Believers in Union with Christ*, Changing Paradigms in Historical and Systematic Theology (Oxford: Oxford University Press, 2007).

31. Sweeney, *Edwards the Exegete*, 207.

instrumental cause of justification, while he would avoid saying that faith is the *only* instrumental cause of justification.

Moreover, the underlying reason why many scholars have failed to correctly assess Edwards's doctrine of justification is that they tend to see Edwards's view of faith only in terms of the doctrine of justification. In other words, the reason Edwards is misunderstood is because the critics fail to see Edwards's view of the doctrinal harmony of the Bible, which connects the doctrine of justification to Christian piety via the doctrine of sanctification. As said earlier, Edwards saw his federal theology as being characterized by both faith and piety. This implies that for Edwards, the doctrine of justification is correlated to the doctrine of sanctification. For example, while Edwards discussed the conditions of justification more than an instrumental cause of justification, as should be clear by now, Edwards understood faith in terms of ministry, exhorting his people to live a life of piety, which had been given to them as a gift of sanctification. In this sense, Edwards's federal theology plays a significant role in establishing a harmonious relationship between justification and sanctification.

Again, Edwards's understanding of the relationship between justification and sanctification is quite similar to that of Calvin. In his definition of justification by faith, Calvin writes, "Christ was given to us by God's generosity, to be grasped and possessed by us in faith. By partaking of him, we principally receive a double grace: namely, that being reconciled to God through Christ's blamelessness, we may have in heaven instead of a Judge a gracious Father; and secondly, that sanctified by Christ's spirit we may cultivate blamelessness and purity of life."[32] Calvin draws his conclusion that justification should be seen just "as the acceptance with which God receives us into his favor as righteous men."[33] Manetsch points out the importance of the close relationship between justification and sanctification in the view of Calvin. Manetsch rightly insists:

> Human sinners whom the Holy Spirit unites to Christ through faith receive a double grace (*duplex gratia*) of justification and sanctification. The gift of justification involves pardon for sin and the

---

32. John Calvin, *Institutes of the Christian Religion*, 2 vols., ed. John T. McNeill, trans. Ford Lewis Battles (Philadelphia: Westminster, 1960), 3.11.1 (725).

33. Calvin, *Institutes*, 3.11.2 (727).

forensic imputation of Christ's righteousness to the believer. The gift of sanctification involves the process of internal transformation that the Holy Spirit achieves through the course of a believer's lifetime. Though justification and sanctification are distinct from one another, they are an inseparable gift received through communion with Christ.[34]

Like Edwards, Calvin emphasizes the role of the Holy Spirit in believers' union with Christ.

The similarity between Edwards and Calvin, however, does not imply that there is no difference between them. Rather, Edwards differs from Calvin when he speaks not just of passive faith but of active faith, by which believers actively participate in union with Christ. In his sermon "Justification by Faith Alone," which served as "one of the sparks for the revival of 1734,"[35] he writes:

> God sees it fit, that in order to an union's being established between two intelligent active beings or persons, so as that they should be looked upon as one, there should be the mutual act of both, that each should receive the other, as actively joining themselves one to another. God in requiring this in order to an union with Christ as one of his people, treats men as reasonable creatures, capable of act, and choice; and hence sees it fit that they only, that are one with Christ by their own act, should be looked upon as one in law.[36]

Edwards continues to argue a similarly detailed exposition of the doctrine of justification, emphasizing an active role of faith on the human side.

This was also the source of Edwards's complaint against the Calvinist understanding of the relationship between perseverance and the covenants. In Miscellany no. 729 of 1740, "Perseverance," Edwards complains

---

34. Manetsch, "John Calvin's Doctrine of the Christian Life," 265. For more on Calvin's view of the relationship between justification and sanctification, see J. Todd Billings, "Union with Christ and the Double Grace: Calvin's Theology and Its Early Reception," in *Calvin's Theology and Its Reception: Disputes, Developments, and New Possibilities*, ed. I. John Hesselink and J. Todd Billings (Louisville: Westminster John Knox, 2012), 49–71.

35. Holifield, "Edwards as Theologian," 152.

36. Edwards, "Justification by Faith Alone," 158.

that "though perseverance is acknowledged by Calvinian divines to be necessary to salvation, yet it seems to me that the manner in which it is necessary has not been sufficiently set forth." He argues that perseverance "comes into consideration even in the justification of a sinner, as one thing on which the fitness of acceptance to life depends." He goes on to assert, "For though a sinner is justified on his first act of faith, yet even then, in that act of justification, God has respect to perseverance, as being virtually in that first act; and 'tis looked upon as if it were a property of the faith, by which the sinner is then justified."[37]

Nevertheless, these statements should not be seen as if Edwards believes that a person is not completely justified until faith results in meritorious works, as Fesko argues.[38] In Miscellany no. 712, "Justification," Edwards argues, "God's bestowing Christ and his benefits on a soul in consequence of faith" is due to "the natural suitableness that there is between such a qualification of a soul, and such an union with Christ and interest in Christ."[39] The imputation of Christ's righteousness to the believer does not occur without union with Christ. More importantly, with respect to the natural fitness of faith, Edwards asserts, "'Tis only from God's love of order and hatred of confusion that [he] bestows these things on the account of faith." God is "a wise being and delights in order," without "confusion." This means that Edwards's appreciation of the act of faith is based on God's love of order. As Carl Bogue points out, while there is "a natural fitness between faith and justification, ... there is no moral fitness in that our faith merits justification."[40]

Edwards in Miscellany no. 726, "Perseverance," maintains a similar position:

> 'Tis one act of faith to commit the soul to Christ's keeping, in this sense, viz. to keep it from falling. The believing soul is convinced of its own weakness and helplessness, its inability to resist enemies, its insufficiency to keep itself, and so commits itself to Christ that

---

37. Edwards, Miscellany no. 729, in The "Miscellanies": Entry Nos. 501–832, 353–54.

38. For a brief review of Fesko's work The Covenant of Redemption, see Thomas Haviland-Pabst, Review of The Covenant of Redemption: Origins, Development, and Reception, by J. V. Fesko, Themelios 43, no. 1 (2018): 123–25.

39. Edwards, Miscellany no. 712, in The "Miscellanies": Entry Nos. 501–832, 341.

40. Bogue, Jonathan Edwards and the Covenant of Grace, 266.

he would be its keeper. The Apostle speaks of his committing his soul by faith to Christ under great sufferings and trials of his perseverance. II Tim. 1:12, "For which cause also I suffer these things: nevertheless I am not ashamed; for I know whom I have believed, and am persuaded that he is able to keep that which I have committed to him against that day." And we are commanded to commit our way and our works unto the Lord (Ps. 37:5, Prov. 16:3). Faith depends on Christ for all good that we need, and especially good of this kind, that is of such absolute necessity in order to the salvation of our souls. The sum of the good that faith looks for is the Holy Spirit—for spiritual and eternal life, perfect holiness in heaven [and] persevering holiness here—for the just shall life by faith.[41]

Edwards articulates that not only does faith depend on Christ who is the mediator for sinners, but also, among the benefits of salvation is the gift of the Holy Spirit himself.[42] A similar emphasis on genuine faith tightly tied to the moral life is found in his sermon "He That Believeth Shall Be Saved." Edwards claims, "We must see our own vileness and wickedness, and lie down in the dust before God, and own we deserve nothing but to be cast into hell. And we must come to Christ and trust in him only, and not in our own righteousness, for salvation."[43]

As suggested above, it is of the utmost importance to see that it is God who initiated Christ's union with believers. In his sermon "God Glorified in the Work of Redemption," Edwards claims, "it is *of* God that we have our Redeemer." God alone provides "a Savior for us." Further, he articulates, "It is of God that Christ becomes ours, that we are brought to him, and are united to him: it is of God that we receive faith to close with him, that we may have an interest in him."[44] Moreover, as seen in chapter 4, Edwards

---

41. Edwards, Miscellany no. 726, in The "Miscellanies": Entry Nos. 501–832, 352–53.

42. Indeed, Edwards considers the Holy Spirit to be "the sum of all that Christ purchased." Edwards identifies "Good things" as the promise of the Father with "the Holy Spirit." Edwards, The "Miscellanies": Entry Nos. a-z, aa-zz, 1–500, WJE 13:466.

43. Edwards, "He That Believeth Shall Be Saved (1751)," in The Sermons of Jonathan Edwards: A Reader, ed. Wilson H. Kimnach, Kenneth P. Minkema, and Douglas A. Sweeney (New Haven: Yale University Press, 1999), 115.

44. Edwards, "God Glorified in the Work of Redemption, by the Greatness of Man's Dependence upon Him, in the Whole of It (1731)," in The Sermons of Jonathan Edwards: A Reader, 68–69.

maintains the Calvinistic doctrine of total depravity. In his letter to the Northampton church in June 1752, in which Edwards warns the church about the errors of Solomon Williams, who misrepresented Edwards's criticism of Stoddard's understanding of communion, he writes:

> You have ever been taught, that the hearts of natural men are wholly corrupt, entirely destitute of anything spiritually good, not having the least spark of love to God, and as much without all things of this nature, as a dead corpse is without life: nevertheless, that 'tis hard for sinners to be convinced of this; that they are exceeding prone to imagine, there is some goodness in 'em, some respect to good in what they do: yet that they must be brought off from such a vain conceit of themselves, and come to see themselves utterly depraved and quite dead in sin. But now this book of Mr. Williams leads you to quite other notions; it leads you to suppose, that some natural men are above lukewarmness in religion, that they may truly profess to be the real friends of Christ, and to love God, more than his enemies, and above the world.[45]

Given his emphasis on God's initiative in salvation and on the total depravity of humanity, it is not surprising that Edwards believes a person cannot be saved by his own disposition or inclination. In "'Controversies' Notebook: Justification," Edwards argues:

> In the method of justification by the gospel, a person is justified before he has any habitual holiness, or any holiness as an established principle of action—not before there has been one act of sincere holiness, an act from the bottom of the heart and with the whole soul—yet the establishing holiness as an abiding principle of spiritual life and action is consequent on justification, as has been shown elsewhere. And in this sense, again, God justifies the ungodly as he justifies persons without any habitual holiness.[46]

---

45. Edwards, "To the First Church of Christ, Northampton," in *Letters and Personal Writings*, WJE 16:481–82.

46. Edwards. "'Controversies' Notebook: Justification," in *Writings on the Trinity, Grace, and Faith*, WJE 21:371.

Edwards is emphatic that the believer's active attendance to union with Christ is bound up with the priority of God's sovereignty through Christ as the mediator and the Holy Spirit as the gift of the covenant of grace, that is, eternal life.

At this juncture, it is worth noting E. Brook Holifield's brief summary of Edwards's doctrine of justification. He states:

> In justification, God accepted the guilty as "free from the guilt of sin" on the grounds of their faith. He defended the idea by recourse to his themes of fittingness and symmetry. Faith did not produce justification but merely made it "fitting." God looked upon it as "fit by a natural fitness" that a faithful relation to Christ should be "agreeable" to justification. It was agreeable to "reason and the nature of things" that God would impute the righteousness of Christ to the faithful since a relation of "union" between a patron and a client made it "fit" to impute the entire merit of one to the other. Christ, moreover, initiated the relation, and the justification resulted from the excellency of the relation, not of the faith. And although he always thought that a genuine faith was united with love, he could still say that faith alone made justification suitable. He opposed New England liberals who contended that faith justified because it included moral obedience in its essence.[47]

Justification is the result of the excellency not "of the faith" but of "the relation" between Christ and the believer.[48]

---

47. Holifield, "Edwards as Theologian," 152.

48. In his exegesis on John 10:4 in his sermon "The Sweet Harmony of Christ," which describes a metaphor of the good shepherd and his sheep, Edwards offers a relational harmony between Christ and believers: "When he calls, they willingly come to him; and when he goes forth, they willingly follow. For they entirely approve of him, and incline to him as their shepherd. Their following is spoken of not as a forced, but a ready and cheerful following of him." From his biblical exposition of the text, Edwards draws this doctrine: "There is a sweet harmony between Christ and the soul of a true Christian." According to Edwards, one can note three harmonious aspects of the relationship: "an harmony of mutual respect," "an harmony of conformity and likeness," and "an harmony of suitableness." With respect to the last aspect of harmony, "suitableness," Edwards details it into three elements. First, there is "a suitableness of temper and behavior to each other's nature and state." While believers are "in themselves so exceeding sinful and unworthy, infinitely undeserving and ill-deserving," Christ is "infinitely rich in free and sovereign grace." Since Christ has "the divine nature," Christians respond fittingly to him, giving "adoring respect to Christ, [paying] him divine honor, and [exalting] him above all." On the other hand, a Christian has "boldness of access" as

One of the great examples of the doctrinal harmony of the Bible is found in Edwards's interpretation of the doctrine of justification in both Paul and James. In a note on Romans 4:3–4, Edwards states, "Abraham's believing God was not righteousness, but was only counted for it. It was of God's grace looked upon as supplying the room of righteousness."[49] However, Edwards's interpretation of the Pauline emphasis on God as the author of righteousness does not contradict his view of James' description of justification through works. In the "Blank Bible" note on Romans 2:13, "For not the hearers of the law are just before God, but the doers of the law shall be justified," Edwards writes:

> By this verse it appears that the apostle Paul and the apostle James were of the same mind in the matter of justification, however their expressions seem to be opposite. Here the apostle Paul says the same thing that the apostle James means, when he says a man is justified by works, and not by faith only. It is doubtless the same thing that the apostle James meant, if we would explain him by himself, for he expresses himself elsewhere almost in the same words that Paul does here.[50]

Edwards made frequent attempts to reconcile James' and Paul's views of justification. Edwards's "Blank Bible" note on James 2:24 introduces three scholars, Glas, Davies of Virginia, and Pfaffius, who sought harmony between James and Paul.[51] Similarly, in Miscellany no. 1130[a], "Justification,"

---

a "true friend and intimate companion" in accordance with Christ's "human nature." Second, there is "a suitableness" of "relation." When Christ is described as "the Christian's head," "there is a spirit of union and dependence in that Christian towards Christ." Edwards claims, "The Christian has a disposition suitable to this relation under all its difficulties to resort to Christ, to go there for counsel, and pity, and help. And Christ is ready to offer it to him as he needs [it]." The last "suitableness of temper and behavior" is related to its own "temper and behavior." For example, as there is "infinite grace toward them" in Christ, there is also "thankfulness and praise towards him" in the believer. Edwards concludes, "The love of God to the Christian exceeds the love of all others. He loves them more than any other friend; and suitably to this, the Christians love Christ, Christ above all." Edwards's interest in the role of faith is how God does not repudiate human activity in their receiving Christ who is the mediator of sinners. Edwards, "The Sweet Harmony of Christ," in *Sermons and Discourses 1734–1738, WJE* 19:439, 445–46.

49. Edwards, *Notes on Scripture, WJE* 15:90.

50. Edwards, *The "Blank Bible," WJE* 24:988–89.

51. Edwards, *The "Blank Bible,"* 1172.

he presents Manton's reconciliation between the two apostles: "If we are charged that we have broken the first covenant, the covenant of works, we allege Christ's satisfaction and merit; if charged not to have performed the conditions of the law of grace, we answer it by producing our faith, repentance and new obedience, and so show it to be a false charge." According to Manton, there are two kinds of righteousness: "First and supreme righteousness," that is, Christ's righteousness, and "our right to impunity and glory." While the former is "our only justification and righteousness," the latter does not belong to "the least part of" the former. On the other hand, "believing, repenting and obeying" becomes "our righteousness" through a way in which Christ's righteousness not only "occurs" but also "continues ours."[52] In this sense, as Sweeney notes, Edwards "refused to settle tensions in the Bible one-sidedly."[53] Edwards's canonical reading of the text allowed him to find harmony between the texts that appear to contradict each other.

As Holifield points out, the reason scholars misunderstand Edwards's doctrine of justification is that they fail to appreciate his view of the harmony in his own theology.[54] Does divine intention contradict the role of human agency in union with Christ? Edwards avoids such an incoherent position in the following way: God never forces believers to follow his word, but rather, union with Christ is pursued and desired by believers according to the will of God as being the sovereign good.

CONDITIONALITY OF THE THREE COVENANTS

CONDITIONALITY OF COVENANTS IN
EDWARDS'S WORK OF MINISTRY

Edwards's understanding of justification, the conditions of faith, and the covenants should be understood in light of his pastoral ministry, in which he attempted to teach and apply his federal theology to the members of his congregation. This is apparent from the changes evident in Edwards's

---

52. Edwards, Miscellany no. 1130[a], in The "Miscellanies": Entry Nos. 833–1152, WJE 20:508–9. For a brief explanation of Manton's view of justification, see 509n1.

53. Sweeney, Edwards the Exegete, 217.

54. Holifield claims, "The critics neglected the themes of excellence, beauty, and proportion that gave unity and force to Edwards' theology." Holifield, "Edwards as Theologian," 158.

thought as the result of his polemics with Arminianism.[55] In a Miscellany from 1723, Edwards stresses that "the wrong distinction" between the covenants of grace and redemption results in all the confusion that could be found in "the foundation of Arminianism and Neonomianism."[56] In "Justification by Faith Alone," Edwards insists:

> One would wonder what Arminians mean by Christ's merits: they talk of Christ's merits as much as anybody, and yet deny the imputation of Christ's positive righteousness: what should there be that anyone should merit or deserve anything by, besides righteousness or goodness? If anything that Christ did or suffered, merited or deserved anything, it was by virtue of the goodness, or righteousness, or holiness of it: if Christ's sufferings and death merited heaven, it must be because there was an excellent righteousness, and transcendent moral goodness in that act of laying down his life: and if by that excellent righteousness he merited heaven for us, then surely that righteousness is reckoned to our account, that we have the benefit of it, or which is the same thing, it is imputed to us.[57]

Edwards opposes Arminianism as he perceived it, claiming that it promoted justification by our own righteousness. Similarly, Edwards argues in his *Faithful Narrative* of 1737 that Arminianism "seemed to appear with a very threatening aspect upon the interest of religion."[58] Against Arminianism, Edwards is clear that the excellent righteousness Christ acquired through his death is imputed to the believer. In a note on Romans 4:5, Edwards insists that God accepts the believer's faith "as though he had righteousness in himself," although his virtue is not perfect. In "'Controversies' Notebook:

---

55. Arminianism stems from the Dutch theologian Jacobus Arminius (1560–1609) and "had spread in England during the 17th century among Anglican divines and, especially after 1689, even among dissenters." As New England clergy "accused their Anglican counterparts of propagating Arminianism," Edwards defended the Calvinistic tenets of salvation—predestination, original sin, total human depravity, the atonement for the elect only, irresistible grace, and Christ's perfect obedience—over against Arminianism. Thomas A. Schafer, "Editor's Introduction," in The "Miscellanies": Entry Nos. a-z, aa-zz, 1–500, 11n3; Kenneth P. Minkema, "Editor's Introduction," in Sermons and Discourses 1723-1729, WJE 14:7–8; Schafer, "Editor's Introduction," 11.

56. Edwards, The "Miscellanies": Entry Nos. a-z, aa-zz, 1–500, 198.

57. Edwards, "Justification by Faith Alone," 199.

58. Edwards, "A Faithful Narrative," in The Great Awakening, WJE 4:148.

Justification," he argues that while "justification" in "the legal way ... is not obtained till a man has actually persevered in holiness through an appointed time of probation," a person "in the way of the gospel" is "justified before holiness." He goes on to claim, "God don't wait till the perseverance of faith has actually existed, the same being made sure in the very first act of faith as though it had existed. But it is not thus in the legal method of justification."[59] Edwards maintains that justification depends on God, who considers faith in union with Christ to be righteousness. Ava Chamberlain rightly notes that it is through his "grounding justification in the reality of union with Christ" that he "rebuts the Arminian objection to imputation without making justification into a reward for meritorious works."[60]

Given his work of ministry, in which Edwards opposed Arminianism, it comes as little surprise that Edwards changed his concept of conditionality in the three covenants. However, this raises an important question: To what extent do the covenants of redemption, works, and grace differ, and to what degree are they similar? This question helps clarify a focal point in Edwards's federal theology. For Edwards, the answer hinges on conditionality.

CONDITIONALITY IN REDEMPTIVE-HISTORICAL PERSPECTIVE

Conditionality for Edwards is fundamental in distinguishing between the covenant of redemption and the covenant of grace. Edwards writes:

> All the promises of each of these covenants [the covenant of redemption and the covenant of grace] are conditional. To suppose that there are any promises of the covenant of grace, or any covenant promises, that are not conditional promises, seems an absurdity and contradiction. These covenants differ in their conditions. The condition of the covenant that God has made with Jesus Christ as a public person, is all that Christ has done and suffered to procure redemption. The condition of Christ's covenant with his people or

59. Edwards. "'Controversies' Notebook: Justification," 371.

60. Chamberlain, "Editor's Introduction," 17. For more on this, see Cherry, *The Theology of Jonathan Edwards*, 187.

of the marriage covenant between him and men, is that they should close with him and adhere to him.[61]

The covenants differ in terms of their conditions. For example, the covenant of redemption is different from the covenant of grace since the conditions of the former are Christ's work on behalf of redemption and the condition of the latter is to be in Christ.

Moreover, the covenants are distinct in relation to their subjects. The covenant of redemption is a covenant that "God makes with believers in Christ [Christ and his people]," while the covenant of grace is "the covenant of union between Christ and his spouse [marriage covenant]."[62] In the covenant of redemption, God transacts with Christ as the head, thereby transacting with believers in Christ. On the other hand, believers in the covenant of grace become "parties contracting" with Christ.[63] Thus, the parties in the covenant of redemption are God and Christ as the head (to whom Christ's posterity belong), and those in the covenant of grace are Christ and his people.

Furthermore, the covenants differ in their promises. The promise in the covenant of redemption is "Christ's reward," that is, "justification, the privileges and benefits of his children, the eternal inheritance and kingdom," all of which come from his work of redemption.[64] On the other hand, "the sum" of rewards in the covenant of grace is "communion," which implies that Christ gives himself to his people.[65] Thus, the covenant of redemption is distinguished from the covenant of grace with respect to its conditions, subjects, and promises.

This does not mean, however, that the covenant of redemption is wholly separate from the covenant of grace. Rather, the former is closely related to the latter. In terms that the promises made to Christ as the head (the

---

61. Edwards, The "Miscellanies": Entry Nos. 501–832, 148.

62. Edwards, The "Miscellanies": Entry Nos. 833–1152, 475; Edwards, The "Miscellanies": Entry Nos. 501–832, 148–49.

63. Edwards, The "Miscellanies": Entry Nos. 501–832, 150; Edwards, "Sermon on Hebrews 9:15–16" (January 4, 1740). This sermon is not yet available online; R. Craig Woods, the editor, kindly shared it with me.

64. Edwards, The "Miscellanies": Entry Nos. 501–832, 148; Edwards, The "Miscellanies": Entry Nos. 833–1152, 475.

65. Edwards, The "Miscellanies": Entry Nos. 501–832, 149.

covenant of redemption) should be "revealed" and "directed" to both the head and members, the covenant of redemption includes promises such as "eternal life," "justification," and "regeneration."[66]

We noted above that the promises in the covenant of redemption are the same as those in the covenant of grace. Edwards writes the following about the covenant of grace:

> This promise of the covenant of Christ with his people, implies eternal life of both soul and body. The happiness of eternal life, it consists in the enjoyment of Christ and in communion with him or partaking with him in the happiness and glory of his reward, who is rewarded with the eternal life and glory of both soul and body. It includes sanctification and perseverance: these are included in the enjoyment of Christ and communion with Christ. It includes justification; this also is a part of believers' communion with Christ, for they in their justification are but partakers of Christ's justification. They are pardoned and justified in Christ's acquittance and justification as Mediator. The promises of the incarnation of Christ and of his obedience and sacrifice, were included in the covenant between Christ and believers before these things were actually accomplished.[67]

As with the covenant of redemption, the promises of God such as "eternal life," sanctification," and "perseverance" are included in the covenant of grace.

However, Edwards maintains that there are some differences in the promises of the two covenants.[68] The promises in the covenant of redemption are occasionally considered by Edwards to be conditions in the covenant of grace.[69] For example, regeneration is considered to be "one of the promises of the covenant of the Father with Christ [the covenant of redemption]," even though it is simultaneously a "condition in the covenant

---

66. Edwards, The "Miscellanies": Entry Nos. 501–832, 149.

67. Edwards, The "Miscellanies": Entry Nos. 501–832, 149.

68. Edwards, The "Miscellanies": Entry Nos. 501–832, 149.

69. Even the promises in the covenant of redemption are conditional. However, the condition of the covenant of redemption is related not to benefits, such as regeneration, but to Christ's redemptive work.

of Christ with his people [the covenant of grace]." The same is true of "the first closing with Christ" and "perseverance," which are conditions of the covenant of grace and at the same time promises in the covenant of redemption.[70]

Edwards believed that human consent plays an important role in the believer's participation in the covenant of grace. "The revelation and offer of the gospel is not properly called a covenant till it is consented to. As when a man courts a woman [and] offers himself to her, his offer is not called a covenant, though he be obliged by it on his part. Neither do I think that the gospel is called a covenant in Scripture, but only when the engagements are mutual," Edwards writes.[71] Edward argues that "the revelation and offer of the gospel" is called a covenant when it is consented to by believers.[72] This mutuality of the covenant of grace indicates that the covenant is actually completed at a specific point in history by Christ's people, as Bogue points out.[73] In this sense, Edwards states that "the condition of Christ's covenant with his people or of the marriage covenant between him and men, is that they should close with him and adhere to him."[74] "Closing with" and "adhering to" Christ do not mean that believers should accomplish the condition by their merit.[75] Rather, conditionality for Edwards is focused on the historical realization of the covenant at a point in time in which the members "come into being."[76] Thus, Edwards writes as follows:

But the covenant of grace, if thereby we understand the covenant between Christ himself and his church or his members, is

70. Edwards, The "Miscellanies": Entry Nos. 501-832, 150.

71. Edwards, The "Miscellanies": Entry Nos. 501-832, 150.

72. Edwards allows a covenant to be called a "free offer and exhibition" from God. Thus, as Van der Knijff and Van Vlastuin have pointed out, the covenant of grace for Edwards is "even synonymous with the gospel." See Van der Knijff and Van Vlastuin, "The Development in Jonathan Edwards' Covenant View," 276.

73. Bogue, Jonathan Edwards and the Covenant of Grace, 127. Cf. The "Miscellanies": Entry Nos. 833-1152, 475.

74. Edwards, The "Miscellanies": Entry Nos. 501-832, 148.

75. Indeed, Edwards says, "If Adam had stood and persevered in obedience, he would have been made happy by mere bounty (and) goodness; for God was not obliged to reward Adam for his perfect obedience any otherwise than by covenant, for Adam by standing would not have merited happiness." Edwards, "Glorious Grace," in Sermons and Discourses 1720-1723, WJE 10:391-92.

76. Edwards, The "Miscellanies": Entry Nos. 833-1152, 475.

conditional as to us: the proper condition of it, which is a yielding to Christ's wooings and accepting his offers and closing with him as a redeemer and spiritual husband, is to be performed by us. ... Propriety in Christ is her believing in Christ, or her [Christ's spouse] soul's active union with him.[77]

As seen in the words "accepting his offers," the condition of the covenant of grace is nothing other than a person's believing in Christ in time. Thus, the covenant of redemption differs from the covenant of grace with respect to the fact that the latter is realized at moments in time.

The historical aspect in the conditionality of the covenant is much more evident in Edwards's view of the relationship between the covenant of works and the covenant of grace. The covenant of works is made with "the first Adam," while the covenant of grace is made "with the second Adam."[78] The condition of the first covenant is "Adam's standing," while the condition of the second covenant is "Christ's standing."[79] However, as seen in chapter 4, the condition in the covenant of works is not contrasted with the condition of the covenant of grace. Rather, Edwards sees the relationship between the covenants of works and grace in terms of the history of redemption. He states that "Christ came into the world to fulfill and answer the covenant of works, that is the covenant that is to stand forever as a rule of judgment, and that is the covenant that we had broken, and that was the covenant that must be fulfilled."[80] This statement contains two crucial points: (1) the covenant of works was fulfilled by Christ's work of redemption, and (2) the conditions of the covenant of works have to do with "a rule of judgment," under which all humanity will be held accountable at the end of the world.[81] Thus, Edwards understands the condition of the covenant of works in terms of the covenant of grace, so that the conditionality of

---

77. Edwards, The "Miscellanies": Entry Nos. 833–1152, 478.

78. Edwards, The "Miscellanies": Entry Nos. a-z, aa-zz, 1–500, 198.

79. Edwards, The "Miscellanies": Entry Nos. a-z, aa-zz, 1–500, 198.

80. Edwards, A History of the Work of Redemption, WJE 9:309.

81. Chapter 4 dealt in detail with these two aspects of the covenant of works.

the covenant of works could be an important means of Christ's fulfilling the work of redemption and judging humanity at the end of the world.[82]

Thus, conditionality for Edwards is important in distinguishing among the covenants of redemption, grace, and works. Moreover, the conditions in the covenants show the historical character of the relationships between the covenants of redemption and grace and between the covenants of grace and works. This reflects his desire for unity and harmony among the three covenants and demonstrates that the doctrinal harmony of the Bible in Edwards's thought is a central interpretive framework, within which human agency actively participates in the history of redemption without destroying God's sovereignty. This, in turn, implies that the conditionality of the three covenants has ecclesiastical and practical significance in Edwards's view of redemption. Now we turn to Edwards's view of redemption within his ecclesiastical perspective, which is rooted in his practical exegesis.

---

82. A similar line of thought is found in Burgess, who emphasizes the significance of good works in the Christian life. He appeals to his predecessors such as Melanchthon and Zanchi, who demonstrated a positive attitude toward good works. According to Burgess, the Reformed tradition understood the law in a twofold nature: "*Bona opera sunt necessaria ad salutem; Bona opera sunt perniciosa ad salutem.*" Burgess quoted Melanchthon as understanding good works to be not "a necessity of merit" but a necessity of "presence," against the antinomians, who do not recognize the presence of good works in human beings. According to Burgess, for the argument that "good works are necessary to salvation," Zanchi wrote, "No man grown up can be saved, unless he give himself to good works, and work in them." For Burgess, these examples demonstrate that good works had been considered an important element in Christian life by earlier Reformers. Obedience to the law goes further than good works, as if "the obedience of the law is a way to heaven, though it be not a *causa*, yet its *via ad regnum.*" A person's good works neither signify a way to salvation like Christ (*causa*) nor operate as "a cause or merit." Rather, good works serve as a metaphor that indicates "actions or course of life." Good works must be evident in the life of those who are justified by the grace of Christ. According to Burgess, Scripture not only expresses "threatnings" against the godly in order that believers not neglect repentance and avoid sins, but Scripture also describes duties, which involve "the promise of pardon, and eternal life, though not because of their worth, yet to their presence." In this view, the law under the covenant of grace leads believers to receive all good things that are promised in the gospel. The divine mercy of the covenant promise is bestowed on those who fulfill the prerequisite condition, not according to "their worth," but based on "the presence" of their good works. In this way, God does not overthrow the requirement to obey the law. See Anthony Burgess, *Vindiciae Legis: or, A Vindication of the Morall Law and the Covenants, From the Errours of Papists, Arminians, Socinians, and More Especially Antinomians* (London: James Young, 1646), 29, 30, 29, 32, 32–34.

THE CONCEPT OF REDEMPTION

Edwards spent his entire ministry emphasizing the meaning of redemption. Admittedly, redemption, for Edwards, is twofold: individual salvation and the progress of redemptive history. However, as chapter 5 showed, Edwards's understanding of redemption is focused on God's grand design as the purpose of redemption rather than on the individual experience of salvation. This suggests that Edwards's concern with redemption lies in the application of redemption to the sphere of the Christian life. One can find supporting evidence from Edwards's works, which emphasize the practical-spiritual significance of redemption. For example, the Redemption Discourse "was intended to eventuate in religious practice or conversion."[83] Similarly, in the sermon, "566. Sermon on Gen. 6:22," Edwards describes Noah as a model for seeking salvation:

> Building the ark at the direction of God embodied that work, for it was a lengthy process—a lifetime and more—expensive in terms of what it cost him financially, and difficult not only because of the extreme labor but the derision he doubtless received from his neighbors, first for believing that a flood, the likes of which had never been seen, was going to come, and then for building so ludicrous a thing as an ark.[84]

Edwards's point here is that the believer should maintain piety, seeking salvation like Noah.

Similarly, Edwards claims in his commendatory preface to *True Religion Delineated* by Joseph Bellamy, "We cannot suppose that the church of God is already possessed of all that light ... that ever God intends to give it." Rather, "we stand in great need of having the certain and distinguishing nature and marks of genuine religion more clearly and distinctly set forth than has been usual." Edwards even thought that if we "do not improve

---

83. John F. Wilson, "Editor's Introduction," in *A History of the Work of Redemption*, 37. In the same vein, Neele argues that Edwards's aim in his sermon series of 1739 was "to awaken New England's congregation of Northampton to the revival." Adriaan C. Neele, "The Reception of Edward's *A History of the Work of Redemption* in Nineteenth-century Basutoland," *Journal of Religion in Africa* 45 (2015): 82.

84. Edwards, "566. Sermon on Gen. 6:22 (September 1740)," (unpublished transcription provided by Ken Minkema of the Jonathan Edwards Center at Yale University).

such an advantage, ... we should be much to blame."[85] Again, in his sermon on Titus 3:5, "None Are Saved by Their Own Righteousness," in which he distinguishes true striving for grace from self-righteousness, Edwards asserts that there is a greater probability that the believers who seek for salvation "with earnestness and diligence ... will obtain [it] than one that is a negligent seeker."[86] As McClymond and McDermott rightly note, Edwards expected God to "give the church more light on important doctrinal issues such as the covenants."[87]

Edwards's emphasis on seeking redemption contradicted Stoddardean practices of church membership and Communion. In "True Grace, Distinguished From the Experience of Devils" (1752), a sermon preached before the Presbyterian Synod of New York, Edwards insists that no "speculative knowledge" of religion can be a sign of "saving grace."[88] Similarly, in his sermon "The Importance and Advantage of a Thorough Knowledge of Divine Truth," he relates redemption achieved by Christ to the application in the believer's "effectual calling and sanctification."[89] Edwards argues, "None of the things which God hath taught us in his Word are needless speculations, or trivial matters; all of them are indeed important points." Indeed, Edwards "rarely taught doctrine in a theoretical manner" but rather "preached first and foremost to inform their daily lives."[90]

Notably, one of the important reasons Edwards emphasizes the true meaning of salvation is his concern about hypocrites. Edwards's interest in true affection is found in his diary of December 1722, in which he made the thirty-fifth resolution. "I fear they [Christian graces] are only such hypocritical outside affections, which wicked men may feel, as well as others. They do not seem to be sufficiently inward, full, sincere, entire and hearty. They do not seem to be substantial, and so wrought into my very

---

85. Edwards, "The Preface to *True Religion* by Joseph Bellamy," in *The Great Awakening*, 570–71.

86. Edwards, "None Are Saved by Their Own Righteousness," in *Sermons and Discourses 1723–1729*, 343.

87. McClymond and McDermott, *The Theology of Jonathan Edwards*, 324.

88. Edwards, "True Grace, Distinguished from the Experience of Devils" "James 2:19," in *Sermons and Discourses 1743–1758*, WJE 25:613.

89. Edwards, "The Importance and Advantage of a Thorough Knowledge of Divine Truth" "Heb. 5:12," in *Sermons and Discourses 1739–1742*, WJE 22:93.

90. Sweeney, *Edwards the Exegete*, 196.

nature, as I could wish," insists Edwards.[91] While this statement shows that Edwards's own experience of conversion in his early age "did not match the conversion narratives he would have heard" from his New England predecessors,[92] it at the same time reveals his constant concern of hypocrisy.

In attempting to set "aside false evidences of grace,"[93] Edwards in *Religious Affections* intends to "test fruits of the Spirit"[94] and identifies true signs of a true religious affection. At the end of *Religious Affections*, Edwards offers a balanced way of thinking with regard to the practice of true religion:

> If we had got into the way of looking chiefly at those things, which Christ and his apostles and prophets chiefly insisted on, and so in judging of ourselves and others, chiefly regarding practical exercises and effects of grace, not neglecting other things; it would be of manifold happy consequence; it would above all things tend to the conviction of deluded hypocrites, and to prevent the delusion of those whose hearts were never brought to a thorough compliance with the straight and narrow way which leads to life; it would tend to deliver us from innumerable perplexities, arising from the various inconsistent schemes that are about methods and steps of experience; it would greatly tend to prevent professors neglecting strictness of life, and tend to promote their engagedness and earnestness in their Christian walk. ... We should get into the way of appearing lively in religion, more by being lively in the service of God and our generation, than by the liveliness and forwardness of our tongues, and making a business of proclaiming on the house tops, with our mouths, the holy and eminent acts and exercises of our own hearts.[95]

---

91. Edwards, "Diary," in *Letters and Personal Writings*, WJE 16:759.

92. Stephen R. C. Nichols, *Jonathan Edwards's Bible*, 163. According to Nichols, Edwards was convinced later that "the steps of conversion are less important than the *nature* of the change wrought in the soul." Nichols, *Jonathan Edwards's Bible*, 164.

93. Stephen J. Stein, "Edwards as Biblical Exegete," in *The Cambridge Companion to Jonathan Edwards*, 189.

94. John E. Smith, "Editor's Introduction," in *A Treatise Concerning Religious Affections*, WJE 2:17.

95. Edwards, *Religious Affections*, 461.

For Edwards, the practical application of faith is based on God's will, according to which the believer is oriented to seek the glory of God. He adds, "Religion would be declared and manifested in such a way … Thus the light of professors would so shine before men, that others seeing their good works, would glorify their Father which is in heaven."[96] Edwards's understanding of ecclesiastical piety is oriented to stimulate the grand design of God, that is, the glory of God as the purpose of all redemptive history. In short, Edwards believes that Scripture teaches us how to glorify God by good works and how true religion in the church can be teleologically manifested through the progress of the history of redemption.

Similarly, in a series of five lectures delivered at the Thursday lecture between February 15 and March 22, 1750, Edwards writes, "Hypocrisy lies in men's pretending to goodness that they have not really. But if God's visible people don't all pretend to godliness, then they are not hypocrites in not being godly."[97] The same is true for "An Humble Inquiry," in which Edwards shows "the intensity of his reaction against what he deemed hypocrisy."[98] In this work, Edwards seeks to make a distinction between "members of the visible church *in general*, and members *in complete standing*."[99] Edwards insists, "The denominations, characters and descriptions, which we find given in Scripture to visible Christians, and to the visible church, are principally with an eye to the church of Christ in its adult state and proper standing." Although "Christian piety or godliness" is a qualification "requisite to communion in the Christian sacraments,"[100] it is not to "be properly the rule of the church's proceeding, in like manner as such a belief and repentance."[101] Instead, it is "a visibility to the eye of a Christian Judgment"

---

96. Edwards, *Religious Affections*, 461. Here, Edwards appears to cite Matthew 5:16.

97. Edwards, "Lectures on the Qualifications for Full Communion in the Church of Christ," in *Sermons and Discourses, 1743–1758*, 379.

98. David D. Hall, "Editor's Introduction," in *Ecclesiastical Writings*, WJE 12:84.

99. Edwards, "An Humble Inquiry," 175. By "members *in complete standing*," Edwards means "those who are received as the proper immediate subjects of all the external privileges, Christ has appointed for the ordinary members of his church." General or ordinary members are meant to be those who need to "qualify themselves for ecclesiastical privileges by making a public profession of the Christian faith, or owning the Christian covenant, or forbear to offer themselves as candidates for these privileges; and not be cast out of the church, or cease to be in any respect its members." Edwards, "An Humble Inquiry," 174.

100. Edwards, "An Humble Inquiry," 176.

101. Edwards, "An Humble Inquiry," 177.

that makes the admission of the believer to Communion possible.[102] Again, it is not by "a private judgment," but by the public judgment that "gives a person a right to be received as a visible saint."[103]

However, Edwards's emphasis on the visibility of faith through profession before the church is grounded upon invisibility of true faith in Christ. Edwards states:

> When it is said, those who are admitted, etc. ought to be by profession "godly" or "gracious" persons, 'tis not meant, they should merely *profess* or *say* that they are converted or are gracious persons, that they *know* so, or *think* so; but that they profess the great things wherein Christian piety consists, viz. a supreme respect to God, faith in Christ, etc. Indeed 'tis necessary, as men would keep a good conscience, that they should think that these things are in them, which they profess to be in them; otherwise they are guilty of the horrid wickedness of willfully making a lying profession. Hence 'tis supposed to be necessary, in order to men's regularly and with a good conscience coming into communion with the church of Christ in the Christian sacraments, that they themselves should suppose the essential things, belonging to Christian piety, to be in them.[104]

Edwards is careful to distinguish between true and false professions. A true profession of faith, Edwards believes, involves the heart and conscience. This is the reason Edwards avoids "any attempt to qualify the meaning of sincerity and visibility," as Hall points out.[105]

Edwards moves on to seek biblical grounds for the argument in which he defends his position of participation in communion through profession of faith as an essential component of church practice. According to Edwards, the word "saints" used in 1 Corinthians 6:2; Ephesians 1:18 and 3:17–18; 2 Thessalonians 1:10; and Revelation 5:8, 8:4, 11:18, 13:10, 14:12, and 19:8 refers "not only to real saints, but to such as were saints in visibility, appearance, and profession."[106] Edwards emphasizes that "the distinction

---

102. Edwards, "An Humble Inquiry," 177.
103. Edwards, "An Humble Inquiry," 179.
104. Edwards, "An Humble Inquiry," 180–81.
105. Hall, "Editor's Introduction," 82.
106. Edwards, "An Humble Inquiry," 182.

of real saints and visible and professing saints is scriptural" and states that only those who are visible and professing believers are "admitted into the visible church of Christ."[107] In opposing Stoddard's work *Appeal to the Learned*, Edwards goes on to claim throughout "An Humble Inquiry" that Scripture provides numerous examples of the significance of professing one's faith in public.

Edwards's view of Communion highlights that ecclesiastical piety is deeply involved in the grand design of redemptive history. "Christ came into the world to engage in a war with God's enemies, sin, and Satan; and a great war there is maintained between them; which war is concerning us; and the contest is, who shall have the possession of *our heart*," he asserts. According to him, people must be on one of two sides: on Christ's side or against Christ. Citing Matthew 12:30, which reads, "He that is not with me is against me," he goes on to argue, "The profession of an intermediate sort of state of our mind, is very disagreeable to the nature of Christ's errand, work and kingdom in the world, and all that belongs to the designs and ends of his administrations."[108] In short, the believer could not accomplish salvation as intended by God's grand design without professing faith. In this way, profession of faith is interwoven with redemption within the framework of the grand design of salvation.

In "Misrepresentations Corrected," Edwards claims that Solomon Williams misrepresented Edwards's rejection of Stoddard's understanding of Communion, as if Edwards forbids believers who do not have "the highest evidence a man can give of sincerity" to participate in the sacraments.[109]

---

107. Edwards, "An Humble Inquiry," 183.

108. Edwards, "An Humble Inquiry," 220–21.

109. Edwards, "Misrepresentations Corrected and Truth Vindicated," in *Ecclesiastical Writings*, 361. While Edwards opposes Stoddard's position on qualifications for church membership, he agrees with Stoddard's understanding of the sinful nature of humanity. He writes, "You know, it was always a doctrine greatly insisted on by Mr. Stoddard as a thing of the utmost consequence, that sinners who are seeking converting grace, should be thoroughly sensible of God's being under no manner of obligation, from any desires, labors, or endeavors of theirs, to bestow his grace upon them; either in justice, or truth, or any other way; but that when they have done all, God is perfectly at liberty, whether to show them mercy, or not; that they are wholly in the hands of God's sovereignty." This is why he, in his epistle to the Northampton congregation, urged the Northampton church to "reject Williams' teaching, which are full of errors, and return to Stoddard." Edwards, "Misrepresentations Corrected," 500; George S. Claghorn, "Editor's Introduction to 'To the First Church of Christ, Northampton,'" in *Letters and Personal Writings*, 479. For more on this, see Cherry, *The Theology of Jonathan Edwards*, 210.

Particularly, Edwards rejects Williams's position that "God requires" believers to demonstrate "credible evidence of true piety" through pious living, not through public confession. The inherent claim of Williams, according to Edwards, is that church members "should be admitted under no other notion than of their being truly godly." Against this position, Edwards asserts that both pious living and public profession is necessary. He insists:

> If some men have a right in the sight of God to sacraments, without true piety, and are fit, and duly qualified without it, in his sight, and by his institution, and yet the church must not admit them unless they are truly pious in their sight; then the eye of man must require higher terms, than the infinitely holy eye of God himself; they must look for something that the eye of God looks not for, and which he judges them duly qualified without.[110]

Edwards is clear that qualification for Communion depends not on some degree of evidence of piety, but on the judgment of God. This means that the final judgement of qualification for participating in Communion hinges not on human beings but on God alone.

Edwards achieves harmony between visible profession of faith and invisible true religious affections. John F. Jamieson provides a good summary of Edwards's change of position on Stoddardeanism: Edwards "had thought out the implications for church polity, of Calvinism as over against Arminianism in its Stoddardean guise, on the one hand, and experimental piety and profession of faith as over against moralism, on the other."[111] Edwards believes "a moral sincerity not springing from faith itself is no sincerity at all in profession," as Cherry points out.[112] It is in this way that the church is never separate from an individual believer's faith and piety, which are involved in the process of redemption.

---

110. Edwards, "Misrepresentations Corrected," 387.
111. John F. Jamieson, "Jonathan Edwards' Change of Position on Stoddardeanism," *Harvard Theological Review* 74, no. 1 (January 1981): 79–99.
112. Cherry, *The Theology of Jonathan Edwards*, 213.

CONCLUSION

Much more could be said about Edwards's ecclesiastical approach in his federal theology, but our concern is this chapter was to note how Edwards's understanding of justification, the conditions of the covenants, and redemption can be understood within his interpretive framework and ministerial context.

With respect to the doctrine of justification, Edwards believes that God does not minimize the role of faith but rather maintains it. God's sovereignty does not come at the expense of the role of human faith. The same principle is true for Edwards's understanding of the relationship between justification and sanctification, which he sees as interconnected because of his understanding of the doctrinal harmony of the Bible. It is through this harmony of Scripture that Edwards has carefully developed the doctrine of union with Christ, which harmonizes God's sovereignty with human active engagement.

We have seen that Edwards draws on a belief in the unity of Scripture as he attempts to harmonize the Pauline doctrine of justification through faith alone with James' description of justification through works. Similarly, Sweeney finds that a series of Edwards's exegetical materials "reinforce Edwards' teaching on the 'natural fitness' of faith as a condition of justification." These exegetical writings, according to Sweeney, show that Edwards believed that "sinners are saved by faith alone not because human faith is 'morally fit' to secure a divine reward, but only because it is 'naturally fit' that God should choose to employ faith as a condition, or the existential means through which the justified receive the gift of saving union with Christ."[113] Therefore, Sweeney concludes that Edwards preached that "God is never obligated to compensate imperfect and inconstant human effort (whether in word or in deed) with the grace of justification, but has

---

113. Sweeney, *Edwards the Exegete*, 207n14. For the materials on the definition of faith and its role in justification, see Edwards, "Sermon on Galatians 5:6" (Winter 1728), Box 10, F. 767, L. 4r.-7r., Beinecke; Edwards, "Sermon on Habakkuk 2:4" (early 1730), Box 6, F. 406, L. 5v., Beinecke; Edwards, "Justification by Faith Alone," in *Sermons and Discourses, 1734-1738, WJE* 19:149-50, 153, 156-58. For Edwards's understanding of "natural fitness" of faith as a condition of justification, see *WJE* 19:159-60, 18:187-88, 341-42, 344-46, 543-46; 20:119-20, 382-83, 479-81, 483-84; 21:339-40; and 23:196. I am indebted to Sweeney's *Edwards the Exegete* for providing these sources. See Sweeney, *Edwards the Exegete*, 207n14.

planned a way of salvation in such a naturally fitting manner, or existen-
tially sensible way, that those who seek it usually find it."[114]

Closely related to the doctrine of justification is Edwards's view of conditionality, which is crucial in distinguishing among the three covenants
(redemption, grace, and works). Here, his conception of the conditions
of the three covenants affirms the doctrinal harmony of the Bible, which
indicates that God is pleased to require an active human faith that aligns
with his sovereignty. Therefore, while Edwards puts an emphasis on the
active role of believers' faith in keeping the conditions of the covenants,
this participation with Christ does not interfere with the priority of God's
initiative.

Finally, we examined Edwards's concept of redemption, which is
focused on the historical progress of salvation in the church, considering
it in light of the controversy that ensued when he attempted to change the
Northampton church's sacramental policy. That historical episode raises
an important question: What is the source of Edwards's attempt to harmonize the outward profession of faith with true or invisible faith? Focusing
on this question, we explored some of Edwards's exegetical and pastoral
works, in which he relates his conception of redemption to the ecclesiastical and practical significance of his federal theology.

Edwards's understandings of justification, the conditionality of the
covenants, and redemption in his ecclesiology suggest that he employs his
interpretive framework, the doctrinal harmony of Scripture, to describe
the relationship between divine sovereignty and human agency as God's
plan of redemption unfolds. Edwards attempts to exhort his people to seek
the purpose of redemption in the grand design of God.

---

114. Sweeney, *Edwards the Exegete*, 207n14.

10
—
CONCLUSION

In bringing this work to a conclusion, it is appropriate to consider whether its analysis has anything to contribute to the significant debates over the nature of Edwards's federal theology. This book, an attempt to explore the pervasive historical aspect of Edwards's doctrine of redemption through examining Edwards's exegetical work in support of federal theology, began by charting the backdrop to Edwards's theological development. Earlier, we pointed out that Edwards inherited his federal theology from seventeenth-century Reformed predecessors. The analysis of these scholastics set out in the second chapter strongly suggests that conceptions of the history of redemption in their writings rest on exegetical, theological, and historical consideration of the federal scheme. Cocceius proceeded to develop his federal scheme according to his abrogation system. Witsius's view of redemptive history was focused on the *ordo salutis* rather than on the grand design, that is, the glory of God, as the ultimate purpose of redemption. Mastricht described how God preserved and intensified the knowledge of salvation within the scriptural accounts of history and secular history. Finally, Turretin opposed making a sharp contrast between the Old and New Testaments' administrations regarding the way of salvation, as he perceived being done by those he called Pelagian. The Puritans' exposition of the history of redemption clearly indicates that they belong to the family of scholasticism, despite the subtle differences among their positions regarding federal theology. Disagreements over smaller points of emphasis ought not obscure the larger consensus on scholastic methods.

The same is true for Edwards, who based his federal theology upon exegetical and theological reflection on redemptive history. However, an examination of Edwards's view of the history of redemption within the federal schema reveals that Edwards differed from his Reformed forebears. First, Edwards did not rest on his own covenant system, but rather, his main concern was to follow the Bible's description of the history of redemption. He believed that every event in history moves the process of salvation history forward toward the glory of God as the purpose of redemptive history, intensifying the light of the gospel. This is hinted at in his unfinished project, *A History of the Work of Redemption*, in which Edwards desired to present an "entire new method" of theology. While this project still invites sharp disagreements among scholars, it is clear that Edwards's main concern for redemptive history within his covenant schema (the covenants of redemption, works, and grace) was to seek the grand design of salvation described in the Bible.

Equally important is the difference between the Reformed Puritans' view and that of Edwards with respect to the essence of the Holy Spirit. As seen in chapter 3, Edwards developed his doctrines of the Trinity and the covenant of redemption from his understanding of redemptive history. In doing so, Edwards emphasized a distinct place for the role of the Holy Spirit. Rejecting the Puritans' description of the Holy Spirit as the applicator of the purchase of salvation by Christ, Edwards claimed that the Holy Spirit is not merely an applicator of the benefits of salvation but is himself, rather, the grace and benefit of salvation. This point of view, for Edwards, manifests the Holy Spirit's equality with the other persons of the Trinity. Moreover, Edwards's exposition of the Trinity and the covenant of redemption is framed within the historical aspect of redemption. In this way Edwards establishes the inherent unity among the persons of the Trinity and identifies subtle relationships of the immanent Trinity *ad intra*, the economic Trinity *ad extra*, the covenant of redemption, and the roles of the three divine persons in this covenant.

In chapter 4, we worked out Edwards's theological framework by examining the doctrine of the covenant of works in his sermons, especially those on Genesis 3:11 and 3:24. Beginning with a historical survey of the idea of the covenant of works in the thought of Edwards's Reformed forebears, we examined the implications of the abrogation of the covenant of works through Edwards's understanding of Adam as the federal head of the covenant of works, the relationship between the law and the gospel, and the Mosaic covenant as a republication of the covenant of works, all of which take a central place in Edwards's doctrine of the covenant of works. The contours of his doctrine of the covenant of works overwhelmingly emphasize the sinful nature of both Adam and his posterity and the human inability to restore the pre-fall state. Particularly, Edwards's desire to emphasize the redemptive work of Christ in the Mosaic covenant led him to diverge somewhat from his Reformed forebears, who did not emphasize the Christological element of the Mosaic law. While he shared a coherent vision for the Mosaic covenant with his Reformed predecessors, Edwards's Christological focus on the covenant of works in the Mosaic administration reveals his concern for the historical reality of redemption.

This is also true for Edwards's doctrine of the covenant of grace (chapter 5), in which Edwards did not merely follow the heritage of Reformed orthodoxy but used his view of salvation history creatively. Although Edwards maintained both the order of salvation and the progressive history of salvation in the world, the driving force for Edwards was not the former but the latter. Particular attention was paid to the pattern with which Edwards defined the structure of the thirty sermons in the Redemption Discourse in describing the scheme of the covenant of grace. Moreover, Edwards followed the biblical story in a way that builds toward the consummation of redemptive history. In other words, the structure of redemptive history, which follows biblical history revealed in the Bible, fleshes out Edwards's commitment to the historical venture. Further, Edwards used three sources of revelation—biblical history, prophecy, and secular history—to develop his understanding of redemptive history. This implies that Edwards used the theme of salvation history as an interpretive grid for understanding all events in both the Bible and secular history.

The doctrinal analysis set out in the second part of this work suggests that while maintaining the federal theology found in the Reformed scholastics, Edwards developed his federal theology from his own understanding of the history of redemption as revealed in the Bible. When Edwards connects his understanding of redemption to federal theology, his concern for a corporate reality of redemptive history is more significant than his interest in individual salvation. This accounts for his summary of redemptive history within his entire scheme of the covenants of federal theology.

As has been suggested already, Edwards grounded his understanding of federal theology on the redemptive-historical aspect of divine revelation. Correcting Kreider's label of Edwards's prevailing interpretive method as Christological typology, Barshinger suggests that for Edwards, the Psalms are understood not merely by Christology or typology but by the redemptive-historical approach as Edwards's encompassing interpretive framework.[1] Barshinger rightly distinguishes between the "'redemptive historical' method" and an "overarching redemptive-historical paradigm of thought." While the former points to a single method of interpretation, the latter signifies a "paradigm" that "guided" Edwards "in unearthing the theological treasures contained within the divinely inspired book of Psalms."[2] Barshinger needs to be credited for discerning the larger interpretive framework through which Edwards read the Bible. However, the theme of redemptive history is not the overall interpretive framework that governed Edwards's whole system of federal theology. Edwards did not pursue a single interpretive framework, but rather, he employed various hermeneutical methods in his attempt to understand the nature of the history of redemption in light of his assumptions about the doctrinal harmony of the Bible.

Of course, the redemptive-historical paradigm could be involved in discerning the doctrinal harmony of the Bible.[3] However, when we explore Edwards's biblical exegesis in support of the federal schema, we should relocate his exegesis within his wider interest in the doctrinal harmony of the Bible, within which the redemptive-historical theme lies. Edwards's view of the harmony of the Bible led him to understand redemptive history as being consistent throughout the Bible. Having noted the difficulty of understanding the nature of the doctrinal harmony of the Bible, chapter 6 demonstrated that the key to understanding Edwards's view of the harmony of the Bible lies in his biblical exegesis in support of the federal schema. Edwards's exegesis regarding the doctrine of the covenant of redemption reveals his own understanding of the history of redemption as the realization of revelation, which integrated biblical and secular history. Again, the various exegetical methods Edwards employed in order to interpret the history of redemption reveal that Edwards looked for a way to bring the covenant system of his federal theology into an organic unity with the Bible.

---

1. David P. Barshinger, *Jonathan Edwards and the Psalms: A Redemptive-Historical Vision of Scripture* (New York: Oxford University Press, 2014), 26, 368.

2. Barshinger, *Jonathan Edwards and the Psalms*, 368.

3. See Barshinger, *Jonathan Edwards and the Psalms*, 368.

This doctrinal harmony of the Bible also plays a significant role in Edwards's exegesis in support of the doctrine of the covenant of works. As chapter 7 showed, Edwards's biblical exegesis of the central themes of the covenant of works, such as federal headship, the distinction between the law and the gospel, and the Mosaic covenant, reveals his endeavors to seek the unity of the Bible. The collations of the central texts for the covenant of works cited by Edwards show that he had a desire to listen to the witness of the Bible itself. Given this, it is not surprising that Edwards's collation of the texts in support of the doctrine of the covenant of works is based on a canonical examination of the Bible. Moreover, for Edwards, the central text of the doctrine appears to be Genesis 3 rather than Genesis 2. Particularly, the correlations of the texts in Edwards's hermeneutic, which is oriented to a textual, linguistical, historical, cultural interpretation, reveal that Edwards considered Christ and his redemptive work as the means of demonstrating the coherent unity of the Bible. Further, Edwards considered authorial intention, a literal reading of the text, and typology to be essential for providing a subsequent narrative of the history of redemption.

Chapter 8 explored how the redemptive promise-fulfillment structure in Edwards's doctrine of the covenant of grace is oriented to demonstrate the doctrinal harmony of the Bible. Edwards employed exegetical methods, perceiving his doctrine of the covenant of grace within the promise-fulfillment structure of redemption. In doing so, he established an organic cohesion of the Bible that permits diverse exegetical methods. He considered the visibility of the church to be important for discerning elements of the revelation of the covenant of grace. Especially when he viewed the visible church in terms of ontology, he found typological, allegorical (spiritual or mystical), and anagogical methods helpful in explaining the church as the mystical body of Christ. Moreover, Edwards's linguistic approach to the text provided him with what he perceived to be clear biblical evidence of the covenant of grace. For Edwards, there is no doubt that typology played a significant role in supporting the promise-fulfillment structure of redemption. The same is true for his pedagogical and redemptive-historical exegetical methods, by which Edwards sought a way in which the continuities between the Old and New Testaments are demonstrated. Furthermore, although there are the microscopic and macroscopic levels of exegetical methods, the most fundamental exegetical principles Edwards maintained are based on the author's intention and the author's interpretation of other texts. This echoes why Edwards continuously sought canonical continuity and employed the analogy of faith in seeking to understand the history of redemption. In sum, Edwards's multidimensional understanding of the visibility of the church, human authorship of biblical texts, languages, biblical genres, and the historical stages of the administration of the covenant of grace—Adam to Noah, to Abraham, to Moses, to David, to the Babylon captivity, and to Christ's incarnation (the intertestamental period)—reveals his desire to demonstrate the history of redemption within the interpretive framework of a presumed doctrinal harmony of Scripture.

Edwards's interpretive method bears great resemblance to the medieval four-fold method of interpretation, which maintained that there were four discernible senses of the biblical texts: (1) the literal sense, which refers to a real event; (2) the allegorical sense, as applied to seeking a spiritual meaning of the text relating to the church or an article of faith; (3) the tropological sense, which deals with morals; and (4) the anagogical sense, which addresses Christian hope.[4] Moreover, Edwards stands within the Puritan tradition in relation to his citations of Scripture and his use of interpretive methods. Despite this fundamental similarity between Edwards and his Reformed forebears, Edwards's exegetical methods are more multidimensional and interwoven with each other when compared with his Reformed forebears. For example, Edwards never repudiated allegory in his advocacy of the literal sense. Moreover, as seen in his exegesis of the doctrine of the covenant of works, a major covenant *locus* in Edwards appears different from Reformed orthodoxy. Why is this so? Edwards's use of the text and his various interpretive methods suggest that he attempted to discern salvation history within his wider interpretive framework, that is, the doctrinal harmony of the Bible.

Finally, the flow of this book focused on Edwards's understanding of the doctrinal harmony of Scripture in relation to his ecclesiastical and

---

4. Roland H. Bainton, "The Bible in the Reformation," in *The West from the Reformation to the Present Day*, ed. S. L. Greenslade, vol. 3 of *The Cambridge History of the Bible* (New York: Cambridge University Press, 1963), 24. See Glenn R. Kreider, *Jonathan Edwards's Interpretation of Revelation 4:1–8:1* (Lanham, MD: University Press of America, 2004), 48.

practical perspective, which focused on the meaning of redemption for his pastoral charge. Edwards encouraged his people to strive for true religion, which involved true faith and piety. This implies that Edwards's federal theology is not an isolated undertaking but rather is rooted in his pastoral ministry, which emphasized the harmony between faith and piety. A primary example of this is found in Edwards's pastoral works, through which he defended the doctrine of justification, in which he changed the concept of conditionality among the covenants of redemption, works, and grace in opposition to Arminianism, and in which he suggested the importance of seeking salvation. Edwards found evidence of divine design in the harmony between faith and piety, making an appeal to the concept of fitness in his doctrine of justification. Edwards's changes to the concept of the conditions of the covenants were primarily based on his concern for redemptive history. In this sense, the meaning of redemption for Edwards played a critical role in the process of redemptive history. For Edwards, God is the one who gives more light to the believer who seeks redemption. Thus, redemption, Edwards alleged, is far from being a finished product achieved by Christ, but rather, it is teleological. That is, redemption is a process continuing through history, a process revealed in Scripture and leading ultimately to the glory of God. It is through his federal theology, particularly his doctrine of the covenant of grace, that Edwards attempted to develop the Christian's practical engagement with redemptive history. Further, Edwards's biblical exegesis, which established the doctrinal harmony of Scripture as an interpretive framework that would avoid potential tensions between biblical texts, demonstrates the inherent unity between faith and piety within his federal theology.

Thus far, this book has argued that there are similarities and differences between Edwards and his Reformed predecessors regarding their respective conceptions of federal theology. However, as has been apparent throughout this book, the admission that Edwards's federal theology is different from his Reformed forebears is not to state that his federal theology is novel. Rather, Edwards's federal theology is inherited from Reformed orthodoxy and should be seen as a significant channel within the wide stream emerging from seventeenth-century federal theology. Like Calvin and Reformed orthodox theologians, Edwards stands in exegetical traditions inherited from the late Middle Ages.[5] In other words, Edwards's assumption of the doctrinal harmony of Scripture within federal theology must be seen as a development within the exegetical tradition from the late Middle Ages, through Calvin and Reformed orthodoxy. At the same time, this book attempts in no way to say that Edwards considered himself a slavish adherent to an unchangeable Reformed orthodoxy. While both Edwards and his Reformed forebears regarded Scripture as the primary source for their federal theology,[6] the former was more appreciative of biblical exegesis than the systematic approaches of the latter. Ultimately, Edwards developed his federal theology from his own biblical exegesis, assuming the doctrinal harmony of the Bible, which proves highly significant in Edwards's dealing with redemptive history embedded within the scriptural accounts of history.

---

5. Muller claims that there is "continuity in development of exegetical method from the late Middle Ages into the sixteenth century." Richard A. Muller, "The Hermeneutic of Promise and Fulfillment in Calvin's Exegesis of the Old Testament Prophecies of the Kingdom," in *The Bible in the Sixteenth Century*, ed. David C. Steinmetz (Durham, NC: Duke University Press, 1990), 82.

6. According to David C. Steinmetz, Calvin considered the Fathers to be "partners in conversation rather than" to be "authorities in the medieval sense of the term." Although the Fathers "presented him [Calvin] with ideas and suggestions he did not find in the writings of his contemporaries," it is not the Fathers but Paul who had "the last word" for Calvin. David C. Steinmetz, "Calvin and the Patristic Exegesis of Paul," in *The Bible in the Sixteenth Century*, 117.

BIBLIOGRAPHY

—

PRIMARY SOURCES

Edwards, Jonathan. *A Faithful Narrative.* In *The Great Awakening,* edited by C. C. Goen, 144–211. Vol. 4 of *The Works of Jonathan Edwards.* New Haven, CT: Yale University Press, 1972.

———. *A History of the Work of Redemption.* Edited by John Wilson. Vol. 9 of *The Works of Jonathan Edwards.* New Haven, CT: Yale University Press, 1989.

———. *An Humble Attempt to Promote Explicit Agreement and Visible Union of God's People in Extraordinary Prayer for the Revival of Religion and the Advancement of Christ's Kingdom on Earth, Pursuant to Scripture-Promises and Prophecies Concerning the Last Time.* In *Apocalyptic Writings,* edited by Stephen J. Stein, 307–436. Vol. 5 of *The Works of Jonathan Edwards.* New Haven, CT: Yale University Press, 1977.

———. "An Humble Inquiry into the Rules of the Word of God, Concerning the Qualifications Requisite to a Complete Standing and Full Communion in the Visible Christian Church. In Ecclesiastical Writings," edited by David D. Hall,167–348. Vol. 12 of *The Works of Jonathan Edwards.* New Haven, CT: Yale University Press, 1994.

———. *Dissertation I: Concerning the End for Which God Created the World.* In *Ethical Writings,* edited by Paul Ramsey, 403–536. Vol. 8 of *The Works of Jonathan Edwards.* New Haven, CT: Yale University Press, 1989.

———. *Freedom of the Will.* Edited by Paul Ramsey. Vol. 1 of *The Works of Jonathan Edwards.* New Haven, CT: Yale University Press, 1957.

———. *Letters and Personal Writings.* Edited by George S. Claghorn. Vol. 16 of *The Works of Jonathan Edwards.* New Haven, CT: Yale University Press, 1998.

———. "Misrepresentations Corrected and Truth Vindicated. In Ecclesiastical Writings," edited by David D. Hall, 351–503. Vol. 12 of *The*

Works of Jonathan Edwards. New Haven, CT: Yale University Press, 1994.

———. *Narrative of Communion Controversy.* In *Ecclesiastical Writings,* edited by David D. Hall, 507–619. Vol. 12 of *The Works of Jonathan Edwards.* New Haven, CT: Yale University Press, 1994.

———. *Notes on Scripture.* Edited by Stephen J. Stein. Vol. 15 of *The Works of Jonathan Edwards.* New Haven, CT: Yale University Press, 1998.

———. *Original Sin.* Edited by Clyde A. Holbrook. Vol. 3 of *The Works of Jonathan Edwards.* New Haven, CT: Yale University Press, 1970.

———. *Religious Affections: A Treatise Concerning Religious Affections.* Edited by John E. Smith. Vol. 2 of *The Works of Jonathan Edwards.* New Haven, CT: Yale University Press, 1959.

———. *Sermons and Discourses 1720–1723.* Edited by Wilson H. Kimnach. Vol. 10 of *The Works of Jonathan Edwards.* New Haven, CT: Yale University Press, 1992.

———. *Sermons and Discourses, 1731–1732.* Edited by Jonathan Edwards Center. Vol. 46 of *The Works of Jonathan Edwards Online.* Jonathan Edwards Center at Yale University, 2008.

———. *The Life of David Brainerd.* Edited by Norman Pettit. Vol. 7 of *The Works of Jonathan Edwards.* New Haven, CT: Yale University Press, 1985.

———. *The "Blank Bible."* Edited by Stephen J. Stein. Vol. 24, Parts 1 and 2 of *The Works of Jonathan Edwards.* New Haven, CT: Yale University Press, 2006.

———. *The "Miscellanies": Entry Nos. 501–832.* Edited by Ava Chamberlain. Vol. 18 of *The Works of Jonathan Edwards.* New Haven, CT: Yale University Press, 2000.

———. *The "Miscellanies": Entry Nos. a-z, aa-zz, 1-500.* Edited by Thomas A. Schafer. Vol. 13 of *The Works of Jonathan Edwards.* New Haven, CT: Yale University Press, 1994.

———. *The "Miscellanies": Entry Nos. 1153–1360.* Edited by Douglas A. Sweeney. Vol. 23 of *The Works of Jonathan Edwards.* New Haven, CT: Yale University Press, 2004.

———. *The "Miscellanies": Entry Nos. 833–1152.* Edited by Amy Plantinga Pauw. Vol. 20 of *The Works of Jonathan Edwards.* New Haven, CT: Yale University Press, 2002.

———. *Writings on the Trinity, Grace, and Faith*. Edited by Sang Hyun Lee. Vol. 21 of *The Works of Jonathan Edwards*. New Haven, CT: Yale University Press, 2003.

———. "082. Sermon on Matt. 12:30 (ca. 1728–1729; September 1756)." In *Sermons, Series II, 1728–1729*. Vol. 43 of *The Works of Jonathan Edwards Online*. Jonathan Edwards Center at Yale University, 2008. http://edwards.yale.edu/archive?path=aHR0cDovL2Vkd-2FyZHMueWFsZS5lZHUv Y2dpLWJpbi9uZXdwaGlsby9nZX-RvYmplY3QucGw/Yy40oMToyNC53amVv (accessed September 10, 2018).

———. "109. Sermon on 2 Samuel 23:5 (Summer–Fall 1729)." In *Sermons, Series II, 1728–1729*. Vol. 44 of *The Works of Jonathan Edwards Online*. Jonathan Edwards Center at Yale University, 2008. http://edwards.yale.edu/archive?path=aHR0cDovL2Vkd-2FyZHMueWFsZS5lZHUvY2dpLWJpbi9uZXdwaGlsby9nZX-RvYmplY3QucGw/Yy40Mjo5LnddqZW8 (accessed September 10, 2018).

———. "139. Sermon on Habakkuk 2:4 (1729–1730)." Jonathan Edwards Collection. Beinecke Rare Book and Manuscript library. Yale University. New Haven, CT.

———. "190. John 15:10 (Mar. 1736)." In *Sermons and Discourses, 1731–1732*. Vol. 46 of *The Works of Jonathan Edwards Online*. Jonathan Edwards Center, 2008. http://edwards.yale.edu/archive?path=aHR0cDovL2Vkd2FyZHMueWFsZS5lZHUvY2d-pLWJpbi9uZXdwaGlsby9nZXRvYmplY3QucGw/Yy40oNDozLnd-qZW8 (accessed September 10, 2018)

———. "470. Sermon on 1 Cor. 13:1–10 (b) (Apr. 1738)." In *Sermons, Series II, 1738, and undated, 1734–1738*. Vol. 53 of *The Works of Jonathan Edwards Online*. New Haven, CT: Jonathan Edwards Center at Yale University, 2008. http://edwards.yale.edu/archive?path=aHR0c-DovL2Vkd2FyZHMueWFsZS5lZHUvY2dpLWJpbi9uZXdwaGlsby9nZXRvYmplY3QucGw/Yy41MToxNi53amVv (accessed September 13, 2018).

———. "495. Sermon on Heb. 9:13–14 (November 1738)." In *Sermons, Series II, 1738*. Vol. 53 of *The Works of Jonathan Edwards Online*. Jonathan Edwards Center at Yale University, 2008. http://edwards.

yale.edu/archive?path=aHR0cDovL2Vkd2FyZHMueWFsZS5lZ-
HUvY2dpLWJpbi9uZXdwaGlsby9nZXRvYmplY3QucGw/Yy41M-
ToyNC53amVv (accessed September 11, 2018).

———. "504. Sermon on Gen. 3:11 (February 1739)." In *Sermons, Series II, 1739.* Vol. 54 of *The Works of Jonathan Edwards Online.* Jonathan Edwards Center at Yale University, 2008. http://edwards.yale.edu/archive?path=aHR0cDovL2Vkd2FyZHMueWFsZS5lZHUvY2dpLWJpbi9uZXdwaGlsby9nZXRvYmplY3QucGw/Yy41Mjo1LndqqZW8 (accessed September 11, 2018).

———. "534. Sermon on Heb. 9:15–16 (Jan. 4, 1740)." Unpublished transcription provided by Ken Minkema of the Jonathan Edwards Center at Yale University.

———. "544. Sermon on Hebrews 12:22–24 (a) (April 1740)." In *Sermons, Series II, 1740.* Vol. 55 of *The Works of Jonathan Edwards Online.* Jonathan Edwards Center at Yale University, 2008. http://edwards.yale.edu/archive?path=aHR0cDovL2Vkd2FyZHMueWFsZS5lZHUvY2dpLWJpbi9uZXdwaGlsby9nZXRvYmplY3QucGw/Yy41MzoxMS53amVv (assessed September 11, 2018)

———. "547. Sermon on Hebrews 12:22–24 (d) (April 1740)." In *Sermons, Series II, 1728–1729.* Vol. 55 of *The Works of Jonathan Edwards Online.* Jonathan Edwards Center at Yale University, 2008. http://edwards.yale.edu/archive?path=aHR0cDovL2Vkd2FyZHMueWFsZS5lZHUvY2dpLWJpbi9uZXdwaGlsby9nZXRvYmplY3QucGw/Yy41MzoxNC53amVv#note10

———. "547. Sermon on Hebrews 12:22–24 (d) (c. Apr.–May 1740)." In *Sermons, Series II, 1740.* Vol. 55 of *The Works of Jonathan Edwards Online.* Jonathan Edwards Center at Yale University, 2008. http://edwards.yale.edu/archive?path=aHR0cDovL2Vkd2FyZHMueWFsZS5lZHUvY2dpLWJpbi9uZXdwaGlsby9nZXRvYmplY3QucGw/Yy41MzoxNC53amVv (assessed September 11, 2018)

———. "566. Sermon on Gen. 6:22 (September 1740)." Unpublished transcription provided by Ken Minkema of the Jonathan Edwards Center at Yale University.

———. "59. Sermon on Galatians 5:6 (Winter 1728)." Jonathan Edwards Collection. Beinecke Rare Book and Manuscript library. Yale University. New Haven, CT.

———. "998. Sermon on Gen. 2:17 (August 1751)." Unpublished transcription provided by Ken Minkema of the Jonathan Edwards Center at Yale University.

———. "A Divine and Supernatural Light." In *Sermons and Discourses 1730-1733*, edited by Mark Valeri, 405-26. Vol. 17 of *The Works of Jonathan Edwards*. New Haven, CT: Yale University Press, 1999.

———. "Apocalypse Series." In *Apocalyptic Writings*, edited by Stephen J. Stein, 125-218. Vol. 5 of *The Works of Jonathan Edwards*. New Haven, CT: Yale University Press, 1977.

———. "Diary." In *Letters and Personal Writings*, edited by George S. Claghorn, 759-86. Vol. 16 of *The Works of Jonathan Edwards*. New Haven, CT: Yale University Press, 1998.

———. "Discourse on the Trinity." In *Writings on the Trinity, Grace, and Faith*, edited by Sang Hyun Lee, 109-44. Vol. 21 of *The Works of Jonathan Edwards*. New Haven, CT: Yale University Press, 2003.

———. "East of Eden" (Gen 3:24)." In *Sermon and Discourses 1730-1733*, edited by Mark Valeri, 329-48. Vol. 17 of *The Works of Jonathan Edwards*. New Haven, CT: Yale University Press, 1999.

———. "Exposition on the Apocalypse." In *Apocalyptic Writings*, edited by Stephen J. Stein, 97-124. Vol. 5 of *The Works of Jonathan Edwards*. New Haven, CT: Yale University Press, 1977.

———. "Glorious Grace (Zech 4:7)." In *Sermon and Discourses 1720-1723*, edited by Wilson H. Kimnach, 388-99. Vol. 10 of *The Works of Jonathan Edwards*. New Haven, CT: Yale University Press, 1992.

———. "God Glorified in Man's Dependence (1 Cor 1:29-31)." In *Sermons and Discourses 1730-1733*, edited by Mark Valeri, 196-216. Vol. 17 of *The Works of Jonathan Edwards*. New Haven, CT: Yale University Press, 1999.

———. "God Glorified in the Work of Redemption, by the Greatness of Man's Dependence upon Him, in the Whole of It (1731)." In *The Sermons of Jonathan Edwards: A Reader*, edited by Wilson H. Kimnach, Kenneth P. Minkema, and Douglas A. Sweeney, 66-82. New Haven, CT: Yale University Press, 1999.

———. "He That Believeth Shall Be Saved (1751)." In *The Sermons of Jonathan Edwards: A Reader*, edited by Wilson H. Kimnach, Kenneth P. Minkema, and Douglas A. Sweeney, 111-20. New Haven, CT: Yale University Press, 1999.

———. "Images of Divine Things." In *Typological Writings*, edited by Wallace E. Anderson, 50–141. Vol. 11 of *The Works of Jonathan Edwards*. New Haven, CT: Yale University Press, 1992.

———. "Justification by Faith Alone." In *Sermons and Discourses 1734–1738*, edited by M. X. Lesser, 143–242. Vol. 19 of *The Works of Jonathan Edwards*. New Haven, CT: Yale University Press, 2001.

———. "Lectures on the Qualifications for Full Communion in the Church of Christ." In *Sermons and Discourses, 1743–1758*, edited by Wilson H. Kimnach, 349–440. Vol. 25 of *The Works of Jonathan Edwards*. New Haven, CT: Yale University Press, 2006.

———. "None Are Saved by Their Own Righteousness." In *Sermons and Discourses 1723–1729*, edited by Kenneth Minkema, 329–56. Vol. 14 of *The Works of Jonathan Edwards*. New Haven, CT: Yale University Press, 1997.

———. "On the Equality of the Persons of the Trinity." In *Writings on the Trinity, Grace, and Faith*, edited by Sang Hyun Lee, 145–48. Vol. 21 of *The Works of Jonathan Edwards*. New Haven, CT: Yale University Press, 2003.

———. "Personal Narrative." In *Letters and Personal Writings*, edited by George S. Claghorn, 790–804. Vol. 16 of *The Works of Jonathan Edwards*. New Haven, CT: Yale University Press, 1998.

———. "The Everlasting Love of God (Jer 31:3)." In *Sermons and Discourses 1734–1738*, edited by M. X. Lesser, 473–90. Vol. 19 of *The Works of Jonathan Edwards*. New Haven, CT: Yale University Press, 2001.

———. "The Importance and Advantage of a Thorough Knowledge of Divine Truth (Heb. 5:12)." In *Sermons and Discourses 1739–1742*, edited by Harry S. Stout and Nathan O. Hatch with Kyle P. Farley, 80–102. Vol. 22 of *The Works of Jonathan Edwards*. New Haven, CT: Yale University Press, 2003.

———. "The Preface to *True Religion* by Joseph Bellamy." In *The Great Awakening*, edited by C. C. Goen, 567–72. Vol. 4 of *The Works of Jonathan Edwards*. New Haven, CT: Yale University Press, 1972.

———. "The Pure in Heart Blessed (Matt. 5:8)." In *Sermon and Discourses 1730–1733*, edited by Mark Valeri, 57–86. Vol. 17 of *The Works of Jonathan Edwards*. New Haven, CT: Yale University Press, 1999.

———. "The Sacrifice of Christ Acceptable (Ps 40:6–8)." In *Sermons and*

Discourses 1723-1729, edited by Kenneth P. Minkema, 437-57. Vol. 14 of *The Works of Jonathan Edwards*. New Haven, CT: Yale University Press, 1997.

———. "The Sweet Harmony of Christ." In *Sermons and Discourses 1734-1738*, edited by M. X. Lesser, 435-50. Vol. 19 of *The Works of Jonathan Edwards*. New Haven, CT: Yale University Press, 2001.

———. "To the First Church of Christ, Northampton." In *Letters and Personal Writings*, edited by George S. Claghorn, 479-84. Vol. 16 of *The Works of Jonathan Edwards*. New Haven, CT: Yale University Press, 1998.

———. "Treatise on Grace." In *Writings on the Trinity, Grace, and Faith*, edited by Sang Hyun Lee, 149-97. Vol. 21 of *The Works of Jonathan Edwards*. New Haven, CT: Yale University Press, 2003.

———. "True Grace, Distinguished from the Experience of Devils (James 2:19)." In *Sermons and Discourses 1743-1758*, edited by Wilson H. Kimnach, 605-40. Vol. 25 of *The Works of Jonathan Edwards*. New Haven, CT: Yale University Press, 2006.

———. "True Saints, When Absent from the Body, Are Present with the Lord (2 Cor. 5:8)." In *Sermons and Discourses 1743-1758*, edited by Wilson H. Kimnach, 222-56. Vol. 25 of *The Works of Jonathan Edwards*. New Haven, CT: Yale University Press, 2006.

———. "Types of the Messiah." In *Typological Writings*, edited by Mason I. Lowance Jr. with David H. Watters, 157-328. Vol. 11 of *The Works of Jonathan Edwards*. New Haven, CT: Yale University Press, 1992.

———. "Types." In *Typological Writings*, edited by Wallace E. Anderson, 145-53. Vol. 11 of *The Works of Jonathan Edwards*. New Haven, CT: Yale University Press, 1992.

———. "'Controversies' Notebook: Efficacious Grace." In *Writings on the Trinity, Grace, and Faith*, edited by Sang Hyun Lee, 191-311. Vol. 21 of *The Works of Jonathan Edwards*. New Haven, CT: Yale University Press, 2003.

———. "'Controversies' Notebook: Justification," In *Writings on the Trinity, Grace, and Faith*, edited by Sang Hyun Lee, 328-413. Vol. 21 of *The Works of Jonathan Edwards*. New Haven, CT: Yale University Press, 2003.

OTHER PRIMARY SOURCES

Anon. *The Confession of Faith and Catechisms, Agreed upon by the Assembly of Divines at Westminster Together with Their Humble Advice Concerning Church Government and Ordination of Ministers*. London: the Sign of the Kings Head, 1649.

Ball, John. *A Treatise of the Covenant of Grace*. London: G. Miller, 1645.

Burgess, Anthony. *Vindiciae Legis: or, A Vindication of the Morall Law and the Covenants, From the Errours of Papists, Arminians, Socinians, and More Especially Antinomians*. London: James Young, 1646.

Calvin, John. *Commentary on Genesis*. Translated by John King. Edinburgh: Calvin Translation Society, 1847.

———. *Commentary on Hebrews*. Translated by John Owen. Edinburgh: Calvin Translation Society, 1853.

———. *Commentary on Zephaniah*. Translated by John Owen. Edinburgh: Calvin Translation Society, 1848.

———. *Commentary on the Epistle of Paul the Apostle to the Romans*. Translated by John Owen. Edinburgh: Calvin Translation Society, 1849.

———. *Commentary on the First Epistle of Paul the Corinthians*. Translated by John Pringle. Edinburgh: Calvin Translation Society, 1848.

———. *Institutes of the Christian Religion 2 vols*. Edited by John T. McNeill. Translated by Ford Lewis Battles. Philadelphia: Westminster, 1960.

Cocceius, Johannes. *The Doctrine of the Covenant and Testament of God*. Translated by Casey Carmichael. Grand Rapids: Reformation Heritage Books, 2016.

Durham, James. *Clavis Cantici, or An Exposition of the Song of Solomon*. Edinburgh: G. Swintoun and J. Glen, 1668.

Dwight, Sereno E. *The Works of President Edwards: With a Memoir of His Life*. Vol. 1. New York: S. Converse, 1829–1830.

Hopkins, Samuel. *The Life and Character of the Late Reverend Mr. Jonathan Edwards, President of the College of New-Jersey*. Boston: S. Kneeland, 1765.

———. *The System of Doctrines: Contained in Divine Revelation, Explained and Defended: Showing Their Consistence and Connection with Each Other. To Which is Added, A Treatise on the Millennium*. Boston: Isaiah Thomas and Ebenezer T. Andrews, 1793.

Mastricht, Petrus van. *A Treatise on Regeneration*. Edited by Brandon Withrow. Morgan, PA: Soli Deo Gloria Publications, 2002.

———. *Theoretico-practica theologia: qua, per singula capita theologica, pars exegetica, dogmatica, elenchtica & practica, perpetua successione conjugantur*. 3rd ed. Utrecht: Apud W. van de Water, 1724.

Schaff, Philip. *The Creeds of Christendom: With a History and Critical Notes*. 3 vols. Reprint, Grand Rapids: Baker, 1983.

Stoddard, Solomon, *The Doctrine of Instituted Churches Explained and Proved from the Word of God*. London: Ralph Smith, 1700.

———. *The Inexcusableness of Neglecting the Worship of God, under a Pretence of Being in an Unconverted Condition....* Boston: B. Green, 1708

———. *An Appeal to the Learned: Being a Vindication of the Right of Visible Saints to the Lords Supper, Though They Be Destitute of a Saving Work of God's Spirit on Their Hearts....* Boston: B. Green, 1709.

Strong, William. *A Discourse of the Two Covenants: Wherein the Nature, Differences, and Effects of the Covenant of Works and of Grace are ... Discussed*. London: J. M, 1678.

Turretin, Francis. *Institutes of Elenctic Theology*. Edited by James T. Dennison Jr. Translated by George Musgrave Giger. 3 vols. Phillipsburg, NJ: P&R, 1992–1997.

Witsius, Herman. *The Economy of the Covenants Between God and Man: Comprehending a Complete Body of Divinity*. 2 vols. Translated by William Crookshank. Edinburgh: John Turnbull, 1803.

SECONDARY SOURCES

Ahlstrom, Sydney E. "Theology in America: A Historical Survey." In *The Shaping of American Religion*, edited by James Ward Smith and A. Leland Jamison, 232–321. Princeton: Princeton University Press, 1961.

Anderson, Wallace E. "Editor's Introduction to 'Images of Divine Things' and 'Types.'" In *Typological Writings*, edited by Wallace E. Anderson and Mason I. Lowance Jr., with David Watters, 3–48. Vol. 11 of *The Works of Jonathan Edwards*. New Haven, CT: Yale University Press, 1992.

Atwood, Christopher. "Jonathan Edwards's Doctrine of Justification." PhD diss., Wheaton College, 2013.

Bainton, Roland H. "The Bible in the Reformation." *In The West from the Reformation to the Present Day*, ed. S. L. Greenslade, 1–37. Vol. 3 of *The Cambridge History of the Bible*. New York: Cambridge University Press, 1963.

Barnes, Michael René. "Augustine in Contemporary Trinitarian Theology." *Theological Studies* 56 (1995): 237–50.

———. "De Régnon Reconsidered." *Augustinian Studies* 26, no. 2 (1995): 51–79.

Barshinger, David P. *Jonathan Edwards and the Psalms: A Redemptive – Historical Vision of Scripture*. New York: Oxford University Press, 2014.

Barth, Karl. *Church Dogmatics*. Vol. 4, *The Doctrine of Reconciliation*, part 1. Translated by G. W. Bromiley. Edinburgh: T&T Clark, 1956.

Bavinck, Herman. *Reformed Dogmatics*. Vol. 2, *God and Creation*. Edited by John Bolt. Translated by John Vriend. Grand Rapids: Baker Academic, 2004.

———. *Reformed Dogmatics*. Vol. 3, *Sin and Salvation in Christ*. Edited by John Bolt. Translated by John Vriend. Grand Rapids: Baker Academic, 2006.

Beach, J. Mark. *Christ and the Covenant: Francis Turretin's Federal Theology as a Defense of the Doctrine of Grace*. Göttingen: Vandenhoeck & Ruprecht, 2007.

———. "The Doctrine of the *Pactum Salutis* in the Covenant Theology of Herman Witsius." *Mid-America Journal of Theology* 13 (2002): 101–42.

Beeke, Joel R. "Editor's Preface." In Petrus van Mastricht, *Theoretical-Practical Theology Vol 1: Prolegomena*, edited by Joel R. Beeke and translated by Todd M. Rester, xi–xiv. Grand Rapids: Reformation Heritage Books, 2018.

———. *Puritan Reformed Spirituality*. Grand Rapids: Reformation Heritage Books, 2004.

Beeke, Joel R. and Mark Jones. *A Puritan Theology*. Grand Rapids: Reformation Heritage Books, 2012.

———. "Puritan Hermeneutics and Exegesis." In *A Puritan Theology*, 27–40. Grand Rapids: Reformation Heritage Books, 2012.

———. "The Puritans on Law and Gospel." In *A Puritan Theology*, 321–33. Grand Rapids: Reformation Heritage Books, 2012.

———. "The Puritans on the Covenant of Grace." In *A Puritan Theology*, 259–78. Grand Rapids: Reformation Heritage Books, 2012.

———. "The Puritans on the Covenant of Works." In *A Puritan Theology*, 217–36. Grand Rapids: Reformation Heritage Books, 2012.

———. "The Puritans on the Third Use of the Law." In *A Puritan Theology*, 555–71. Grand Rapids: Reformation Heritage Books, 2012.

Bezzant, Rhys S. *Jonathan Edwards and the Church*. New York: Oxford University Press, 2014.

Bierma, Lyle D. *German Calvinism in the Confessional Age: The Covenant Theology of Caspar Olevianus*. Grand Rapids: Baker, 1996.

———. Review of *The Origins of the Federal Theology in 16th Century Reformation Thought*. by David A. Weir. *Calvin Theological Journal* 26, no. 2 (1991): 483–85.

Billings, J. Todd. *Calvin, Participation, and the Gift: The Activity of Believers in Union with Christ*. Oxford: Oxford University Press, 2007.

———. "Union with Christ and the Double Grace: Calvin's Theology and Its Early Reception." In *Calvin's Theology and Its Reception: Disputes, Developments, and New Possibilities*, edited by I. John Hesselink and J. Todd Billings, 49–71. Louisville, KY: Westminster John Knox, 2012.

Bogue, Carl W. *Jonathan Edwards and the Covenant of Grace*. Cherry Hill, NJ: Mack, 1975.

Bozeman, Theodore Dwight. *To Live Ancient Lives: The Primitivist Dimension in Puritanism*. Chapel Hill: University of North Carolina Press, 1988.

Brown, Robert E. *Jonathan Edwards and the Bible*. Bloomington: Indiana University Press, 2002.

Butler, Diana. "God's Visible Glory: The Beauty of Nature in the Thought of John Calvin and Jonathan Edwards." *Westminster Theological Journal* 52 (1990): 13–26.

Caldwell, Robert W., III. *Communion in the Spirit: The Holy Spirit as the Bond of Union in the Theology of Jonathan Edwards*. Eugene, OR: Wipf & Stock, 2007.

———. "Original Sin." In *A Reader's Guide to the Major Writings of Jonathan Edwards*, edited by Nathan A. Finn and Jeremy M. Kimble, 153–74. Wheaton, IL: Crossway, 2017.

Casselli, Stephen J. *Divine Rule Maintained: Anthony Burgess, Covenant Theology, and the Place of the Law in Reformed Scholasticism.* Grand Rapids: Reformation Heritage Books, 2016.

———. "Anthony Burgess' *Vindiciae Legis* and the 'Fable of Unprofitable Scholasticism': A Case Study in the Reappraisal of Seventeenth Century Reformed Scholasticism." PhD diss., Westminster Theological Seminary, 2007.

Chamberlain, Ava. "Editor's Introduction." In *The "Miscellanies": Entry Nos. 501-832*, edited by Ava Chamberlain, 1-47. Vol. 18 of *The Works of Jonathan Edwards.* New Haven, CT: Yale University Press, 2000.

Cherry, Conrad. *The Theology of Jonathan Edwards: A Reappraisal.* Bloomington: Indiana University Press, 1990.

———. "Justification by Faith." In *The Theology of Jonathan Edwards: A Reappraisal*, 90-106. New York: Doubleday, 1966.

———. "The Puritan Notion of the Covenant in Jonathan Edwards' Doctrine of Faith." *Church History* 34, no. 3 (September 1965): 328-41.

Cho, Hyun-Jin. *Jonathan Edwards on Justification: Reformed Development of the Doctrine in Eighteenth-Century New England.* Lanham: University Press of America, 2012.

Claghorn, George S. "Editor's Introduction to 'To the First Church of Christ, Northampton.'" In *Letters and Personal Writings*, edited by George S. Claghorn, 479-84. Vol. 16 of *The Works of Jonathan Edwards.* New Haven, CT: Yale University Press, 1998.

Claghorn, George S. "Editor's Introduction." In *Letters and Personal Writings*, edited by George S. Claghorn, 3-27. Vol. 16 of *The Works of Jonathan Edwards.* New Haven, CT: Yale University Press, 1998.

Clark, Stephen M. "Jonathan Edwards: The History of the Work of Redemption." *Westminster Theological Journal*, 56, no. 1 (1994): 45-58.

Cole, Victor Babajide. *Training of the Ministry.* Bangelor, India: Theological Book Trust, 2001.

Collins, C. John. *Genesis 1-4: A Linguistic, Literary, and Theological Commentary.* Phillipsburg, NJ: P&R, 2006.

Cotterell, Peter, and Max Turner. *Linguistics and Biblical Interpretation.* Downers Grove, IL: InterVarsity Press, 1989.

Crisp, Oliver D. *Jonathan Edwards and the Metaphysics of Sin*. Burlington,
VT: Ashgate, 2005.

———. "Jonathan Edwards on the Divine Nature." *Journal of Reformed
Theology* 3 (2009): 175–201.

———. "The Moral Government of God: Jonathan Edwards and Joseph
Bellamy on the Atonement." In *After Jonathan Edwards: The
Courses of the New England Theology*, edited by Oliver D. Crisp and
Douglas A. Sweeney, 78–90. New York: Oxford University Press,
2012.

Cunnington, Ralph. "A Critical Examination of Jonathan Edwards's
Doctrine of the Trinity." *Themelios (Online)*, 39, no. 2 (July 2014):
224–40. http://themelios.thegospelcoalition.org/article/a-criti-
cal-examination-of-jonathan-edwardss-doctrine-of-the-trinity.

Danaher, William J. *The Trinitarian Ethics of Jonathan Edwards*. Louisville,
KY: Westminster John Knox Press, 2004.

De Jong, Peter Y. *The Covenant Idea in New England Theology, 1620–1847*.
Grand Rapids: Eerdmans, 1945.

Dennison Jr, James T. "The Life and Career of Francis Turretin." In *Institutes of Elenctic Theology*, Vol. 3, edited by James T. Dennison Jr.,
translated by George Musgrave Giger, 639–58. Phillipsburg, NJ:
P&R, 1997.

Emerson, Everett H. "Calvin and Covenant Theology." *Church History* 25,
no. 2 (June 1, 1956), 136–44.

Erskine, John. "Unpublished Letters of the Late Rev. Dr. Erskine." In
Church of Scotland Magazine and Review, 329–38. Palala Press, 2015.

Eusden, John Dykstra. "Introduction." In *The Marrow of Theology*, by William Ames, edited and translated by John D. Eusden, 1–66. Boston:
Pilgrim Press, 1968.

Ferguson, Sinclair B. *John Owen on the Christian Life*. Carlisle, PA: Banner
of Truth, 1987.

Ferry, Brenton C. "Cross-Examining Moses' Defense: An Answer to
Ramsey's Critique of Kline and Karlberg." *Westminster Theological
Journal* 67 (2005): 163–68.

———. "Works in the Mosaic Covenant: Reformed Taxonomy." In
The Law is Not of Faith: Essays on Works and Grace in the Mosaic

Covenant, edited by Bryan D. Estelle, J. V. Fesko, and David Van Drunen, 76–103. Phillipsburg, NJ: P&R, 2009.

Fesko, J. V. *The Covenant of Redemption: Origins, Development, and Reception*. Göttingen: Vandenhoeck & Ruprecht, 2016.

Fisk, Philip John. *Jonathan Edwards's Turn from the Classic-Reformed Tradition of Freedom of the Will*. Göttingen: Vandenhoeck & Ruprecht, 2016.

Gay, Peter. *A Loss of Mastery: Puritan Historians in Colonial America*. Berkley and Los Angeles, CA: University of California Press, 1966.

Gerstner, John H. *Steps to Salvation: The Evangelistic Message of Jonathan Edwards*. Philadelphia: Westminster Press, 1960.

———. *The Rational Biblical Theology of Jonathan Edwards*. Vol. 2. Powhatan, VA: Berea, 1991.

———. "The Church's Doctrine of Biblical Inspiration." In *The Foundation of Biblical Authority*, edited by James Montgomery Boice, 23–58. Grand Rapids: Zondervan, 1978.

Gibson, J. C. L. *Canaanite Myths and Legends*. Edinburgh: T&T Clark, 1977.

Goudriaan, Aza. *Reformed Orthodoxy and Philosophy, 1625–1750: Gisbertus Voetius, Petrus van Mastricht, and Anthonius Driessen*. Leiden; Brill, 2006.

Hall, David D. *A Reforming People: Puritanism and the Transformation of Public Life in New England*. New York: Knopf, 2011.

———. "Editor's Introduction." In Ecclesiastical Writings, edited by David D. Hall, 1–90. Vol. 12 of *The Works of Jonathan Edwards*. New Haven, CT: Yale University Press, 1994.

Haroutunian, Joseph. *Piety Versus Moralism: The Passing of the New England Theology*. New York: Harper & Row, 1970.

Helm, Paul. "Jonathan Edwards and the Parting of the Ways?" *Jonathan Edwards Studies* 4, no. 1 (2014): 42–60.

———. "Turretin and Edwards Once More." *Jonathan Edwards Studies* 4, no. 3 (2014): 286–96.

Heppe, Heinrich. *Geschichte des Pietismus und der Mystik in der reformierten Kirche namentlich in der Niederlande*. Leiden: Brill, 1879.

———. *Reformed Dogmatics: Set out and Illustrated from the Sources*. Edited by Ernst Bizer. Translated by G. T. Thomson. London: Allen & Unwin, 1950.

Hesselink, I. John. *On Being Reformed: Distinctive Characteristics and Common Misunderstandings*. Ann Arbor, MI: Servant Books, 1983.

Hoadly, Charles J., ed. *Records of the Colony and Plantation of New Haven*. 2 vols. Hartford: Case, Tiffany, 1857.

Holbrook, Clyde A. "Editor's Introduction." In *Original Sin*, edited by Clyde A. Holbrook, 1–102. Vol. 3 of the *The Works of Jonathan Edwards*. New Haven, CT: Yale University Press, 1970.

Holifield, E. Brooks. "Edwards as Theologian." In *The Cambridge Companion to Jonathan Edwards*, edited by Stephen J. Stein, 144–61. Cambridge: Cambridge University Press, 2007.

Holmes, Stephen R. *God of Grace and God of Glory: An Account of the Theology of Jonathan Edwards*. Grand Rapids: Eerdmans, 2001.

———. "Does Jonathan Edwards Use a Dispositional Ontology? A Response to Sang Hyun Lee." In *Jonathan Edwards: Philosophical Theologian*, edited by Paul Helm and Oliver D. Crisp, 99–114. Aldershot: Ashgate, 2003.

———. "Three Versus One? Some Problems of Social Trinitarianism." *Journal of Reformed Theology* 3 (2009): 77–89.

Horton, Michael S. *Covenant and Salvation: Union with Christ*. Louisville: Westminster John Knox Press, 2007.

———. *God of Promise: Introducing Covenant Theology*. Grand Rapids: Baker Books, 2006.

———. "Obedience Is Better than Sacrifice." In *The Law is Not of Faith: Essays on Works and Grace in the Mosaic Covenant*, edited by Bryan D. Estelle, J. V. Fesko, and David Van Drunen, 315–36. Phillipsburg, NJ: P&R, 2009.

Hunsinger, George. "Dispositional Soteriology: Jonathan Edwards on Justification by Faith Alone." *Westminster Theological Journal* 66, no. 1 (2004): 107–20.

Isbell, R. Sherman. "The Origin of the Concept of the Covenant of Works." Master's thesis, Westminster Theological Seminary, 1976.

Jamieson, John F. "Jonathan Edwards' Change of Position on Stoddardeanism." *Harvard Theological Review* 74, no. 1 (January 1981): 79–99.

Johnson, Thomas H. *The Printed Writings of Jonathan Edwards, 1703–1758: A Bibliography*. Princeton: Princeton University Press, 1940

Karlberg, Mark W. *Federalism and the Westminster Tradition.* Eugene, OR: Wipf & Stock, 2006.

———. "Justification in Redemptive History." *Westminster Theological Journal* 43 (1981): 213–46.

———. "Moses and Christ—The Place of Law in Seventeenth-Century Puritanism." *Trinity Journal* 10, no. 1 (Spring 1989): 11–32.

———. "Recovering the Mosaic Covenant as Law and Gospel: J. Mark Beach, John H. Sailhamer, and Jason C. Meyer as Representative Expositors." *EQ* 83, no. 3 (2011): 233–50.

———. "Reformed Interpretation of the Mosaic Covenant." *Westminster Theological Journal* 43 (1981): 1–57.

———. "The Mosaic Covenant and the Concept of Works in Reformed Hermeneutics." PhD diss., Westminster Theological Seminary, 1980.

———. "The Original State of Adam: Tensions within Reformed Theology." *EQ* 87 (1987): 291–309.

———. "The Search for an Evangelical Consensus on Paul and the Law." *Journal of the Evangelical Theological Society* 40 (1997): 563–79.

Kevan, Ernest F. *The Grace of Law: A Study in Puritan Theology.* Grand Rapids: Baker, 1965.

Kline, Meredith G. *By Oath Consigned: A Reinterpretation of the Covenant Signs of Circumcision and Baptism.* Grand Rapids: Eerdmans, 1968.

———. *Kingdom Prologue: Genesis Foundations for a Covenantal Worldview.* Overland Park, KS: Two Age, 2000.

———. *Treaty of the Great King: The Covenant Structure of Deuteronomy: Studies and Commentary.* Grand Rapids: Eerdmans, 1963.

———. "Covenant Theology Under Attack." *New Horizons* 15 (February 1994): 3–5.

———. "Gospel until the Law: Rom. 5:13–14 and the Old Covenant." *Journal of the Evangelical Theological Society* 34 (1991): 433–46.

Kling, David W., and Sweeney, Douglas A., eds. *Jonathan Edwards at Home and Abroad: Historical Memories, Cultural Movements, Global Horizons.* Columbia, SC: University of South Carolina Press, 2003.

Knight, Janice "Learning the Language of God: Jonathan Edwards and the Typology of Nature." *WMQ* 48 (1991): 531–51.

Kraus, Hans Joachim. "Calvin's Exegetical Principles." Translated by
    Keith Crim. *Interpretation* 31, no. 1 (1977): 8–18.

Kreider, Glenn R. *Jonathan Edwards's Interpretation of Revelation 4:1–8:1.*
    Dallas, TX: University Press of America, 2004.

Landrum, Doug. *Jonathan Edwards' Exegesis of Genesis: A Puritan Herme-
    neutic?* Mustang, OK: Tate Publishing & Enterprises, 2015.

Lee, Brian J. "Biblical Exegesis, Johannes Cocceius, and Federal Theology:
    Developments in the Interpretation of Hebrews 7:1–10:18." PhD
    diss., Calvin Theological Seminary, 2003.

— — —. "The Covenant Terminology of Johannes Cocceius: The Use of
    Foedus, Pactum, and Testamentum in a Mature Federal Theology."
    Mid-America Journal of Theology 14 (2003): 11–36.

Lee, Sang Hyun, ed. *The Princeton Companion to Jonathan Edwards.* Princ-
    eton, NJ: Princeton University Press, 2005.

— — —. "Does History Matter to God?: Jonathan Edwards's Dynamic
    Re-conception of God's Relation to the World." In *Jonathan
    Edwards at 300: Essays on the Tercentenary of His Birth*, edited by
    Harry S. Stout, Kenneth P. Minkema, and Caleb J. D. Maskell, 1–13.
    Lanham: University Press of America, 2005.

— — —. "Editor's Introduction." In *Writings on the Trinity, Grace, and Faith*,
    edited by Sang Hyun Lee, 1–106. Vol. 21 of The Works of Jonathan
    Edwards. New Haven, CT: Yale University Press, 2003

— — —. "God's Relation to the World." In *The Princeton Companion to
    Jonathan Edwards*, edited by Sang Hyun Lee, 59–71. Princeton, NJ:
    Princeton University Press, 2005.

_____. "Introduction." In *The Princeton Companion to Jonathan Edwards*,
    edited by Sang Hyun Lee, xi–xx. Princeton: Princeton University
    Press, 2005.

Lesser, M. X. *Reading Jonathan Edwards: An Annotated Bibliography in
    Three Parts, 1729–2005.* Grand Rapids: Eerdmans, 2008.

Letham, Robert. "Not a Covenant of Works in Disguise." *Mid-America
    Journal of Theology* 24 (2013): 143–77.

— — —. "The Trinity between East and West." *Journal of Reformed Theol-
    ogy* 3 (2009): 42–56.

Lewalski, Barbara Kiefer. *Protestant Poetics and the Seventeenth-Century
    Religious Lyric.* Princeton, NJ: Princeton University Press, 1979.

Lillback, Peter A. *The Binding of God: Calvin's Role in the Development of Covenant Theology*. Grand Rapids: Baker, 2001.

Lim, Won Taek. "The Covenant Theology of Francis Roberts." PhD diss., Calvin Theological Seminary, 2000.

Logan, Samuel T. Jr., "The Doctrine of Justification in the Theology of Jonathan Edwards." *Westminster Theological Journal* 46 (1984): 26–52.

Loonstra, B. *Verkezing, verzoening, verbond: beschrijving en beoordeling van de leer van het "pactum salutis" in de gereformeerde theologie*. Gravenhage: Boekencentrum, 1990.

Lowance, Mason I. Jr., "'Images or Shadows of Divine Things' in the Thought of Jonathan Edwards." In *Typology and Early American Literature*, edited by Sacvan Bercovitch, 209–44. Amherst: University of Massachusetts, 1972.

Lowance, Mason I. Jr., and David H. Watters. "Editor's Introduction to 'Types of the Messiah.'" In *Typological Writings*, edited by Mason I. Lowance Jr. with David H. Watters, 157–328. Vol. 11 of *The Works of Jonathan Edwards*. New Haven, CT: Yale University Press, 1993.

Lucas, Sean Michael. *God's Grand Design: The Theological Vision of Jonathan Edwards*. Wheaton, IL: Crossway, 2011.

———. "A History of the Work of Redemption." In *A Reader's Guide to the Major Writings of Jonathan Edwards*, edited by Nathan A. Finn and Jeremy M. Kimble, 175–92. Wheaton, IL: Crossway, 2017.

Macedo, Breno. "Covenant Theology in the Thought of John Calvin From the Mosaic Covenant to the New Covenant." *Fides Reformata* 21, no. 1 (2016): 121–48.

Manetsch, Scott M. "John Calvin's Doctrine of the Christian Life." *Journal of the Evangelical Theological Study* 61, no. 2 (2018): 259–73.

Marsden, George M. *Jonathan Edwards: A Life*. New Haven, CT: Yale University Press, 2003.

McCarthy, Dennis J. "Běrît and Covenant in the Deuteronomistic History." In *Studies in the Religion of Ancient Israel*, edited by G. W. Anderson, et al., 65–85. VTSup 23. Leiden: Brill, 1972.

McClenahan, Michael. *Jonathan Edwards and Justification by Faith*. Aldershot, UK: Ashgate, 2012.

McClymond, Michael J., and Gerald R. McDermott. *The Theology of Jonathan Edwards*. New York: Oxford University Press, 2012.

McClymond, Michael J. *Encounters with God: An Approach to the Theology of Jonathan Edwards*. Religion in America. New York: Oxford University Press, 1998.

———. "Of His Fullness Have All We Received." In *Jonathan Edwards and Scripture*, edited by David P. Barshinger and Douglas A. Sweeney. New York: Oxford University Press, 2018): 163–81.

McCoy, Charles S. "Johannes Cocceius: Federal Theologian." *Scottish Journal of Theology* 16 (1963): 352–70.

———. "The Covenant Theology of Johannes Cocceius." PhD diss., Yale University, 1956.

McDermott, Gerald R. *Jonathan Edwards Confronts the Gods: Christian Theology, Enlightenment Religion, and Non-Christian Faiths*. New York: Oxford University Press, 2000.

———. *One Holy and Happy Society: The Public Theology of Jonathan Edwards*. University Park: Pennsylvania State University Press, 1992.

———. "Jonathan Edwards on Justification by Faith—More Protestant or Catholic?" *Pro Ecclesia* 17, no. 1 (2008): 92–111.

———. "Salvation as Divinization: Jonathan Edwards, Gregory Palamas and the Theological Uses of Neoplatonism." In *Jonathan Edwards: Philosophical Theologian*, edited by Paul Helm and Oliver D. Crisp, 127–38. Aldershot: Ashgate, 2003.

McGiffert, Michael. "From Moses to Adam: The Making of the Covenant of Works." *Sixteenth Century Journal* 19, no. 2 (1988): 131–55.

———. "Grace and Works: The Rise and Division of Covenant Divinity in Elizabethan Puritanism." *Harvard Theological Review* 75, no. 4 (1982), 463–502.

McLoughlin, William G. *Revivals, Awakenings, and Reform: An Essay on Religion and Social Change in America, 1607-1977*. Chicago: University of Chicago Press, 1978.

McNeill, John T. "The Church in Post-Reformation Reformed Theology." *Journal of Religion* 24 (1944): 96–107.

Mead, Sidney Earl. *Nathaniel William Taylor, 1786-1858: A Connecticut Liberal*. Chicago: University of Chicago Press, 1942.

Miller, Perry. *Jonathan Edwards*. New York: William Sloan Associates, 1949. Reprint. Amherst: University of Massachusetts Press, 1981.

———. "Roger Williams: An Essay in Interpretation." In *The Complete Writings of Roger Williams*, Vol. 7, edited by Perry Miller, 5–25. New York: Russell & Russell, 1963.

———. "The Marrow of Puritan Divinity." In *Errand into the Wilderness*, 50–98. New York: Harper and Row, 1964.

Minkema, Kenneth P. "Editor's Introduction." In *Sermons and Discourses 1723–1729*, edited by Kenneth P. Minkema, 2–46. Vol. 14 of *The Works of Jonathan Edwards*. New Haven, CT: Yale University Press, 1977.

———. "Jonathan Edwards in the Twentieth Century." *Journal of the Evangelical Theological Society* 47, no. 4 (2004): 659–87.

Moody, Josh. "Edwards and Justification Today." In *Jonathan Edwards and Justification*, edited by Josh Moody, 17–43. Wheaton, IL: Crossway, 2012.

Morimoto, Anri. *Jonathan Edwards and the Catholic Vision of Salvation*. University Park: Pennsylvania State University Press, 1995.

Morris, William S. *The Young Jonathan Edwards: A Reconstruction*. Brooklyn, NY: Carlson, 1991.

Muller, Richard A. *After Calvin: Studies in the Development of a Theological Tradition*. Oxford: Oxford University Press, 2003.

———. *Dictionary of Latin and Greek Theological Terms: Drawn Principally from Protestant Scholastic Theology*. Grand Rapids: Baker Academic, 2017.

———. *Post-Reformation Reformed Dogmatics: The Rise and Development of Reformed Orthodoxy, ca. 1520 to ca. 1725*. Vol 1. *Prolegomena to Theology*. Grand Rapids: Baker Academic, 2003.

———. *Post-Reformation Reformed Dogmatics: The Rise and Development of Reformed Orthodoxy, ca. 1520 to ca. 1725*. Vol 2. *The Holy Spirit: The Cognitive Foundation of Theology*. Grand Rapids: Baker Academic, 2003.

———. *Post-Reformation Reformed Dogmatics: The Rise and Development of Reformed Orthodoxy, ca. 1520 to ca. 1725*. Vol 4. *The Triunity of God*. Grand Rapids: Baker Academic, 2003.

———. "Covenant and Conscience in English Reformed Theology: Three Variations on a 17ᵗʰ Century Theme." *Westminster Theological Journal* 42, no. 2 (Spring 1980): 308–34.

———. "Giving Direction to Theology: The Scholastic Dimension." *Journal of the Evangelical Theological Society* 28, no. 2 (1985): 183–93.

———. "God as Absolute and Relative, Necessary, Free, and Contingent." In *Always Reformed: Essays in Honor of W. Robert Godfrey*, edited by R. Scott Clark and Joel E. Kim, 56–73. Escondido: Westminster Seminary California, 2010.

———. "Jonathan Edwards and Francis Turretin on Necessity, Contingency, and Freedom of the Will: In Response to Paul Helm." *Jonathan Edwards Studies* 4, no. 3 (2014): 266–85.

———. "Jonathan Edwards and the Absence of Free Choice: A Parting of Ways in the Reformed Tradition." *Jonathan Edwards Studies* 1, no. 1 (2011): 3–22.

———. "The Covenant of Works and the Stability of Divine Law in Seventeenth-Century Reformed Orthodoxy: A Study in the Theology of Herman Witsius and Wilhelmus à Brakel." *Calvin Theological Journal* 29, no. 1 (1994): 75–101.

———. "The Hermeneutic of Promise and Fulfillment in Calvin's Exegesis of the Old Testament Prophecies of the Kingdom." In *The Bible in the Sixteenth Century*, edited by David C. Steinmetz, 68–82. Durham, NC: Duke University Press, 1990.

———. "Toward the *Pactum salutis*: locating the origins of a concept." *Mid-America Journal of Theology* 18 (2007): 11–65.

———. "'Either Expressly Set Down … or by Good and Necessary Consequence': Exegesis and Formulation in the Annotations and the Confession" in *Scripture and Worship: Biblical Interpretation and the Directory for Public Worship*, edited by Richard A. Muller and Rowland S. Ward, 59–82. Phillipsburg, NJ: P&R, 2007.

Neele, Adriaan C. *Before Jonathan Edwards: Sources of New England Theology*. Oxford University Press, 2018.

———. *Petrus van Mastricht (1630-1706): Reformed Orthodoxy: Method and Piety*. Leiden: Brill, 2009.

———. "Petrus van Mastricht (1630–1706): Life and Work." In Petrus van Mastricht, *Theoretical-Practical Theology*. Vol. 1, *Prolegomena*, edited by Joel R. Beeke and translated by Todd M. Rester, xxv–lxiii. Grand Rapids: Reformation Heritage Books, 2018.

———. "Appendix VIII: Mastricht and Edwards." In *Petrus van Mastricht (1630–1706): Reformed Orthodoxy: Method and Piety*, 316–20. Leiden: Brill, 2009.

———. "The Reception of Edward's *A History of the Work of Redemption in Nineteenth-century Basutoland.*" *Journal of Religion in Africa* 45 (2015): 68–93.

Nichols, Stephen R. C. *Jonathan Edwards's Bible: The Relationship of the Old and New Testaments in the Theology of Jonathan Edwards*. Eugene, OR: Pickwick, 2013.

Pabst, Thomas Haviland. Review of *The Covenant of Redemption: Origins, Development, and Reception*, by J. V. Fesko. *Themelios An International Journal for Students of Theological and Religious Studies* 43, no. 1 (2018): 123–25.

Pauley, Garth E. "Soundly Gathered Out of the Text? Biblical Interpretation in 'Sinners in The Hands of an Angry God,'" *Trinity Journal* 76 (2014): 95–117.

Paulson, Steven D. "Law and Gospel." In *Dictionary of Luther and the Lutheran Traditions*, edited by Timothy J. Wengert, 414–18. Grand Rapids: Baker, 2017.

Pauw, Amy Plantinga. *The Supreme Harmony of All: The Trinitarian Theology of Jonathan Edwards*. Grand Rapids: Eerdmans, 2002.

———. "The Trinity." In *The Princeton Companion to Jonathan Edwards*, edited by Sang Hyun Lee, 44–58. Princeton, NJ: Princeton University Press, 2005.

Poole, David N. J. *The History of the Covenant Concept from the Bible to Johannes Cloppenburg: De Foedere Dei*. San Francisco: Mellen Research University Press, 1992.

Ramsey, D. Patrick. "In Defense of Moses: A Confessional Critique of Kline and Karlberg." *Westminster Theological Journal* 66 (2004): 373–400.

Ramsey, D. Patrick, and Joel R. Beeke. *Analysis of Herman Witsius's The Economy of the Covenants*. Grand Rapids: Reformation Heritage

Books, 2003.

Ramsey, Paul. "Appendix III: Heaven Is a Progressive State." In *Ethical Writing*, edited by Paul Ramsey, 706–38. Vol. 8 of *The Works of Jonathan Edwards*. New Haven, CT: Yale University Press, 1989.

———. "Appendix IV: Infused Virtues in Edwardsean and Calvinistic Context." In *Ethical Writing*, edited by Paul Ramsey, 739–50. Vol. 8 of *The Works of Jonathan Edwards*. New Haven, CT: Yale University Press, 1989.

Rast, Lawrence R. Jr. "Jonathan Edwards on Justification by Faith." *CTQ* 72 (2008): 347–62.

Rester, Todd M. "Translator's Preface." In Petrus van Mastricht's, *Theoretical-Practical Theology*. Vol. 1, *Prolegomena*, edited by Joel R. Beeke, translated by Todd M. Rester, xvii–xxiv. Grand Rapids: Reformation Heritage Books, 2018.

Richardson, Herbert W. "The Glory of God in the Theology of Jonathan Edwards: A Study in the Doctrine of the Trinity." PhD. diss, Harvard University, 1962.

Robertson, O. Palmer. *The Christ of the Covenants*. Grand Rapids: Baker, 1980.

Rohls, Jan. *Reformed Confessions: Theology from Zurich to Barmen*. Translated by John Hoffmeyer. Louisville, KY: Westminster John Knox Press, 1998.

Rolston, Holmes, III. *John Calvin Versus the Westminster Confession*. Richmond, VA: John Knox, 1972.

———. "Responsible Man in Reformed Theology." *Scottish Journal of Theology* 23, no. 2 (1970), 129–56.

Régnon, Théodore De. *Études de théologie positive sur la Sainte Trinité*. 4 vols. Paris: Victor Retaux, 1892–1898.

Sairsingh, Krister. "Jonathan Edwards and the Idea of Divine Glory: His Foundational Trinitarianism and Its Ecclesial Import." PhD. diss, Harvard University, 1986.

Scheick, William J. "The Grand Design: Jonathan Edwards' History of Redemption." *Eighteenth-Century Studies* 8, no. 3 (Spring, 1975): 300–14.

Schnabel, Eckhard J. *Acts*. Zondervan Exegetical Commentary on the New Testament. Grand Rapids: Zondervan, 2012.

Selvaggio, Anthony T. "Unity or Disunity? Covenant Theology from Calvin to Westminster." In *The Faith Once Delivered: Essays in Honor of Dr. Wayne Spear*, edited by Anthony T. Selvaggio, 217–45. Phillipsburg, NJ: P&R, 2007.

Shafer, Thomas A. "Editor's Introduction" In *The "Miscellanies": Entry Nos. a-z, aa-zz, 1–500*, edited by Thomas A. Schafer, 1–38. Vol. 13 of *The Works of Jonathan Edwards*. New Haven, CT: Yale University Press, 1994.

———. "Jonathan Edwards and Justification by Faith." *Church History* 20, no. 4 (1951): 55–67.

———. "Jonathan Edwards' Conception of the Church." *Church History* 24, no. 1 (1955): 51–66.

Smith, John E. "Editor's Introduction." In *A Treatise Concerning Religious Affections*, edited by John E. Smith, 1–83. Vol. 2 of *The Works of Jonathan Edwards*. New Haven, CT: Yale University Press, 1959.

Stahle, Rachel S. "The Trinitarian Spirit of Jonathan Edwards' Theology." PhD. diss, Gordon-Conwell Seminary, 1999.

Stein, Stephen J. "Editor's Introduction." In *The "Blank Bible,"* edited by Stephen J. Stein, 1–117. Vol. 24 of The *Works of Jonathan Edwards*. New Haven, CT: Yale University Press, 2006.

———. "Editor's Introduction." In *Notes on Scripture*, edited by Stephen J. Stein, 1–46. Vol. 15 of the *The Works of Jonathan Edwards*. New Haven, CT: Yale University Press, 1998.

———. "Edwards as Biblical Exegete." In *The Cambridge Companion to Jonathan Edwards*, edited by Stephen J. Stein, 181–95. Cambridge: Cambridge University Press, 2007.

———. "Jonathan Edwards and the Rainbow: Biblical Exegesis and Poetic Imagination." *New England Quarterly* 47, no. 3 (Septempber 1974): 440–56.

———. "The Quest for the Spiritual Sense: The Biblical Hermeneutics of Jonathan Edwards." *Harvard Theological Review* 70, no. 1 (1977): 99–113.

———. "The Spirit and the Word: Jonathan Edwards and Scriptural Exegesis." In *Jonathan Edwards and the American Experience*, edited by Nathan O. Hatch and Harry S. Stout, 118–30. New York: Oxford University Press, 1988.

Steinmetz, David C. "Divided by a Common Past: The Reshaping of the Christian Exegetical Tradition in the Sixteenth Century." *Journal of Medieval and Early Modern Studies* 27, no. 2 (Spring 1997): 245–64.

Stout, Harry S. "The Puritans and Edwards." In *Jonathan Edwards and the American Experience*, edited by Nathan O. Hatch and Harry S. Stout, 142–59. New York: Oxford University Press, 1988.

Strobel, Kyle. *Jonathan Edwards' Theology: A Reinterpretation.* London: Bloomsbury T&T Clark, 2013.

———. "By Word and Spirit: Jonathan Edwards on Redemption, Justification, and Regeneration." In *Jonathan Edwards and Justification*, edited by Josh Moody, 45–69. Wheaton: Crossway, 2012.

Studebaker, Steven M., *Jonathan Edwards' Social Augustinian Trinitarianism in Historical and Contemporary Perspectives.* Piscataway, NJ: Gorgias Press, 2008.

———. "Jonathan Edwards' Pneumatological Concept of Grace and Dispositional Soteriology: Resources for an Evangelical Inclusivism." *Pro Ecclesia* 14, no. 3 (2005): 324–39.

Studebaker, Steven M., and Robert W. Caldwell III. *The Trinitarian Theology of Jonathan Edwards: Text, Context, and Application.* Burlington, VT: Ashgate, 2012.

Sweeney, Douglas A. *Edwards the Exegete: Biblical Interpretation and Anglo-Protestant Culture on the Edge of the Enlightenment.* New York: Oxford University Press, 2016.

———. *Jonathan Edwards and the Ministry of the Word.* Downers Grove, IL: IVP Academic, 2009.

———. "Edwards and His Mantle." *New England Quarterly* 71 (1998): 93–115.

———. "Justification by Faith Alone? A Fuller Picture of Edwards's Doctrine." In *Jonathan Edwards and Justification*, edited by Josh Moody, 129–54. Wheaton, IL: Crossway, 2012.

———. "The Church." In *The Princeton Companion to Jonathan Edwards*, edited by Sang Hyun Lee, 167–89. Princeton, NJ: Princeton University Press, 2005.

Todd, Obbie Tyler. "What is A Person? Three Essential Criteria for Jonathan Edwards's Doctrine of Personhood." *Journal of the Evangelical Theological Society* 61, no. 1 (2018): 121–35.

Torrance, James B. "Calvin and Puritanism in England and Scotland—Some Basic Concepts in the Development of 'Federal Theology.'" In *Calvinus Reformator*, edited by B. J. van der Walt, 264–77. Potchefstroom: Potchefstroom University for Christian Higher Education, 1982.

———. "Covenant or Contract: A Study of the Theological Background of Worship in Seventeenth-Century Scotland," *Scottish Journal of Theology* 23, no. 1 (1970): 51–76.

———. "Strengths and Weaknesses of the Westminster Theology." In *The Westminster Confession in in the Church Today: Papers Prepared for the Church of Scotland Panel on Doctrine*, edited by Alisdair I. C. Heron, 40–53. Edinburgh: Saint Andrews Press, 1982.

———. "The Covenant Concept in Scottish Theology and Politics." In *The Covenant Connection: From Federal Theology to Modern Federalism*, ed. Daniel J. Elazar and John Kinkaid, 143–62. Lanham, MD: Lexington, 2000.

Turnbull, Ralph G. *Jonathan Edwards: The Preacher*. Grand Rapids: Baker, 1958.

———. "Jonathan Edwards: Bible Interpreter." *Interpretation* 6, no. 4 (October 1952): 422–35.

Valeri. Mark. "Editor's Introduction to 'East of Eden' (Gen 3:24)." In *Sermon and Discourses 1730–1733*, edited by Mark Valeri, 329–30. Vol. 17 of *The Works of Jonathan Edwards*. New Haven, CT: Yale University Press, 1999.

Van Asselt, Willem J. *The Federal Theology of Johannes Cocceius, 1603–1669*. Translated by Raymond A. Blacketer. Leiden: Brill, 2001.

———. "Covenant, Kingdom, and Friendship: Johannes Cocceius's Federal Framework for Theology." In *The Doctrine of the Covenant and Testament of God*, translated by Casey Carmichael, xv–xxxviii. Grand Rapids: Reformation Heritage Books, 2016.

———. "Johannes Cocceius Anti-Scholastic?" In *Protestant Scholasticism*, edited by Willem Van Asselt and Eef Dekker, 227–52. Grand Rapids: Baker, 2001.

Van Drunen, David. "Israel's Recapitulation of Adam's Probation under the Law of Moses." *Westminster Theological Journal* 73 (2011): 303–24.

———. "Natural Law and the Works Principle under Adam and Moses." In *The Law is Not of Faith: Essays on Works and Grace in the Mosaic Covenant*, edited by Bryan D. Estelle, J. V. Fesko, and David Van Drunen, 283-314. Phillipsburg, NJ: P&R, 2009.

Van Vliet, Jan. *William Ames: Marrow of the Theology and Piety of the Reformed Tradition*. PhD. diss, Westminster Theological Seminary, 2002.

———. "Covenant and Conscience: Amesian Echoes in Jonathan Edwards." In *The Rise of Reformed System: The Intellectual Heritage of William Ames*, 233-65. Eugene, OR: Wipf & Stock, 2013.

Van der Knijff, Cornelis, and Willem van Vlastuin. "The Development in Jonathan Edwards' Covenant View." *Jonathan Edwards Studies* 3, no. 2 (2013): 269-81.

Vanhoozer, Kevin J. *Is There a Meaning in This Text?* Grand Rapids: Zondervan, 1998.

Venema, Cornelis P. "Recent Criticisms of the 'Covenant of Works' in the Westminster Confession of Faith." *Mid-America Journal of Theology* 9, no. 2 (1993): 165-98.

———. "The Mosaic Covenant: A 'Republication' of the Covenant of Works?" *Mid-America Journal of Theology* 21 (2010): 35-101.

———. "Union with Christ and the 'Twofold Grace of God.'" In *Accepted and Renewed in Christ: The "Twofold Grace of God" and the Interpretation of Calvin's Theology*, 83-94. Reformed Historical Theology Series. Göttingen: Vandenhoeck & Ruprecht, 2007.

Von Rohr, John. *The Covenant of Grace in Puritan Thought*. Atlanta: Scholars Press, 1986.

Waddington, Jeffrey C. "Jonathan Edwards's 'Ambiguous and Somewhat Precarious' Doctrine of Justification?" *Westminster Theological Journal* 66 (2004): 357-72.

Weber, Richard M. "The Trinitarian Theology of Jonathan Edwards: An Investigation of Charges against Its Orthodoxy." *Journal of the Evangelical Theological Study* 44, no. 2 (June 2001): 297-318.

William, C. J. "Good and Necessary Consequences in the Westminster Confession." In *The Faith Once Delivered: Essays in Honor of Dr. Wayne Spear*, edited by Anthony T. Selvaggio, 171-90. Phillipsburg, NJ: P&R, 2007.

Wilson, John F. "Editor's Introduction." In *A History of the Work of Redemption*, edited by John F. Wilson, 1-109. Vol. 9 of *The Works of Jonathan Edwards*. New Haven, CT: Yale University Press, 1989.

———. "Jonathan Edwards as Historian." *Church History* 46, no. 1 (1977): 5-18.

———. "Jonathan Edwards' Notebooks for 'A History of the Work of Redemption.'" In *History of the Work of Redemption*, edited by John F. Wilson, 543-56. Vol. 9 of *The Works of Jonathan Edwards*. New Haven, CT: Yale University Press, 1989. Reprint, with minor editorial changes, from *Reformation, Conformity and Dissent, Essays in Honour of Geoffrey Nuttall*, edited by R. Buick Knox, 239-54. London: Epworth, 1977.

Wilson-Kastner, Patricia. "Jonathan Edwards: History and the Covenant," *Andrews University Seminary Studies* 15 (1977): 205-16.

Woo, Byunghoon. "The *Pactum Salutis* in the Theology of Witsius, Owen, Dickson, Goodwin, and Cocceius." PhD. diss., Calvin Theological Seminary, 2015.

Yazawa, Reita. "Covenant of Redemption in the Theology of Jonathan Edwards: The Nexus between the Immanent and the Economic Trinity." PhD diss., Calvin Theological Seminary, 2013.

———. "Federal Theology," In *The Jonathan Edwards Encyclopedia*, edited by Harry S. Stout, 118-22. Grand Rapids: Eerdmans, 2017.

Yarbrough, Stephen R. "The Beginning of Time: Jonathan Edwards' Original Sin." In *Early American Literature and Culture: Essays Honoring Harrison T. Meserole*, edited by Kathryn Zabelle Derounian-Stodola, 149-64. Newark: University of Delaware Press; London and Toronto: Associated University Press, 1992.

Yoo, Jeongmo. "Edwards's Interpretation of the Major Prophets." *Puritan Reformed Journal* 3, no. 2 (2011): 160-92.

SUBJECT/AUTHOR INDEX

—

SCRIPTURE INDEX

—